Managers and Work Reform

Managers and Work Reform

A Limited Engagement

Ivar Berg,
Marcia Freedman,
and Michael Freeman

THE FREE PRESS
A Division of Macmillan Publishing Co., Inc.
NEW YORK

Collier Macmillan Publishers
LONDON

658.315
B 493

The Free Press
A Division of Macmillan Publishing Co., Inc.
866 Third Avenue, New York, N.Y. 10022

Collier Macmillan Canada, Ltd.

Library of Congress Catalog Card Number: 77–83165

Printed in the United States of America

printing number

1 2 3 4 5 6 7 8 9 10

Library of Congress Cataloging in Publication Data

Berg, Ivar E
    Managers and work reform.

    Includes bibliographical references and index.
    1. Labor and laboring classes--United States.
2. Job satisfaction--United States. 3. Labor
productivity--United States. 4. Personnel management--
United States. 5. Industrial relations--United States.
I. Freedman, Marcia K., joint author. II. Freeman,
Michael, joint author. III. Title.
HD8072.B358   658.31'5   77-83165
ISBN 0-02-902900-7

For Howard Rosen

The dedication of this book to Howard Rosen, of the Department of Labor, reflects our admiration and affection for a man who has given so much of himself to his social science colleagues and to the larger public he serves so honorably.

Contents

Foreword

Eli Ginzberg

A useful foreword should tell how the work came to be written; something about its special qualities; and something about its potential impact on policy.

The roots of the present work can be found in the research strategy of the Conservation of Human Resources Project, Columbia University, under whose auspices the study was carried out. The financing of the project by the Office of Research and Development, Employment and Training Administration of the U.S. Department of Labor and the Ford Foundation reflects the concerns of the two sponsors with the subject of "work and values," which served as the working title for the present investigation. The earlier work of the senior authors helped to bring them to the questions that are the focus of the present undertaking. A few words about each of these three strands.

When the pioneering research into human resources was expanded at Columbia University in 1950 with the establishment of the Conservation of Human Resources Project, the agenda included three themes: the study of the talented, of the disadvantaged, and of work. This book represents the most recent, the most ambitious, and the most penetrating effort of the conservation staff to understand the forces operating to alter the structure and functioning of work, one of the most important of all societal arrangements. Earlier contributions of the conservation staff to this theme included a historical treatment of *Women and Work in America* (Robert Smuts); a book tracing, through a study of arbitration awards, how changing values were altering the workplace (*Democratic Values and the Rights of Management*, Eli Ginzberg and Ivar Berg); and *The American Worker in the Twentieth Century: A History Through Autobiographies* (Eli Ginzberg and Hyman Berman), which illuminated the changing conditions of work as seen through the eyes of three cohorts of American workers.

When, in the early 1970s, the Conservation Project approached the U.S. Department of Labor and the Ford Foundation for financial support to undertake the investigations that form the core of this book, the responses were favorable because of their current programmatic and policy efforts. Both the Department of Labor and the Ford Foundation had engaged in exploring issues that were grouped under the rubric of the "quality of working life." The high level of employment in the late 1960s provided the backdrop for this new focus—or, as our authors point out, for a renewed focus on work and its satisfactions. The meat and potatoes of industrial relations—job security, high wages, and good retirement benefits—were apparently being taken care of through the processes of a steadily expanding economy. The setting was favorable for new initiatives.

Ivar Berg and Marcia Freedman, the senior authors, had through their earlier research brought themselves to a favorable starting point from which to launch the present effort. Berg had looked at the work–value interface in his study of arbitration awards and had explored another dimension in *Education and Work: The Great Training Robbery*. In that study, he was impressed with the difficulties that managers made for themselves by hiring individuals whose education was in excess of the requirements of their jobs. He also reassessed the conventional wisdom about worker satisfaction and performance, a theme that looms large in the present study.

Marcia Freedman was well into her reformulation of processes in the labor market when the present study was launched. In effect, her 1976 publication, *Labor Markets: Segments and Shelters,* is a companion piece to this book, because it contains a fuller development of the influence of macro factors than could be encompassed here. One of her findings, for example, concerns the intensity of the struggle among workers to find job shelters—that is, jobs with relatively good wages, fringes, and security. The pursuit of such shelters, with its implications for satisfaction, contrasts with the theme of work reformers, which is focused on enlarging satisfaction through changes in the workplace.

Consideration of the origins of the present study helps to reinforce a basic fact about any large-scale research effort in the social sciences. Such an undertaking can be launched and carried out to a successful conclusion only if the intellectual interests of the principal investigators find a favorable response from sponsors who have the resources and the risk-taking proclivities to underwrite their proposal, even one whose conclusions may be antithetical to their program initiatives. Researchers who find such sponsors are twice blessed, for only then can they pursue their inquiries secure in the knowledge that their conclusions will be assessed by the strength of their evidence and logic, not by whether they reinforce the assumptions of the sponsors.

In describing some of the special qualities that characterize the present work, I shall review briefly the central theme that the study addresses, the methods employed to explore it, and the conclusions that emerge from the sifting of the evidence.

The central theme, here oversimplified, is the potential for managers to intervene in the work setting to increase the satisfactions that workers can derive from their jobs and, further, whether such interventions, when successful, are likely to lead to desirable outcomes from the viewpoint of the firm in terms of reduced labor costs and labor strife, increased productivity and profits.

The theme has intrinsic as well as institutional relevance. Intrinsic because class conflicts, muted or explosive, have been inherent in modern industrialism as in all other forms of economic organization from peasant societies to modern communist states. The institutional emphasis derives from the cross-national concern with the quality of working life that has been engaging at least small numbers of industrialists, labor leaders, professors, and government officials since the mid-1960s, an effort that may be exaggerated through media attention but one that has achieved some social momentum.

The authors' approach is multidimensional. In fact herein lies their major contribution. They look at work reform through a wide lens. Specifically, they trace its origins back to the human relations work at the Harvard Business School of the 1930s, when Elton Mayo and his disciples first looked at the work environment from a sociopsychological vantage and concluded that managers were in a position to introduce changes that would be welcomed by the workers and would be reflected in higher output.

But the authors insist on broadening the framework of analysis far beyond the direct intervention of managers. They lead the reader to consider a host of macro factors that impinge on the workplace, including wage determination in a competitive or oligopolistic economy, the educational capital that a society invests in successive cohorts of workers, changes in family structure and working behavior that have vastly increased the number of two-worker families, changing societal expectations about work and income, the importance of trade unions in redefining power relations among major groups, and still other influences which managers have little or no ability to affect.

But in broadening the framework, the authors do not lose their focus on the central theme of managers and work reform. Their introduction of historical, theoretical, comparative, and still other approaches is undertaken to illuminate different dimensions of their subject in which plant and company specifics are set within the larger social and economic context. In finding a way of moving back and forth between the specifics of the workplace and the large macro determinants of work and life satisfactions the authors are both ingenious and productive.

If the micro-macro treatment of work reform is one important advance, the broadened treatment of the role of managers is another. Berg and his associates are more realistic than most earlier investigators in seeing managers as constrained by their environment rather than as a group of disembodied decision makers responding to the cold logic of profit-maximization.

What are some of the findings that grow out of this expanded treatment of work reform? The following brief comment is highly selective and reflects my view of what is new and important. Others might draw up a different list.

On the critical issue of the relation between workers' satisfaction and their productivity, the authors conclude that the linkage between the two is hard to measure, harder to establish conceptually, and almost impossible to affect through direct interventions.

What they offer in its place is a more complex and sophisticated paradigm in which worker satisfaction is seen to depend on the interaction between the demands of the job and the education and skill the person brings to the job, as well as on his or her expectations of what is an adequate family income. It is further influenced by the challenge of the work assignment, the quality of supervision, and the resources that management makes available. Poor supervision and inadequate resource support—two important contributors to worker dissatisfaction—are interpreted as managerial responsibilities.

The authors also call attention to the role that equity plays in worker satisfaction. As every employer knows, the surest road to increasing worker dissatisfaction is to upset long-standing relative wage relationships among different groups. Berg and his associates present some interesting analyses that should remind all reformers that increasing one person's satisfaction may not be possible without reducing another's.

The authors raise the important question whether the new cohort of American workers now entering the labor force are overeducated for the jobs available to them and conclude that, while they should not be considered overeducated (since education should not be judged solely by occupational imperatives), they *are* underutilized because their jobs do not make adequate demands on their education and skill. The authors review the evidence, and add some of their own, to show that jobs formerly filled by persons of lesser qualifications are now being filled by persons of higher qualifications. They see trouble ahead if the discrepancy widens and if certain moderating influences such as paying the educated group more than they are worth cannot be maintained.

In emphasizing the importance of managers, the authors first make the telling point that in most large U.S. companies the majority of executives have little freedom to alter anything. Here is one major constraint to work reforms. A second is the role of the trade union whose members are locked with management in a continuing battle over rights, privileges, and rewards, where armistices are called but no permanent treaty is ever concluded. While some naive managers may fantasize about a world without unions, the authors insist that such a world would not be the imperfect democracy that we know but something much less attractive.

Through imaginative use of content analysis of arbitration awards, the authors see the heart of the manager–worker conflict in the scope of managements' rights to give orders and the obligations of workers to follow them. Over time, the boundary line shifts: managers are no longer permitted to take the whip to their workers, but workers who break discipline can still be fired and lose a lifetime of accrued benefits.

The focus on collective bargaining is the way in which the authors seek to remind the more enthusiastic work reformers to tread warily, for whatever other purposes unions serve, they always seek to protect their members against changes introduced by management to which workers have not been party. Here is a potent micro-level constraint on work changes. In unionized plants and industries all such changes must be negotiated. And negotiation is at best no fast track to fundamental reforms.

Enough has been extracted from the book's account to make the simple point that for the first time, I believe, the subject of work reform has been placed in context. Many will see the book as an unjustified attack on a desirable societal effort. Others will read it for the illumination it brings to a field long confused by slogans, enthusiasm, and false claims. But much of the value of the work must be found in the light it throws on current issues of manpower and broader social policy. These policy concerns will be the focus of my concluding observations, for which the authors bear no responsibility.

The U.S. government has in past years directed some modest resources to demonstrations aimed at enhancing productivity and the quality of working life. The burden of this book's analysis suggests to me that such efforts can be continued and even enlarged only so long as they stop far short of moving to center stage in collective bargaining. As marginal experiments, they may have a future. As a critical thrust of public policy, they are doomed from the start since they involve the undermining of positions that no union and no management can afford to yield. In fact, the withdrawal of government from the arena might encourage both management and unions to adopt a more venturesome stance.

A major source of present, and even more of potential, discontent among workers reflects the widening discrepancy between their education and training and the requirements of the jobs they fill. What does this imply for educational policy, in the public and business arenas? At a minimum the correction now under way—which the authors support—moderates the prevailing ideology that education pays off in terms of future income. It may, but then it may not. It all depends on what one studies, what one learns, the future state of the labor market, the prejudices of employers, and still other factors. The simple criterion for an affluent society such as the United States is to provide reasonable opportunities for higher education for all who are able to pursue it and interested in doing so. But the risk that graduates will be overeducated for the world of work should be publicized, not muted. The choice of more education at the risk of greater underutilization at work must be the individual's; he should recognize that no social policy is likely to enlarge significantly the challenge of routine jobs, no matter what the quality-of-working-life enthusiasts promise.

The situation is equally ambiguous when it comes to the growing investment of business in the continuing education of their staffs, especially those on the managerial ladder. With more middle managers than they know what to do with, and with many still in their forties, large and even medium-sized organizations have an excess of trained people. Education for self-development is one out, but it must be made clear by top management that more education will not necessarily, and perhaps only infrequently, lead to rapid promotion. Once again, the education—work link must be loosened if not broken.

If there is little prospect that our society will be able to increase substantially the challenge that people find in their work, and if further our society is unlikely to be able to use constructively in the work arena all of the education that the younger age groups are acquiring, what options remain? The most obvious is a reduction in the amount of time that people are forced to devote to their work, per day, per week, per month, per year, per lifetime. Of course, Western industrial societies have been altering over the past century the proportions devoted to preparation, work, leisure, and retirement. But if education and work reform prove as intractable as appears likely, then a more direct and aggressive attack on the time—value axis must be launched. Education can prove rewarding for life off the job when many new challenges can be found. A move in this direction need not threaten the work ethic. Expanding the sights of people to seek satisfactions in areas other than their work holds promise of adding to total satisfaction.

Action in these directions is much more urgent in a society that faces marginally high unemployment rates, more costly inputs, and the rapid consumption of irreplaceable natural resources.

There are reformers who believe that omnipotent managers can alter the work environment to the point where most workers will be able to gain more satisfaction from their work. In contrast, the road to which the present study points goes in the direction of reforms which, in transcending the workplace, broaden the options that workers need and want.

Preface and Acknowledgments

"Ever since the Munich Olympics," writes Peter Black in the *Manchester Guardian*,[1] "the thought has worried me that television has become so huge and interlocked that ordinary standards of human behavior cannot be applied to it. The human response to the murder of the Israeli team would have been to abandon the games. The complexity and expense of dismantling the TV structure made it impossible." It is only a little unfair to compare the movement to "redesign," "restructure," "enrich," and "enlarge" work with the television industry.

The evolving movement is now over twenty years old, employs a very large corps of social scientists and social scientists manqués in corporations and government bureaus, and is led by a phalanx of academicians in universities and colleges, especially in business studies. And just as television can spark in us the sense that we are there, in Ed Murrow's fine phrase, and that we are thereby doing something—at least as legal witnesses to Joe McCarthy's loathsome ways, to Jack Ruby's insanity, to urban rioters' desperations—so the work reform movement can engender a feeling that something useful can be done to make all our work a bit less tedious by holding conferences and publishing endlessly optimistic reports about the ease with which we can reverse trends toward workplace specialization and heavy-handed supervision. Getting there or being there may be half the fun, but it is not, by any means, doing something.

It has not been our intent, by our work, to stop the work reformers. Rather, we have sought to open the matter of working conditions somewhat wider than it is their disposition to do; we felt it would be useful to focus less on the psychology of work. While much can be and has been said about the contribution of psychology as the dominant discipline in setting standards for behavior in the workplace, especially managers' behavior, more needs to be said about the circumstances surrounding the psyches of workers and bosses. Indeed, top managers in America, pressed on one or another social issue, regularly tell us that the comings and goings of men and women in the nation's workshops, mills,

1

stores, and offices are of less concern, are less important, than the "tough" problems they themselves face in financing, merchandising, forecasting, and other arcane aspects of entrepreneurship and economic derring-do.

It would, of course, simply not be useful to argue that psychology should be dropped and attention be directed entirely to the correlates of business cycles, for example, or that we should ignore worker "motivation" in favor of studies of mergers. Clearly it is as sanguinary a prospect nowadays to be "split by a false dichotomy" as it used to be to be "impaled on the horns of dilemma." There are, after all, subtleties beyond juxtapositions of persons and structures, and it was a number of these subtleties we sought to delineate and investigate.

Consider, in this context, that talking with European managers is like looking in the mirror. What we see there is a picture of American managers as superior, hard-driving decision makers, unbound by tradition and brimming over with willingness to change. As the Europeans see it, Americans operate in a range between flexibility and ruthlessness; Americans are much envied for their consequent opportunities and admired for their skills in exploiting them.

American students of the European scene, but far less often American managers, have a complementary view. They see a hard-working European labor force that compares all too favorably to the American labor force with its penchant for paid holidays and coffee breaks, and a benevolent management that somehow inspires greater productivity. Well, we have all seen holes cut in this tapestry; everyone, for example, finds the British to be ineffective. But somehow our stories about industrial relations, about techniques for getting along in the workplace, and about ultimate satisfaction and dissatisfaction with work maintain a naive quality.

Our own efforts to look beyond these conventional pictures, to examine some of the conflicts in ends and in means, are reported in this book. Given the large number of topical areas, we can be accused of being interdisciplinary. (We say "accused" because, as Philip Handler has put it, interdisciplinary research programs are often contrived "as if, by the pooling of ignorance, one might successfully address otherwise intractable problems." [2]) We hope we will be cleared of this basic charge on the grounds that, while we have only sampled the work in the fields from which we draw, we have drawn on the fine work of experts. We accordingly will plead guilty to the lesser charge of doing injustices by oversimplification or omission to the deeper-going, more extensive studies by investigators in each of the many subdisciplines on which we lean. It is clearly not possible to attend to every relevant study in each of so many fields; we hope that the utilities of a preliminary effort to synthesize will offset the intellectual-informational losses that accompany representative sampling techniques applied to knowledge, however thoughtfully they are applied.

Readers given to leafing through the notes, meanwhile, will discover that we mean what we say about sampling! The fact is, however, that we intend no slight to the many important investigators whose works are not cited; we chose the works we did cite for specific reasons, often rhetorical ones, and seek in this passage to honor the others whose influences, though implicit, will be detectable throughout. Among them the names of Robert Kahn, Barrington Moore, C. Wright Mills, Robert Merton, Harold Wilensky, Eugene Schneider, Robin Williams, Peter Blau, Michael Crozier, William Domhoff, Wilbert Moore, William Faunce, Amitai Etzioni, William J. Goode, S. M. Miller, Delbert Miller, Talcott Parsons, and Bernard Rosenberg come readily to mind.

An uncommonly large number of references have been made to our own work. The simple fact is that this volume represents a kind of summary of our work as much as a report on the specific problems we formally undertook to investigate. Our references to our earlier work are therefore substitutes for detailed restatements of specific materials that readers can, if they need them, obtain either from us or from libraries; we mean by these references to convey no special respect, as such, for our earlier labors.

This volume first began taking shape in 1956–57 when I was privileged to serve, with David Rogers, now of New York University, as a teaching fellow in George Homans's lecture series to Harvard undergraduates on industrial sociology. These scholars will have little difficulty in identifying the effects of our encounters on the main line of the discussion reported in these pages. Both subscribed to our central thesis that there are forces operating on managers and their charges at what we term macro-, mezzo-, and microscopic levels, and that the would-be analyst must constantly be mindful of the importance of forces beyond those singled out for specific attention by an investigator or teacher, lest he mislead himself and thus his audience. We have sought to live quite literally by this dictum; my collaborators and I accordingly offer our readers tentative conceptualizations. While our conceptualizations perforce do less than the fullest honors to those people who study specific phenomena, they are designed to stress the holism in the events of industrial sociology.

Teaching and research experiences since those Harvard days encouraged me many years ago to conceive of this volume pretty much as it developed. I always hoped, in short, that an opportunity to draw together the numerous piecemeal and particularized efforts in which I was engaging and to pull together some of the representative work of others in a more synoptic overview would someday materialize. I am happy to acknowledge the encouragement of many former colleagues at Columbia University who saw utilities in the approach, most especially Courtney C. Brown, William Newman, Leonard Sayles, James W. Kuhn, B. J. Widick, Ernest Williams, Clarence Walton (now of Catholic University), Roger Murray, David Dodd, the late Roger Flynn, Roy Blough, Samuel Richmond (now of Vanderbilt), Neil Chamberlain, and Eli Ginzberg. These men were among the principal architects of a graduate business curriculum in 1958–59 at Columbia University that was basically constructed around the premises of this volume, and they were much more than tolerant of my intellectual inclinations, however much they would dissent from some of the conclusions drawn in this volume.

In specific terms the book reflects the significant influences of James Kuhn, with whom I have often collaborated, of Leonard Sayles (and, indirectly, of his frequent collaborator, George Strauss of Berkeley), and of Eli Ginzberg. Dr. Ginzberg, who was kind enough to write the Foreword to this volume, has been a friend, mentor, colleague, and (permissive) boss during the eighteen years of my association with his Columbia University Conservation of Human Resources Project. This association was as significant intellectually as it was emotionally gratifying. My collaborators join me in thanking him for his splendid good offices in assisting us to obtain support for our work from the Ford Foundation and the Department of Labor. Kuhn, Sayles, and Ginzberg live very literally by the intellectual principles informing this volume, though they would not necessarily practice at the multiple analytical levels quite as we have done in these pages.

Next, it is relevant to comment on my collaborators, who tolerated my often ambiguous formulations with patience and forebearance. Mr. Freeman undertook the many months of work that are here greatly distilled in the discussions in Chapters 4, 5, 7, and 8, and taught all who were connected with it many important social science lessons. He never had doubts about the usefulness of our "model," but he served an enormously practical function in highlighting the difficulties in our strategy and tactics that we might otherwise have played down. In addition to the specific contributions I have noted, he played an important part in the discussions that fed into the development of other chapters in other parts of the book.

Marcia Freedman, who essentially wrote Chapters 6 and 9 and drafted lengthy memos that were eventually the spines of several other chapters also brought experiences from her ongoing research on macroscopic labor-force developments to the study's main story line. Those investigations, though conducted and written up during the present study and published separately, as Eli Ginzberg notes in the Foreword, helped us to remain loyal to our convictions that the work reform movement's prospects in organizational settings are best assessed while keeping a weather eye on social, economic, and occupational developments. Our collaborative efforts over the past decade, meanwhile, make it very difficult for me to separate the strands of our thoughts; her perceptions are enough a part of my own to make it an only slightly awkward pleasure to acknowledge that her ideas, phrases, and words appear throughout a report for which I was and am the responsible agent. Neither of us, I would judge, could readily make many clear claims to a number of the segments of the work. But I must absolve her from the sins of authorship, and I would prefer to do so in a way that stresses my debts to a most competent colleague, collaborator, and friend.

I wish also to acknowledge the important contribution made by Patricia Bonfield, who undertook, under my direction, to code and analyze the awards of arbitrators and then to draft the memoranda from which Chapters 10 and 12 were finally constructed. Her work made it possible to include a discussion of workers' and managers' rights and claims about which work reformers tend to be almost silent. As it happens, she augmented these efforts with careful assessments of the linkages between arbitrators' backgrounds and their awards that are not reported in this volume, but which she and I will seek to publish separately. By excluding that portion of her good work we also exclude a good deal of the very competent industrial-sociological analysis with which she surrounded the analysis of arbitrators' logics, for this analysis would have been a digression in a book in which we were already obliged to make enough "side trips" to tax the patience of readers.

Next, I am obliged to John Fietze and Geoffrey Berg for the spade work they did in anticipation of Marcia Freedman's discussion of strikes (Chapter 9). Mr. Fietze's ambitious and disciplined efforts went well beyond the discussion here reported; I hope that these efforts will be published separately, in a specialized scholarly journal. In the meantime, Mr. Fietze was an active participant in the early stages of our secondary analyses of worker survey data, reported in Chapters 5, 7, and 8.

We were also the beneficiaries of the time, data, thoughts, and technical skills of competent colleagues at Ann Arbor: Robert Quinn, Martha deBaldi Mandilovitch, Linda Shephard, and Peter Joftis. Gerald Gurin and Arthur Miller at Ann Arbor were extraordinarily helpful. We are also indebted to Eric Trist, Richard Shore, Donald Warren, Eugene Litwak, Harry Levinson, Albert Cherns, Douglas Bray, Harold Sheppard, Louis Davis, and Stanley Seashore, all of whom joined us for an informal meeting to discuss our work and to offer advice.

Among those people who gave the three of us substantive help were Jack Bailey and Samuel Peng of the Research Triangle Institute, the anonymous corporation personnel who provided us with restricted data, and Edward Rogoff, who analyzed data on self-employed workers in a memorandum that will likely be published separately.

I was also aided most significantly by William Rushing's careful reading of an early draft of Chapters 1–5 and 7–12, though he asked many more tough-minded questions than we could answer in kind. He made many corrections, spotted many logical flaws, and offered us many criticisms precisely on the issues we sought to join in our effort to derive the preliminary conceptual scheme we here describe. I am grateful, too, for helpful comments by Mayer Zald and Joachim Singlemann on Chapters 1–12, and by Rendig Fels and Malcom Getz on Chapter 6. Last, but by no means least, I would like to thank Anna Dutka for her meticulously professional help with the manuscript's preparation. While all three of us are beneficiaries, they were essentially my scribblings that she worked over.

Thanks go, as well, to the staff personnel at the United Auto Worker's Union's Walter and May Reuther Camp and to the rank-and-file members of the UAW and their families who tolerated my intrusions into their "working vacations" at Black Lake, Michigan, in 1973. The experience was a most valuable one, indeed. During my stay I benefited greatly from the help of B. J. Widick, a Columbia colleague who has a long association with the UAW, and of Bill Goode, then a UAW official.

To our sponsors at the Ford Foundation we owe many debts—intellectual no less than financial. Thus Basil Whiting, Robert Schrank, and Mitchell Sviridoff facilitated our work, read and commented on progress reports, and gave generously of their time as helpful listeners and commentators.

I am personally indebted to the Rockefeller Foundation for my share of a fellowship in the Foundation's Humanities Program, held jointly with James Kuhn in 1975–76. Much of the material in Chapters 4, 5, 8, 10, 12, 13, and 16 were collected as part of the research the Foundation supported; they are among the larger corpus of materials collected for a volume that I am preparing with James Kuhn on value dilemmas in business. My debts to Gladys Topkis, of The Free Press, are both numerous and individually large ones. As many social scientists have come to know, she belongs in the select company of editors who consistently seeks to protect authors from their worst instincts while making them her life-long friends . . . a "pro" among the best of "pros."

Finally, our thanks to John Deegan and Robert Burgelman for the help they gave all of us indirectly and more directly to Michael Freeman. To Joanne Koeller we owe thanks for typing and technical assistance in New York. To my wife, Winifred Berg, I owe thanks not just for library assistance and for providing me with clean typescript all day long, each day—an author's dream—but for many, many more gifts than either an author or a husband deserves.

Ivar Berg
Nashville, Tennessee

This study was prepared for the Employment and Training Administration, U.S. Department of Labor, under research contracts 21–36–73–47, 21–36–73–51, and 21–36–75–20—authorized by Title I of the Manpower Development and Comprehensive Employment and Training Act. Since contractors performing research under government sponsorship are encouraged to express their own judgment freely, this report does not necessarily represent the Department's official opinion or policy. Moreover, the contractor is solely responsible for the factual accuracy of all material developed in this report. Reproduction in whole or in part is permitted for any purpose of the U.S. Government.

Articles based on several chapters of this book have appeared prior to publication in this edition in *transaction/Society* and *Change* magazines.

1. Faith and Evidence: Will Patience Have Her Perfect Work?

A majority of people who have considered the inherent problems of worker morale and productivity in America have long shared a faith that workplace reforms would reduce workers' complaints while increasing their output. The faith came easily to Americans; it was consistent, after all, with biblical prescriptions about work making a moral virtue out of economic necessity, even as it allowed managers to claim a humane interest in employee welfare. Both elements of the faith, first enunciated clearly in the late 1930s, were attractive indeed to those disciples who were groping for rhetoric that might compete with that of a minority in America who saw revolutionary change as the only hope for workers' redemption. The ranks of the faithful believers in work reforms expanded greatly during the early years of the present decade, when, it was widely argued, the level of malaise among older workers had increased precipitously even as legions of youths were bringing new and challenging values to the nation's shops, mills, stores, and offices.

It was our judgment, as the paeans to work reform increased in volume, that the bases of this faith deserved systematic study to the end that we could make some estimates of the realistic prospects for improvements in the ways and means of work in America, of the degree to which the faith, so to say, will be matched by good works. We report here upon a series of the explorations we conducted, on several fronts, of the validity of a number of strategically important articles of the faith among optimists about jobs, workers and, especially, about managers.

Among the issues we sought to join are those that arise in connection with the following specific questions:

1. How well established are the direct and indirect relationships between the state of workers' well-being and organizationally relevant patterns of worker behavior? The answer to this question would presumably have considerable bearing upon one's assessment of the responses of

policymakers, public and private, to the options they have to affect workers' experiences in favorable ways.

2. Assuming that one may obtain decent relative if not absolute measures of different workers' discontents, what portions of these discontents are amenable to remediation specifically by the workers' own employers? To put this in another way, are there margins beyond which even managers who are engaged in the reform movement are limited?

3. Assuming that some worker discontents are in some measurable degree linked to arrangements over which employers *do* have managerial responsibility, how *deeply* engaged are managers in work reform efforts?

4. What reasons for managers' reactions to reform schema can be inferred from actual applications of social science-inspired reforms? These inferences should help one to gauge the depth of managers' interests in reform while adding to our sense of the functions of the American executive.

To put it succinctly, we are concerned with both the prospects for and the relevance of work reforms, especially those that have recently gained wide attention in the United States and Western Europe. The fact is that the steady flow of studies and discussions on work, workers, and work reform that began in the late 1930s has become a torrent. And there is promise of a great deal more to come. What, we ask, does it all mean?

In this first chapter we shall comment briefly on the current clamor over worker discontents and on the approaches to the problem offered over the past forty years. We shall then pass to an outline of the underlying assumptions of our explorations. Finally, we shall present the plan of this volume.

CONCERNS NEW AND OLD

Some of the language is new, to be sure, and a few new imperatives may be discerned in the flood of materials that have appeared since the matter of "worker alienation" moved toward the top of nearly everybody's list of America's crises in the late 1960s.

The contemporary version of the old concern with work stresses the errant ways of youth and the increasingly benighted place apparently assigned by them to economic growth and productivity; the work ethic, whose health has always attracted a certain concern, is now perceived in some quarters to be dying and has lately become the subject of eulogies in many others. Even some liberal skeptics have publicly mourned the passing of a moral imperative they once saw to be rooted more in profane economic necessity than in sacred precept.

It is something of a novelty, too, that the problem of worker discontent has not been pushed by besetting economic problems to a far less prominent place on the national agenda—as has been regularly the case with reform urgings in the past. Thus, TV documentaries and news magazines continue to tell us of "work enlargement" and "work enrichment" and of "sociotechnical-systems" approaches to "worker alienation," even in the face of chronically high unemployment rates. Somewhat less romantic pragmatists regularly assure us that while these and other workplace reforms are not likely to revive the "dying work ethic" in America, they are at least responsive to the demands of a growing number of employed citizens whose consciousness about work, like their consciousness about the environment and consumer rights and gender roles, has been "raised."

But the new brand names cannot obscure the generic quality of the drugs currently being prescribed for workers' malaise. Nor can hyperbole about heightened consciousness in the Age of Aquarius obscure the fact that "change agents" and their corporate clients in earlier times also had an interest in absenteeism and turnover (in periods of peak employment) and (in all periods) in the threats of unionists or the specter of union organizers.

Even the new endorsement of "business responsibility," often expressed by aspiring work reformers along with friendly business critics, has a historical analogy. As Reinhard Bendix has shown,[1] American business interest in human relations preachments, emanating from Harvard Business School professors and associates in the 1930s, reflected a long-time anxiety of professional managers who were embarrassed by the fragile logic linking their considerable authority over human and other resources to the property rights of the widows and orphans on whose putative behalf they directed our great enterprises. The problems of legitimacy, professional managers recognized, are less easily resolved in a democracy then elsewhere; authority was accordingly conceived by them to be far more acceptably linked simultaneously to noblesse oblige and to social-science research findings than to classically arrogant insistence on the legal rights and prerogatives of rulers. Professional managers' authority could be exercised more legitimately if it were rooted in expertise and generosity than in the property rights of stockholders.

The industrial conflicts of the 1930s added to earlier managers' interests in programs designed by social scientists and aimed at reducing employee "hostility." The effort to mobilize social-science wisdom in support of novel management tactics, meanwhile, was understandably viewed by unionists in this period as an expedient quest for any port in a storm.

The fact is that the underlying logic of numerous current Scandinavian workplace-reform experiments, and of a few celebrated attempts l States, publicized by Tom Wicker and others in the *New* by the task force responsible for the widely noted *Work* by expert witnesses appearing before a Senate subcom- n International Council for the Quality of Working Life,[4] ard Business School's Research Director,[5] even by UAW t Irving Bluestone—derives almost entirely and in a straight e investigations, articles, and books by Harvard Business ssors, their associates, and their students in the period be- ing World War II.

current version of the human-relations movement is not, aking, a recrudescence of the doctrines of that movement movement itself (discussed in Chapter 2) never abated. In- re scarcely any among the millions of graduates of business er the past thirty years who have not taken courses ac- m with applications of the behavioral sciences to the end in an organization may at once be better satisfied and more d that the organization's managers may be more sensitive, "nondirective," and otherwise benign.[6] On one side em- aced on the needs for redesigning job tasks so that workers specialized, less bored, and less constrained. On the other s are placed on the hazards of managerial officiousness and ism.

ved and far more broadly based interest in human relations- ions of work in recent years and the prescription of homeo- ies for the disorders allegedly bred by bureaucratic struc- odern production techniques would seem to suggest, how- are at last on the eve of a new age. As antidotes to work ackbreaking, is for most of us only a little less dull than pin- observed to be by Adam Smith in 1775, surely "work re- rticipatory democracy," and improved worker morale are time, finally, has really come. Or so we have been urged to vay, by a remarkable coalition of researchers, writers, think- a few consultant-practitioners.

nism of reformers, however, is grounded in studies in which have focused systematically on only a few aspects of eriences, and upon workers' attitudes rather more than r. The general tendency among reformers has been to em- e aspects of work and reactions to work that *seem* amenable ion in the interests of *both* employees and employers. The of reform-related research has thus been allocated to the f democratic over autocratic supervision, of work arrange- centive systems that facilitate the formation of work groups s may, with the help of social-psychological techniques, be fluenced), and of organizational designs that allow some involvement on the part of employees in procedures by which decisions affecting their work are reached.

AN APPROACH TO THE STUDY OF WORKING CONDITIONS: INITIAL ISSUES

Unlike many optimists, we see only dim prospects for much meaningful reform, particularly along the lines staked out in either the older or the newer versions of human relations. Our misgivings stem most immediately from our reading of the materials we have collected and on which we report in this volume. They are related more fundamentally, however, to the conceptions that informed our judgments about the types of evidence deserving consideration. These conceptions, which often compete with but sometimes augment those of human relationists, derive from social-science traditions in the industrial-relations and human-resources schools.

In contrast to the human-relations school, we attach considerable explicit importance to some issues that, as we see them, are beyond the scope of particular managers to join or resolve. Still other issues are beyond what managers themselves apparently consider to be their pale: they are not matters of management interest. While a number of these issues are often recognized in the abstract by work-reform enthusiasts, they are regularly ignored in intraorganizational studies by researchers who nevertheless would have managers act decisively on the basis of their particularized findings. In a similar way, a number of intraorganizational forces and factors are defined in question-begging fashion. For example, sloppy and inept supervision, often the scourge of a workplace, is rarely blamed on those higher up who screen, select, train, and govern supervisors.[7]

The traditions from which we draw lead us to be skeptical of the curiously two-valued view of managers and workers, the ingenuousness about efficiency and the distaste for conflict that characterize those who believe that a new day would dawn in America's shops, mills, and offices were it not for (1) managers' lack of scientific awareness of their opportunities, (2) the lack of union support, and (3) the need for further social science research designed to quicken managers' interests and to reassure resistant union leaders.

The approach in human relations, about which we have misgivings, differs from that in industrial relations and human resources, first of all and most important in breadth of focus. Human relations is concerned with the proximal, "micro" setting, while the others are concerned with "macro" aspects, common to a number of settings. Human relations, furthermore, is far more preoccupied with psychological and social-psy-

ces and with their management than with the structures of
and industries and the rights of persons.

ifference is rooted in the widely held conception among the
nists that there is an essential harmony in the interests of
managers. This conception is related in a critically impor-
o the perspective from which collective bargaining, includ-
navior, is viewed. Thus, in the human relations approach,
strikes are generally taken as evidence of logical defects in
-bargaining process rooted in the fact that bargaining il-
resupposes adversarial relations requiring adjudications of
ims and interests. In the industrial relations approach, on
, which accepts the legitimacy of fairly basic conflicts and
versarial interests between employers and employees, the
wed more favorably. Strikes in particular are taken to be
ions of bargaining rather than evidence of the deficiencies
ning process, extensions that constructively force negotia-
ver ever more inventive bargaining methods the better to
ks of strikes and lockouts.

ifference derives from the relative weights assigned to in-
l economic rationality, on the one hand, and to what the
onomist Pareto called nonlogical sentiments, on the other.
ied by our industrial relations—human resources approach,
ur reading of the evidence, to attribute more rationality to
d to expect somewhat less from managers than is typical
ations studies. To put it another way, we do not so readily
' conceptions of the world of work to be grounded essen-
rance, in their feelings, and in incompetent readings of
interests. In the other approach, workers' perceptions are
iewed as misperceptions, as "gut reactions" to a reality
they are inadequately informed and about which they are
rood unintelligently.

e are concerned with at least one set of issues that are not
uced to dichotomous formulation, issues involving concep-
sources of productivity, the linkages between productivity
y, and the "appropriate" balances to be struck between
and stability and between equity and efficiency. As it hap-
nceptions are widely shared by students of all persuasions,
strial-relations and human-resource students are more in-
uman relationists to ponder the complexities in the linkages
.

e have misgivings about the human relations tradition, we
in our explorations to deal simultaneously with issues and
ed in each of the two main schools. Our selection of spe-
variables, data limitations and specific misgivings about

some interpretations aside, has thus been influenced by human relations research as well as by industrial-relations and human-resources research. We have also sought to treat a few issues raised by eclectics who quite consciously borrow from the data and the interpretations offered by the more loyalist members of the two larger groups.

The distinctions in scope and interests to which we refer do not, it should be emphasized, describe a division of labor uniquely to be found in studies and writings about workers and working conditions. It is a common one in economic analysis generally and is especially well developed in the curricula of business schools. Indeed, the macro-micro distinction which we take to be a most critical one in work studies parallels a general distinction in academic social science.

Consider that proximal, local, intraorganizational issues are taken up by university teachers who teach micro-economics, organization theory, and management in curriculum offerings that emphasize the firm and the options available to the firm's managers in their planning, direction, and control functions. In these classes, managers are said to act decisively and to decide actively about choices whose larger parameters are described by external forces. Managers must simply accept these wider forces, but *within* their organizations, it is postulated, they can do good works.

Concurrently, diverse courses in macro-economics—national income accounts, economic theory, business cycles, public finance, and labor economics, for example—are taught by pedagogues and practitioners whose interests are heavily institutional rather than organizational in nature. The emphases in these courses are accordingly on the secular, cyclical, and programmatic developments in society, and on the political processes, statutory arrangements, and administrative initiatives about which organized interest groups make representations.

The topics addressed in these two broad curriculum areas are rarely considered simultaneously, a fact that reflects the practical difficulties of undertaking to "do everything." It is, after all, not obvious how one can go about melding relevant materials in a way that permits one to speak coherently about administered prices in the steel industry and, at the same time, about the effects of local union elections on managers of a steel mill; about the "conceptual foundations of business" and the "social responsibilities" of the businessman, on one side, and the status insecurities and "role strains" of shop foremen on the other; about the business cycle's principal determinants and the inventory problems of a middle-sized firm.

To put the matter in slightly different terms, our research efforts have been directed in large measure to problems that fall between those addressed in the narrower and wider perspectives alluded to here. Indeed, the problems to which we have been attracted are those engaging of a number of policy-oriented colleagues, including those at Columbia University's Conservation of Human Resources Project, who seek to the conclusions of "macro" *and* "micro" research strategies, one against the other. Our interests have accordingly been with theoretical constructions that are more integrated than those to which separate "macro" and "micro" traditions generally point. It has been a major and conscious aim of two of the authors for nearly twenty years to divine lessons from research, "macro" to "micro," on the economy's main sectors; on occupational segments; on industry, regional, and community settings; on work rules; on employer organizations; on corporate strategies; on unions; on job clusterings; on company work forces; and on the occupationally relevant educational achievements of employees in the aggregate and in particular work settings.

In all of this, teaching experience provokes intellectual discomfiture because so little literature is available that can help students of the business of America to assign priorities to the allegedly different forces that competing scholars and consultants hold to be nearly sovereign in their effects.[8] Interpretative problems are, however, more serious as one moves from the academy to the real world of managers and workers, the world in which commentaries on worker discontent are widely published. It is clear that the opposing perspectives of friendly professional antagonists have their homologue in the discussions about work and workers among those who manage.

As one might expect, however, there are some differences in the nature of these academic and "practical" debates: the institutional (macroscopic) and the organizational (microscopic) traditions gain approximately equal time in academic circles, but the debates in management circles and in the media tend to focus exclusively upon microscopic issues. The larger stage is thus held by social scientists who would equip managers from the scientific armamentarium stocked from studies of organizations, not from studies of the larger society; by human relations students, not by students of industrial relations and human resources.

PROBLEMS IN SYNTHESES

There is, as these remarks suggest, no well-developed sociology of knowledge based essentially on industrial-sociological problems; hence no theoretical apparatus is conveniently available for a systematic ordering of issues and empirical materials bearing upon work and its reform from the entire spectrum, "macro" to "micro." Indeed, such an apparatus would have to take account precisely of the problem to which we refer; it would have to help us get around the discontinuities, conceptual and otherwise, that become visible when the work in macro and micro studies are compared and contrasted.

A useful theoretical apparatus would also have to facilitate the ordering and synthesis of *historical* materials, going back to the Encyclopedists, who wrote about the division of labor in the production of pins thirty-eight years before Adam Smith made so much of the matter in 1775.[9] An examination of some of these materials strongly suggests, for example, that grossly misleading characterizations can readily creep into assessments of work-related conditions or circumstances when these are viewed in essentially ahistorical terms.

We may, in fact, illustrate our concerns, dramatize a major reason for our restiveness about the character of current discussions about work, and anticipate some of our conclusions by pausing to note the case of the Luddites who broke the machines in the shops of masters in the British cottage industry in the late eighteenth and early nineteenth centuries. The wage rates of these angry cottage workers had been cut by cottage masters hard-pressed in their turn by higher rents for the equipment they leased from "putters-out." These machine-owning "factors," who also put out the raw materials to cottage masters and then collected and sold the finished goods, had increased the rents on their machines as a result of adjustments required when Napoleon blockaded their European markets by the imposition of the Continental System.[10] Thus, the Luddites, whose very name has joined the language as a (usually pejorative) description of the psychology of those who dare to resist change, were actually fighting wage-rate cuts and anti-union sentiments, not technological change. The psychological assessment, emphasizing fear of change, has survived for over a century and is an attractive and apparently parsimonious evaluation when one's focus is upon microphenomena and when larger institutional and economic developments are ignored

In modern analysis, it is similarly too easy to impute fearful and therefore resistant attitudes to workers who, for example, simply husband the property investments in their jobs by collectively protecting hard-won workrules that have been bargained over long periods. Rarely are such phenomena as workrules examined in an historical context; such an examination might distinguish between fully rational economic behavior and psychologically irrational responses to "change."

Thus a number of students have, for example, pitied railroad firemen who tend no fires on diesel locomotives and printers who were for years entitled to reset advertising matrices—the notorious "bogus type" rule—in agreements that were viewed as protecting would-be Luddites. The facts of the matter, carefully considered, suggest that firemen and printers anticipated the relevant changes long before their employers did, acted inventively on their forecasts, and, finally, sold their rules for a price when employers' interests led *them*, decades later, to see an enterpreneurial advantage in making the purchase.[11]

A synthesizing apparatus would also have to order available empirical materials about a large number of occupations, not to mention specific jobs, and thereafter to offer some clues to the sources of similarities and differences among the attitudes and behaviors of workers in different employment settings and, indeed, in different nations.[12]

As our brief discussion of macro and micro approaches and our examples of difficulties facing a would-be industrial-sociological theorist suggest, we have here eschewed any ambitious venture in theory construction or into the sociology of knowledge. Colleagues in business no less than in the academy would of course be grateful to anyone who could move us closer to a formal theoretical apparatus suggesting resolutions regarding work that could be translated into public and private policies for enhancing the freedom, happiness, and productivity of the work force. The facts of occupational injuries and diseases; worker malaise; technological change; industrial conflict; inter- and intragroup tensions among persons of different ages, sexes, and races that are work-related; absenteeism; unfair labor practices; industrial sabotage; and the portion of inflation attributable to wasted talent and inadequate productivity, to name a few problems, need no detailed rehearsal in this introductory context. Nevertheless, we have avoided formal theorizing; we see our efforts as prerequisite steps toward a policy-relevant conceptual scheme, and we recognize that many more such steps need to be taken.

OUR APPROACH TO MANAGERS AND WORKING CONDITIONS: SOME SPECIFICS

Rather than attempt a fully developed version of the desired synthesis, then, we have joined a few of the issues we take to be critical for a realistic assessment of the prospects for constructive interventions calculated to affect and balance interests in the attitudes, behavior, and productivity of American workers. It is a main purpose of this book to explore an alternative to the prevailing view, especially in the most popularized literature on work, that managers alone seek to maximize (or at least optimize) efficiency and productivity, while they must simply adapt to forces that effectively limit the commitment of workers to work industriously. Our long associations with managers and aspiring executives and with the world in which they operate have left us highly skeptical of the first part of this perspective.[13] It is one of our main objectives to stake out the implications of our contention, for example, that tendencies to tame, temper, and traduce the production process are not one whit less developed among owners and managers than they are among workers. As we see matters it is simply unproductive to differentiate workers' and managers' stances toward production and to focus exclusively on reforms targeted on workers.

Old hands at the craft will recognize that our misgivings about the assumptions of Left and Right regarding managerial rationality and worker's psychology necessarily owe more to John R. Commons and to William Leiserson than they do to our own work. Commons, a leader of the "Wisconsin School" in economics, was the first (and one of the few) to examine work systematically from the perspective we have adopted, in an analysis for the old Bureau of Labor in the Department of Labor and Commerce. The study, published by the Government Printing Office in 1904, under the direction of Commissioner of Labor Carroll D. Wright,[14] is even-handed in its treatment of the reasoning of managers and workers. Its title, *Regulation and Restriction of Output*, refers first to employers and then to employees in more than thirty trades.

The second patron saint of the present study, William Leiserson, wrote an essay in Stanley B. Mathewson's classical study of 1931, *Restriction of Output Among Unorganized Workers*, in which he offered the then novel (and now neglected) interpretation of Mathewson's findings that workers who restricted output, nonunion no less than union, were "in good company when they limit production. . . . They appear to be following sound business principles." He added that among the "general kinds" of immediate stimuli to restriction of output was "unintelligent management."[15]

Our involvements in the human-resources field have therefore led us to view jobs and jobholders primarily in their larger economic-sectoral and occupational contexts, while striving to keep an eye on the key local organizational, "proximal," and intraorganizational contexts in which employees find themselves, upon which most investigators have focused, and to which reformers regularly bring a kind of "tunnel vision."

THE PLAN OF THE BOOK

We may view workers and their jobs, in metaphorical terms, as though they are and have been caught up in the vortex of a slow-moving whirlpool.[16] In one ring, so to speak, workers are significantly influenced by the characteristics of their employers' organizations and the technologies they utilize. We are respectful, in short, of an obligation to consider the "effects," reported in an extensive literature on workers' attitudes and behavior, of diverse structural features and of work methods and technological arrangements descriptive of an employment setting. Specific attention will be paid in Chapter 3 to the reported effects of what may be called the major indicia of organizations.

The consequences of some of the ways and means of managers, another of the rings in the spiraling whirlpool, will concern us in Chapters 4, 7 and 8, in which we consider evidence bearing upon the competence of supervisors, on managers' use of workers' educational achievements, and on managers' provisioning of workers on their jobs.

A third and a fourth ring are taken to represent the influence of the values of the larger American society. In the third ring are the values in America, on one side, that inform the standards by which we judge our achievements. The influence of these balances we examine in Chapters 5 and 6, dealing with the assessments Americans make of (1) the occupational advantages born of their educational achievements and (2) the (rather closely linked) relative income benefits perceived to be the rewards of workers and their families.

On another side are values having to do with the rights, privileges, and immunities of citizenship in what the late Adolf A. Berle called the American Economic Republic, values that need to be balanced against those underlying the rights, privileges, and immunities of property owners and the authority of their professional-managerial representatives. These balances, occurring in the fourth ring, we examine in approximate terms in Chapters 9 through 14 on the conflicts between unionized workers and managers that are manifest in strikes and grievances and the specific interests of managers in work reforms. In the final chapters we consider a few relevant lessons from overseas, examine the question of productivity, and proceed to summarize our efforts.

The foregoing will suggest that we are a good deal more concerned with managers—their interests, logics, options, and competencies—than with work satisfaction *as such*. While we hope to contribute to the discussion of worker discontent, our intent is to use the innumerable issues attaching to that question as vehicles, to shift metaphors, for an excursion into the other, the management side of the institutional landscape. To that end we have conducted a series of distinguishable studies or reports which are the stuff of Parts III through V. After organizing and packing the baggage in Chapters 2, 3, and 4, we stop at various points to view numerous terrain features in Chapters 5 through 15. While we do not turn over every stone or look behind every boulder during these stops, we have been obliged to do a fair amount of lifting and peering. We hope that our frequent introductions and summaries will serve to keep the main path of our analysis fairly clearly in view. A few of the more important of our conclusions, meanwhile, may be summarized in advance:

On one hand, managers are largely powerless to deal with many worker discontents and are largely uninterested in or ambivalent about some apparently important and potentially remediable complaints. The drama of the work-reform movement is best described as a limited engagement.

Workers, on the other hand, appear to be acting fairly rationally, under the circumstances, to protect their interests in situations in which their employers have comparable (rather than more highly developed) concerns about productivity and efficiency, as these values are conventionally defined. Finally, we regard recent and highly publicized West European experiences with work reforms as having only limited relevance to the American case.

The reference in the introductory chapter's title, meanwhile, to the Apostle James's preachment that the testing of faith produces steadfastness and that patience's work is made perfect by such trials is a pointed one. It is quite possible that the faith of true believers in reform will not be much tempted, in the Apostle's terms, by the trials we have conducted; those who lose faith, as Publilius Syrus (and Janis Joplin) have pointed out, often "have nothing left to lose." On one side, believers readily construct their faith, as perhaps salesmen-consultants must, to think highly of themselves.[17] Their expedience in the matter, however, leads them to confuse faith with piety and piety with godliness.

On another side, the more sincerely faithful reformers may argue that the trials we conducted are simply no match for their patience, that the trials have not been—and cannot be—conducted in a sufficiently rigorous fashion, and that the case for work reform remains as compelling in strict scientific terms as it is expedient in economic and attractive in moral terms.[18] We may accordingly be well advised to use the term "testlike" to describe our multiple ventures: the relevant data are perforce scattered, imprecise, and tentative and may not be assessed in accordance with methods that are either experimental or otherwise unambiguously valid and reliable.

Nevertheless, we invite the reader to consider the cumulative weight of the evidence we discuss. It is our sense that the evidence thus conceived is *at the very least* an inconvenience to uncritical convictions about work reform.

PART I

WORKERS, MANAGERS, AND THE SOCIAL SCIENTIST: WHAT IS PAST AND WHAT IS TO COME

In this first part we pursue in more detail the approaches to work to which we have already alluded. Our purpose in this section is to clarify and interrelate some of the key issues that adherents of different schools of thought have tended to explore separately.

The continued prominence of diagnoses and prescriptions deriving from research along the lines first staked out in the human-relations tradition leads us to give somewhat more critical attention in Chapter 2 to this position than to the perspectives of the industrial-relations and human-resources traditions.

Inferences about the sources of worker discontent, about the relationship of worker discontent to productivity, and about prospectful managerial strategies lead us to a discussion, in Chapter 3. of relevant research findings.

2. Two Perspectives on Saturday's Children: Rendering to Man According to His Work

To argue that an intellectually adequate and policy-relevant synthesis of materials on workers and their discontents is elusive is not to deny the efforts by social scientists and others who have sought to impose some order on these materials. It is our purpose in this chapter to define and narrow somewhat further the issues identified in general terms in Chapter 1 by reviewing studies with an institutional character and, somewhat more intently, studies with a more micro-sociological and psychological cast. Our discussion is not intended as a contribution to intellectual history, however. Indeed, our undertaking here has borrowed from the work of many others and is designed as an overview of a number of intellectual-historical ventures that have helped direct us to the distinctions we now hope to clarify.[1]

MARXIST, ECONOMIC, AND REVISIONIST APPROACHES

Work under Capitalism

Marxists, whatever their sectarian differences, have taken as their main concern the assertedly overriding effect on workers of the institutional character of capitalism; they have focused especially upon the principle of private property. There is, indeed, a long tradition of industrial-sociological and economic analysis in which the surplus produced by workers is elevated to ontological status in what is nominally a theory of value.[2]

According to some members of this school, the margins for countering the alienation that grows out of the separation of workers from the means of production [3] are limited in capitalist societies. The state, in this view, has among its major specific functions the preservation of private ownership, the incentive values perceived to inhere in the un-equal distribution of wealth, the *formal* freedom of labor, and the legal protection of labor's status as something very much like a commodity.[4]

To the extent that workers do not give conscious and organized expression to the estranging effects of these and related institutional arrangements and fail to identify the exploitative and repressive quality of their circumstances, they are said to suffer, in this perspective, from "false consciousness." Interventions on behalf of workers that do not encroach upon the legal and normative sanctity of private property miss the essential point: These interventions can function, at best, as pacifiers of workers whose productivity inheres in their dependence, their vulnerability, and their "false consciousness"—not in their satis-factions or their interests. Workers, in a word, produce out of necessity.

The Marxist tradition is well represented in Harry Braverman's work and, far less adequately, by a team of Soviet sociologists at Lenin-grad State University.[5] The latter study of 2,665 workers in Leningrad enterprises will receive attention in Chapter 15, in which we consider the relevance of comparative findings to the American case. Perhaps oddly, the authors are Marxists largely in the sense, one judges, in which most Americans are Democrats or Republicans. As garden-variety party members in America pay ritual obeisance to Lincoln and other saints, so the Soviet authors honor Marx or Lenin. The assessments, however, read like those to be found in a good American business school. The Braverman volume, on the contrary, goes far beyond the issues typically discussed in studies of work representing a position that goes well beyond contemporary discussions of workplace reforms.

Dignity, Democracy, and Bargaining

In a second institutional view, intellectually akin to but politically unallied with the Marxist version, most of the interest of property owners–employers and their highest-level representatives are conceived to be in substantial (though not in total) conflict with those who toil and trouble. The interventions endorsed by adherents of this position are designed to foster peaceful or constructive conflict in the form of collective-bargaining arrangements, grievance and arbitration proce-dures, and, ultimately, nonviolent strikes.

While adherents of a conflict model of industrial society vary in their detailed views, they tend to avoid the assignment of priorities to possible explanations of workers' attitudes and behavior, though considerable emphasis is placed on workers' interests in wages, salaries, and benefits, in work rules, and in the maintenance of the bargaining machinery through which these interests are represented and pursued. Rather less emphasis is placed on such other occupational aspects as intra-work-group relations and psychological responses to authority.

Workers' interests in work satisfaction, in this second institutional version, are informed by hard-headed assessments of the best that is possible—which is to say, negotiable or bargainable. As gains are won piecemeal, and with an eye to the strategic and tactical uses of economic power, new objectives will be identified and pursued by both parties. Simultaneous efforts are made by workers and their representatives to secure desirable and safer working conditions and larger economic benefits through public policy—that is, through the mobilization of political action.[6] Great emphasis is placed by analysts in this tradition on the overall demand for labor, on the "tightness" and "looseness" of the labor market, in shaping worker attitudes and behavior.

Matching the entirely open-ended views of worker satisfaction in this second institutional approach are highly pragmatic views of productivity. Thus, most members of the industrial-relations fraternity draw upon a large and complex body of economic science in which productivity is the result of a host of forces, arrangements, and decisions. These forces, while reducible to *theoretically* parsimonious categories like "labor," "capital," and "entrepreneurship," are not amenable to simple prescriptions for day-to-day actions.[7]

The fact that labor economics, a special area in economics that is close to industrial relations, has stood outside the field's mainstream reflects the extraordinary difficulties economists have confronted in assimilating workers' involvements in the production process into the neoclassical model with which they work. Even efforts to comprehend the labor sector in work on human capital, its formation, and its utilization, are acknowledged to be inadequate to the assimilative task.[8] The issue is a vexed one indeed.

This is not to say that industrial relationists have been oblivious to the satisfaction-productivity question. The point is, rather, that both worker satisfaction and work productivity are taken by them to be highly complex matters: workers' concern with the first and their commitment to the second are taken at face value, as the outcome of bargaining processes. Interests change in a changing society, and productivity is the result of bargains with workers, as well as of a large array of decisions (such as those governing capital investments) that lie substantially beyond the pale of labor-management relations.

Finally, it needs to be added that, in this conflict view, few assumptions are made about differences in rationality between workers and employers. Rather, the actions of both are taken to be rationally informed by accurate perceptions of their respective interests. While normative judgments about the parties intrude into the analysis in many instances, the model underlying the second institutional approach aspires to deal with behavior as events occur.

A third institutionally linked view may be quite literally attached to the second; it is associated with the name and the work of Frederick W. Taylor, and it focuses on the prospects for enlarging the economic pie (and thus the size of absolute shares) through more effective production techniques, in the hope of obviating battles between labor and management over relative shares. While the specific prescriptions of Taylor and his followers, involving the detailed analysis of jobs, the application of work-simplification techniques, time-and-motion studies, and more, have a major place in the history of the subject of this chapter,[9] they will not concern us for the moment. The "larger pie" notion *does* concern us, but is best juxtaposed with the less institutional views outlined below because it has been largely incorporated by the human relationists and their successors. The other scientific management point, about work simplification, is most clearly represented in engineering studies; like the economists' "economic man," routinized man finds no admirers among human relationists and their sundry intellectual kin. Indeed, many of the major figures in human relations and related reform groups began in other days and today begin their theoretical assessments with castigations of both "Taylorism" and economists' postulates.[10]

Human Relations and Beyond: Here Today and Here Tomorrow

The second of the two *main* approaches that concern us, is most conveniently dated from the work in the 1930s and 1940s by Elton Mayo, a lay psychoanalyst, Fritz Roethlisberger, and George Lombard, all of the Harvard Business School; L. Henderson, a physical scientist;[11] and several students of Mayo and Roethlisberger, including a number of today's senior social scientists. Like the "sociotechnical systems" and the "work-enrichment" enthusiasts of the 1960s and 1970s, these social scientists of the 1930s and 1940s had followers in industry. Just as today articulate business leaders with eyes for social-science solutions and strategic positions at General Foods have joined forces, in celebrated experiments in the Gainesburger plant at Topeka, Kansas, with Richard Walton of the Harvard Business School, so Professors Mayo, Roethlisberger, and Lombard earlier joined with Chester Barnard, James Worthy, and W. J. Dickson of New Jersey Bell, Sears Roebuck, and Western Electric, respectively.

Mayo and Roethlisberger were quite taken with several sets of ideas that are crucial to understanding the aspirations of those who have continued to work in their tradition. First, they were influenced by

Freud's explanations of unconscious processes, especially the so-called defense mechanisms. Second, they were impressed by Emile Durkheim's notions about anomie and the social circumstances that produce the sense of loneliness and isolation comprehended by the French socio-logist's term. Third, they were taken with a central proposition among anthropologists: that all social activities of people, no matter how ap-parently trivial, serve to maintain the ongoing functioning of a social system.[12] Mayo, who had worked as a psychoanalyst in Australia, had met countless "functionalist" anthropologists on their way to and from studies of the social life and rituals of aborigines in the hinterlands, and he was struck by their ideas.

Finally, Mayo and his colleagues were in debt to two Harvard Business School articles of faith: first, that men could be trained to be-come managers through academic programs that go well beyond ac-counting, finance, and marketing, to include psychology;[13] second, that the urge of workers to organize themselves into unions could be coun-tered by "making the pie larger"—that is, by increasing the productivity of the factors of production, especially the human factor, and by help-ing workers to consider the work organization as a membership group.

The influences on Mayo, presented here only in their barest outline, were neatly articulated: workers' lack of cooperation with managers, or outright opposition to them, was a special case of an unresolved author-ity problem, probably with parents; life in industrial society was anomic, and the workplace was a potentially therapeutic setting in which com-pensatory social relations would emerge; workers' behavior, finally, would be understandable to employers if clique formation, output re-striction, and other "defensive" acts were viewed, like behavior patterns in a preliterate culture, in functionalist anthropological, sociological, and psychological terms.

Of the businessmen, it was Chester Barnard of AT&T who seized upon the notions of the Harvard Business School professors, and wove these ideas together in *The Functions of the Executive*, one of the most influential books ever published about business[14] Drawing heavily on his mastery of Ma Bell and of the New Jersey Telephone Company apparatus, Barnard argued that managers should deal with worker dis-content by applying social-science knowledge regarding workers' needs for social affiliations and more "democratic" supervision.[15] Both of these could be provided to workers so that they would be happier, more pro-ductive, and less interested in conflict. "Conflict," with its insidious overtones, was in this tradition clearly a euphemism for unions, a fact not lost upon trade-union critics before World War II.

Unions were ignored in other studies as well. The published report on the now celebrated Hawthorne experiments appeared in 1938, but the experiments were completed much earlier. Restriction of output, in 1929, was attributed to "nonrational" workers who, according to Roethlisberger and Dickson, mistakenly feared that management would revise piece rates if workers produced at higher levels.[16] The effects of depression fears, like the potentially functional roles of unions, were ignored by these scholars. The older inclination to package anti-union-ism and managerial apologetics reappears, sometimes quite explicitly, in the contemporary work of those with interests in organizational development and sociotechnical systems.[17]

Like Barnard, the professors discovered workers' "social needs" by the bagful, though the research had initially concerned the effects of the physical environment (heat, ventilation, illumination, and so forth) on industrial fatigue. Mayo, in a series of books as influential on management theory as those by Barnard, preached the need for arranging equipment and organizing supervisory functions in such a fashion that workers' social and psychological needs could be filled.[18]

An "informal system," said the early human relationists, would develop among employees anyway; the wise manager would recognize that these systems tempered emotional reactions to managerial rewards and punishments. Work-group members, they reminded students, would adhere to group production standards and to other problematical norms lest they incur the wrath of the system's other members. This informal system could be of considerable value to sophisticated managers, wrote both Mayo and Barnard, in that the loyalty of individuals to the work group was of greater influence in shaping the behavior of employees than were management sanctions—and perhaps a good deal greater than marginal increases in managements' rewards to individual workers.

An employee, for example, would let his co-workers down only under penalty of social isolation; thus, attendance and production rates were a function of social needs and of the degree to which work-group norms were well developed. Such assertions were borne out, at least in the short run, in studies like those by Mayo and Lombard of air-frames manufacturing,[19] where the Harvard professors constructed what is now called a "sociotechnical system" solution: machines were placed sufficiently close together for workers to talk with each other. The result of this intervention during World War II was a workers' "social system" whose sanctions against absenteeism were far more effective than those of managers.

Mention of the war is relevant here because it was a time during which industrial sociologists with these perspectives became the beneficiaries of two unrelated developments: a change in union attitudes and ongoing changes in cultural anthropology. The icy opposition of unions and leftist intellectuals to the human-relations movement temporarily melted when all parties agreed that productivity needed to be increased if the United States was to succeed in the great war against fascism. Clinton Golden and Harold Ruttenberg were among the first trade-union converts, and their writings incorporated all the relevant citations of studies showing that it was possible to make work-life better while making workers more productive. Indeed, the latter was held to be dependent on the former.[20]

Secondly, a group of anthropologists, whose work on Pacific island cultures helped shape Navy and Marine Corps policies designed to win over or neutralize indigenous populations on the "stepping stones" to Tokyo, came into their own. Their ethnographic methods had already incorporated Freudian thinking, the family being so obviously an important unit in the cultural transmission process, and they set about enlarging their intellectual sphere by applying their psychocultural approach to the problems of totalitarianism, anti-Semitism, and militarism in Europe and Asia.

Leading political scientists, too, were for a time taken with the promise that employment of the "culture concept" would facilitate dealings with the Soviet Union and reform of Japan and Germany along more democratic lines. A whole shelf of books helped explain that the swaddling of Soviet infants contributed to stoicism—and vodka consumption—among Soviet adults; that early toilet training in Japan contributed to the orderly—that is, militaristic—Japanese character; and that the patriarchal nature of the German family contributed to the authoritarian German personality to which Hitler successfully appealed.

The data supporting these and related simplifications of complex social systems were scant, if imaginative.[21] Much was made, for example, of an early German film, *The Cabinet of Dr. Caligari,* in which all the themes later embodied in the person and role of Adolph Hitler appeared. The investigators' methods were those of the ethnographer who was accustomed to characterizing a whole preliterate culture on the basis of a period of participant observation with a few families and individuals of a particular tribe of South Pacific islanders.

It did not take long after the war ended for the approach to be called into question. Teams of Soviet specialists at university research centers found only modest hope in these undertakings in their own interdisciplinary efforts to understand the USSR; and they practically wrote off the "culture and personality" approach, with its emphases on child-training techniques, as "Scott Tissue Sociology." Back at the factory, however, the message of the national-character studies fell on the interested ears of human-relations enthusiasts.

ORGANIZATION DEVELOPMENT

Unions were here to stay after World War II, and it became inappropriate to regard workers as neurotic aborigines. By adopting the psychocultural model, it would be possible for sociologists and anthropologists who studied organizations to reorganize the concepts of three decades of work, including the wartime work at the Tavistock Institute in the United Kingdom.

Of great moment here was the investigators' sense of the need to preserve the psychological component while dropping the questionable pejorative implications of the earlier model's view of individual workers. The redeeming solution involved taking two relatively simple steps. First, do psychological studies of organizations rather than of individuals, and do them in plants or in worker groups rather than in whole nations. In each of several subsequent studies the organization was characterized in terms of the psychological demands it made upon individuals, and efforts were made to determine whether or not the personalities "fit" the structure; incongruencies between structures and personalities would only evoke defense mechanisms, conflict, alienation, and all the rest. The second step was to do psychological studies of managers.[22]

Critics were disarmed by this new synthesis. Whereas the older model made a great deal of the rationality of managers and the nonrational behavior of workers who failed to respond to incentives, absented themselves, and restricted output (and thereby irrationally lost income), the new model at least made room for the nonrationality of managers. According to the organization-development writers, workers might be driven to alienation and low productivity by managers who, in psychologically self-serving ways, structured organizations so as to isolate themselves from employees and thereby deny workers the "self-actualization" they sought.

Human relations had entered a new era, in which its practitioners could follow a doctrine that was apparently even-handed and thus more attractive to professional academics with "applied" interests. A number of contemporaries have become prominent spokesmen for this position. One of them, Scott Myers, operates a nationally known consulting service that specializes in detailed applications of the approach and sponsors conferences on these techniques aimed at audiences interested in, for example, "How to Avoid Unions." Another, Louis Davis, directs a center at UCLA that is devoted to improving the quality of working life and organized around frameworks first staked out in the 1930s, embellished in the late-1950s, and currently being fully codified. Myers, according to the Columbia Business School's associate dean for continuing education, "offers practical top executives a very important and useful perspective" at the school's executive programs.[23] Davis is a senior staff advisor to the Organisation for European Economic Cooperation in Paris, lectures and publishes widely on work structure and worker malaise, enjoys the support of governments and foundations, and is a leader of an international organization of work reformers. His work will concern us in Chapter 16 and elsewhere.

Chris Argyris has applied his version of the evolving techniques and perspectives to highly placed officers in hospitals, corporations, and the U.S. Department of State. His work has been admired equally by the editors of the *Harvard Business Review* and by leaders of the Students for a Democratic Society. It is accordingly something of an oversimplification to argue that today's human relationists could appeal only to those bent on preserving the status quo.

The point is that the heirs of the original Hawthorne investigators are by now well established indeed; their students and teachings are distributed across the globe, and their audiences are equally international in composition.

By implicating management, the newer investigators appear to have reduced their vulnerability to critiques grounded in modern liberal economic thought [24] and to have broadened the front across which we might look for solutions to the industrial problems of workers. Indeed, the failures of management to apply the human-relations approach were seen, in rather strict psychological terms, as results of the hierarchical, bureaucratic, rule-ridden, "punishment-centered," psychologically insensitive, and even repressive structures designed by managers who mistrusted employees, feared candor, and were led by their authoritarian instincts to seal themselves off in the executive suite.[25]

In *current* discussions, managers are assumed to have the capacity to overcome their irrationality and to build new organizational and technical systems. Researchers share with business audiences the promising data on the new Gaines pet-food plant in Topeka, on Western European experiments at the Volvo, Saab, Porsche, and Olivetti plants, and at a couple of Norwegian locations, as well as data on earlier experiments in collieries in the English Midlands and at the Lincoln Electric Company in the United States. The point of these discussions is to demonstrate that social and technical systems must be *articulated* in order to produce a single "sociotechnical system" that simultaneously serves human and production goals.[26] Managers are thus stimulated to think of their options, and conference discussions are conducted by investigators on how presentations may be made to avoid promising too much to would-be clients.[27]

While the perspectives, from Hawthorne to Topeka, have undergone a kind of linear evolution, present-day audiences are made up of substantially the same kinds of people who have shown interest in these issues since the earliest days of human-relations efforts: business journalists on assignment from their editors; a random assortment of people from universities and foundations; a few staff personnel from the labor movement; and, finally, a large number of personnel executives from U.S. corporations. In recent years these audiences have heard lectures on restoration of the work ethic, on "managerial grids," on "sensitivity training," on therapeutic versus autocratic management modes, on "dollarizing personnel investments," and much more.[28] The fact that these audiences rarely include managers from either the private or the public sector who have line responsibilities [29] is relevant to an understanding of the modest degree to which the ideas presented are applied in the world of work (a matter which is addressed in Chapters 7 and 10).

PERSPECTIVES, PROSPECTS, AND PROBLEMATIC ISSUES

If we leave aside the Marxist approach [30] and recognize that the scientific management school's essential strands have been selectively incorporated in the industrial-relations and human relations–organization development approaches, we are left with (1) the perspective in the latter two approaches regarding work and regarding intervention schema addressed to improving the conditions of American workers, and (2) a residual perspective we identified in the introductory chapter by the term "eclectic."

Improving Working Conditions

Many investigators would indulge us in the use of this threefold characterization for rhetorical and expository purposes but would be understandably uneasy about being pigeonholed. It is true, after all, that a great many investigators do not pursue in their research *all* of the issues about work that they think important in this area of scholarship; it is unfair to interpret a researcher's focus on a single problem as evidence that the scientist has rejected other problems as unworthy of study.

Nor are scientists, whatever their particular research interests or relative breadth of outlook, responsible for the excesses and exaggerated claims of their many colleagues—called academic entrepreneurs by the late C. Wright Mills—who simplify and merchandise social-science findings as consultants, without inhibition or reservation. It is accordingly appropriate to suspend concern with innumerable value-laden dimensions of the industrial-relations and the human relations–organization development schools and to disregard the differences, both gross and subtle, between the two approaches in favor of a more general discussion. We may then confront these approaches, and especially the intervention schemes of the latter-day human relationists with what we suggest are relevant findings. We will accordingly return later to the differences between the major points of view where these differences are highly developed and productive of insights.

Thus, it has been commonly held that a major prerequisite to increases in the productivity of American workers is that they be satisfied and, furthermore, that managers' concerns with productivity are by and large consistent with workers' concerns with their own well-being. But, it is often added, managers and American society would benefit from the improvement of workers' well-being even if productivity gains did not result.

It has been argued repeatedly that workers' satisfactions and dissatisfactions are both "intrinsic" and "extrinsic." Characteristically, socioeconomic issues (like salaries and wages) are conceived to be "extrinsic," while sociopsychological issues (like group memberships and authority relationships) are conceived to be "intrinsic" in character.

Next, it has been held that managers are capable of identifying and dealing with both types of satisfaction and dissatisfaction whose sources are anchored in arrangements vulnerable to decisive interventions. These interventions, in turn, are calculated, on the one hand, to increase satisfactions and, on the other, to reduce dissatisfactions.

By way of sampling some of the specifics, it has been argued that a consideration of technology's role is indispensable in efforts to identify the causes of dissatisfaction. The *type* of technology,[31] the spatial location of technical means—from Xerox machines to drill presses [32]—and the spatial-temporal discontinuities or linkages of machine-related units of work flow [33] are among the key structural "givens" that shape intergroup relations as well as the attitudes and the behavior of workers.

It has also been reported that the effectiveness of the grievance process in organized work settings is of strategic importance to workers; [34] that many unhappy workers are afflicted with structurally induced inconsistencies among the multiple indices of what would otherwise be gratifying organizational statuses; [35] and that workers have needs that are of a hierarchical character, such that higher needs like the need to "self-actualize" appear after lower-level needs are met.[36]

Of critical interest here are the underlying principles associated with the human relationists, especially, in their several incarnations: that a significant number of issues which are problematical (or worse) for employees arise in the actual work setting; that these are to a very large extent rooted in organizational size and technology and the job methods related thereto; and that there are wide margins for sensible managerial interventions into offensive intraorganizational causes of discontent.

These interventions may be successfully designed and beneficially applied to the degree to which managers are sympathetically disposed toward behavioral-science perspectives, methods, and findings. Managers, it is widely believed, would in most instances enthusiastically embark upon and seek to maintain workplace and organizational reforms in order to gain either direct or indirect benefits. Finally, it is argued, worker representatives are too often chary of interventions for accountable but largely and ultimately inexcusable reasons.

A critical evaluative treatment of these approaches awaits more detailed discussion in Chapter 3 of the underlying relationships between satisfaction and productivity, the sources of satisfactions and their ordering, and a preliminary discussion of the observed impacts of intervention strategies on workers' satisfactions and dissatisfactions. We turn now to that discussion.

3. Productivity, Satisfaction, and Intervention: Forty Years in the Wilderness

The brief overview of underlying assumptions in Chapter 2 was intended to spotlight issues rather than to illuminate specific intramural differences among social scientists and practitioners about the questions to which the chapter alluded. Fortunately, there is available a review of these differences that provides descriptive and critical orientations toward the human relationists, the organizational behaviorists, and the organizational development ("OD") groups, specification of the implications for the industrial- relations approach, and a helpful bibliography.[1]

Our more pointed concerns leave us with relatively fewer issues than are reviewed by Strauss and his colleagues, as follows:

1. To what extent are the satisfactions and dissatisfactions of workers related to their performance in general and their productivity in particular?
2. To what extent can the sources and determinants of workers' satisfactions and dissatisfactions be pinpointed, whatever their implications for worker performance?
3. To what extent can the sources of satisfaction and dissatisfaction be ordered in respect to their importance as "explanations" of observed variations in worker reactions to the world of occupational experiences generally and concrete work experiences in particular?[2]
4. To what extent are the forces, circumstances, and events that appear, in statistical and analytical terms, to reduce dissatisfactions and heighten satisfactions amenable to influence and intervention?

And finally,

5. To what extent are employers particularly and worker representa-

tives to a lesser degree concerned about and capable of acting upon options suggested in answers to the previous question?

The first three of these issues are addressed in this chapter.

SATISFACTION AND PRODUCTIVITY

We may some day discover the simultaneous equations that express the complicated interactions among workers' performance patterns and their satisfactions and dissatisfactions. The first of the questions above, however, cannot be answered affirmatively. There is something resembling a network of relationships among the relevant variables; it is exceedingly hard, however, to construct even an approximation of a matrix from available materials.

Consider, first, the conceptual and methodological difficulties of defining and measuring "productive" performance in a world in which the long run is a succession of short runs; in which the energy of managers and their charges can flag as well as peak; in which machines can break down for lack of "unproductive" maintenance work; in which customers seek a personal touch, and in which quantity and quality may be reciprocals; a world, finally, in which haste often makes waste. It is a world also in which the demands for some products are sufficiently price-inelastic to protect an enterprise against the costs of occasional miscalculations, just as market imperfections may otherwise protect employers from having to absorb all or most of the costs of what Thorstein Veblen called workers' "strategies of independence" and "withdrawals of efficiency."

Robert Quinn and his colleagues in The Survey Research Center, a component of the Institute for Social Research of the University of Michigan, put the matter well: "It may be doubted," they point out,

> whether there is any empirical justification for assuming a unidimensional construct representing "overall job performance" or "net performance," and whether various separate measures of performance can be legitimately regarded as independent estimates of such a single variable.[3]

One may question the validity of such a construct and the measurement tactics it implies for logical reasons arising in part

> from the common finding that some elements of performance may be *negatively* correlated, that the elements interact, and that the resulting single measure does not reflect well the values implied by the initial choice of elemental measures.[4]

Quinn and his colleagues cite data from each of two studies on the interrelationships among workers' effectiveness ratings, productivity, accidents, absences, and errors, in twenty-seven organizational settings.

These indicate that the relationships "were generally small, and that the size and direction of relationships were generally more variable than could be accounted for on the basis of measurement and sampling errors."[5]

Summaries of relevant research appeared in studies by Victor Vroom in 1964 and by Frederick Herzberg in 1957. Vroom concluded that

> there is no simple relationship between job satisfaction and job performance. Correlations between these variables vary within an extremely large range and the median correlation of .14 has little theoretical or practical importance.[6]

In the earlier summary statement, Herzberg and his colleagues said substantially the same thing: of twenty-six studies, fourteen showed that positive job attitudes were related to higher productivity; nine showed no relationship; and three, that workers with positive job attitudes had poorer production records than those with negative attitudes.[7]

Where Herzberg and his colleagues suggest that "job satisfaction may indeed affect performance but *only under certain limiting conditions*,[8] Vroom pursues a more basic line of analysis which leads him to question whether job satisfaction should even be *expected* to be related to performance. The key point of his skepticism is that keeping a job usually requires performance far short of the potential of the worker, and most workers reach or exceed the minimal level of performance necessary to avoid being fired.[9]

More recently, Katzell, Yankelovich, *et al.*, in reviewing studies of the relation of job design to motivation, performance, and satisfaction, concluded that, while "intrinsic aspects of job *content* associated with enlarged challenge or difficulty, diversity, identity, control, and work-cycle time" are correlated with higher job satisfaction, the relationships of satisfaction to productivity, absenteeism, and turnover are more complex. As for the claim that "productivity is greater in enlarged or enriched jobs, the supporting evidence is sparse, at best."[10]

The reading of these reviews and of their own findings by Quinn and his colleagues is probably the best that can be rendered. When all is said and the research is done, the relationships between workers' satisfactions and their performance are concomitant in nature: the two are conditioned by the extent to which high productivity is a value in itself and by the extent to which productivity is valued as a means to workers' other aims.

As we will see again later, there can be reasoned disagreements between workers and managers—and even among workers—about precisely what productive behavior is, a fact that makes for considerable difficulties in studying the role of satisfaction in workers' performance. In addition, there are conceptual and methodological difficulties in efforts to measure dissatisfactions, since dissatisfactions begin to register at different points depending upon the questions asked of respondents.

Thus, in the 1969 Working Conditions Survey, the percentage of satisfied workers varied from 48 to 86 on a half-dozen relevant questions. The "thresholds of discontent" can therefore be seen to have a considerable range depending on the nature of the question. More dissatisfaction is reported—

1. when workers are asked whether they enjoy their jobs than when "satisfaction" with the job is asked about specifically.
2. when the question concerns another—even a hypothetical—worker than when the question focuses on the respondent.
3. when the question raises the (hypothetical) issue of the worker's reliving his or her life than when it directs attention to the worker's present reaction to the job.
4. when workers are invited to consider attractive alternatives to their present jobs than when they are asked for their reactions to their present jobs on a noncomparative basis.[11]

Thus the Ann Arbor researchers conclude that:

Except for recent and anticipated improvements of measures, there is no reason to expect that future investigations will be any more consistent in identifying substantial positive relationships between job satisfaction and performance than other investigations have been hitherto.

There is no compelling theoretical reason for expecting any sort of across-the-board relationship between satisfaction and performance.

Even when such relationships *are* identified they cannot automatically be interpreted as indicating that high satisfaction is a cause of good performance. There are two competing interpretations:

1. it is actually the good performance that is creating the high satisfaction;
2. there is no causal association between satisfaction and performance but both are in fact the product of some third factor.[12]

We will return to the performance-productivity issue in later chapters in which other correlates of worker behavior are assayed. We may suggest even this early in our discussion, however, that available evidence hardly supports the bold claims that investments by managers in intervention techniques proposed by social scientists will yield palpable benefits.

WORKER SATISFACTION AND DISSATISFACTION

It should by no means be inferred from the foregoing that workers' attitudes and feelings are unrelated to the quality of their jobs or to the myriad immediacies that shape their occupational experiences. At the same time, in a civilized society, it does not gainsay the desirability of humane reforms to argue that the costs and benefits thereof are incalculable.[13]

As a matter of fact, there are *some* discernible relationships between work experiences and work attitudes. To rely once again on Quinn and his colleagues, satisfaction seems, on the one hand, to be most closely related to demographic factors and, on the other, to be rooted in working conditions. Younger workers, blacks, and other minorities are consistently less satisfied with their jobs, as are blue-collar, service, and clerical workers. Women, except those with preschool children, register about the same degree of satisfaction as men. And while college graduates have high satisfaction levels, there is little relationship among non-college graduates between years of schooling and job satisfaction.[14]

As we shall observe in Parts II and III, the relationships between satisfaction and age, race, sex, education, and occupation are somewhat more complicated than these simple statements might imply, particularly because of the occupational distribution of young workers and minorities and because of the earnings patterns associated with this distribution. But demography aside, the Working Conditions Survey and the subsequent Quality of Employment Survey found that workers accorded overriding importance to such job facets as the "challenge" of the job, the availability of resources needed to perform well, and the quality of the supervision they received. In citing these findings we invite particular attention to the fact that major academic surveys gave a representative sample of employed Americans opportunities never before given them *as workers* to speak to questions about the quality of their managers *as managers*.

Even when questions about workers' supervisors have been raised in surveys, they have never been conceived as indicators of the quality of leaders higher up, who have responsibilities for selection, assignment, and monitoring activities in the enterprise. The underlying issues of the quality, the competence, and, ultimately therefore, of the very legitimacy of managers are almost totally ignored in the abundant writings since Elton Mayo and Chester Barnard. In 1969 and again in 1973, however, workers were afforded multiple opportunities to express themselves on matters intimately related to the legitimacy of their managers, and from 61 to 68 percent reported these items as very important to them.[15] As we shall see, the facts regarding managers' uses of resources in employment settings suggest that the terrain—even in organizations that have been well surveyed and regularly observed in the past forty-odd years—contains features yet to be adequately identified and charted on the way to a more complete conception of worker discontent.

Of course, there are some factors known to affect the contents and discontents of workers, though they tend to be viewed as part of a psychological hierarchy of workers' concerns rather than as elements of the social and organizational structures in which workers find themselves. Thus, it has been repeatedly shown that workers are more satisfied to the degree to which they feel secure in their economic circumstances and to the degree that their efforts are well rewarded; to the extent to which they enjoy their obligatory relationships with their peers; to the degree to which they feel the risks to their physical safety are both predictable and minimized; to the extent to which they feel their work is challenging and genuinely skilled rather than tedious and simplified; to the degree to which they enjoy some opportunities for personal development; and to the degree to which they feel they have a say in the way things are done.[16]

THE ORDERING OF WORK SATISFACTION

Many words have been written about these satisfactions and dissatisfactions as orderly and ordered outcomes of diverse experiences. It is, however, not easily established that either the attitudes or the behaviors of workers are amenable to hierarchical differentiation. Thus it has been argued that "satisfiers" and "dissatisfiers," among workplace attributes, are of essentially different natures, an argument that has been most effectively questioned by Katzell and Yankelovich.[17]

Finally, as we have suggested, it is an article of faith among many employers and social scientists that workers' "needs" and their reactions to work are arranged hierarchically. As "lower-order" needs are satisfied, it is argued, "higher-order" needs are admitted to consciousness, a kind of evolution of rising expectations. Attractive on its face, the argument gains no endorsement from Porter, Lawler, and Hackman:

> There is strong evidence to support the view that unless the existence needs are satisfied none of the higher-order needs will come into play. There is also some evidence that unless security needs are satisfied, people need not be concerned with higher order needs. . . . There is, however, little evidence to support the view that a hierarchy exists once one moves above the security level. . . . Thus, it probably is *not* safe to assume more than a two-step hierarchy, with existence and security needs at the lower level and all the higher-order needs at the next level.[18]

The most pervasive mobilization of evidence that there are *some* orderings in the discontents of workers may be found in the Working Conditions Survey of 1969–70. The investigators refined thirty-three predictors from their data that accounted for 53 percent of the variance in a composite measure of job satisfaction. The results, involving assignment of priorities to a variety of what they call job facets, represent great improvements over previous efforts. Nevertheless, the investigators sensibly insist that " a good deal of model development and refinement remains to be done." [19]

Again we emphasize that the only issues about work that may be joined are those about which investigators have gathered direct information or about which valid and reliable indicators can be constructed. It is also the case that many aspects of work are intertwined; worker surveys are chronically rife with collinearities: a great many variables go together. And work satisfactions are themselves elusive targets, especially among the members of a survey population assembled with an eye toward statistical representativeness. A great deal of information must be sacrificed if we are to gain comparable and revealing occupational data on workers as disparate as Girl Scout executives and YMCA locker-room attendants.

Finally, we suspect that workers engage in a kind of "trading off" of work experiences. At one extreme, one person's psychic income is another person's occupational neurosis. At the other extreme, an individual comes to despise what, earlier in life, was valued.[20] More appositely, the members of an organization's labor force have individually variable preferences, tastes, and thresholds; to complicate matters further, these may be balanced out in both the long *and* the short run.

ORGANIZATIONAL ATTRIBUTES AND EMPLOYEE ATTITUDES

The evidence adduced so far suggests that though employee satisfactions are *not* linked to worker performance in any simple or obvious ways, they *are* related to a great variety of particular worker experiences and traits. While a number of these relationships will continue to concern us, it is important in the present context to consider evidence bearing upon the relationship between worker attitudes and two organizational characteristics that have been singled out especially often: "size" and "technology."

Large organizations and work-simplifying technology, it is regularly argued, are the two key elements in bureaucratization. Whatever else impinges on workers, it is argued further, the quality of work experience is largely governed by size and technology. Differentiated, simplified labor may be a boon to managers in the folklore of capitalism, but to Saturday's hardworking children it is a bane. The view of bureaucracy as a false talisman is explicit in the work of human relationists and most would-be change agents and implicit in the views of many others.[21]

The issue needs attention in the present context because of claims that managers can and should temper the impersonal, bureaucratic effects of size and technology on worker attitudes (and behavior). A-meliorative interventions, it is widely believed, would be productive of "sociotechnical" subsystems in organizations to which workers may attach themselves in ways that are personally gratifying and organizationally functional. Similarly, the work flows that condition the interactions within and among worker and supervisor groups are held to be themselves governed by technological circumstances amenable to redesign and restructuring within fairly broad limits.[22]

Empirical evidence that managers have largely untapped and relatively low-cost opportunities for reforms of the two putatively offensive organizational traits is far rarer, however, than the popularity of the position and the amount of literature on the subject would suggest.

There is some evidence from a 25-year-old study of 82 manufacturing plants in the Trenton, New Jersey, labor market that smaller plants are less likely than larger ones to be unionized and more likely to have older and more conservative union leaders, to have fewer opportunities for promotion, and to "promote from within"; the smaller plants, finally, tend to have more intimate interpersonal and industrial relations, to have a cohesive work force, and to have fewer strikes. The only prospects suggestive of managerial options in the Trenton investigation are those that attach to larger firms willing to reorganize operations into separate branch plants. The flowering of advantages from such reorganizations would be largely dependent upon the willingness of central managers actually to delegate authority to branch managers, as Cleland points out.[23]

In the first of two reviews, summarizing work completed before 1962, the attack on "size" appears to be joined to some degree by the investigators in twenty-six of thirty-nine discrete reports. But the discrete studies are far from conclusive: correlations between size and such variables as satisfaction, absenteeism, turnover, accidents, labor disputes, and productivity were observed in factories and mines (15); stores (2); "divisions" and "departments" (11); work groups (7); and "other" (4). It is difficult to determine much about the effect of organizational size, per se, from studies of organizations and of organizations' suborganizations.[24]

A later review of the literature on the effects of size appears as a part of a study by Geoffrey Ingham of work orientations, expectations, rewards, deprivations, absenteeism, and turnover among employees of various departments in one large and eight smaller British firms.

From his own work (in which technology was held constant) and from the work of others, Ingham concludes that "size" produces ambiguous results. His interpretation of the ambiguities in the data is that workers are, among themselves, of different orientations—" economizers-instrumentalists" and "identifiers"—in organizations both large and small.

> [In] *both* large and small organizations there was a high level of congru-
> ence between the workers' wants and expectations (orientations) and the
> organizational rewards structure. This kind of approach went some con-
> siderable way toward explaining why there was no significant difference
> between the labour turnover rates of the small and large organizations.[25]

Ingham's explanation, which is not inconsistent with the hypothesis of some of the "organization-personality" writers to which we alluded in Chapter 2, leans on the observed distributions of "congruent" and "incongruent orientations," on workers' "definitions of situation," among employees in organizations that afford relatively more or fewer "eco-nomic-instrumental" versus "noninstrumental" rewards. He argues quite reasonably that larger organizations offer relatively more "instrumental" (economic) rewards and tend to retain workers with complementary "orientations"; smaller organizations offer greater noneconomic, more "expressive" opportunities and rewards, and they more often retain workers for whom higher wage demands are relatively less important than social-psychological rewards.

While we have not examined American "workers' orientations" and their "definitions of their situation" in precisely these terms, our assess-ments in subsequent chapters are entirely in line with the implicit view of workplace trade-offs discernible in Ingham's analysis. Indeed, the re-sponses of self-employed workers in the Working Conditions Survey suggest that wholly analogous self-selection processes have led some Americans to opt for occupations that are situated almost entirely "out-side" organizations.[26]

Where the effects of size have been a matter of industrial-sociologi-cal concern in modern times, interests in the oppressive consequences of technology go back to very early days and have been the subject of formal social-scientific study since Marx distinguished between the fac-tory system as a technique of production and capitalism as a mode of "production relationships" among citizens. Marx was not concerned with either managers or technology per se. But when he wrote about capitalists he could as easily have been speaking about technology, as in the following passage in which "technology" may be readily substituted for "capitalists," "landlords" and "individuals":

> To prevent possible misunderstanding, a word. I paint the capitalist and
> the landlord in no sense *couleur de rose*. But here individuals are dealt
> with only in so far as they are the personifications of economic categories,
> embodiments of particular class relations and class interests. My stand-
> point from which the evolution of the economic formation of society is

viewed as a process of natural history, can less than any other make the individual responsible for relations whose creature he socially remains, however much he may subjectively raise himself above them.[27]

The citation from Marx on managers and "the system" is not so forced as it might appear in the present circumstance: A kind of neo-Marxist model, in which technology *is* substituted for capitalism, has grown up in recent years, a model that has attracted a significant number of social scientists who seek to bypass the original Marxist concern about the "economic formation of society." It is as if Marx both saw and overlooked technology in his related assessments of capitalism and the "factory system," as if one can quietly retain his critique of *capitalism* while explicating assessments of the effects of *technology*, and substituting the latter for the former. The effect—a kind of legerdemain—is to honor the dogma, in Joseph Schumpeter's fine phrase, by simply "fingering the Marxian rosary."

For example, in a widely cited study, Blauner substitutes the separation of workers from *control* over their work and their working conditions in different technological settings for Marx's separation of workers from *ownership* of the means of production, in an effort to account for observed differences in worker satisfaction.[28]

We would urge that the explicit thesis linking technology and workers' control over their work is not nearly so well established as one is often asked to believe. Sufficient evidence may yet be gathered and published to show that "the industrial system distributes alienation unevenly among its blue-collar force, just as our economic system distributes income unevenly."[29] And it may be the case, indeed, that the key factors differentially endowing industries with their capacities for "alienating" workers may be defined as "the complex of physical objects and technical operations (both manual and machine) regularly employed in turning out the goods and services produced by an industry."[30]

An examination of Blauner's analysis casts some doubt on his conclusion that "alienation" varies "in form and intensity" depending upon technology. Although evidence from his case studies supports such a conclusion, the analysis of the Roper survey data is inconclusive. There are eighteen questions in the survey dealing with work experience. Table 3.1 shows (a) whether the percent of satisfied workers observed in the four industries postulated to represent three different types of technology (with different job requirements and different degrees of worker control over their work processes) are consistent with Blauner's thesis and (b) whether the items were used systematically or selectively in support of his assessments.

It will readily be seen that the distributions of responses to the eighteen items are consistent with the technology hypothesis across the

TABLE 3.1. Response to 18 Items in Blauner's Study Grouped by Agreement with His Hypothesis

Table No. in Blauner	Items[a]	Degree of Agreement with Hypothesis		
		Yes	Ambiguous	No
	A. *Responses Presented Systematically*			
34	Job leave you too tired?	*		
35	Chance to try out ideas of your own?	*		
42	Job interesting . . . monotonous?	*		
45	Job lead to a promotion?	*		
46	Factors involved in advancement		*	
	B. *Responses Presented Selectively*			
31	Can have present job as long as you want it?	*		
32	Likely to be laid off temporarily during next six months?	*		
33	Job make you work too fast?	*		
49	Chance to get above foreman?	*		
52	Adequate financial provision for retirement?	*		
36	Can let work go for a half an hour and catch up later?		*	
41	Job let you keep your mind on other things?		*	
43	Job too simple to bring out best abilities?		*	
37	Wish you had chosen different trade or occupation?			*
38	Better companies to work for?			*
39	Job essential to success of company?			*
40	Length of tenure, current job.			*
48	Prefer another job in your company with similar pay?			*

[a] Paraphrased

three-way technology distinctions (Printing and Chemicals, together, versus Autos and Textiles) in nine instances (items 34, 35, 42, 45, 31, 32, 33, 49, and 52). In one of the five items that are systematically compared in Blauner's discussion, the results are ambiguous if not contradictory.

Of the items that he discusses selectively—i.e., items examined in fewer than the four industries about which he writes—five are consistent with his thesis when systematically compared (31, 32, 33, 49, and 52); ten are ambiguous (36, 41, 43, and 46) or inconsistent (37, 38,

39, 40, 47, and 48). When item 43 (job "too simple for abilities") is disaggregated by skill level, the results are less ambiguous within industries but no less ambiguous between industries (see Blauner, Table 50).

A reasonable verdict from our reading of what is so widely cited as evidence of the impact of technology on work and work attitudes is, at best, a Scottish "not proven."

The same ambiguous results occur elsewhere. Thus, two British sociologists report that while some differences in the attitudes and behavior of workers vary with work obligations attributable to different technologies, others are more clearly correlated with differences in backgrounds, attitudes, previous work experiences, and expectations. Some attitudes could be linked to differences in workers' tasks, but not to technology, as Blauner and many others use the term.[31]

Among the reasons: while some "technologies" are "pure," others are not easily classified. Thus, the majority of these workers performed functions and operations that were shaped by a variety—sometimes a mixture—of "pre"-technological processes. While some shops appeared to be using "the same dominant technology, when a relatively crude classification was used, [they] were revealed on further investigation to be different in important respects." Investigators thus run the risk of oversimplification in analysis of the autonomous effects of technology and work flow when, as in the Roper data, workers are members of different firms and subfirm work units, as well as of different industries.

There are two suggestive studies of the impact of work flows: Sayles and Kuhn, in parallel studies in the auto and rubber industries conducted in the late 1950s, reported that some workers—those with higher-level skills and in locations that permitted considerable latitude in managing their work—used grievances concerning their working conditions as highly effective adjuncts to their bargaining strategies. Workers with more modest skills and with fewer options in the management of their tasks had similar dissatisfactions but were either apathetic toward or more undisciplined in their use of the grievance machinery provided in their union agreements.[32]

It should be emphasized that while technology, in generic terms, largely determined the viability of the unionists' strategies and tactics observed by Sayles and Kuhn, the data actually refer to units of work flows. These investigators thus conceive of technology in rather broad analytical terms; their concerns lead them to avoid identifying technology with machines, as such, and their specific operations.

In a more recent and path-breaking study, William Form reports on the effects of the "complexity of technology" on work values among workers in auto factories in Bombay, Cordoba (Argentina), Torino and

Lansing, Michigan. In the major portions of Form's analysis, the data for which were collected by him and Steven Deutsch, Richard Gale and Balder Sharma, the *skill level* of workers becomes a measure of technical complexity in a discussion that is entirely in line with the argument we develop in Chapter 4. It should be noted here that Form's analyses of survey data, unlike Blauner's, are conducted consistently across the four-country worker samples. Form concludes that as industrialization progresses, skill differences become greater, not smaller.[33] Since these investigations were conducted, Strauss and Sayles have elaborated upon the work-flow notion and now suggest that the most recurrent of relationships defined by technology (in its widest meanings) may usefully be classified into "work flows," "advisory flows," "audit flows," and "stabilization flows." Their analysis is suggestive of a number of relevant managerial opportunities for intervention.[34]

CONCLUSIONS

We have reviewed representative materials that bear directly upon three of the five questions raised at the chapter's outset and at least indirectly on those having to do with managers. If policymakers and their advisers, public and private, seek to improve worker morale, they may by and large not expect that success will lead to measurable shifts in the behavior or productivity of workers.

There is evidence that some worker attitudes that have been regularly studied are indeed vulnerable to "positive" management efforts aimed at improved morale, at least in the short run. Less clear is the ordering of the weights that should be assigned to these attitudes: some are interdependently contingent; others suggest a kind of benefit-cost analysis in which agreeable and disagreeable job experiences are "traded off" by workers, one or more against others.

We have noted that different appraisals of satisfaction result when new questions are asked of workers—for example, about the adequacy of their resources at work. Such questions afford a view of workers' perceptions of higher-level managers' *competencies*, in contrast to the usual survey items, which elicit assessments of business leaders as a class.

Furthermore, it appears that neither organizational size nor "technology," other than as broadly conceptualized in the studies by Sayles and Kuhn, are especially powerful predictors of worker behavior or attitudes. Survey responses are sufficiently variable *within* organizations matched for their sizes and technologies to leave one unimpressed by variations among workers in *different* organizations.

We will return later in less elliptical fashion to the fourth and fifth questions with which we opened this chapter, concerning the margins for managers' interests in and capacities for interventions designed to reform the workplace.

In Part II we turn to an approximation—but only an approximation—of a model that will carry us a bit beyond the essentially microscopic model that has informed much of the research discussed in this chapter.

PART II
MERCY, TRUTH, AND THE REALITIES BETWEEN

The evidence presented in Part I does not provide much assurance about the validity of the claims made by intellectually responsible work reformers on behalf of various interventions. Our restiveness stems specifically from the problematic assumptions underlying the definitions of the situation that have been basic to the human-relations school since its earliest days, from the measurement difficulties that attend research in this area, and from the often tenuous and anomalous findings of studies bearing on work satisfaction and worker performance. It also derives from the lack of clarity in even the best studies of worker attitudes regarding the relative weights of matters that are within and beyond managers' control.

In this second part of our analysis we report on our efforts to develop a "mezzoscopic" perspective from which to view the impingement upon American workers of forces both broader and narrower than those regularly contemplated in the micro- and macroscopic perspectives.

In Chapter 4 we commend a view of workers' experiences in which emphases are placed on their occupations, in general, and the skills linked to their jobs, in particular. The perspective we endorse is closely akin to one presented by Lester Thurow according to which the labor market is seen not as an auction market but as one in which opportunities for training, and thus for skill acquisition, are allocated.[1] At the end we present a tentative paradigm for examining workers' attitudes.

In Chapters 5, 6, and 7 we look at the components of the paradigm developed at the end of Chapter 4. Thus, in Chapter 5 we look at the impact on worker satisfactions and dissatisfactions of their own and their families' incomes, their claims to job security, and their perceptions of the equity accorded them in the marketplace.

In Chapter 6 we address the role that their educational achievements play in helping Americans procure jobs to which skills or skill-enhancing training and experience are attached. It is our thesis that effects of educational achievements on workers' perceptions are helpfully gauged through assessments of the chain: education-skill-job attitudes.

In Chapter 7 we present a discussion of the ways in which a few of the most strategic proximal and local working conditions—conditions favored as determinants of satisfaction by those who tend to view work almost entirely in microscopic perspective—may be integrated with the materials in Chapters 5 and 6, thereby to flesh out, in some measure, our middle-range approach.

4. Macro-, Mezzo-, and Microscopic Approaches to Managers, Workers, Jobs, and Tasks: Spying Out the Land

While the work of many social scientists was considered in Part I, the emphasis was on studies of workers in the workplace, their relationships, their attitudes, and their satisfactions. We mentioned industrial-relations and human-resources research, and a current example was commended in Chapter 2,[1] but in comparative terms scant attention was paid to the apparent effects on workers of such variables as their occupations, their earnings, the prevailing management practices to which they are subject, and numerous other fairly stable workplace givens.

In this chapter we begin to combine key conceptions of labor economists and occupational specialists with the behaviorist approach outlined earlier. Our goal is to widen the scope of typical inquiries into work by suggesting how structural factors[2] influence worker attitudes, how these attitudes in turn are related to measurements of job satisfaction, and, finally and most important, to draw out implications for interventions in the workplace itself aimed at improving worker satisfaction, morale, and performance.

To understand fully the relationship of the individual to the job, it would be desirable to construct a comprehensive model of the effects of all these structural factors, the characteristics of particular job settings, and the subjective dispositions of workers as these interact over time. Precise tests of such a complex model would have to include a great number of simplifying assumptions, even if reliable and distinct measures for these effects were at hand. In the absence of longitudinal data on individuals that would allow for close comparisons within and between differing employment conditions, we must base our conjectures not on such ideal data but on existing survey materials. We judge

51

these to be indicative, not conclusive, and our approach, therefore, has been to use these data to suggest some of the important conceptual concerns that we think an ideal model must eventually comprehend.

Thus, we are mindful of several limitations in using a cross-sectional survey and its attitude measures as the touchstone for our elaborations. It may be objected that, as work is at the core of life and life values, "self-esteem colors the response to job satisfaction attitude surveys" [3]: to admit dissatisfaction in work is to admit failure in life. In addition, the context of the worker's expectations for satisfactions may influence his response at various life-cycle stages. Expectations change: younger workers particularly expect more satisfaction from work, whereas older ones may have over the years accommodated their aspirations to their jobs. Furthermore, several empirical studies have indicated that the disregard for intrinsic job satisfaction among many workers is generated by competing pressures for economic advancement.[4]

It may be further argued that those who see work as a valued end in itself—professionals, many managers, skilled craftsmen—have jobs that offer the experience of primary satisfaction. As work itself is salient to this group, so may be their perceptions and responses about the satisfactions it brings. When work tasks offer *little* opportunity for expression or intrinsic satisfaction, work will be tolerated, at best,[5] and answers to questions about satisfaction will consequently reflect the lesser salience of work activity.

Clearly, workers' expectations will also be affected by the rise and fall of the business cycle. In tight-employment years in which work-satisfaction surveys were conducted, intrinsic factors may have become more important in producing overall job satisfaction because the majority of workers felt financially secure and the sense of entitlement to a challenging job had grown.[6]

In the next sections we will continue our discussion of the view that structural factors provide only marginal prospects for the kind of general workplace improvements that the work interventionists promise us.

"TRADE-OFFS" IN THE WORKPLACE

The notion of trade-off is familiar in the work of economists who think of tastes and preferences as important influences on individual choices. They differ, of course, in the amount of attention they pay to the forces shaping choice and the weights that should be assigned to these forces—for example, the roles of unions and of discrimination. But they agree that some margins exist for individual occupational choice and that, insofar as workers have choices, their choice of an employer for whom they will work is wider than the choice of the kind of work that they will do.

The probability that a good many workers have at least marginal choices suggests the possibility that they may balance out the good and the bad facets of their jobs in accordance with a "calculus" of some kind, and that some of the terms in this "calculus" may be identified.

Our experience suggests that an approach drawing on the economist's trade-off model *and* upon constructs rooted in theories of personality, organization, small-group dynamics and leadership may be crudely applied to illuminate issues bearing upon employment in America. The merger or synthesis of these two strains of thinking must, we repeat, be primitive, however, for the following reasons.

First, not many of the data relevant to such an effort are available. A number of issues, like the demand for specific skills, must be studied from data collected in accordance with schemata that are substantially influenced by investigators' values; we may here suggest and later develop the point that the selective and value-laden quality of these schemata may not be overlooked without problematic consequences. In Parts III and IV, for example, we dwell on the rather different value positions assumed by many investigators toward the obligations, motives, sensitivities, and loyalties of managers and workers, respectively. The fact of the matter is that values affect the ways labor markets operate and the ways in which we collect and classify data on labor market processes.[7]

Second, while the concept of trade-offs makes intuitive sense, it is an economic abstraction impossible to demonstrate firsthand. Concretely, not all jobs, even were they all realistically available to job seekers, contain the same inventory or "mix" of "good" and "bad" facets.

Related difficulties in pinpointing even gross elements in the trade-offs among different types of work rewards and benefits are inherent in the facts that (1) units of tastes or preferences are typically measured in dollars; (2) each individual has an "indifference curve" describing preferences for one or another facet in each of multiple pairs taken one pair at a time; these curves cannot be aggregated; and (3) since many "good" job features cluster together in the world of work it is a corollary of the second fact that some "pairs" of trade-off choices simply do not exist. Consider that clean jobs *tend* to be better paid, *and* offer more promotion opportunities, *and* afford more skill-learning prospects, and so on.

These difficulties aside, the trade-off model of job selection holds that, if a worker is paid less than he could earn in another job, and assuming that the worker actually has a choice, then the residual funds are treated as income forgone in favor of either (1) other aspirations, such as helping one's fellow man ("pychic income"); (2) nonpecuniary benefits, like those attaching to regional preferences ("amenities"); and (3) a residual category of benefits we may identify with the minimization of psychic expenditures. (Thus one may suffer psychologically as a result of taking up residence near an obnoxious mother-in-law, but one's guilt feelings are reduced by the sense that one has performed filial sacrifices in a praiseworthy manner.) [8] The dollar values ascribed to these choices are at best indirect estimates that do not lend themselves to clear-cut classifications.

Third, from the noneconomists' side, specific trade-offs are only inferable from data on the behavior and attitudes of employees toward specific working conditions, taken one or very few at a time. Workers are not often asked directly by survey researchers or participant observers how many units of increased job hazard or deficient supervision they have traded or would trade for increased pay and fringe benefits, for better tools and equipment, or for fuller utilization of their educational achievements.

When workers *are* asked, as they rarely are, for answers to specific propositions, the questions and responses imply that trade-offs do exist in the real world. Yankelovich found in a survey of American youth aged sixteen to twenty-four that

> Sixty-eight percent of the young blue-collar workers and 65 percent of white-collar workers report they would be willing to take a 20 percent pay cut in order to take advantage of a six-month training program (sponsored by employer, government, or union, etc.) which might lead to a promotion or a better job.[9]

As this type of evidence indicates, analysts usually have available only weak and indirect, if suggestive, measures of individual and aggregated trade-offs.[10]

GROUNDS FOR DIALOGUE

Given our own predilections and the suggestive findings of human-relations research, it seems reasonable to us that trade-offs, even measured only indirectly, are crucial to an understanding of workers' reactions to their jobs. The problem of synthesis might be approached, at least, if we could identify a common ground between investigators whose research efforts normally do not intersect. If one approach emphasizes macroscopic forces and the other more proximal or microscopic events in explanations of workers' circumstances, then we should be seeking to identify what we may call mezzoscopic forces affecting workers. These forces and the processes resulting therefrom should have some ascertainable, interdependent relationships with developments examined in macroscopic *and* microscopic approaches to people at their work.

We have accordingly borrowed, on one side, from relevant studies in economics in which heavy emphasis is placed, not only on income-distributive forces, but also on the implication of workers' incomes for occupational choice, job satisfaction, and job performance. We have borrowed as well from studies of the social and private returns to investments in formal education and training. Economists stress in these studies the ways in which individual income relates to education, intelligence, aptitude, ability, and productivity. A number of sociologists interested in the subject add what they take to be the important intervening effects of the *occupational* determinants of earnings.[11]

From the predominantly human-relations tradition we have borrowed, on a second side, the logic implicit in the longtime emphasis upon the working conditions that are immediate and proximal to workers, including the quality of their supervision, and, in more recent studies, in emphasis on the availability of resources for getting their work done.

We have also borrowed from the industrial-relations students who assign considerable weight in their assessments of workplace questions to the realities of labor markets and the treatment in these markets accorded persons of different traits, attributes, and, in particular, different educational achievements.[12]

OCCUPATIONS AND SKILLS

We suggest that an analytical linchpin that can help hold such a loose but suggestive middle-range theoretical apparatus together is the concept of occupation. The intersection of economic factors—like technological developments, the aggregate demand for goods and services, and the overall pace of an economy's development, differentiation, and growth[13]—with the traits, capacities, and aspirations of workers comes at the points where productive activities are sorted into sectors, industries, and occupations. To think about these questions at all requires a set of categories, whether to pursue labor-market research, to publish governmental statistics, or to place individuals in jobs.

Occupation is also a critical variable in the major types of studies to which we refer throughout this book. First, it appears in research that uses large samples to study wage determination and income distribution. Second, it is an element in labor-market studies, both for the distribution of job opportunities among population groups and for assessing the influence of educators, employers, legislators, and licensing bodies on the relative bargaining strength of worker groups. Third, occupational level plays a differentiating role in intraorganizational studies of stress, of status, and of job satisfaction among both individuals and groups.

Individuals no less than researchers are given to the use of occupational categories in their thinking, especially if they are in a position to make career choices. One trains after all to be a physician, and only thereafter to work in a particular hospital; one prepares first to be a lawyer and only later perhaps to become a member of the House Committee on the Judiciary. The point is simply that we generally think about our work in occupational terms, and when we compare our earnings and our working conditions with those of other workers, our reference groups are more likely to be made up of people doing the *same* kind of work than of people doing *other* kinds of work in our own organizations.

The categories used to designate "occupation" vary from the 20,000 or so distinct job titles in the *Dictionary of Occupational Titles* to the ten major decennial census classes. In between, there are other, more or less aggregated classification schemes and related subschemes.[14] The best known subscheme, used in the census, was developed originally to reflect social status as well as activity differences; other schemes are related to task analysis, to the matching of jobs and personality traits, or to facilitate occupational choice. For our purposes, however, the most important attribute of occupation as a concept is skill level.

Like the occupation to which it may be attached, skill level can describe both job and worker, but it has further advantages as an aggregating device. Earlier investigations had led us in the late 1960s to view the sorting of workers among differentially skilled jobs in partial accordance with their educational achievements as a determinant of their future in the labor market.[15] The use of estimates of the skills attached to jobs enabled us at that time, as it does in the current effort, to consider workers' educations across occupations along a critical dimension.

For present purposes, we have used the assignment of skill level to jobs from the *Dictionary of Occupational Titles*. In this scheme, skill theoretically has two aspects, the general educational development (GED) and the specific vocational preparation (SVP) required to perform a job according to an acceptable standard. GED is a six-point scale, and SVP is expressed in categories of training time.[16] It is clear to us that education facilitates the acquisition of a job that provides skill and skill training. The SVP gives us a measure, albeit a crude one, of the skills people have as distinct from their formal educational achievements. We emphasize that it is crude and that the separation of education from skill is difficult in particular occupations such as physician, lawyer, or academician, in which skill acquisition is entwined with schooling. A more detailed discussion is presented in Chapter 6 and its addendum.

UTILIZATION

In the area where the macro parameters of people's lives are determined, education and training, access and placement, and worker and job come together. In our version of how worker satisfaction enters this process, we considered the match between worker and job—the utilization of the individual's education and training—to have critical importance.

Just as workers classified according to the degree of their "utilization" would respond differently to questions about experiences shaped by *larger* social and economic forces over which managers have little control, so we expected that they would respond differently to questions about conditions specific to their work settings, conditions over which managers do have options. "Utilization" itself we conceived to be a variable between macro and micro. We expected its effects on worker satisfaction to be less conspicuous than the effects, for example, of major economic downswings, because the degree of utilization may be perceived in accordance with shifting social definitions of appropriate jobs and occupational requirements. Utilization is also in the mezzoscopic range in the sense that the degree to which educational achievements are utilized is neither wholly within nor wholly without the scope of a given manager to specify. Consider that the labor force was a good deal less heterogeneous in point of its members' educational achievements in the 1950s and 1960s than it is today. Where they could choose whether to have a high-school dropout, a high-school graduate, and so on, in the earlier period, managers now come to a labor market sufficiently crowded with high-school and college graduates to reduce the margins for choice; a high-school diploma has become the minimum standard for most employments, and a college degree for a large number of others. The point is that utilization patterns are shaped by employers—at the micro level—only in part.

We have accordingly pursued the earlier concern in the present research, elaborating upon and making more current estimates regarding the utilization of differentially educated Americans,[17] and then going on to examine what bearing utilization has on perceptions of working conditions. In terms of the match between worker and job, the analysis of aggregated data (in Chapter 6) confirms the existence of a sizable and growing amount of underutilization. But the effects of utilization on job satisfaction turned out to be far more complex in character.

In the chapters that follow, we explore several of the possibilities for these outcomes, including those that seem to result from the kinds of trade-offs described above. But these very complexities suggested a more general approach to the question, "How do people interpret the large structural factors, the macro forces, that impinge on their jobs?" To explore this question, we chose illustrative survey items to represent elements of structure that seem at face value to be important, as well as attitude items and indexes found by other researchers to have an important bearing on job satisfaction. A further criterion for selection was to lay the groundwork for exploration of the possibilities for intervention.

We have exploited and stitched together the findings from three different bodies of data. The richest of these is the Working Conditions Survey (WCS) on which we have relied to explore the linkages between education, occupation, and satisfaction. Since the WCS did not contain items relating to equity, we have introduced a supplementary data source, the Institute for Survey Research 1972 Election Study (ES). Finally, we used data from the decennial census and Current Population Survey for macro estimates of the utilization of education and for a brief discussion of projections of utilization.

We start with "job satisfaction" at the heart of our elaboration. In our presentation of some survey findings, we have used the traditional (and conservative) single-item global measure, which asks the worker directly how satisfied he is with his job, on the assumption that it is possible for individuals to express some vaguely defined attitude toward a total job situation. In addition, we use a more indirect index of job satisfaction, composed of several single-item attitude measures, to capture the range of job satisfaction which different questions may elicit. The measures in this index have been averaged by the designers of the WCS according to the weights on each response shown in the addendum to this chapter.

Our thesis about the connections among these selected variables is most clearly expressed in Figure 4.1. The variables within the circle are expressions of attitudes drawn from the Working Conditions Survey and will be more fully described in subsequent chapters. Their connection with an index of overall job satisfaction can be expressed as a multiple correlation of .554. If we posit that the responses to these indicators of the challenge of the job, perception of family income, the adequacy of resources to do the job, and quality of supervision are all "predictive" of job satisfaction, then taken together they "explain" about 30 percent of the variance in satisfaction. We assume here that the direction of influence goes from the specific facets to the overall estimate of satisfaction.[18] More interesting from our point of view are the partial correlation coefficients (that is, the specific weights of the component

Figure 4.1: Interconnectedness of Variables Drawn from the Working
              Conditions Survey*

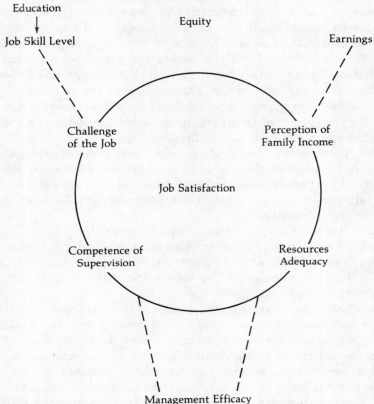

*We may note here that the four items in the circle are not independent of each other. It should also be noted that while age is positively associated with satisfaction overall, the effect of age is essentially wiped out by the four items in the circle; i.e., if respondents enjoy benefits represented by the four items, they are satisfied with their jobs overall, a proposition that applies to youths and nonyouths alike. By and large, youths receive a bit less of each of the four types of benefits because of the types of jobs youths obtain compared to older respondents.

measures within the overall multiple correlation); these tell us the relative importance of the items when they are considered together. In a standardized form, these weights are as follows:

Challenge Index	.352
Perception of Family Income	.192
Supervisor Competence	.154
Resources Adequacy	.144

Outside the circle are those constructs that we perceive to have important influence from the structural side on the formation of the attitudes inside the circle. First, long-abiding interests in the utilization of human resources—and particularly in the education that workers bring to jobs and the skills that those jobs require—led us to consider the impact of education on the allocation of workers among skill groups, and of the relationship of skills to worker attitudes. Insofar as this relationship can be established, we believe that this is the link between the skill level of the job and the inherent interest and challenge.

Second, we are concerned about the relationship of individual earnings to the perceptions of family income among respondents in a society with a growing number of multi-earner families.

Third, our concern with issues growing out of the equity workers perceive to be accorded them in labor markets that offer disparate returns to different occupations, and even to the same occupations in different settings, led us to examine these perceptions to the extent permitted by available data.

Fourth, we postulate variation in management efficacy as a strategic force related to the quality of supervision and the adequacy of resources provided to workers to carry out their jobs, issues that human-relations theory and responses to worker surveys, respectively, suggest are critical to worker satisfaction.

Once again, we have invested considerable confidence, given our research purposes, in the proposition that occupational and skill differences are among the critical ones on which to focus in an effort to open up questions about the interplay of macroscopic social and economic forces with microscopic, job-related experiences. We are arguing that the study of work can best move ahead if the issues are defined in what are conventionally called middle-range theoretical terms or, in our usage, mezzoscopic terms.

It seems to us that occupation-as-skill is a key concept, linked as it is to family income, to prestige, to status, to labor markets, to productivity, to education and training, to division of labor—all subjects of related research. It can also be readily related to industry, to organization, and, apparently for some time to come, to age, sex, and caste.

Regrettably, we do not have a highly refined and widely accepted way of looking at occupations and their skill components, though suggestive segments of a unified perspective on occupation and skill have been developed. Sociologists generally have emphasized the prestige attaching to occupations; a valuable treatment of occupations and organizations appears in a discussion by Zald;[19] and labor economists have always worked with data aggregated into occupational categories and clusters.[20] Other economists who focus on the structure and functioning of labor markets—and the patterning of wage contours, especially—typically employ occupations as basic units of analysis.

We are pleased, meanwhile, to note that recent studies by Kohn and Schooler and by Kalleberg have adopted a similar perspective. Thus Kalleberg, working quite independently with the Working Conditions Survey data and with measures constructed, as ours were, from the *Dictionary of Occupational Titles,* reaches conclusions very much like those we report in this chapter and in Chapters 5, 7, and 8.

Indeed, the only immediately relevant differences between our efforts and Kalleberg's result, first, from our attempt to distinguish measures of work satisfactions, per se, from perceptions of employed Americans of the degree to which they feel their occupations, compared to their jobs, are equitably rewarded—an attempt that could be conducted only by resorting to data other than those in the Working Conditions Survey. Our work differs from Kalleberg's, secondly, in our incorporation of supervision as an issue adjunctive to our notions of occupation.[21] We do so because employees' prospects for skill learning, through training and promotional opportunities, are influenced in strategic ways by their supervisors.

ADDENDUM TO CHAPTER 4

Facet-free Job Satisfaction Index Components with Numerical Weights Assigned to Responses (in Parentheses)

Response Categories for Questions Comprising Facet-free Job Satisfaction

All in all, how satisfied would you say you are with your job—very satisfied, somewhat satisfied, not too satisfied, or not at all satisfied?

a) Very satisfied (5)
b) Somewhat satisfied (3)
c) Not too satisfied (1)
d) Not at all satisfied (1)

Before we talk about your present job, I'd like to get some idea of the kind of job you'd *most* like to have. If you were free to go into any type of job you wanted, what would your choice be?

a) Worker would want the job he or she now has (5)
b) Worker would want to retire and not work at all (1)
c) Worker would prefer some other job to the job he or she now has (1)

Knowing what you know now, if you had to decide all over again whether to take the job you now have, what would you decide? Would you decide without hesitation to take the same job, would you have some second thoughts, or would you decide definitely not to take the same job?

    a) Decide without hesitation to take same job (5)
    b) Have some second thoughts (3)
    c) Decide definitely *not* to take the job (1)

In general how well would you say that your job measures up to the sort of job you wanted when you took it? Would you say it is very much like the job you wanted, somewhat like the job you wanted, or not very much like the job you wanted?

    a) Very much like the job worker wanted (5)
    b) Somewhat like the job worker wanted (3)
    c) Not very much like the job worker wanted (1)

If a good friend of yours told you (he/she) was interested in working in a job like yours for your employer, what would you tell (him/her)? Would you strongly recommend this job, would you have doubts about recommending it, or would you strongly advise (him/her) against this sort of job?

    a) Worker would strongly recommend it (5)
    b) Worker would have doubts about recommending it (3)
    c) Worker would advise friend against it (1)

5. Earnings, Security, Equity, and Job Satisfaction: Work as an Investment

Nonpecuniary or "psychic" returns are undoubtedly important to many employed Americans, and a variety of such rewards are unquestionably available in many jobs. Indeed, one could not otherwise readily explain the willingness of the 435 members of the House of Representatives, of the one hundred senators, of the justices of the Supreme Court, of cabinet members, of fifty state governors, of the president and of the vice-president of the United States—a total of over six hundred persons —to serve in their respective offices while they earn less, collectively, than the seventy-odd officers and directors of General Motors.

Still the link between income and well-being for earners and their dependents remains a central one. In the preceding chapter, earnings were related to the skill level of the job in a scheme according to which our crude measure of skill was taken as a surrogate for the positions of respondents in an occupational hierarchy. The strength of the relationship is represented by a zero-order correlation of .40 between skill level and earnings for both wage and salaried workers. When we go on to examine the linkage between individual earnings and job satisfaction the correlation, using the index, is much smaller (.17).

Table 5.1 shows that increased earnings are associated with increases in the proportion of "very satisfied" responses to the single, global question on satisfaction with the job "all in all," but that the proportion expressing themselves to be "somewhat satisfied" is very nearly the same in all earnings categories. Furthermore, there is very little difference in size between the "somewhat satisfied" and "very satisfied" groups, except for the highest earnings bracket in the table, $10,000 or more. The largest difference in the table is between those with less than $5,000 and those with $10,000 or more in earnings: about 38 percent of the former are very satisfied with their jobs compared to 54 percent of the latter. These results encouraged us to pursue a more complex model of the place of earnings and income.

TABLE 5.1. Job Satisfaction According to Individual Earnings, Wage and Salary Workers—Percent Distribution

	Individual Earnings				
Job Satisfaction	Less than $5000	$5000–7499	$7500–9999	$10,000 or more	Total
Not Satisfied	22%	14%	14%	10%	16%
Somewhat Satisfied	40	43	44	36	41
Very Satisfied	38	43	42	54	44
Total	100%	100%	100%	100%	100%
N =	398	346	245	260	1249
(NA =	78)				

Tau–$c = .12$, significant at .01 level.

PERCEPTION OF FAMILY INCOME

As we have already indicated, we understand earnings to make their contribution to job satisfaction through family income. Given the growing prevalence of two-earner families, we expected that individuals' assessments of their own economic welfare would be shaped in part by the contributions of other family members and that the importance of their own earnings to that extent would be reduced as a correlate of job satisfaction. The Working Conditions Survey enabled us to pursue the matter because it permitted us to estimate differences among workers in the degree to which they perceive their family incomes as adequate "to meet monthly bills and expenses" and in the degree to which they feel this total income is enough "to live as comfortably as [they] would like." It was possible, in the face of modest correlations between respondents' incomes and their work satisfactions, we reasoned, that satisfactions with life, with work, with pay, and with family experiences are intertwined. Our thoughts led us specifically to the possibility that family well-being is critical to work satisfaction, especially in an age of multi-earner families.

A three-point scale for perception of family income, described below, has a correlation of .20 with individual earnings. Table 5.2 shows the relationship in more detail. In each of the four individual earnings classes, the same proportion (about one-third) of the respondents perceived their family incomes as adequate but not comfortable.[1] On the other hand, there was a large difference in reports on job satisfaction among those who perceived their family incomes to be inadequate compared to those who perceived their incomes to be both adequate and comfortable.

TABLE 5.2. Perception of Family Income According to Earnings, Wage, and Salary Workers—Percent Distribution

Family Income is "Adequate?" "Comfortable?"	Individual Earnings				
	Less than $5000	$5000– 7499	$7500– 9999	$10,000 or more	Total
Not Adequate	35%	28%	24%	10%	27%
Adequate or Comfortable	34	34	35	33	33
Adequate *and* Comfortable	31	38	41	58	40
Total	100%	100%	100%	100%	100%
N =	394	343	243	261	1241
(NA =	86)				

Tau–c = .20, significant at .01 level.

If we scale the responses to the adequacy-comfort questions by scoring a one for each yes answer and a zero for each no, we find that the correlation of this scale with the job satisfaction index is .27. The relationship between this scale and the global question on job satisfaction is displayed in Table 5.3. Respondents who found their family incomes adequate and comfortable were twice as likely to be very satisfied with their jobs as those whose family incomes were neither.

One may speculate about the relation between family income and job satisfaction. It is our best estimate that a wife or a young worker may be satisfied with a job that contributes secondary earnings to make the family more comfortable or to make family members more independent, even though those earnings may be relatively small. The benefits accruing to two or more family members by virtue of the participation of either earner in a health or pension plan, or some other job

TABLE 5.3. Job Satisfaction, According to Perception of Family Income, Wage, and Salary Workers—Percent Distribution

Job Satisfaction	Perception of Family Income			
	Not Adeq	Adeq or Comf	Adeq and Comf	Total
Not Satisfied	27%	15%	10%	16%
Somewhat Satisfied	46	44	34	40
Very Satisfied	27	41	56	44
Total	100%	100%	100%	100%
N =	335	441	536	1312
(NA =	15)			

Tau–b = .23, significant at .001 level.

benefit, influence the importance attached to salary increments accruing to either one alone.

Furthermore, the alleged development of new attitudes toward self-fulfillment in work for women is reflected in data suggesting more explicit recognition of the place of trade-offs between income received and satisfaction or career forgone. According to Yankelovich, these new attitudes have a special effect on some men in the "non-college majority who work hard, manage to make a living, and seek their personal fulfillment through their families"; Yankelovich considers that a wife who is a good earner could, of course, "threaten a precarious social balance":

> Many men learn to accept the frustrations of boring work and lack of involvement in the decisions that make work meaningful precisely because they accept the necessity of making sacrifices for their family. As long as the money comes in, and as long as the family provider is not threatened, most men will go along, often cheerfully, with the work routine, however arduous it is. If, however, the man's role as he-who-makes-sacrifices-for-his-kids'-education-and-his-family's-material-well-being grows less vital, the whole fragile bargain threatens to break down.[2]

For young workers who are assimilating these new values and who now face a time when orderly career prospects are threatened, a resolution of this issue would seem more urgent now than it was for Working Conditions Survey respondents in 1969. The evidence presented by Yankelovich, meantime, clearly shows that most Americans, males only a little more than females, are pleased with the prospects afforded by dual incomes.[3] In another survey, Campbell and his colleagues report that men with working wives welcome the additional income and report about their marital attitudes in terms similar to those of employed males whose wives are not gainfully employed.[4]

The fact that the WCS questions go to general *perceptions* of the adequacy and comfort provided by family incomes may reassure one that abundant room was left for the play of idiosyncratic differences in consumption aspirations and preoccupations with creature comforts, status yearnings, and needs for the setting-by of stores for bleaker days.[5] Although the direction of the influence is by no means clear, we should point out here that—predictably in aphorisms if not always in life—good things tend to go together. There is, for example, a regular increase in reports of job satisfaction as workers assess not only their family incomes but also their job security. Table 5.4 shows that only 13 percent of those who perceive family income to be inadequate *and* have little confidence in the security of their jobs report that they are very satisfied with their jobs. As positive perceptions of both family income and job security increase, so too does the proportion of "very satisfied"

TABLE 5.4. Job Satisfaction According to Job Security and Perception of Family Income, Wage, and Salary Workers—Percent Very Satisfied

Family Income is "Adequate?" "Comfortable?"	"The Job Security Is Good" (How True?)		
	Not at all/ A Little	Somewhat True	Very True
Not Adequate	13% (90)[a]	18% (84)	40% (155)
Adequate or Comfortable	23% (87)	34% (109)	53% (236)
Adequate and Comfortable	35% (77)	43% (137)	67% (313)
N = 1291 (NA = 36)			

[a] Number in parentheses is base N for the reported percentage.

workers. At the upper limits shown in the table, where job security is very good and family income is both adequate and comfortable, two-thirds of the respondents report themselves to be very satisfied with their jobs.

The reader will recall that we have been concerned with the impact of macro and micro forces on worker satisfaction. Earnings together with perceptions of the adequacy and comfort of family income and of job security have been taken here to represent the more important of the macroscopic social and economic forces impinging upon workers. We should add that the margins within which employers might intervene to increase job satisfactions shaped by these macro income forces are decidedly narrower than those they could exploit, say, in connection with proximal and therefore unique job conditions.

Americans' perceptions of the adequacy of the gains they receive from their occupations, no less than their views of what levels of living standards are "comfortable," are conditioned, if not largely determined, by influential forces operating in the larger society. Among these are forces that shape expectations, such as formal educational achievements and the persons and reference groups with whom respondents are disposed to identify. It is both easy and correct, moreover, to credit (or blame) managers and business leaders for encouraging favorable and invidious intergroup comparisons and for endorsing elevated expectations and ambitions—through advertising, for example. But it is fatuous to assign overriding influence to individual employers for socially shared norms and values that shape perceptions of wage and salary scales, or of the absolute wages, salaries, and benefits themselves. To put this differently, economists are undoubtedly correct in assigning to larger labor-market forces the collective potency to establish the parameters within which employers make marginal adjustments; survey respondents are faced primarily with realities affected by these parameters and only secondarily by individual employers.

Even where employers have a significant if not dispositive influence over the direct and most of the indirect costs of their wage bill—such as, for example, to pay workers in amounts that are significantly different from those paid by similarly situated employers—they do not individually determine the conditions that increase or decrease the job security of their employees; economic conditions, after all, play notoriously important parts in setting limits: Employers enjoy marginal, not global, initiatives in this respect, as well as in respect to wages, salaries, and benefits.[6]

Employers have some room to influence the wages and salaries workers receive, of course. Most readers are aware, for example, of "sweetheart" agreements, embodying arrangements that may be more convenient for employers and their labor-leader opposites than they are productive of workers' well-being. And we have all learned that there can be great discrepancies in the returns received by different individuals and groups in "internal" labor markets doing very similar jobs. But we are also aware that many employer practices are mandated by public regulations and influenced by negotiations. It is also worth noting that the more employers or employer groups can influence the larger outside forces, either by their influence on norms, on general economic conditions, or on cyclical labor market developments (because of their market positions and their tastemaking capacities for the creation of images), the more likely it is that these employers will be obliged to confront collectively bargained limitations on their unilateral powers to shape internal–labor-market characteristics, reward structures, and the rest.

Once again, the point is not that managers have *no* options as regards work and workers' reactions. As we shall see, managers appear to have a number of workplace opportunities to shape working conditions; though there are real limitations even at the proximal, micro level, these constraints are by no means as limiting as those affecting managers' capacities to direct the multiple and complex forces shaping wider-going labor-market processes and general economic conditions.

There are of course arguments to the contrary, and the auto and steel industries are favorite cases in point for those who regard the collective-bargaining agreements between the United Auto Workers and the United Steel Workers with large firms in their respective industries as the result of near-conspiracies. According to skeptical critics, the costs of settlements in steel and autos are simply transmitted by economically autonomous actors to defenseless customers. In the case of autos, it has been argued that even strike actions are simply part of what these days are cynically called "scenarios."

Thus the great 116-day steel strike of 1959 was only ostensibly over working rules, according to some skeptics. Consider, they say, that steel output and the utilization of steel capacity were about the same in the years before, during, and after the strike, suggesting that the great (and last) steel strike was not really a classical industrial conflict over worker demands and production aims but a convenient way for managers to dramatize the issue of allegedly inefficient work rules and to sound a clarion call to managers everywhere to defend management's "rights to manage"—at literally no cost to production or sales.

The great 1970 UAW strike against General Motors is often taken as a parallel case. When strike benefits had exhausted the union's strike fund, it negotiated loans from the Teamster's Union, with the UAW's Walter and May Reuther Camp at Black Lake, Michigan, as collateral, and later with General Motors itself, at the then-prevailing commercial interest rates, to sustain the union's strike position. That the company was willing to forgo alternative increments of earnings on these funds and was thereby actually willing to *assist* their union antagonists' capacities to continue striking, it is argued, is circumstantial evidence of the company's autonomous position in labor and other markets.[7]

Similar arguments are made by others on the left and right who focus specifically on the broad institutional and market powers of the leaders of large unions and their equivalently well-situated management peers.[8] These arguments clearly cannot be dismissed out of hand, but two points can be made by way of qualification. First, significant orders of autonomy attach to the parties in relatively few bargaining arrangements and, directly at least, to the advantage of relatively few workers.

Second, there are times when even the most heavily shielded oligopolists find themselves vulnerable to the inclemencies of economic storm seasons. We recall, for example, that the first and second liveliest issues among UAW members in the spring and early summer of 1973, as the union headed into its contract negotiations, were "thirty and out" and "compulsory overtime." The first of these referred to the union's proposed efforts to eliminate the age requirement (fifty) for retirement after thirty years' service. The second referred to the desire of workers to make their obligations to work overtime more voluntary than the existing contract allowed, though there was practically no interest in contesting overtime work per se.

Attendance at the UAW Collective Bargaining Convention and a few weeks later, residence at the encampment of UAW members and their families at Black Lake, Michigan, respectively, persuaded us of the great strength of both of these issues among the rank-and-file. But the ink on the 1973 agreement, signed in August, was barely dry when auto owners and prospective auto buyers were introduced to OPEC. Venezuelan oil barons, Arab sheiks, the Shah of Iran, and their Harvard Business School–trained advisers (!) made a sad footnote of the overtime issue, reduced the hopes and prospects for many autoworkers that they would *ever* reach thirty years' service, and for a time rocked even the big-three auto makers.

Our own conclusions in this much debated area are not easily drawn. On the one side, we argue here that managers' freedom of action in respect to the rewards they afford their workers is limited. In Parts III and IV we will argue that managers often do not act on the proximal issues about which they *do* have some options; among other reasons, they often have sufficient market power, in the short run, certainly, to pass on to consumers the costs of buying out worker dissatisfactions.

We suggest that these holdings are not contradictory: to the extent that there are "excess" labor costs, they are low compared to other costs that trouble business leaders in the short run; and labor costs can be passed on in an inflationary economy, even by employers who do not enjoy fully oligopolistic market positions.

At the same time, the market powers of corporations, evident even in the least competitive industries, are sufficient in neither magnitude nor temporal duration to assure managers ready control of workers' incomes. Loans to striking auto unions, finally, are perhaps good investments over the longer pull, by business standards, given the goodwill generated and the perceived need for collaboration among auto companies and unions—for example, in battles against environmental restrictions that threaten car sales.

EQUITY

Workers' perceptions about the adequacy of their incomes and their sense of job security are interesting in absolute terms; they are interesting, as well, in relative terms. Indeed, the concept of "relative deprivation" may be considered one of the most important of those derived and developed in social science since World War II.

The idea is that subjective findings of well-being depend on how one's own experiences compare to those close at hand, what one anticipates for the future, or what one may have been accustomed to in the past. Thus, degradation may seem tolerable if others close at hand fare no better, or if one never had reason to expect any better. Similarly, an "absolute" advantage will appear less satisfying in comparison to the advantages enjoyed by others. Indignation, for example, over the high wages reputedly enjoyed by plumbers is regularly expressed by college professors. The real question for us would be to what extent, if at all they might blame their own employer-administrators for what they perceive to be inequitable treatment.

It was our expectation that workers would be more inclined to perceive their rewards to be in line with the earnings of others in similar *jobs* and less inclined to regard their earnings as fair in comparison to those in other *occupations*. Thus, we hypothesized, workers have a well-developed sense of approximately what their employers can pay, but far less developed and satisfying explanations of the patterns according to which earnings are distributed among occupations in the American economy. In general, we tend to view favorably the occupational returns we receive relative to those accorded our fellows who earn less and to view more skeptically the equity of rewards accorded those in better-paid occupations.[9]

Once again, testable hypotheses about work satisfaction are limited by the types of data that have been collected. The Working Conditions Survey did not lend itself to an examination of the fairness of earnings, but the Post-Election Survey of 1972 did contain items on workers' perceptions of their earnings relative to those of others in the same jobs and to others in different occupations.[10] Unfortunately, these items did not appear in the same form on the survey as the item on overall job satisfaction, so that it was impossible to cross-tabulate them directly. We include some discussion of the items and the issues to which they relate here because we think there is a plausible, if undemonstrable, connection between equity and satisfaction, and because the locus of perceptions of inequity has a bearing on our concern for the margins of managerial intervention.

The Election Survey showed that whereas 28 percent of employed workers believed that they were paid less than others in the same jobs, 39 percent felt that their earnings were unfairly low compared with those of incumbents of other occupations. The pay ranges for doing the same kind of work tend to some local uniformity, but for different kinds of work the disparities are not only greater but are also more likely to be perceived as unfair.

This relationship holds across the board for subgroups of workers, but there are several differences in the patterns of response to the two questions. Young workers (whether defined as under twenty-five or under thirty-five) are more likely than older workers to question the equity of their job earnings, but there is no difference by age in perception of occupational earnings. Workers in low-income families (less than $4,000) are more likely than high-income ($15,000 or more) families to view both their job and occupational earnings as inequitable.

More interesting is the fact that while the perception of job earnings is the same by achieved education, 54 percent of college graduates feel their occupations to be unfairly rewarded compared to 36 percent of those less educated. And those who perceive themselves as middle-class are less satisfied than those who perceive themselves as working-class in response to questions about both job and occupational earnings.

Burkhard Strumpel has explored these issues by comparing the responses in 1972 and 1973 to the same questions concerning job and occupational returns. In Table 5.5, "within" and "between" groups' comparisons correspond to our "job" and "occupational" comparisons.

He explains the increase of "felt inequity" and the considerable reaction of older blue-collar workers and blacks as follows:

> In 1973 real income increases were harder to come by. Survey findings suggest a conspicuous failure of political leaders to explain the present economic difficulties and convince the public that they were shared by all. A particularly large proportion of older blue-collar workers and blacks report being worse off than 12 months ago. White-collar workers tend to be somewhat shielded from adverse developments in the economy by more job security, a larger margin of discretionary income, and the more frequent availability of liquid assets. Younger workers, white- or blue-collar, are more likely to receive pay increases in excess of price increases than older workers.[11]

This interpretation is consistent with the assessment we have made, quite independently, regarding the real and perceived roles of employers

TABLE 5.5.   Feelings of Inequity,[a] Selected Population Groups—Percent Feeling They Get Less than They Deserve

	Within-Group Equity ("Job" Comparison)		Between-Group Equity ("Occupation" Comparison)	
	Fall 1972	Fall 1973	Fall 1972	Fall 1973
All workers	28%	43%	39%	53%
Less than 35 – white collar	28	42	41	51
35 and over – white collar	28	38	40	48
Less than 35 – blue collar	37	42	37	49
35 and over – blue collar	20	50	36	62
Blacks	26	66	36	69

[a] The questions in Fall 1973 were: "How fair is what you earn on your *job* in comparison to others doing the same type of work you do? How fair is what people in your line of work earn in comparison to how much people in other *occupations* earn? Do you feel that you get much less than you deserve, somewhat less than you deserve, about as much as you deserve, or more than you deserve?" The Fall 1972 questions were similar but referred to getting more or less than your "fair share." Source: Burkhard Strumpel, "Inflation, Discontent and Distributive Justice," *Economic Outlook USA* 1 (Summer 1974), p. 12.

and the system in matters of equity. The findings are in line with our suppositions concerning the associations between work satisfactions and perceptions of the degree to which rewards are, in our language, equitably distributed. We are mindful that the broader issue of economic justice is a vexed one in a society in which meritocratic, individualistic, and democratic values are in such delicate balance. The debate, sometimes angry, that followed the publication of John Rawls' widely discussed book, *A Theory of Justice,* is sufficient to warn against glib treatment of the complexities involved in identifying what is most equitable about economic rewards, a warning we are prepared to honor.

We are, however, quite willing to endorse a congenial treatment of the matter by Lester Thurow, who merges economists' conceptions of "wage contours" with sociologists' "relative deprivation" in an essay in which he writes that "the social specification of equity is a problem in relative income distribution" [12] and that Americans make estimates of their circumstances in relative terms—which is to say, in terms of their perceived memberships in reference groups. We Americans wish to receive rewards similar to those accorded to others perceived as "close" to ourselves. We accept modest rewards compared only to those of others whose "efforts, talents, hardships, and the like" are "legitimate"—i.e., not subject to invidious comparison. [13]

The meaning of all this is not elusive: on one side, there are both economic and social restrictions on the degrees of managers' unilateral freedom to alter the incomes or job security of American workers. To the extent to which workers' satisfactions are related to their perceptions of security and the "adequacy and comfort" of their incomes, managers are constrained by market and legal forces beyond their control from applying fully appropriate remedies. To the extent that workers view their circumstances in relative terms, managers are further constrained by norms influential in defining social and economic justice, norms that are themselves potent in shaping workers' judgments about the fairness of the allocations of economic and therefore social rewards.

It follows, to the extent that relative conceptions of income allocation are related to work satisfaction, that efforts to reorder economic and social rewards might produce a redistribution of satisfactions; but it is most unlikely that satisfactions would increase across the board were the incomes of all uniformly raised. [14]

In the next chapter we will examine aggregate data bearing on the utilization of the labor force's educational achievements and the role of those achievements in facilitating opportunities for moving into preferred occupations. This macro-level assessment will help to clarify the roles of skills and occupations in the structure of workers' attitudes toward work. It will help, furthermore, to clarify the possible relevancies of reformers' ideas.

Mention of reformers' ideas serves to remind us of the relevance of our story line as we expand upon the discussion of macro and micro factors. Thus it is one of the prevailing views among would-be work reformers and their followers that we face problems in America of work adjustment, that work dissatisfaction is essentially an intra-job phenomenon. We suggest, on the contrary, that job attitudes should be conceived to relate also to wider-going experiences, that workers' assessments of their jobs are colored by their circumstances as industrial citizens, and that workers' assessments of macro, mezzo, and micro forces interpenetrate, one with each of the others. One facet of our analysis is thus nicely summarized by Patricia Smith, who, after a careful review of relevant evidence, writes that

> . . . above a certain minimum, for example, a given annual income is a positive source of satisfaction, a source of dissatisfaction, or irrelevant to an individual, depending upon what other jobs might pay, upon what other people of comparable training, skills, and experience are obtaining (in the same labor market), upon what the same individual has earned in the past, and upon the financial obligations he has assumed and the expenditures to which he has become accustomed.[15]

We may end this discussion by adding that employed Americans have well-developed notions of labor-market offerings and rewards beyond those prevailing in their immediate, local settings. We may also note the evidence that one's overall satisfactions with life, in general, are influenced not only by perceptions of how well one is doing relative to those in other occupations but, as William Rushing has shown in a study of farmers and farm workers, by perceptions of how well one is doing compared to widely shared cultural standards governing achievement and performance.[16]

6. The Demand for and Utilization of Differentially Educated American Workers

Much has been said in recent years about the extent to which the educational achievements of Americans have come, in a narrow, technical, sense to exceed those needed to staff the economy. The argument that college-trained Americans, for example, are "overeducated" has even come to the surface in the work of economists who, after imputing great value to formal schooling in the 1960s, see its value declining as the actual prices paid to educated Americans for their schoolroom achievements, in a classic supply-demand model, begin to decline.[1] The implication is that education's economic values are as the marketplace says they are, neither more nor less, questions of content, quality, and so on quite aside. An entirely parallel set of conceptions underlies a large segment of recent discussions of work satisfaction, arguing for a considered treatment of the ways in which Americans' educational achievements are utilized and rewarded by employers.

In its most general form, the question before us here is: How much of the demand for formal schooling has been and will be generated by relatively arbitrary employer decisions to upgrade educational requirements for jobs as compared to changes in actual job tasks? In the following sections we first discuss a little of the question's background and the principal ways in which the general question may be addressed; we then present the methods we used to prepare our estimates of the answer to the question. While these estimates are sufficiently interesting to justify chapter-length treatment, they were derived with the specific intention that we would juxtapose them, as we have done in Chapters 7 and 8, with data on work satisfaction from the Working Conditions Survey.

Our specific interest in simplifying and updating our own earlier estimates [2] is thus to provide a basis for considering the relationships between workers' educational achievements and the skill levels called for by their jobs. *Because the acquisition and use of skills involve experiences both inside and outside of employment settings*, a consideration of skill-related issues as they are joined in the workplace facilitates simultaneous assessments of the relative influences on worker sensibilities of employers' ways and extra-organizational forces. It may be recalled that our approach to the research problem required us to seek opportunities for conducting precisely such micro, mezzo, and macro assessments.

The educational achievements of Americans have, of course, always been of interest to social scientists, especially to students of social stratification. Among economists, technically detailed concerns about a broad array of the correlates and consequences of formal schooling emerged in the 1960s. Groundbreaking efforts by Schultz,[3] Denison,[4] and Becker [5] were aimed at filling the lacunae in neoclassical economic theory, especially those relating to international differences in economic growth rates and intranational differences in income distribution.[6] These studies and discussions have been collectively grouped under the rubric "human capital theory." The studies we have cited have helped us to understand the implications of investments in education for workers and their reactions to work, but because it is to these implications that our own materials and concerns relate we have been obliged to develop alternative methods to those favored in human-capital studies in order to pursue our concerns more expeditiously.

EDUCATIONAL ACHIEVEMENTS AND PRACTICAL JOB REQUIREMENTS

We may say at the outset that we have no argument with the popular position that the cultural or "consumption" benefits of schooling are as important as the economic and skill returns. Nor would we take exception to the idea that higher levels of education may be necessary to cope with bureaucratic organizations that "are perhaps the major vehicle for producing and sustaining the class system in the modern welfare state. Nowhere is this more transparent than in the income tax structure. Persons who have the means . . . employ specialists . . . to help them take advantage of the rules." [7] Nor would we be inclined to contest the scientist who sees, among the external benefits of education, the simplifications in income tax collection that an educated population makes possible.[8] We are not at all discomfited by the urge to remember education's cultural and other roles. We do not, in short, wish to consider here education's "noneconomic" roles in society, important as such issues are.[9]

On the economic side, we are made uncomfortable by the debate over education's purported "production" and "consumption" benefits, its external benefits, and the relative weights of "social" and "private" rates of return in calculations of education's worth. It strikes us as interesting but highly problematic *for our purposes*, for example, that in the work on education by some economists, workers' educational achievements are seen to be differentially utilized "in terms of the marginal social product of education in comparison with the opportunity cost of capital." [10] One difficulty with such formulations for our purposes is that they are predicated on the undocumented assumption that the dollar values of employees' wages and salaries are "rationally" allocated to them over the longer run on the basis of their productivity. Even a view of education as an overall screening device—as an indicator of the quality of employees—absent more empirically detailed studies of workers' performance, is subject to doubt. Indeed, a crude test we conducted in the late 1960s of this increasingly popular assumption of economists provided no evidence whatever that marginal increments of education are predictive of proportionate improvements in the performance of employees. [11] We emphasize that the test was a crude though quite extensive one; the fact is that there is little usable, detailed information available for testing the meaning of the high positive relationship between the incomes of workers and workers' educational achievements. It has also been suggested that education, on the other side, may not adequately represent the most important worker traits. Thus formal education, in the views of some, has been taken altogether uncritically as a surrogate measure of ability in the education-income model. [12]

As these misgivings suggest, we have avoided the temptation, in dealing with aggregate data, to use wages and salaries as indicators of workers' performance and of the extent to which their formal educations are being utilized. While objections to what is known as the indirect approach have been made on other grounds, [13] our objection is informed by our earlier experiences, which is to say by the need to move, directly, to detailed occupational data in order to identify more precisely the proportion of jobs that have been "educationally upgraded" because their *content* has changed and the proportion that have been "educationally upgraded" in ways unrelated to content. [14]

Efforts paralleling our approach have, of course, been made by others, and they suggest—as we will—that a considerable number of persons will be "occupationally downgraded." [15] We offer a discussion of our own specific assessments because they permit us to estimate the additional effects in aggregate data of past "occupational downgrading," as some other essentially direct estimates do not, and because they are based on methods that permit us, though somewhat tentatively, to deal with workers' educational achievements in juxtaposition with the skills required in their jobs. The fact that our measures of skill apply *across* jobs in our economy makes it possible, finally, to compare the perspectives of workers in different occupations in accordance with a common, albeit crudely conceived, denominator.

ESTIMATING THE "MATCH-UP" BETWEEN JOB REQUIREMENTS AND EDUCATIONAL ACHIEVEMENTS

Data on the educational achievements of workers are readily available; more problematic, as we have already implied, are estimates of actual educational requirements for jobs. In our earlier work we presented five different "matches" of achievements and requirements, with the latter based on the General Educational Development (GED) level for the job. Figure 6.1 is a version of earlier estimates for 1950 and 1960 updated to include 1970 data. Despite methodological flaws—the estimates are crude—these data are the only ones available with which to represent longitudinal developments.

In Figure 6.1, the experienced civilian labor force is allocated among three levels, with an assumed match between educational achievements and requirements.[16] The two distributions in the columns do not relate to the same individuals; they simply show the proportions of the labor force with various levels of schooling, compared to the proportion of jobs at various levels of GED. Thus, in 1950, the majority of workers were in the low-education group, but the proportion of low-level jobs was only about one-third of the total. Since 60 percent of the jobs (but only one-third of the workers) were in the middle level, there would seem to have been considerable room for "upward mobility" in 1950. In 1960, the favorable aspects of this "mismatch" were even more pronounced. By 1970, however, there was a reversal: the upper level included 10.1 percent of all jobs but 12.6 percent of all workers. In absolute numbers, the disparity between workers and jobs was about two million, or one-fifth of the ten million college graduates in the labor force at that time.

It is apparent from these retrospective data that the upward shift in the occupational structure was largely a phenomenon of the 1950s, while the more striking increase in educational achievements occurred in the 1960s. In the 1970s, not surprisingly, the returns to investment in education began to drop. Insofar as market forces may be said to govern in matters of education, job requirements, and returns on education, these data suggest that they do so with a ten-year lag. Even assuming that aggregate adjustments are finally completed for any given age

Figure 6.1: Percentage Distribution of General Educational Development (GED) Level of Job Requirements and Years of Schooling for the Civilian Labor Force, 1950, 1960, and 1970.

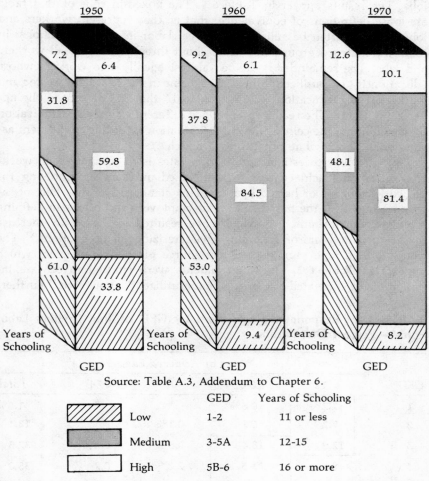

Source: Table A.3, Addendum to Chapter 6.

	GED	Years of Schooling
Low	1-2	11 or less
Medium	3-5A	12-15
High	5B-6	16 or more

group, ten years, in human terms, represents an expenditure of one-quarter of a typical worker's life in the process of getting disentangled from the cobweb quality of the market.

Education, Jobs, and Workers

A more direct set of comparisons between educational achievements and requirements is available for 1971 as a result of a unique data source: a Current Population Survey, coded not only in census categories but also in *Dictionary of Occupational Titles* categories. The existence of this "bridge tape" makes it possible to cross-tabulate the educational achievements of workers with the GED of their particular jobs. The results appear in Table 6.1. The boxed-in cells of that table are loose definitions of equivalence; that is, they represent workers and jobs that can often be substituted in real labor-market transactions. In total, the matched groups constitute about three-quarters of all workers and jobs. The remainder is divided almost equally into workers whose education is "overutilized," the 13.1 percent in the lower-left sector and workers whose education is "underutilized," the 12.8 percent in the upper-right sector. The reader can produce different estimates of utilization by recombining the cells of the cross-tabulation according to different assumptions about what constitutes a match.

Another way to estimate utilization rates is to compare each worker's educational achievement with the median years of schooling for all workers in his or her occupation. This standard has the effect of incorporating all of the past practices of employers and others in defining job requirements, practices which have resulted in the steady increase in the median years of schooling characterizing all occupations.[17] The same "bridge tape" for 1971 is the source of this comparison, which appears in Table 6.2. Full-time students were omitted to obviate inflation of the estimated size of the "underutilized" labor force.[18] Further-

TABLE 6.1. Respondent's Education by GED of Job, Civilian Labor Force[a]—Percent Distribution

GED[b]	Years of Achieved Education				
	< 12	12–15	16	17+	Total
1	1.2%	0.6%	c	c	1.8%
2	7.2	5.1	0.1%	c	12.4
3	12.9	18.4	0.8	0.2%	32.3
4	8.6	23.5	2.2	0.7	35.0
5					
A	0.8	3.2	1.8	1.3	7.1
B	c	2.4	2.3	1.7	6.4
6	0.2	1.1	1.1	2.6	5.0
Total	30.9%	54.3%	8.3%	6.5%	100.0%

[a] Full-time students excluded.
[b] General Educational Development required for job. For full definition, see Addendum.
[c] Less than 0.1.

Source: 1971 Current Population Survey Bridge Tape.

TABLE 6.2. Respondent's Education by Median Education of Respondent's Occupation, Civilian Labor Force[a]—Percent Distribution

Occupation—Median Educ.	Years of Achieved Education				
	< 12	12–15	16	17+	Total
< 12	**21.1%**	16.1%	0.5%	0.1%	37.8%
12–15	9.7	**37.0**	4.9	1.7	53.3
16	0.1	0.9	**2.0**	1.5	4.5
17+	b	0.4	1.0	**3.2**	4.6
Total	30.9%	54.4%	8.4%	6.5%	100.2%

[a] Full-time students excluded.
[b] Less than 0.1 percent.

Rows and columns do not add precisely because of rounding.

Source: 1971 Current Population Survey Bridge Tape.

more, the aggregations are confined to four categories to allow room for the play of ambiguity in the requirements–achievements matching process, since the labor market actually differentiates at the diploma- or degree-granting points (high school, college, and post-graduate) in the screening and allocation of workers.

Using this standard, 63.3 percent of the labor force were appropriately matched with their jobs (the sum of the underlined cells on the diagonal); 12.1 percent were overutilized (below the diagonal); and 24.8 percent, underutilized (above the diagonal). The bulk of the underutilization in this table was among high-school graduates, including those with one to three years of college. As yet, the underutilization of these workers has received little attention. Among women clericals, the upgrading process has long been completed, as jobs have been filled by high-school graduates; the medians for the occupations in question therefore cluster at twelve years, and the close correspondence between requirements and achievements reflects this homogeneity.

Given the great popular interest in college graduates, it is useful to look attentively at that population group. The 1971 data (Table 6.2) show about 15 percent of the labor force with at least four years of college. Divided into those with college 4 and college 5+, and measured by the median education achievement for their jobs, 35 percent were equal and 7 percent were overutilized (college graduates in jobs requiring college 5+); 51 percent were underutilized.

Of the underutilized, the single largest group (2.4 million, about one-third of all college graduates) were in jobs where the median was somewhere in the high-school-plus-some-college range (twelve to fifteen years of schooling). This is obviously a mixture that includes some occupations on the way up in point of their credentials. A clear-cut example is nursing, an occupation in which the former fifteen-year standard has been rapidly moving to sixteen years as long-familiar "diploma schools" have been dispossessed of their credentialing role by baccalaureate programs.

Finally, it is possible to incorporate both standards—GED and median education of occupations—in making utilization estimates (Table 6.3). We begin with the data in Table 6.2, which provide three categories —equal, overutilized, and underutilized—and then disaggregate by GED to create a control for job level. In addition, Table 6.3 shows the results separately for men and women.

As we have seen, 63 percent of the civilian labor force, excluding full-time students, are in jobs consonant with their educational level. At the top (GED 6) and the bottom (GED 1–3) of the occupational structure the proportion of workers who are matched with their jobs is about the same. The matched proportion is higher in GED 4 because of the preponderance of high-school graduates in the population and the large number of GED-4 jobs. On both the "requirements" and the "achievements" side, the modal categories are joined together in the middle of the distribution. The matched proportion is the smallest among GED 5s, as might be expected in a category largely composed of two disparate occupational types—professionals (engineers and teachers) and managers (both salaried and self-employed).

Looking at the detailed comparisons by sex, utilization patterns are

TABLE 6.3.   Utilization[a] by GED by Sex—Percent Distribution

	General Educational Development				
			MALES		
	1–2[b]	3	4	5	6
Equal	61.8%	59.2%	61.0%	54.7%	62.6%
Overutilized	3.2	8.8	14.6	14.0	15.6
Underutilized	35.0	32.0	24.4	31.3	21.8
Total	100.0%	100.0%	100.0%	100.0%	100.0%
			FEMALES		
Equal	60.7%	65.8%	80.0%	58.0%	65.7%
Overutilized	4.2	17.7	10.0	16.8	17.0
Underutilized	35.1	16.5	10.0	25.2	18.3
Total	100.0%	100.0%	100.0%	100.0%	100.0%

[a] The utilization standard is the median education of the respondent's education. See Table 6.2.
[b] GED 2 is 88 percent of this category.

similar in GED 1–2 and GED 6. What is most striking in the middle categories is the significantly larger underutilization among men. Again, this outcome is related to the large number of high-school graduates (without college degrees) in these data. Among men, they are spread relatively widely among jobs where the median education has not yet reached twelve years because of the dominance of older blue-collar men with relatively little schooling. Among women, on the other hand, occupational designations are much more homogeneous; on balance, more high-school graduates are in GED-4 jobs and more college graduates (mainly teachers) in GED-5 jobs. Again, it should be noted that these are 1971 data, gathered before the underutilization of college graduates was of serious magnitude.

What we can expect in the future is that the rising educational achievements of American workers will shift the median to high-school graduation for groups below that standard in 1971, so that the growing population of college graduates, some of whom will occupy nonprofessional, nonmanagerial positions, will become the bulk of the underutilized workers.

THE FUTURE SUPPLY AND UTILIZATION OF COLLEGE GRADUATES

The maintenance of a high rate of return to higher education depends in general on the assumption of economic growth and, in particular, on an ever-expanding market for the specific "products" of the knowledge industry. The optimism of the 1960s has been displaced in many quarters by reservations about the market for technical and professional education at all levels and by pessimism about the market for baccalaureates.[19] Beginning around 1970, with the increasingly depressing reports on the market for college graduates, it has become accepted that institutions of higher education are producing more degree holders than can be "appropriately" absorbed by the labor market. It is by now well understood that the leveling-off in the exponential increases in the demand for scientific personnel as a result of research and development cutbacks in both the military and civilian sectors of the economy, together with the unusually large demographic cohort born immediately after World War II and their high levels of enrollment in colleges, have created a serious imbalance.

Folger *et al.* in 1968 estimated a "residual" of 2.6 million college graduates for the period 1970–1980.[20] They interpreted their data to mean that the jobs in the American occupational structure had been substantially upgraded in the period 1950 to 1960, but that the rate of change in the occupational structure had slowed down in the succeeding decade. Meanwhile, colleges were producing graduates at accelerating rates. What, then, are the employment prospects of this "residual"? The *Manpower Report of the President for 1972* [21] projected that the 2.6 million graduates in the "residual" would be absorbed into "newly upgraded" jobs and that an additional 0.2 million would simply be pushed out into the rest of the market. The Carnegie Commission on Education Report, *College Graduates and Jobs,* [22] estimated that 25 percent of all college graduates in the seventies would be employed in jobs previously performed by noncollege graduates. Since some of these jobs will be truly "upgraded," the Commission offers a "*very rough guess*" that 1 to 1.5 million would remain in jobs that "have not been or cannot be upgraded."

Folger, in a later projection, estimated that in the 1980s, fewer than half of the college graduates could expect to find jobs in the professions even if the assumption were made that a higher percent of entrants into the professions were college graduates, something on the order of 70 to 80 percent.[23] Rosenthal's projections for a different time period (1972 to 1985) show a larger number of new entrants (15.3 million), but also greater growth (7.7 million) and greater replacement (6.8 million), leaving a much smaller "problem" residual of under a million.[24] Joseph Froomkin, on the other hand, concluded that by 1985 "roughly a third of college graduates will be in positions which were hitherto held by persons with less education." [25]

Apart from the differences in magnitudes, the most interesting aspect of these projections is that they assume that at the beginning of the period—that is, at the time the estimate was made—all college graduates were appropriately situated in the job market with respect to the match between their achieved education and the education required for their jobs.

CROSS-SECTIONAL ESTIMATES OF UNDERUTILIZATION

In the previous section we presented estimates of underutilization using different standards for three decades. Those data showed the historical development of high-school graduation as a criterion for employment; but even with the steady increase in average years of schooling, substantial numbers of high-school graduates were employed, as late as 1971, in occupations where the median number of years of schooling was below twelve. Those same data showed that 58 percent of college graduates were underutilized, with a small offset of 7 percent who were "overutilized" (a group of workers with four years of college in jobs where the median education was five years of college or more).

One may conclude, if the 7 percent is netted out, that approximately half of all college graduates were underutilized in 1971.

Using the same standard of underutilization (median educational achievement), data for 1975 show that about 45 percent of the almost fourteen million employed college graduates were underutilized (48 percent of the men and 40 percent of the women). The detailed occupational composition of this underutilized group appears in Table 6.4. We know that salaried managers and salespeople in occupations other than retail trade are increasingly likely to be college graduates upon entry into the labor force. If one removes these "transitional" occupations, the percentage of underutilization falls to 19 percent for the men, 33 percent for the women, and 24 percent for all employed college graduates.

Using a different method, the original team that conducted the 1969 Working Conditions Survey cross-tabulated the completed years of schooling for each of their respondents with respondents' answers to the question, "What level of formal education do you feel is needed by a person in your job?" The responses were coded into eight categories: "no special level"; 1–7; 8; 9–11; 12; 13–15; 16; and 16-plus years of schooling. The matched cells in the resulting 8 × 8 matrix

TABLE 6.4. Number of College Graduates in Occupations with Median Years of School Less Than 16, by Sex, 1975

Occupation	Number College Graduates (in thousands)		
	Total	*Men*	*Women*
Health Workers[a]	452	90	362
Engineering, Science Technicians	135	111	24
Salaried Managers	2,302	2,009	293
Self-Employed Managers	203	167	36
Retail Sales Workers	182	95	87
Other Sales Workers	723	661	62
Clerical Workers	1,127	407	720
Craft Workers	421	321	100
Operatives	208	165	43
Laborers	85	78	7
Private Household Workers	3	—	3
Service Workers	327	201	126
Farm Workers	128	113	15
	6,296	4,418	1,878

[a] Except practitioners.

Source: Bob Whitmore, "Educational Attainment of Workers, March 1975," *Special Labor Force Report 186* (Washington, D.C.: U.S. Government Printing Office, 1976), Table I, pp. A 19–20.

were considered to be a perfect fit, with the off-diagonal cells "under-utilized" where the respondent's education was higher than his estimate of job requirements and "underqualified" where the respondent had less education than his estimate of job requirements.[26]

This method presents three problems. First, it is based on a judgment by the respondent rather than a more objective standard; second, the fact that there are eight categories automatically inflates the proportion of underutilization since there are more possibilities for mismatch than in a simpler schema; and third, the inclusion of "no special level," which accounted for 10 percent of the total sample, obscures the meaning of the rest of the categories. The result is that 55 percent of the sample showed an exact match, 19 percent were "overqualified," and 27 percent "underutilized." Of the college graduates in the sample, 31 percent were "underutilized" by the same criterion.

No matter what the standard, substantial numbers of college graduates are underutilized in any given cross section. The additions to this cohort in the form of new entry workers is illustrated in a survey reporting the employment experience of those who received baccalaureate and advanced degrees between July 1971 and June 1972. About 70,000—9.4 percent of the total—were unemployed. Of those who were working, 82 percent had jobs "directly or somewhat related to their majors." Of the approximately 200,000 in work not directly related, about half reported that they could not find jobs in their fields. We will leave to the reader the question of assessing the utilization levels involved when the *type* of education rather than the number of years of education is taken into account.

More significant, however, is the distribution by gross occupation category of the employed. Fifty-eight percent of the men and 71 percent of the women were in "professional, technical, or kindred" jobs. The utilization pattern for women seems more favorable, but it should be recalled that "professional, technical, and kindred" includes a large number of women in health occupations, most of them nurses and technicians, in addition to elementary–school teachers, the traditional profession for which women prepare and in which they are employed.

Fourteen percent of the men but only 6 percent of the women were employed as managers, while the proportions for sales workers were 7 percent and 4 percent. All other occupations, including clerical, blue-collar, and service jobs, accounted for 20 percent of the total sample (21 percent of the men and 19 percent of the women).[27]

PROJECTIONS

Trend lines in the data presented so far underscore the importance of future developments affecting manpower utilization. As we shall see, the relationship between underutilization and worker attitudes is at best indirect because of the intervention of skill level. But if in fact education's role is to provide access to skilled jobs, as we argue, the relationship will likely be a good deal less subtle in the realities of the next several years.

Thus, it has been demonstrated by several investigators that the big increase in demand for college-educated workers in the post–World War II era stemmed from the expansion of education-intensive industries, such as education itself, rather than from pronounced shifts in the occupational structure within industries.[28] True upgrading of occupations, in the sense of increasing the complexity of tasks, is a limited solution for utilizing more highly educated workers. Adequate increases in demand would depend on continued expansion of specific industries in addition to real changes in occupational structures, neither of which seems likely in the near future. True upgrading cannot be inferred from a mere rise in years of schooling. Rawlins and Ulman, for example, showed a large increase in achieved education for selected low-level jobs, an increase that bore little relationship to the requirements for those jobs.[29]

Table 6.5 shows the educational distribution of the labor force in 1970 and 1975 with projections for 1980 and 1990. According to these figures the proportion of college graduates will almost double from 1970 to 1990, and the absolute number will rise from 10.4 to 24.7 million.

Economists, who have observed both the mismatch and the decline in enrollment rates, predict a smaller supply of entering graduates in the future. Richard Freeman concluded that there was a significant decline in both salaries and job opportunities for college graduates in the 1969–1974 period; that, as a consequence, the rate of return was reduced from the 11–12 percent of the early 1960s to about 8 percent in the early 1970s; and that with these events, enrollments in college began to decline, "apparently as a rational supply response to changed market incentives." [30]

Freeman does not make specific estimates but simply predicts that a decline in enrollments will follow the decline in earnings with a four-year lag. Stephen Dresch, who has experimented with models for prediction, also criticizes the assumption of static enrollment rates that has characterized standard projections of enrollment produced by the National Center for Educational Statistics and by the Carnegie Commission. The inadequacies of this "trend-demographic" approach, in which future variation depends entirely on the size of the college-age population, according to Dresch, "have been permitted and to a degree justified by the emphasis in the human-capital literature on the estimation of static rates of return to investments in education." Instead, Dresch relies on relative wages and the achievement of a wage equilibrium be-

TABLE 6.5 Civilian Labor Force 16 Years Old and Over, Years of School Completed by Sex, 1970, 1975 Actual; 1980, 1990 Projected

	Total N (in thousands)	Total	11 or less	12	13–15	16 or more
			Percent Distribution by Years of School Completed			
1970 Total	82,714	100	39.3	35.0	13.1	12.6
Male	51,194	100	41.7	31.5	13.0	13.8
Female	31,520	100	35.3	40.8	13.4	10.5
1975 Total	92,613	100	29.2	39.7	15.4	15.7
Male	55,615	100	30.9	36.3	15.5	17.3
Female	36,998	100	26.6	44.8	15.3	15.3
1980 Total	101,673	100	27.3	40.4	15.9	16.4
Male	60,000	100	28.4	37.2	16.3	18.1
Female	41,673	100	25.6	45.3	15.2	13.9
1990 Total	113,839	100	19.8	40.5	18.0	21.7
Male	66,947	100	19.9	38.0	18.8	23.3
Female	48,619	100	19.6	44.3	16.8	19.3

Source: Civilian labor force: Howard N. Fullerton, Jr., and Paul O. Flaim, "New Labor Force Projections to 1990," *Monthly Labor Review* 99 (December 1976), Table 3, p. 7. Education: 1970, 1980, 1990: Denis F. Johnston, "Education of Workers: Projections to 1990," *Monthly Labor Review* 96 (November 1973), Table 2, p. 24. 1975: "Educational Attainment of Workers, March 1975," *Special Labor Force Report 186* (Washington, D. C.: U.S. Government Printing Office, 1976).

tween college graduates and other workers as the major forces affecting enrollment rates in the future.[31]

Dresch's original model produced approximately the same level as the projections he criticized until 1985, when his enrollment estimates dropped off sharply. A subsequent revision of the model reduced the projected 46 percent decline between 1980 and 1990 to 18.5 percent.[32]

While predictions of lower enrollments on the grounds of declining rates of return or the convergence of relative wage rates are intuitively plausible, other factors clearly affect the decision to enroll in college. First, the cost of higher education is reduced when unemployment is high because earnings for alternative activities are low. Furthermore, unemployment affects the less educated disproportionately:

> On both counts even temporarily high rates of unemployment can be expected to encourage further schooling on the part of significant numbers of young people who, in a more stable, full-employment environment would have considered work a preferable alternative.[33]

The decision to continue in school under these circumstances is a response to the segmentation of the labor market and the sheltering processes that take place there. What seems most likely is that college graduates will continue to enjoy advantages over noncollege graduates, but some will be competing for lower-wage positions with less-educated workers.[34] The possibility that some will be chosen despite a shortfall in the aggregate demand for their education lies behind the idea that people will continue to enroll as a defensive measure. The rationality that the economists impute to the market may or may not lower rates of return, but there is no guarantee that it will weaken employers' requirements for credentials in a growing number of occupations.

While the predictions for college enrollments are important in the long run, it is very difficult to foresee the shape of opportunity for college graduates after 1990. The entering cohorts of the total work force are bound to be smaller because of the current decline in the birthrate, but we have very little basis for speculation on the level or the quality of demand. However optimistic the forecast for the year 2000, the problem of underutilization is bound to be severe at least for the next decade.

Those who have made projections with respect to utilization have to bear in mind that, in addition to the excess of well-educated new entrants for whom demand is insufficient on a current basis, there is another group, already in the labor market, competing for better jobs. The backlog is, of course, not homogeneous. Some may find that experience puts them ahead of new graduates, while others may find that their skills and credentials are obsolete by the time opportunities arise. Interestingly enough, it has been suggested that college enrollment levels may be maintained if individuals in the maturing baby-boom cohorts turn to adult education to update their skills when confronted by the anticipated competition.[35]

The severity of this competition, which is due to the relative youth of the labor force as well as to its high educational achievements, is graphically portrayed in Figure 6.2. Sixty-two percent of the total labor force was under forty-five in 1960 and 66 percent in 1975. Official projections, heavily influenced by actual population changes, forecast a leap to 71 percent in 1990.[36] Put another way, the ratio of persons 30–44 to those aged 45–49 is expected to rise from 1.07 in 1975 to a peak of 1.62 by 1990.[37] It is not only the absolutely large size of the younger cohorts that matters but also the smaller number of positions being vacated. A relatively young labor force minimizes the effect of attrition in creating new job openings. Dresch estimates that the rate of attrition will be only 1.1 percent between 1980 and 2000. "Only as the war and post-war cohorts begin at last to experience significant mortality in late middle age will 'replacement' provide substantial opportunities for young people."[38]

Figure 6.2: Four Age Cohorts and the Growth of the College-educated Labor Force, 1950-1990

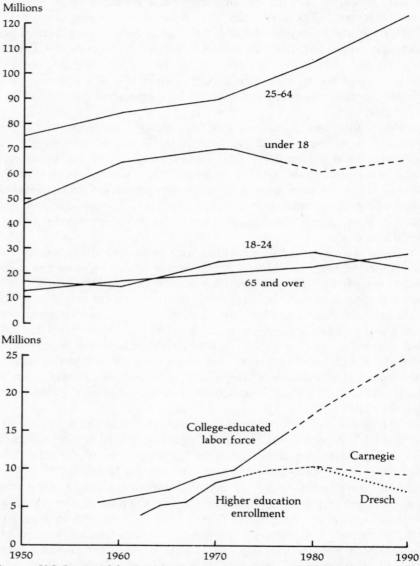

Sources: U.S. Bureau of the Census, "Projections of the Population of the United States: 1975 to 2050," *Current Population Reports*, P-25, No. 601, (October 1975); *Projections of Educational Statistics to 1983-84* (1974 ed.) (U.S. Office of Education, Washington, D.C., 1975), Table 5, p. 22; Denis F. Johnston, *Monthly Labor Review* 96 (November 1973): Table 2; Carnegie Commission on Higher Education, *College Graduates and Jobs* (New York: Mc Graw-Hill, 1973); Stephen P. Dresch, "Ability, Fertility, and Educational Adaptation," in *Research in Population Economics*, Vol. I, edited by Julian L. Simon (Greenwich, Conn.: JAI Press, 1977).

CONCLUSION

Because marginal misgivings about the subject of this chapter may remain, we tried to leave room for different assumptions in identifying the parameters of underutilization. It may be argued, however, that the evidence is methodologically circumstantial. If so, we believe with Thoreau that "some circumstantial evidence is very strong, as when you find a trout in the milk."

We also believe that underutilization is a serious problem for a large number of expectant and hopeful young people affected by the glacial but inexorable movements of market forces. In terms of attitudes, we had some reason to expect that individuals whose education was greater than the median for others in their occupations would be significantly less satisfied with their jobs than individuals whose education was either congruent with or less than the typical educational achievement of their occupational peers. How this expectation turned out, in detail, is a subject of the next chapter.

ADDENDUM TO CHAPTER 6: THE MEASUREMENT OF UNDERUTILIZATION

THE GED SCALE

The scale of General Educational Development (GED) embraces three types of development: logical, mathematical, and linguistic. In the Worker Traits studies, each of these dimensions was estimated separately on a scale from 1 (low) to 6 (high); the final estimate of the requirement of each job in the analysis was the highest of the three. For this reason, and also because of variation in the quality of schooling and the possibility of learning from nonschool experience, GED was defined as a measure independent of actual years of schooling.

In an earlier work, shifts in job requirements (GED estimates) from 1950 to 1960 were juxtaposed with shifts in achieved education. To obviate direct translation of GED into years of schooling we proposed five different ways of matching these distributions, thus presenting a choice of assumptions upon which to base an overall judgment on the utilization question.[39] Since that time, additional data have become available for extending the analysis.

CURRENT POPULATION SURVEY "BRIDGE TAPES"

The Bureau of the Census, in collaboration with the Bureau of Employment Security, prepared two bridge tapes for Current Population

Surveys of 1966 and 1971. From these samples (approximately 50,000 records each), the jobs held by respondents were coded not only by their census occupation group but also by their *Dictionary of Occupational Titles* designation. The error attached to this complex procedure is unknown. Although most well-populated three-digit census occupational groups showed a central tendency with respect to GED, the fundamental differences in the two classification schemes make an average GED somewhat suspect. For 1970 only these data make it possible to estimate the distribution of GEDs either directly by aggregation or indirectly by calculating the mean GED for each census group and weighting by the population of each group before aggregating. The direct method is obviously preferable since the result is closer to the original data. Comparison with earlier years, however, requires using the indirect method.

The bias involved in the indirect method is probably consistent for the three decades, but there are two other sources of difference. First, the 1950 distribution is based on GED estimates from the first Worker Traits Analysis of 1956, while both 1960 and 1970 rely on the second Worker Traits Analysis of 1966. We have discussed the differences in some detail elsewhere,[40] where we demonstrated a certain amount of upgrading of the formal requirements from the first to the second analysis. This source of difference has its greatest effect on the distribution of GEDs 1, 2, and 3 and, to a lesser extent, GED 5.

The other major difference in the data base affecting the relative distributions is the change in the census classification of occupations from 1960 to 1970. The creation of more groups in 1970 by breaking up certain large aggregations resulted in an overall shift of about 10 percent among major census groups. More important for the estimates presented here, 3.5 million retail managers were broken out of the Managers, not elsewhere classified, category in 1970. Taken alone, their GED mean was 4, while in the 1960 aggregate they were part of a larger group whose mean was 5. This shift, about 3.6 percent of the labor force, accounts for the differences observed in the GED-4 and GED-5 percentages from 1960 to 1970 (Table 6A.1).

REQUIREMENTS AND ACHIEVEMENTS AT THE GED-5 LEVEL

Because GED and years of schooling are not congruent, there is also a problem of overlap between educational requirements and achievements that is particularly troublesome for GED 5 jobs. For presentation of these historical data we have employed an earlier solution to the problem of an appropriate division of the GED 5s. The procedure is straight-

TABLE 6A.1.   General Educational Development[a] of Jobs Held by the Experienced Civilian Labor Force, 1950, 1960, 1970—Percent Distribution

GED Level	Year		
	1950	*1960*	*1970*
1	b	—	b
2	32.9%	9.4%	8.2%
3	27.8	42.3	42.9
4	31.2	30.9	34.2
5	6.6	15.1	11.3
A	1.7	11.3	4.5
B	4.9	3.8	6.8
6	1.5	2.3	3.4
Total	100.0%	100.0%	100.0%
N = (000s)	57,247	64,528	80,071

a Calculated from the GED mean for disaggregated census occupational groups, weighted by experienced civilian labor force.
b Less than 0.5 percent.
Source: 1950 and 1960, Berg, *Education and Jobs*, Chapter 3; 1970, 1971 Current Population Survey Bridge Tape.

forward: each census occupational group with a GED mean of 5 is assigned for purposes of aggregation to one of two groups according to the median years of schooling of that group for the appropriate census year. The 5A subset includes those jobs where the median years of schooling of the incumbents is *less* than 16, while the 5B subset includes those jobs where the median years of schooling is *more* than 16. It is important to note that this division introduces a moving standard, thus subsuming much of the upgrading of the past that has produced current definitions of appropriate educational credentials.

GED DISTRIBUTIONS

The most striking feature of Table 6A.1 is the greater overall similarity of the 1960 and the 1970 distributions compared to the 1950 and 1960 distributions. The changes in the basic assessments from the first to the second Worker Traits Analysis undoubtedly contribute to the 1950–1960 disparity, particularly at the lower GED levels. There is in this difference a hint of a "catch-up" with the increased schooling of the population. But if we conclude that the data reflect real shifts in the occupational structure in the first full decade after World War II, then the gross similarity of the 1960 and the 1970 distributions at the lower levels argues a leveling off during the second decade.

The 1960 and 1970 distributions do, however, diverge at the upper levels. The difference in the proportions of GED 4 and 5, as explained above, was an artifact of a change in census classifications. The increases in 5B and 6, however, were largely a result of the expansion of education at all levels, with elementary and secondary school teachers swelling the ranks of the 5Bs, and college teachers contributing to the 6s.

EDUCATION DISTRIBUTION

Meantime, the trend in the production of highly educated workers rose more sharply in the second decade than in the first. Table 6A.2, which includes the entire civilian labor force sixteen years and older, shows an average increase of 5.1 percent in the first decade and 6.3 in the second. Considering only the employed, the number of men twenty-five years and over increased by 19 percent between 1950 and 1970— 0.9 percent a year on the average—while college-graduate men increased 134 percent. For women, the comparable figures were an 89 percent increase in employment—an average gain of 3.2 percent a year—and a 147 percent increase in college graduates, or an average of 4.5 percent a year.

If we think of the data in Table 6A.1 and the GED distribution of jobs held by the labor force in 1950, 1960, and 1970 as representing the demand for workers at various levels of educational development, and the data in Table 6A.2 on educational achievement for the three decades as representing the supply of workers, we may then consider these distributions side by side to obtain a rough notion of the match between supply and demand at various levels of schooling. Because GED was designed as a measure independent of years of schooling, the way in which these distributions are juxtaposed depends on the assumptions, or even the predilections, of the investigator. As an example of the technical problem, GED-3 jobs have for some time, in fact, been filled half by high-school graduates and half by high-school dropouts. The choice, therefore, of either level of education does violence to the reality of the labor market.

There is no consensus among employers, job analysts, or labor economists on an appropriate way to equate GED and years of schooling, but a three-level array, while lacking precision, does least violence to the data. In Table 6A.3, GED-1 and GED-2 jobs are matched with workers who have had less than twelve years of schooling; GED-3 through GED-5A jobs, with twelve to fifteen years of schooling; and GED-5B and

TABLE 6A.2. Years of School Completed, Civilian Labor Force, 1950, 1960, 1970—Percent Distribution

Years of Schooling	Year		
	1950	*1960*	*1970*
11 or less	61.0%	53.0%	39.3%
12	23.8	27.6	35.0
13–15	8.0	10.2	13.1
16 or more	7.2	9.2	12.6
Total	100.0%	100.0%	100.0%
N = (000s)	57,141	67,545	80,393

Source: Denis F. Johnston, "Education of Workers: Projections to 1990," *Monthly Labor Review* 96 (November 1973), Table 2, p. 24.

GED-6 jobs with sixteen or more years of schooling, i.e., college graduates. The data presented in Table 6A.3 are the source of the bar graphs in Figure 6.1 (p. 79).

DIRECT COMPARISON OF EDUCATION AND JOB REQUIREMENTS

A direct comparison between educational achievements and requirements appears in the text (Table 6.2). That analysis was made possible by using the 1971 bridge tapes referred to earlier. An earlier version (1966) was analyzed by Ann Miller, who concluded that achieved education seemed to bear little relationship to the requirements of the occupational structure: "The high level of educational attainment in the country reflects a much broader set of social values than those related to purely occupational requirements." [41] This conclusion was based on a comparison of GED distributions (grouped 1–3, 4, 5–6) with educational attainment distributions (grouped eight years or less; high school, one to four years; and college, one year or more). While the two distributions are indeed quite disparate, the education groups leave much to be desired for purposes of assessing utilization patterns especially in respect of the college–graduate population.

Unfortunately, information on achieved schooling was not included on the computer tape of these 1966 data made available for public use. The project was, however, repeated in 1971, and this time all of the data from the Current Population Survey are on the tape, thus providing the opportunity to develop the direct estimates presented in Tables 6.1 and 6.2 (pp. 80 and 81).

TABLE 6A.3. **Education Required (Mean GED) and Education Achieved, Civilian Labor Force, 1950, 1960, 1970**

	1950		
GED		*Years of Schooling*	
Level	Percent	Percent	Level
1–2	33.8	61.0	11 or less
3–5A	59.8	31.8	12–15
5B–6	6.4	9.2	16 or more
	1960		
GED		*Years of Schooling*	
Level	Percent	Percent	Level
1–2	9.4	53.0	11 or less
3–5A	84.5	37.8	12–15
5B–6	6.1	9.2	16 or more
	1970		
GED		*Years of Schooling*	
Level	Percent	Percent	Level
1–2	8.2	39.3	11 or less
3–5A	81.4	48.1	12–15
5B–6	10.1	12.6	16 or more

Source: Tables 6A.1 and 6A.2.

THE SVP SCALE

In addition to the GED scale, the *Dictionary of Occupational Titles* has abstracted from the particular exigencies of skill acquisition another variable which provides a common dimension along which jobs may be ranked. This Specific Vocational Preparation (SVP) scale is the required training time for average performance in a specific job situation. To be sure, this is only one approximation of skill requisites, but it is a useful one.

We combined the last two categories of SVP when we assigned the SVP values to the Working Conditions Survey respondent's occupations according to the *Dictionary of Occupational Titles*. We quote in its entirety the description of SVP: [42]

> Specific Vocational Preparation: The amount of time required to learn the techniques, acquire information, and develop the facility needed for average performance in a specific job-worker situation. This training may be acquired in a school, work, military, institutional, or avocational environment. It does not include orientation training required of even every

fully qualified worker to become accustomed to the special conditions of any new job. Specific vocational training includes training given in any of the following circumstances:

a. Vocational education (such as high school commercial or shop training, technical school, art school, and that part of college training which is organized around a specific vocational objective);

b. Apprentice training (for apprenticeable jobs only);

c. In-plant training (given by an employer in the form of organized classroom study);

d. On-the-job training (serving as learner or trainee on the job under the instruction of a qualified worker);

e. Essential experience in other jobs (serving in less responsible jobs which lead to the higher grade job or serving in other jobs which qualify);

The following is an explanation of the various levels of specific vocational preparation.

Level	*Time*
1	Short demonstration only.
2	Anything beyond short demonstration up to and including 30 days.
3	Over 30 days up to and including 3 months.
4	Over 3 months up to and including 6 months.
5	Over 6 months up to and including 1 year.
6	Over 1 year up to and including 2 years.
7	Over 2 years up to and including 4 years.
8	Over 4 years up to and including 10 years.
9	Over 10 years.

7. Utilization, Skills, and the Challenge of the Job

Our intent in the preceding chapter was to prepare the way for an exploration of the relationship between the patterns of on-the-job utilization of workers' educational achievements and the patterns of worker responses to questions about their job experiences. In the conduct of this exploration, in which the skill levels of their jobs are taken to be the critical issue, we experimented with both of the standards against which utilization, in our restricted usage, was measured in our aggregate analysis.

More specifically, we judged utilization according to the match between (1) achieved education and the General Educational Development required for job performance in the occupation and (2) achieved education and the median years of schooling for all incumbents of the occupation. Using the data from the Working Conditions Survey, the "underutilized," measured by either standard, were only a little less satisfied on several measures of job satisfaction.

A look at the underutilized population might suggest how certain of their characteristics worked to offset the anticipated dissatisfaction. Consider that the underutilized tended to be better paid: their median annual earnings were $7,500 compared to $6,121 for the rest of the sample. It is accordingly the case that many workers whose educations are underutilized by our skill- and job-related standards are, in fact, currently reaping benefits by economic standards from their investments in education, benefits that very likely contribute to a sense of relative advantage in a world in which coercive or invidious comparisons are conducted across occupational and income lines.

The larger their earnings and the better their educations are utilized, the more likely workers are to report greater satisfaction, "all in all," with the job. Table 7.1 shows this additive relationship: the "very satisfied" proportion increases, regardless of the utilization level, for

TABLE 7.1. Job Satisfaction According to Earnings and Utilization, Wage and Salary Workers—Percent Very Satisfied

| | Individual Earnings | |
Utilization	Below $6,500	$6,500 or more
Overutilized	48.6	52.3
	(72)	(65)
Matched	38.9	49.2
	(411)	(378)
Underutilized	34.9	42.3
	(126)	(196)
N = 1248		
(NA = 79)		

Number in parentheses is base N for the reported percentage.

respondents above the sample median of $6500. Similarly, holding income constant, there are increases in satisfaction across levels of utilization.

The answer to the question of why those who are underutilized by our standards should be better paid was also revealing: we found a large concentration of relatively high-skill jobholders among blue-collar workers. These tended to be high-school graduates in occupations in which the median educational achievement had not yet reached twelve years of schooling. On the scale used to measure skill (see addendum to Chapter 6), their mean was 6 (out of a possible 9), compared to 2.5 for other blue-collar workers. Given this higher skill level, it is not surprising that they were more satisfied on a number of items, including "pay," "challenge," and "job security." Furthermore, as with earnings, skill level was more highly related to job satisfaction for the underutilized population (both blue- and white-collar) than for the rest.

It is important to keep in mind that the bulk of the workers defined as underutilized among the wage and salary workers of the Working Conditions Survey were high-school graduates. In 1969, when the data were gathered, most college graduates or persons with advanced degrees were employed in occupations where the median years of schooling matched their own educational achievements. This matching of workers to jobs argues that expansion at the top of the occupational structure was sufficient in the earlier period to absorb the highly educated workforce. Furthermore, underutilized high-school graduates were acquiring the more highly skilled jobs *within* occupational classifications, a fact that would seem to bear out the argument of employers that better-educated people are more promotable. Given the aggregate shifts in the distribution of education *and* of occupations described in Chapter 6, there is some question as to whether this kind of upgrading can continue; but whatever the outcome, there are several possibilities as to how the resolution will affect job satisfaction. We may defer our own speculations on this subject until we address other issues suggested by these findings.

OTHER APPROACHES TO THE UTILIZATION-SATISFACTION NEXUS

The attempts we have described so far to relate utilization of education to satisfaction by no means exhaust the possibilities. Quinn and Mandilovitch investigated the relationship between education and job satisfaction through reanalysis of several bodies of data, including the Working Conditions and Quality of Employment surveys.[1] They found, as we did, that education expressed in terms of utilization is a better predictor than absolute level of education.

To estimate "job satisfaction and relative levels of education" [utilization], they used four different measures developed to express "a worker's years of education in terms of deviation from the following standards": (1) the six-point scale of General Educational Development; (2) the worker's own estimate of how many years of education the job required; (3) the median years of education attained by others in a worker's occupation; and (4) the median years of education attained by others in a person's work group.

The first two of these measures present certain difficulties. Their own estimates of their job requirements, juxtaposed with their achieved education exaggerate differences by workers' effective insistence on too close a match. A similar problem arises when the GED scale is translated so as to make each interval equivalent to a specific number of years of schooling—e.g., GED 1 = 4, GED 5 = 16.[2] It is a consequential effect of such a translation of the scale that it groups people with GED 2 jobs who had ten or more years of schooling and people with GED 6 jobs with four or more years of postgraduate education together. The last group presumably would include doctors, dentists, and veterinarians, although lawyers might miss the underutilized group because their total years of schooling would not reach twenty.

Using the measure developed as a "deviation" from the same conservative standard we had used in (3) above, they did not find a significant relation with job satisfaction.

The most promising of the Quinn and Mandilovitch estimates derived from the Survey of Organizations, another product of the Michigan Institute for Survey Research. These data permit comparison of individual workers' educations with the median for others in their own work group, giving closer assessment of the effect of utilization than by an occupation or by the subjective standards required in the other analyses, both by us and by Quinn and Mandilovitch. Their judgment of the effect of utilization agrees with our own findings:

> Strikingly, it was not deviation *per se* that was associated with dissatisfaction, but only deviation in a particular direction—where a worker was *too* highly educated for his or her work. . . . It may therefore be concluded that the relatively small payoffs in job satisfaction that accompany increasing education can be more than offset when job demands fail to keep pace with educational attainment.[3]

Complicating the picture further is their estimate that "any effect that education level had on overall job satisfaction was explainable in terms of education helping its recipients to secure better jobs." [4] We would add the specification that "better" jobs are jobs with *skill* requirements, requirements enabling their incumbents to shelter their employment more readily. That there are positive interactions between schooling increments and work experiences seems indeed to be the case in a study of "postschool human investments" by economists.[5]

A picture emerges from all this according to which education is antecedent to skill acquisition; but in a situation where there is more education than there are skilled jobs, those who are left out should be more dissatisfied. We have already indicated some of the reasons why the differences in the 1969–72 period were small, but there are other possible explanations that are more subjective in nature. By the evidence of the 1972 Election Survey, the educationally underutilized were optimistic in about the same proportion as the rest of the population, an inference we drew from similarity in responses to subjective items.

It should be emphasized that we are not here concerned with the absolute proportions of the responses but only with the fact that the underutilized responded according to the same pattern as other workers. They were, however, disproportionately younger: 39 percent were under thirty. In contrast, 24 percent of the group whose education and jobs were matched and 12 percent of the overutilized were under thirty. Taken together, these findings suggest that those who were both underutilized *and* young had not yet given up, that their dissatisfaction was being traded off for their confidence in themselves and their ability to carry out their plans.

Older respondents might be expected to reduce their aspirations and their expectations in a process of accommodation.[6] But apart from any possible aging effect, there remains the possibility that if economic conditions and the occupational structure do not produce the hoped-for improvement in opportunity, Americans will fall back upon a more relativistic interpretation of their situations. The fact that a significant number are underutilized, when we evaluate their circumstances in accordance with our measurement standards, does not mean that they are underutilized in accordance with critical social norms.

A large body of social-science literature, meanwhile, supports the proposition that the meanings of deprivations and advantages in society are defined in terms of reference-group standards; these standards, moreover, spread rapidly. The term "relative deprivation," most often used in this context, is rooted in the observation that there are no intrinsic *a priori* criteria for judgments of status. Thus, if many college graduates do not get the jobs they expected, both surprise and disappointment are likely to diminish as the popular standards governing public opinion in the matter change. Consider, in this context, that few Americans under forty have doubts about the essential legitimacy in the shift in the training of nurses in the last dozen years away from diploma schools in favor of collegiate programs. Nursing has simply become a college-level occupation.

EDUCATION, SKILL, AND CHALLENGE

If comparing education with education, so to speak, leaves us uncertain, what happens when the worker's education is juxtaposed with the skill level of the job?

In a previous study, we analyzed job satisfaction among men with blue-collar jobs in sixteen industries according to their responses when asked whether the "jobs [were] too simple for their abilities." [7] Our hypothesis, sustained at the time, held that workers would view their abilities as being used in proportion to the degree to which the respondents' educational level was matched with the skills required in their jobs. Responses were cross-tabulated by this match, defined in four utilization categories: low education–high skill; high education–high skill; low education–low skill; and high education–low skill.

The operational definition for education for those 1947 data was a dichotomy split at nine years of schooling and, for skill, three months of training time. In retesting the hypothesis, two important changes were made in these definitions: (1) Because of the increasing years of schooling in the population and changes in the standards of acceptability for employment, we made the cutoff point twelve years of school or high-school graduation. This means that the lower education category now included those workers with nine, ten, and eleven years of schooling, as well as those with fewer than nine. (2) We maintained the three-month training-time dividing point employed in the earlier study. However, in the 1947 data, the training time was *self-reported*, whereas the "specific vocational preparation" (SVP) code was assigned to occupations in the Working Conditions and Quality of Employment Surveys.[8]

We combined both the Working Conditions and the Quality of Employments Surveys to yield a sample of blue-collar men to compare with the earlier study. Using the four utilization categories described above, we examined responses to two questions comparable to the 1947 "Is [your job] too simple to bring out your best abilities or not?" These asked, "How true [do] you feel each is of *your* job?": (1) "I have an opportunity to develop my own special abilities" and (2) "The problems I am expected to solve are hard enough." Here again we found that those with more education working in lower-skill jobs expressed significantly less satisfaction with this dimension of job experience. This finding is interesting because it suggested a connection with another finding that holds an important place in other analyses of job satisfaction: that the challenge of the job has more power to predict satisfaction than almost any other factor.

The "challenge index" which we used was constructed by Quinn *et al.* and includes the two items above for our retest of the utilization thesis. The responses to the question "How true is this of your job?" were averaged for the following:

I can see the results of my work.
I have enough authority to do my job.
The problems I am expected to solve are hard enough.
I am given a chance to do the things I do best.
I am given a lot of freedom to decide how I do my own work.
The work is interesting.
I have an opportunity to develop my own special abilities.

We would expect higher-skill jobs, associated below with more training time (Table 7.2), to provide more opportunities for the "challenge" comprehended by these questions. Similarly, the higher the skill level, the more the job itself is "satisfying" (Table 7.3). At whatever skill level, our initial framework leads us to expect diminished job satisfaction when the worker is denied adequate resources or support to do the job properly, when the worker's skills and training far exceed the job requisites, or when the effort expended is seen as inequitably rewarded. But in these regards as well, higher-skill jobs are generally "better" than lower-skill jobs.

Table 7.2 shows the relationship between SVP and challenge. The "medium" category of challenge reflects about the same proportion of both blue-collar and white-collar workers regardless of SVP category. "High challenge" is associated with high SVP, and "low challenge" with low SVP.

TABLE 7.2.   **Relationship between Specific Vocational Preparation (SVP)**[a] **and Challenge Index by Collar Color,**[b] **Wage and Salary Workers—Percent Distribution**

Blue Collar
Level of Specific Vocational Preparation

Challenge	3 Months or Less	3 Months– 2 Years	Over 2 Years	Total
Low	43%	39%	24%	36%
Medium	36	38	36	37
High	20	24	40	27
Total	100%	100%	100%	100%
N =	261	202	198	661
(NA =	15)			

Tau -b = .13, significant at .01 level.

White Collar

Low	43%	30%	15%	26%
Medium	38	39	37	38
High	19	31	48	36
Total	100%	100%	100%	100%
N =	88	279	249	616
(NA =	7)			

Tau -b = .17, significant at .01 level.

[a] For full definition, see addendum to Chapter 6.
[b] This table excludes 28 respondents who were in farm occupations or who could not be classified by collar color.

The direct relationship between skill (SVP) and satisfaction emerges in Table 7.3. Note the regularity of this connection: about 40 percent of the low-skilled are low in satisfaction, and 40 percent of the high-skilled are high in satisfaction. The general relationship is similar to that of SVP and the challenge index in Table 7.2.

UNUTILIZED SKILLS AND DECLINING KNOWLEDGE

So far, the evidence regarding underutilization and its correlates are more suggestive of what may come to be than of immediate problems of worker morale. Even though opportunities for skill utilization as well as on-the-job skill acquisition are constrained, at least for this decade, we need not exaggerate the worst possible hypothetical consequences—alienation, political cynicism, and the like; the fact is that there are less dramatic but still significant losses that may result from

TABLE 7.3. **Relationship Between Specific Vocational Preparation (SVP)[a] and Job Satisfaction by Collar Color,[b] Wage and Salary Workers—Percent Distribution**

Blue Collar
Level of Specific Vocational Preparation

Job Satisfaction Index	3 Months or less	3 Months– 2 Years	Over 2 Years	Total
Low	41%	34%	26%	34%
Medium	34	42	34	37
High	25	24	40	29
Total	100%	100%	100%	100%
N =	264	204	201	669
(NA =	7)			

Tau -*b* = .14, significant at .01 level.

White Collar

	3 Months or less	3 Months– 2 Years	Over 2 Years	Total
Low	38%	24%	18%	23%
Medium	42	45	43	44
High	20	31	39	33
Total	100%	100%	100%	100%
N =	89	279	251	619
(NA =	4)			

Tau -*b* = .15, significant at .01 level.

[a] For full definition, see addendum to Chapter 6.
[b] This table excludes 28 respondents who were in farm occupations or who could not be classified by collar color.

underutilization. One consequence is a kind of intellectual atrophy in which people whose education is underutilized, who are not challenged by the work they do, fall to the level of their jobs. Employers, who for a long time thought they were buying promotable workers at a discount, for example, may find them not so promotable over the longer haul as these workers lose control over the content of their knowledge. This inference is suggested by Hyman, Wright, and Reed,[9] who explored the extent to which citizens of diverse educational backgrounds differ systematically in their knowledge about all manner of things. After examining the responses of four age cohorts to two hundred and fifty discrete items of information asked in fifty-four different surveys, they concluded that the knowledge of those queried did indeed reflect differences in formal schooling. This finding holds, moreover, in each of an extraordinarily long list of circumstances for which the investigators introduced controls.

The expectation they uncovered is of immediate relevance to the present discussion. In their words:

> When the detailed distributions are examined, there is considerable evidence that education, although significantly effective no matter what the opportunities and life style available, functions differently depending on the circumstances. The effects of education are frequently enhanced among those whose circumstances are advantaged and attenuated among those in less-advantaged positions. This pattern occurs on a substantial number of discrete items of knowledge. . . . *What is suggested is that it is harder for the educated to obtain and maintain their knowledge under stringent conditions of life.* Evidently, their greater knowledgeability is whittled away but not to the extent that it withers or vanishes.[10]

We do not know, from the analysis in *The Enduring Effects of Education*, the extent to which being underutilized "causes" significant reductions in the effects of education.[11] The fact that many of the older cohort of well-educated respondents enjoyed entry into the economy when it *was* growing and when the number of "high-level" jobs especially ("professional, technical, and managerial"), *was* expanding apace suggests that self-selection factors probably were at work among the "declining knowledge" respondents. Such information would be very hard to retrieve. Looking ahead, however, we may anticipate a more refined test of the effects of underutilization on differentially educated Americans; prospective investigators may be assured that there will be greater numbers of persons in "less advantaged positions" for analytical use than in the period 1950–1960.

The questions involved are by no means trivial. The finding that education has enduring effects on knowledge but, as an important example of potential problems, a declining effect on incomes and upon occupational status [12] could take us in several different directions. Consider that, on the one hand (and all other things being equal), we may move toward more income equality between high-school and college graduates in a nation of increasingly knowledgeable citizens facing a stabilized occupational structure. On the other hand, the reduced rates of return to college educations may contribute to reductions in the proportion of high-school graduates who go to college. We would then have reductions in the underutilization of college educations, but not necessarily reductions in the underutilization of ability.

Whose ability is utilized depends in the first instance on who is able to attend some kind of postsecondary institution in a society where job competition has grown ever keener. Wide gaps still exist in the probabilities of college attendance between whites and blacks or Hispanics. Blacks of high ability and high socioeconomic status, although they are not numerous, are more likely than other groups to attend college. The problem in recent years has not been outright discrimination alone but rather the disproportionate incidence of poverty among black families.[13]

The general relationships between family income, high-school scholastic achievement, and college attendance emerges clearly from Table 7.4. Enrollment rates go up with both achievement and income; but while achievement has the stronger influence, even among the highest achievers 86 percent of 1972 graduates from families in the top-income class enrolled in college compared with 64 percent of graduates from the poorest class.

There is a grave issue in all this, enrollment differences by ability and race aside: the sons and daughters of lower-income families, and especially of the blacks among them, who for long have been encouraged to stay in school and continue their educations as long as possible, are now finding it increasingly difficult to reap the rewards that had been promised them by anti-poverty warriors and others. Either way, therefore, many of them are in difficulty—if they attend a two-year or four-year institution, they may have diminished hope; if they do not attend, they may have no hope at all.

Is it fair to lay any of the blame for the underutilization of educated manpower at managers' doorstep? Our answers to the question in the earlier study to which references have been made and earlier in this volume were guarded.

The conservative argument on hiring people with higher education than the jobs require, we have said, is based on (a) an allegedly lower

TABLE 7.4. **Enrollment Rates of 1972 High School Graduates by Income Class and Achievement Level, Fall 1972—Percent Postsecondary Enrollment**

Family Income Class	High School Achievement Level				
	Bottom 30	Second 20	Third 30	Highest 20	All Achievement Levels
$0– 7,500	30%	41%	47%	64%	45%
7,500–10,500	32	48	58	70	53
10,500–15,000	35	49	64	75	59
15,000 and up	47	64	77	86	72
All Incomes	35	50	62	75	57

Source: Congressional Budget Office, *Postsecondary Education: The Current Federal Role and Alternative Approaches* (Washington, D.C.: U.S. Government Printing Office, 1977), p. 13.

information cost (about worker capacity) to employers;[14] (b) the fact that there is, after all, some occupational mobility after the entry level; (c) the fact that the underutilization of individuals is not properly measured cross-sectionally. (Substantiation of applicability of the term "underutilization," especially to younger workers, requires follow-up over life cycles during which some, at least, are upgraded); (d) the fact that the graduates of high schools are a salmagundi of abilities and ambitions: thus employers are told that "years of schooling" means less nowadays than it did in other times and, to that extent, they tend to look for certified graduates only;[15] (e) it pays an employer to recruit at a community college because the students there have exhibited evidence of self-denial, the capacity to defer gratification, and the willingness to undertake the opportunity costs of education; (f) furthermore, the proportion of bright, low-income young people going to college is increasing, and education undeniably does make *some* contribution to "productivity." Taking all these things into account for the middle levels of the occupational structure, could employers be seen to be "democratizing" the system by insisting on better-educated workers?

We think not, but readers will have to draw their own conclusions. We have, we submit, made allowances for the most critical points listed, in what we will term a conservative argument regarding education and work, by such manipulations of the data as left a smaller residual of underutilized workers than would otherwise be the case in our tables. We still find considerable underutilization and sufficiently consequential correlates of underutilization, both in being and in prospect, to urge that the issue be taken quite seriously.

Overall, the mixed evidence presented in this chapter and in the previous ones leaves us with a sense that this is a transitional period. Looking back, the intent of the subtitle *The Great Training Robbery* [16] is even clearer now than in 1970, when it was our purpose to focus on the degree to which formal education was displacing alternative entry routes to work in America. Our related point in 1970 was simply that in order for workers to gain access to jobs presenting an opportunity for skill acquisition, they had to present educational credentials— whether or not these were appropriate or necessary for the positions they would occupy. The word "credentials" is intended to connote more than a screening device. It implies completion of a degree program—not just additional increments of schooling to which regular increments of productivity and pay could be attached, but diplomas, the possession of which separated differentially eligible pools of workers.

In the seventies, educational credentials are still necessary, either for further professional training or for procuring jobs in which training is an integral part. The difference, of course, is that the "most" eligible pools are now conspicuously larger than the available opportunities. This changed picture implies, first, a decline in returns in investments to education, a matter to which we referred earlier.

Second, the fact is that while the returns to education are dropping, it is not necessarily the case that they will drop much more than they have. As long as educational achievements per se are rewarded among the underutilized in such a way as to assure some relative income (and promotion) advantages over their less-educated workmates, they would appear to be "bought off." The fact that many of the underutilized in our data were in relatively higher-skilled, better-paid jobs than their less-educated peers points directly to the possibility that education can continue to offer a measure of economic redemption, if not the near-total salvation assured by educational achievements in earlier years.

Third, there are the ebbs and flows of economic circumstances. Underutilized workers, like other employed citizens, probably compare their lots with those of the less fortunate unemployed when the economic tides are low and of their better-matched and better-utilized peers when these workers' ships are more visibly riding high.

Fourth, "status inconsistency" stemming from underutilization on the job may have been overtaken, in the perspective of many Americans, by larger status discrepancies in the society. This, after all, is the thrust of our and Strumpel's reading of the differences between job and occupational dissatisfactions, discussed in Chapter 5. Note, for example, that the attention of women is increasingly on sex-linked discrimination in labor markets rather than on the bigoted attitudes of particular employers at their own workplaces.

Finally, and most important, the effects of underutilization of education on satisfaction are transmitted through a chain of relationships that take us from the wider, macro considerations of educational outcomes and labor market opportunities for acquiring and enhancing skills to micro factors in the job setting itself. The major link is between skill, its utilization, job challenges, and job rewards—and an overall sense of job satisfaction. The kinds of interventions, like job enlargement and job enrichment programs, aimed at creating variety and challenges in jobs that are intrinsically unskilled would seem to be doomed to failure. To make a silk purse out of a sow's ear, one is well advised to start with a silk sow. Unskilled work could and should be made safer, pleasanter, and, for many logical reasons, better paid— all improvements that might buy off a good deal of dissatisfaction. But the satisfactions that come from skill and challenge probably cannot be artificially induced. Managers, in fine, may not be able to affect the matters discussed here unless they continue to buy off the underutilized while simultaneously engaging in the actions urged by work reformers.

In Part III we turn to some limited data on worker attitudes and on behavior suggestive of worker concerns that are more amenable to managerial interventions than those reviewed in this section.

PART III

MANAGERS AND
WORKING CONDITIONS

Managers do not emerge from the assessments in Part II as potent leaders of private governments within which they can move freely, as is so commonly supposed, to improve worker morale. The evidence points strongly to the conditioning effect on workers' overall satisfaction of developments rooted in arrangements and processes transcending those that are typically organizational in character and therefore well beyond managements' parietal walls.

The data considered in this third part of our study, however, point more directly toward the opportunities managers do have in shaping workers' job satisfactions.

MANAGERS AS BUSINESS LEADERS

It is not news that business leaders as a class have had their sophisticated critics, especially from the articulate ranks of the political and economic left, and that they have suffered their share of more popular criticism as well. By and large, however, they have enjoyed secure roles in a nation given to doing, to making, to inventing, to improving, and to producing.

The evidence of the general approval of managers' roles, as contrasted with the critical perspectives, is all about us. We see it in the legal care our society has taken to preserve the proprietary rights of those in whose names managers perform their duties; in our highly developed concern with balancing society's welfare with the protection of both managers' incentives and their rights to manage; in our readiness to put business leaders in charge of public policy-implementing machinery; and in our faith that public administrators schooled in managers' techniques can flesh out and apply vague laws that inexpert members of Congress are unable to specify.[1]

Even now, at a comparatively low point in the history of businessmen's respectability, the American people have a singularly respectful attitude toward management. Thus, although Louis Harris and other public pulse-takers have documented the increase in criticisms of American business in the period 1966–1973, these criticisms are not accompanied by a collapse in the population's confidence that business can and should exercise "special leadership in the broad issues of the day" [2] or by a reversal in the public's commitment to capitalism. Indeed, the decline in America's confidence in the businessman—from 55 percent to 27 percent in the period 1966 to 1973—was tempered by hope. From the solid increases in expressions of the need for business to take leadership in diverse areas, Harris concludes:

112

The strong implications of these results were that the American people had come to believe that business should take the lead, not only in its daily behavior but also as advocates for raising moral standards, for curbing crime, for wiping out poverty, and for rebuilding cities. Certainly this was not a mandate from a people who were spoiling to overthrow the private business system. Instead, it was a blunt statement that, given their disenchantment with government, their skepticism about union leadership, if the most powerful elements in the private sector did not step forth with leadership, who else could?[3]

EXECUTIVES AS MANAGERS

In the Harris survey, as in many others, respondents are invited to reply as citizens to questions about business executives as members of a stratum in American society. In the following chapters we consider evidence bearing rather more directly on executives as managers than as the prospectively helpful national leaders who could act to move the Republic forward on many fronts.

In Chapter 8 we review briefly the contributions to overall job satisfactions of workers' reactions to the quality of their supervisors and the resources afforded them by their managers.

In Chapter 9 we attempt to infer lessons about the performance of managers from data on industrial conflicts.

Chapter 10 dwells on managerial capabilities that may be construed from the formal grievances of organized workers that have gone to arbitration. The data point to a two-valued logic regarding workers' and managers' roles that distracts us from seeing how managers' interests limit the prospects for work reform. This interpretation, in turn, serves as a bridge to the more explicit discussion, in Part IV, of further reasons for despairing of a new workday in America.

8. Managers at Work—After Their Own Manner

We have already seen that responses to the items in the Working Conditions Survey that focused on the degree to which jobs are "challenging" correlate very strongly with overall job satisfaction. We have also been at some pains to make clear our conception that the responses to these "challenge" items are most fruitfully regarded as reflecting the skill levels of respondents' jobs. Finally we have emphasized that there are real restraints upon managers that effectively limit the freedom they have to determine the skill mix of their individual enterprises.[1]

Our analysis accordingly led us to regard survey questions having to do with job challenges as helpful in illuminating the meaning of utilization, since the job challenges respondents reported varied in significant ways with their skill levels. Again, we see these relations to be lengthened shadows of workers' experiences in the social and economic system rather than simply, or even mostly, clear reflections of experiences in the organizations run by their managers.

In contrast, there are activities in the workplace for which managers have direct responsibility and over which they exercise considerable control. The Working Conditions Survey included several items specifically concerned with the provision of resources and the quality of supervision.

Quinn and his colleagues asked the WCS sample how important— very, somewhat, not too important or not at all important—they found each of 23 job facets. The items with the highest mean rating for the whole sample were "the work is interesting" followed by two items in the resource adequacy index: "enough help and equipment" and "enough information." Quinn explains:

> Since adequate resources are vital for adequate job performance, resources may be viewed as instrumental to the procurement of many economic and non-economic occupational rewards. Whether a worker performs ade-

quately, is, at least in principle, one determinant of the income he or she receives. Likewise, the intrinsic satisfaction a worker obtains from his or her job is likely to be quite limited if the work is not done well. Securing adequate resources for job performance may thus be important both to workers who are extrinsically motivated to work and to those who are intrinsically motivated. Since resource adequacy may be essential to workers with a variety of motivational orientations toward their jobs, it plausibly emerged as an aspect of the job that was of considerable importance to workers as a whole.[2]

Administration is a much admired and rewarded art in America. Top managers are *responsible* economic agents. Even if the particular systems we use in America to measure managers' performance fail to take full account of this fact, especially in the short run, the deficiencies of inept selection and sloppy training of their lower-level supervisors, of badly organized and badly scheduled work, of failure to invest in [3] and maintain needed equipment and supplies must be laid at management's doorstep. The survey items presented below show that most workers were satisfied that they had enough resources to do their work. But among those who report that they are given inadequate resources, job satisfaction is appreciably lower.

When these items were combined to form our "adequacy of resources index" (Chapter 4), the overall correlation with the general index of job satisfaction was about .3. The correlation of our supervision index with job satisfaction was about the same.

Table 8.2 shows how job satisfaction levels vary according to the competency of supervision. In all, we see no hazards in viewing questions

TABLE 8.1. Job Satisfaction According to Adequacy of Resources, Wage, and Salary Workers—Percent Very Satisfied

Type of Resource	"Given Enough or Not Enough to Work Your Best?"		
	Enough	Not Enough	
Help or Assistance	49	24	
	(1055)	(262)	(NA = 10)
Authority	47	32	
	(976)	(312)	(NA = 39)
Time	48	29	
	(1004)	(309)	(NA = 14)
Facts and Information	47	30	
	(1084)	(234)	(NA = 9)
Machinery, tools, equipment	47	22	
	(1083)	(234)	(NA = 10)

Numbers in parenthesis are base Ns for the reported percentages.

TABLE 8.2.   Job Satisfaction According to Competence of Supervisor, Wage, and Salary Workers—Percent Distribution

	"My Supervisor is Competent in Doing His Job" (How True?)			
Job Satisfaction	Not at All/A Little	Somewhat True	Very True	Total
Not Satisfied	34%	16%	11%	16%
Somewhat Satisfied	46	51	35	41
Very Satisfied	20	33	54	44
Total	100%	100%	100%	100% *
N =	180	329	776	1285
(NA =	42)			

Tau -b = .26, significant at .01 level.

* This percentage totals more than 100% because of rounding.

about supervisors (their standards, their competence, and their knowledge of their jobs), the adequacy of job-relevant information supplied to workers, the extent to which workers are supplied with adequate help and equipment to do their jobs, and the extent to which workers' responsibilities are clearly defined as meaningful indicators of *managers'* performance. Workers in the WCS are more satisfied when they have supervisors with high rather than low standards. In Table 8.3, they are clearly not looking for a "soft touch," even allowing for the yea-saying inclinations and socially approved response sets among worker respondents to surveys.

Even more telling, there is a growing body of research that shows the important effects of supervision on work satisfaction. While we have

TABLE 8.3.   Job Satisfaction According to Performance Standards, Wage, and Salary Workers—Percent Distribution

	Supervisor "Maintains High Standards of Performance in His/Her own Work" (How True?)			
Job Satisfaction	Not at All/A Little	Somewhat True	Very True	Total
Not Satisfied	35%	22%	10%	16%
Somewhat Satisfied	42	51	36	40
Very Satisfied	24	27	54	44
Total	100%*	100%	100%	100%
N =	144	301	796	1241
(NA =	86)			

Tau -b = .27, significant at .01 level.

* This percentage totals more than 100% because of rounding.

conjectured from a sample survey about the meaning of zero-order associations, other researchers have found "some experimental evidence that extensive changes in satisfaction follow changes in supervision." [4] The relationships between supervisory arrangements and productivity are notoriously anomalous, to be sure. And it is clear, from the mass of evidence assayed by Dubin, Homans, Mann, and Miller, that the specific supervisory techniques that work best in a given setting are those designed to fit particular technical and organizational realities. [5]

At the same time, however, it is evident that the supervisors whom workers consistently praise are those in whom human-relations skills are coupled with relevant technical know-how and with skills in planning and scheduling work, in making sensible job assignments, in maintaining work flows by managing the necessarily complicated lateral relations of work groups, in making accurate time and cost estimates, in anticipating supply and parts requirements, in teasing away resources from the chary chieftains of stock and toolrooms, in renegotiating work standards with production engineers and revising production quotas, in trades with hard-pressed plant "supers," and in bargains with the officers, business agents, and shop stewards of unions, democratic and otherwise. [6]

Our own marginal misgivings about the interpretation of workers' perceptions of supervisors and the provisioning of work-related requirements as measures of top management, meanwhile, were additionally dissipated upon discovering that top-level executives in one of the largest corporations in the nation had viewed these issues in exactly the same perspective. These corporate officers combined selected "resources" and "supervision" items—similar to those in the WCS but with a few additional questions—to form a "Management-Style Index" in a study of work satisfaction. [7] These executives expressed no doubts whatever about the responsibilities of top management for the conduct of supervision and their obligations to provide employees with the wherewithal of productive work.

The study involved about 3,500 workers in both assembly and non-assembly operations. It measured job satisfaction with an eighteen-item index, described as primarily a measure of satisfaction with the job itself and, to a lesser degree, with the work environment. The predictor variables were: demographic characteristics such as respondent's age; technology, (i.e., type and location of work assignment); the *importance* of positive job characteristics; the positive job characteristics themselves; and the Management-Style Index (MSI).

At one extreme, job satisfaction was greatest among employees with all the following characteristics:

1. was thirty-five years old or older;
2. had an idea of what kind of job he or she wanted;

3. did assembly- or nonassembly-type work off a production line or did support work on or off the line;
4. definitely had an opportunity to develop his or her special skills and abilities;
5. had more effective supervisors and people-oriented management (as measured by the MSI).

The greatest job dissatisfaction tended to be present if the employee had these characteristics:

1. was thirty-four years old or younger;
2. had some college education;
3. saw no chance to do the things he or she did best.

It is worth noting that of two other highly dissatisfied groups that emerged from the analysis, one was composed of workers over thirty-five who had a clear idea of the job they wanted, were on production lines, had below-average "Management-Style-Index" scores, and saw no chance "to do the things [they] did best." The other was composed of workers under thirty-five, with no college, who were on production lines, felt it important to see the results of their work, and had below-average "Management-Style-Index" scores.

Interactions among job-related and non-job-related factors in these findings support the researchers' conclusion that neither the prediction nor the generation of job satisfaction is a simple task: "Arguing that job satisfaction is primarily a function of age, work assignment, or any other single factor is not supported by the results from this study." They also concluded, in any case, that:

> In general, the perceived work environment better explains differences in level of job satisfaction than biographical, technological or other psychological information. Specifically, *a people-oriented management system is the one best contributor to high job satisfaction.* However, its contribution can vary under different conditions which moderate its influence.[8]

That the problematical capacities of the very top managers may stand high on employee complaint lists is readily established with the help of data from another survey at one of the nation's largest retail organizations.[9] The data are especially interesting for four reasons: they are descriptive of the attitudes of anonymous managers as *employees* at the level of the company's retail outlets; they are descriptive of a population of employees in a prototypical segment of the so-called service sector, a sector in which some suggest there are relatively few worker complaints;[10] the managers come from retail stores that may be classified by size, thus permitting another test of the effect of a "bureaucratic" factor in respondents' discontents; and finally, the survey instrument afforded these managers-as-workers specific opportunities to respond to questions about their immediate, intermediate, *and* topmost (headquarters) managers.

Respondents in this survey were asked "to indicate to what extent representatives of the administrative levels listed are described by each of the seven statements" for their immediate, intermediate, and head-quarters managers on this five-point scale: "almost always, usually, at times, rarely, and almost never." We were particularly interested in responses as to how these managers, in the words of the survey:

1. Provide help needed to strengthen or maintain my store's performance.
2. Provide support of my decisions or actions aimed at strengthening my store's performance.
3. Provide accurate information about things that affect my store.
4. Criticize my store's performance fairly.
5. Seek my opinion on decisions which affect my store.
6. Lead by fear and threats.
7. Lead by encouraging my full involvement in programs.

First, differences in responses to these questions by age were few and small.

Second, respondents were far more critical of the ways and modes of top-level managers than of intermediate and immediate superiors, and their criticisms in the event were hardly misdirected. Thus, follow-up interviews with a member of the company's headquarters staff, about the transition in the corporation from decentralized to centralized decision making in the areas of sales promotion, regular advertising, and inventory policies, reassured us that the most essential doings of store-level managers had indeed been more pervasively influenced by policies initiated by headquarters executives than by the two groups of lower-level executives.

Third, and perhaps in reverse of the sapient orthodoxy, discontents about managers at all corporate levels were regularly and systematically greater in the smaller stores. We were unable to identify an unambiguous explanation for this last finding, but there is internal evidence to suggest that the managers of larger stores may have simply been "validating" the higher-level logic according to which the less critical respondents themselves had been promoted into better-paid, more responsible positions, which is to say positions in the large stores.

We were particularly interested in the responses to an invitation to the 700 store managers in the study to make open-ended remarks at the end of the survey. While seventy-four chose to make comments about the questionnaire or about the company in general terms—usually quite favorable—282 made substantive comments that could be roughly divided into issues about compensation, promotion, and hours of work, on the one hand, and about management problems, on the other.

Two major themes in these remarks concerning management problems involved uncertainty about change and about the competence of upper levels of management. Several of the comments refer to the company's aforementioned historical decentralization, which they fear is being threatened:

> The single one thing that can hurt our company and keep it from progressing is centralized control. We must keep our company decentralized; and . . . the stores should have direction not directives.

While they see customer service as a traditional source of strength, these store managers fear the competition of discount stores.

> Our future will depend upon our ability to introduce more self-service and mechanization. Largely we are operating as we have for many years. I believe there is an intelligent compromise available in the self-serve area. . . . Customers more and more are willing to serve themselves in certain merchandise. We must explore new and better store designing instead of updating old ideas. We have much work to do in material handling and marking. While some progress has been made in mechanizing record procedures, it has been too little and too slow.

They complain of "overbilling":

> Due to overbilling practices I think we are in great danger of being outsold by some discounters. In some instances, their prices to the public are as low as our costs. . . . Store managers do not know the true costs, yet they are charged with the responsibility of being competitive.

Most of all, these managers report that they feel out of control. As one put it:

> There is less control exercised by managers today. There is a trend toward centralization. In a group operation, the manager's job re: promotional opportunities, credit and service has been assumed by group personnel. Therefore, there is less flexibility at management level.

And another:

> Store manager's responsibility is increasing, but his authority is decreasing along with his compensation. We have too many programs—sometimes it appears that everybody in headquarters has a program, and they all land up on the manager's desk at one time.

Longer store hours mean part-time people, and part-time people mean problems:

> Our turnover is extremely high among part-time people. It is a constant problem to find, hire and train good dependable salespeople who have a real desire to be of service to the customer a few hours each week.

Merchandising uncertainty:

Lack of assortments. . .is becoming an adverse factor. We go from "too fat" to "too lean." Discounts and other chains are capitalizing on this weakness.

Too much overhead:

The retail store is not the only place to cut payroll costs. Regional and central headquarters must also cut costs, both in payroll and operations. We seem to make it—they seem to spend it.

Why do we continue to add non-selling jobs at the expense of floor coverage? We are a selling organization just loaded with non-selling people. Every time we are forced by system changes or embellishments to add non-sellers, we go to the sales floor and reduce people or hours there. This immediately reduces our chances to separate customer from money to pay for these non-sellers. I would like to know the ratio of selling people to non-selling people. We've got non-selling people in regional and central headquarters we don't need.

And, finally, too much direction from higher levels means:

The company has worked itself into a position of the so-called inverted triangle—hundreds in headquarters merchandising—30 or so regional merchandising—only 2 in the retail store to carry out the programs of so many—impossible. The same is true of all staff jobs—too many directors with directives; too few to carry them out—too much centralization—store managers have too many bosses.

There is a strong trend the last few years to run the company by policies and systems rather than the judgment of local people. I hope we don't carry it too far. Too many programs from headquarters requiring store manager personal involvement. The store manager is responsible, but can't personally handle all that is asked. Department managers are often overworked and underpaid and they are keys to our company success.

None of the information available to us from an informed company spokesman led us to believe that these respondents' comments were misdirected. As we will note in a later chapter, however, in one sense they were wide of the actual mark: while top managers did not deny the accuracy of the complaints, the company, they maintained, was doing very well on the so-called bottom line. Their feeling was that personnel experts should be contented doing surveys but were "not to worry" about reforms aimed at improving morale. So it apparently is with moving targets, a point that may be inferred from the reactions generally of managers to workplace reforms, which we will review in Part IV.

Once again, our interest in the "supervision" and "resources" questions, whether examined in the configuration of the indexes we used or those used by Quinn and his colleagues, resides in the clues they provide about managers' performance and the closely related prospects for managerial efforts to increase workers' satisfactions. Unlike situations involving socially influenced conceptions of the relative equity they enjoy or the socially defined norms governing workers' sense of utilization in an education-conscious society, organizational circumstances, strictly speaking, are at least within managers' theoretical capacities to control significantly, if not absolutely. "Challenge" factors may fall somewhere between the more and the less controllable matters. We will return in Parts IV and V to these opportunities and to some of the reasons they so often go unexploited.

In Chapter 9, meanwhile, we move to a discussion of the behavioral indicators of worker concerns discernible in data on industrial conflicts and to the prospects these data suggest for managerial interventions designed to improve the quality of working life.

9. The Crucible of Conflict: The Reconciliation of Interests

The data considered in Part II and in Chapter 8 have come in very large part from attitude-gathering efforts and from the work of investigators in or close to the human-relations tradition. In this chapter we turn to data on the behavior of workers—at least organized workers—data that enable us to consider a number of issues typically addressed by investigators in the industrial-relations and human-resources fields, and not so typically by human relationists and their nearest of intellectual kin.

This is not to say that those trained in labor economics are averse to gathering attitude data, for they certainly are not. It is simply to say that they draw from different intellectual wellsprings, including those in which industrial conflict enjoys a somewhat better reputation than it does among human-relations investigators. Of central concern in this chapter will be the lessons about the prospects for improving work and reducing workers' discontents that may reasonably be inferred from data on strikes.

A NOTE ON BEHAVIOR AND ATTITUDES

Behavioral data, as we shall see, do not correlate at all well with attitude data, even when these data are disaggregated by industry. The logic supporting an examination of data disaggregated in this fashion, meanwhile, follows in part from the emphasis on industry differences in some other studies, especially Blauner's study of the role of technological differences in respect to worker discontents (discussed in Chapter 3).[1] In part, the logic follows from findings in studies of strikes reported by Kerr and Siegel and by Kuhn,[2] stressing differences in strike behavior attributable to technological differences as well as other interindustry differences in workplace conditions that bear upon the character of worker experiences. We will return to the matter of industry-related data at appropriate points in this chapter. Our concern at this point is with issues cutting across the detailed discussions that follow.

The fact that the best available data on worker attitudes aggregated by industry do not correlate with interindustry differences in selected behavioral domains does not argue compellingly that no such association theoretically exists. On the one side, the actual workers questioned in national probability samples are not necessarily representative of workers prone to strike, to absent themselves from work, or to change jobs. Even high correlations among the relevant statistics could be quite fortuitous.

Of more immediate interest is the possibility that the factors contributing to the patterns discernible in behavioral data are simply not among those touched upon in survey studies of worker discontent. The reader will recall that we have been at pains to emphasize the hazards in confusing the innumerable irritations of many American workers delineated in surveys with *all* the irritations of these workers. It may indeed be the case, for example—faulty methodology and deficiencies in experimental control conditions quite aside—that the ambiguous relationships discussed in Chapter 3 among worker attitudes, work-redesign efforts, and worker productivity are in some measure attributable to the fact that some critical attitude domains, like resource management, were simply not taken into account. Sometimes important domains are excluded even when their importance has been identified. Thus, when Quinn's and Seashore's colleagues at Ann Arbor adapted the Working Conditions and Quality of Employment Surveys to a section on work in their survey of Americans' views of the general quality of life in America, they were obliged, for logistical reasons, to omit what in our perspective are the critically important "resources" items discussed in our Chapters 4 and 8 and by Quinn *et al.*[3]

At the same time, however, we cannot deny the difficulties in identifying the causes of the distributions described in the substantive sections of this chapter. The patterns in the data, insofar as we are able to delineate them, suggest problematic issues; moreover, these issues appear, like those we dealt with in examining attitude data in Chapters 4 through 8, to be differentially amenable to managerial influence.

THE USES OF STRIKE DATA

Strikes are dramatic but relatively infrequent manifestations of worker discontents. Although there is a substantial literature that attempts to explain and predict fluctuations in strike activity, it is important to note at the outset that since World War II the number of man-days idle as a proportion of available work-time has consistently been less than 1 percent and far below that level in most years.[4] A collective-bargaining agreement, whether or not a strike is involved in its consummation, often has far-reaching effects on wage levels and wage structures within a particular industry and sometimes on the economy as a whole. Disruptions due to strikes are, however, not the norm in our economy or in most industries.

The literature on the causes of strikes in recent years includes some important comparative studies, a large body of literature on historical trends in the United States, and a small number of studies focused on interindustry variations in the United States. The two major conceptual approaches may be roughly identified with economics and political sociology: one seeks the causes of conflict in the bargaining process, the other in the capacity of worker groups to take collective action.[5]

Studies of strikes in the United States have focused on disputes in connection with the negotiation or renegotiation of labor agreements. In view of the fact that the most lost time is associated with such disputes, the focus is understandable. In 1961, Arthur Ross made the point that if the four major active strike cycles in the basic steel, construction, electrical equipment, and machinery industries became dormant and no new ones emerged, the residual level would be about 18,000,000 man-days a year, an amount that would not generate any real pressure for changes in the industrial-relations system.[6]

In fact, a number of events combined to keep man-days idle above this residual level, even though the last steel strike was in 1959. But it is well to bear Ross's assessment in mind in evaluating the major contributions to strike activity, even though it by no means tells the whole story.[7] About one-third of all strikes occur while a contract is in effect; on balance these are shorter than between-contract strikes. It is among these less readily definable disputes that we find clues to the proximal discontents of worker groups. And it is to these proximal discontents and the prospects for their remediation that we are directing our attention here.

We know from a resurvey of job-satisfaction studies since 1958 that the distribution of responses to questions on overall job satisfaction have been remarkably positive and steady.[8] As we have indicated, however, one cannot empirically pinpoint the causes of dissatisfaction by the expedient juxtaposition of strike data with responses from national-sample surveys of workers. Most workers are not union members and therefore lack the capacity for collective action; yet surveys ask questions applicable to all workers. By casting a wide net with large holes one loses many concerns of the 27 percent of the labor force that *is* organized, concerns that simply fall through the net.

Nevertheless, it has seemed to us that strike data are a useful guide to dissatisfaction. Whether the operative issues have to do with explanations of patterns in time series, differences among industries in a given time period, or the significance of short versus long strikes, we view them, and the bargaining with which they are associated, moreover, as forms of worker participation that are at least competitive with proposals for new "participatory" schemes. To put it another way, strikes may be revealing not only of worker dissatisfactions but of the utility of the collective-bargaining machinery of which they are organic elements. The fact that human relationists take a dim view of strikes as important vehicles for worker participation in an industrial democracy does not make the forms of participation they commend—worker councils, quality of work committees and what all—automatically preferable.

The point is an important one because of the blatant antiunionism of some would-be reformers and the less manifest, but nonetheless real, antipathy of others. In fairness, it should be pointed out that some intervention enthusiasts, most notably those connected with official organizations like the National Commission on Productivity, explicitly stress the importance of union involvement. Nevertheless, the assumed linkages in many proposals for work enlargement, work enrichment, and participatory management run, as we noted earlier (in Chapters 1, 2, and 3), from the enhancement of satisfaction to the reduction of overt conflict and, finally, to increased productivity. The intellectual room left over for unions is exceedingly small.

THE CAUSES OF STRIKES: A SYNOPTIC OVERVIEW

The most influential study of recent years, a model for predicting the number of strikes, was constructed by Ashenfelter and Johnson for the years 1952–1967.[9] Their explanation attributes considerable force to changes in the unemployment rate and to an "expectation-achievement" gap in real-wage rates of change. They conclude that unions are more likely to conduct strikes in periods of prosperity and tight labor markets, when their wage expectations have been influenced by actual increases in the recent past.

This "bargaining model" has been amplified in two ways. Robert Stern identified standard metropolitan areas in which strikes are most likely to occur and explained the variation among these "conflict" areas by references to their population size, the extent of their unionization, plant size, and a measure of "economic vulnerability."[10] Stern considers this last variable, a relative measure of earned income that represents the ability of high-wage earners to endure a strike through their superior economic resources, as a further specification of the Ashenfelter-Johnson model.

David Snyder has placed the Ashenfelter-Johnson discussion in a comparative political-organizational context by comparing U.S. data before and after World War II with data for France and Italy.[11] The "economic" explanation of strikes depends on a particular context—one in which the collective-bargaining process is well established and in which aggregate economic changes affect the costs and benefits of striking to all parties. Snyder points out that the institutional context of labor relations reflecting these assumptions describes the postwar situation in the United States fairly well, but not the prewar situation in the United States or the French and Italian situations over the entire period (1900–1970). His two political variables, "percent Democrats in Congress" and "the party of the President," were chosen to indicate favorable government attitudes toward labor in the United States. Together with "extent of unionization," they had strong positive effects on year-to-year fluctuations in the prewar period. These results support the imputation of significance to the organizational capacity of workers for collective action as a precondition for their conducting "economic" strikes, on one side, and the importance of this capacity as a variable in theories of strike fluctuations, on the other.

These studies offer plausible explanations of the overall variations in strike activities in the postwar period in the United States.[12] They do not, however, deal directly with the question of interindustry differences.[13] Stern, in fact, assigns little weight to industry alone as a variable. He uses industry mix as a first step in sorting the 248 cities in his sample into "low conflict" and "conflict" groupings. After that step, he finds that industry does not make a significant contribution to variations within the "conflict" set.

In the search for the causes of strikes, industry by itself may not be so informative as other, more abstract and disaggregated measures, particularly because of intraindustry variation in unionization. But in the search for clues to dissatisfaction and the relationship between dissatisfaction and behavior, interindustry differences serve as convenient surrogates for the relative capacity for collective action at the micro level and for observing changes in the bargaining process, the uneven development of union-management relationships, and the effects of the maturation of the bargaining process.

Stages in labor-management relations at the plant or company level follow a developmental pattern:

1. Metaphorically, the initial stage has often been described as armed conflict: with the initiation of labor-management relations, a battle begins in which neither party accepts the legitimacy of the other.

2. This stage may be succeeded by an armed truce, where skepticism remains but legal requirements force reluctant adjustments, and bargain-

ing involves an increasing degree of accommodation, still accompanied by relatively high levels of mutual suspicion.

3. At a later stage, bargaining takes place more or less continuously, with the atmosphere varying from very good to only slightly less icy than in stage two. This stage may be characterized as one of Weberian legitimacy: each party sees benefits in the arrangement and agrees that conflict, as long as it is formalized, may have creative uses. Developing mechanisms for handling grievances begin to drain off poisonous suspicions and, at this stage, one may discern the beginnings of the building of trust and even mutual respect.

Short of a notorious "sweetheart" contract, there is a further stage in which unions and managements may see their interests more in terms of collaboration than of conflict. This stage may produce several seemingly divergent patterns. Even if one accepts the notion that as unionism takes hold in a firm or in an industry, as the result of a long period of a benign governmental climate, and as labor organizations become part of the polity,[14] it does not follow that all unions can exert the same influence either in the private bargains they arrive at with employers or in the political activities they undertake. An institutional context that supports bargaining leaves the way open for relative bargaining power to emerge; at the same time, it does not obviate the possibility that unions and managements may join together for purposes they define as essential to their survival.

As we suggested earlier, interindustry comparisons provide useful clues to the patterning of conflict behavior over time. Postwar studies of interindustry differences began with Kerr and Siegel in 1954. While they postulated a number of possible contributors to their differential propensities to strike, they concluded that industries tend to be "strike-prone" when workers form relatively homogeneous groups whose cohesiveness is enhanced by geographic isolation, as in the lumbering and mining industries.[15]

While the Kerr-Siegel study is always cited in the literature, the actual placement of industries in the five categories of strike propensity they created is seldom reproduced nor are their results brought up to date. To be sure, their method was crude, not only because of the relatively early date of the study, but also because of differences in the type and quality of data available from the countries they examined. Essentially, they ranked industries on the basis of the relationship between man-days idle in strike activity and the volume of employment. We conducted a "replication" for the period 1949–1973 by calculating man-days idle as a percent of industry employment. The results appear in Table 9.1.

It should be pointed out that mining, which has made the largest per-capita contribution to strike activity over the years, is *sui generis*: work sites in deep-coal mining are isolated, there is a tradition of worker

TABLE 9.1.   Interindustry Propensity to Strike, United States, 1927–1973

	1927–1941	1942–1948	1949–1973
High	Mining[a]	Mining[a] Auto Rubber Stone, Clay, Glass	Mining Primary Metals Rubber Transport. Equip.
Medium High	Apparel Furniture Leather Lumber Miscellaneous Mfg. Textiles Transport. Equip.	Fabricated Metals Leather Lumber Primary Metals Textiles	Construction[b] Electrical Machinery Fabricated Metals Machinery, exc. Elec. Petroleum Stone, Clay, Glass
Medium	Construction Transportation, Util. Electrical Machinery Fabricated Metals Machinery, exc. Elec. Tobacco Primary Metals Stone, Clay, Glass	Construction Transportation, Util. Electrical Machinery Food Furniture Machinery, exc. Elec. Paper Petroleum Tobacco Transport. Equip., except Auto	Transportation, Util. Chemicals Furniture Lumber Paper
Medium Low	Services Chemicals Food Paper Printing, Publishing	Chemicals Miscellaneous Mfg. Printing, Publishing	Food Leather Miscellaneous Mfg. Printing, Publishing Textiles Tobacco
Low	Trade (Wholesale and Retail) Other Non- manufacturing	FIRE Services Trade (Wholesale and Retail) Apparel	FIRE Services Trade (Wholesale and Retail) Apparel

[a] Coal mining only.
[b] Contract construction only.
Source: 1927–1948, Clark Kerr and Abraham Siegel, "The Interindustry Propensity to Strike: An International Comparison," in Arthur Kornhauser, Robert Dubin, and Arthur M. Ross (eds.), *Industrial Conflict* (New York: McGraw-Hill, 1954), and 1949–1973, calculated from U.S. Bureau of Labor Statistics, *Analysis of Work Stoppages*, annual publication.

solidarity and a long history of corrupt union leadership in the postwar period, and the work is very dangerous, both in terms of disaster and severe injury and in terms of health in general.

At the other extreme, unionization in trade, in finance, insurance, and real estate (FIRE), and in services has been too low for these industries to make sizable contributions to any measure of strikes. This is in part an artifact of classification: teacher strikes accounted for a large number of man-days idle in recent years but are counted in the service industry rather than in government and are therefore lost to view in aggregated statistics.

Kerr-Siegel's second highest category for the period 1927–1941 included lumber, furniture, textiles, apparel, and leather, all industries characterized by high competitiveness, small plant size, but relatively early unionization. The presence of the transportation equipment industry in this category was due to the large scale organizing efforts of the period.

An examination of the Kerr-Siegel list of high-strike-propensity industries up to 1942, in comparison with the positions of these industries in later periods, supports Snyder's conclusion that in the United States up to 1948 workers did not act as if they made the economic calculations attributed to them in studies based on postwar data.

By the 1942–48 period, Kerr-Siegel found apparel to be in the low-strike-propensity category. Two things accounted for this transformation. First, the industry began to move out of its traditional centers and to become fragmented: a substantial amount of high-skill work remained in traditional locations like New York City, but sewing operations were increasingly contracted out to smaller towns, where they were often performed in unorganized shops. Perhaps more important, in locations that were organized the union began to play a different role as the bargaining process matured. This is an industry characterized by work-sharing, a practice dictated not only by the seasonal nature of employment but also by the rapid formation and disappearance of many small firms. In effect, the union became the personnel manager for the splintered industry and, as such, established elaborate procedures for handling not only grievances but also the allocation of the work itself.

Textiles is a case of a weakened union, again caught in the runaway-shop squeeze: by the middle of the postwar period this industry had practically abandoned its traditional locations in the Northeast and became concentrated in states such as North Carolina with strong open-shop laws and an antiunion ambience.

Meanwhile, in the 1942–48 period, rubber, stone/clay/glass, fabricated metals, and primary metals moved into the higher strike-propensity categories, followed by construction, electrical equipment, machinery, and petroleum in the postwar years. While there was considerable year-to-year variation in strike activity from 1949 to 1973, there seems to have been more variation within years than between years, probably because of shifts in the bargaining strategies of strike-prone industries in a period that included, after all, an unusually long business upswing (from 1961 to 1969).

Comparing the entire period from 1949 to 1973 with the last five years of the period, one can observe some of the more recent changes in institutional context. Table 9.2 shows the ratio of man-days idle to employment for selected industries. What is significant is that in a period when strike activity was generally on the upswing, primary metals and rubber showed a decline. One can only speculate about the latter—the likelihood is that as employment increased in the plastics sector, strike activity declined because a good deal of plastics fabrication is performed in shops that are small, economically marginal, and unorganized, compared to the traditional Akron-based rubber plants with which plastics are grouped in published strike data.

In primary metals, however, the case is clear. After the 116-day industry-wide strike in 1959, union-management relations in steel, the largest sector of primary metals, became more collaborative than in any other industry. Over a number of years the United Steelworkers and the companies were engaged in joint activities, spurred on in particular by the threat, real or imagined, of foreign competition. Thus, joint committees that were established in 1971 to further employment security

TABLE 9.2. **Man-days Idle Due to Strikes, Rates per 1000 Workers, by Selected Industries,**[a] **1949–1973 and 1968–1973**

| | Mean Number Mandays Idle | | |
Industry	1949–1973	1968–1973	Percent Difference
Primary Meals	3.90	1.98	−49
Mining	3.24	3.35	3
Transportation Equipment	1.95	2.81	31
Rubber and Plastics	1.91	1.29	−32
Construction	1.80	3.41	89
Machinery, except Electrical	1.62	1.64	1
Petroleum	1.33	1.47	11
Fabricated Metal Products	1.25	1.45	16
Electrical Machinery	1.10	1.62	38
Stone, Clay, Glass, Concrete	1.06	1.42	34
Transportation, Communications	.82	1.68	105
Tobacco	.40	1.38	245

[a] Criterion for choice: Rate per 1000 > 1.
Source: Calculated from U.S. Bureau of Labor Statistics, *Analysis of Work Stoppages*, annual publication.

and plant productivity had a complex job-classification system, a highly developed abitration system, and a Joint Basic Education Program as their forerunners. The most important sequel was the 1973 Experimental Negotiating Agreement that provided a procedure for voluntary arbitration of any unresolved bargaining issues, a procedure that survived a substantial attack by intraunion critics in steel negotiations in 1977. The object is to eliminate "the uncertainty at each negotiating period that encouraged inventory buildups and increased steel imports, followed by higher unemployment and low productivity after contract settlements." [16]

An agreement like the ENA goes well beyond concerns about the economic calculations and vulnerabilities of worker groups that are considered in assessments of propensities to strike. Steelworkers, having negotiated supplementary unemployment benefits, early retirement, a thirteen-week vacation for high-seniority workers, and other measures that can cushion the impact of change, entered a new phase of concern about job security. The response, appropriate enough in a society dedicated to political bargaining, is to join with employers in matters of mutual interest. In the case of steel, the union has lent its support to the industry's successful campaign for import quotas under the job-protection provisions of the 1962 Trade Expansion Acts.[17]

Where industries showed large increases in the strike index in the last five years of the period, the major contributions came from activity between 1968 and 1971. The number and volume of strikes had begun to increase in 1964 and reached a peak in 1971, when the Bureau of Labor Statistics' measure of percentage of working-time lost (.37) was the highest since 1959. As economic conditions became more straitened, strike activity declined markedly in line with the models cited above, but again, organizational context may be seen to play a role.

The well-documented history of the construction industry affords an illustration.[18] As in all industries, most strikes are due to disagreement over wage and benefit changes at contract time. In construction these have been relatively short, but major strikes (those involving 10,000 workers or more) became increasingly severe during the 1960s, influenced not only by the favorable economic conditions of the period but also by the fact that the industry experienced a steady trend toward the formation of larger bargaining units.

After 1971 all measures of strike activity showed marked reductions because of continued high unemployment in the industry, increasingly successful competition from nonunion contractors, and anticipation of the development of federal regulation in the industry. A review of interstate variations in recent years showed several variables that strongly influenced the occurrence and severity of work stoppages: the annual value of new construction put in place, the level of union penetration, the existence of "right-to-work" statutes, the level of employment, and the degree of maturity of the collective-bargaining relationship. Again, we observe the combination of factors from both economic and organizational contexts. The development of conflict-mitigating arrangements is illustrated on the local level in Detroit, which experienced a notable decrease of strike activity in the construction industry after 1970, the year 25 building-trades employers formed an association to engage in multitrade bargaining with local building unions.

Strikes occur more frequently during the contract term in construction than in most other industries. The data suggest that there was no overall improvement in settlement machinery of "noneconomic" disputes in the latter half of the sixties, especially as evidenced by a marked rise in strike duration. The frequency of job-assignment and jurisdictional disputes is related to the blurring of craft lines, especially with the emergence of new technology. Vague job boundaries cause serious difficulties in making clear work assignments, and even though the Taft-Hartley Act makes it an unfair labor practice for a union to strike over work assignments, the act's settlement machinery is too complex to resolve such issues legally. Of central importance here are the interests of workers in protecting the advantages their skills afford them in labor markets, a worker-satisfaction concern that is bypassed in surveys and treated by many of the rest of us, rather too one-sidedly, as one that nurtures inefficient work methods. When, in a similar fashion, publishers protect their capital by copyright laws or a corporation protects its technology by patents and licensing arrangements, we applaud the role these restrictions play in our system of business incentives.

Procedures established by unions themselves through the National Joint Board for the Settlement of Jurisdictional Disputes in 1948 and subsequently refined, have met with only partial success.[19] As evidence of the Joint Board's inability to enforce its determinations, man-days idle resulting from interunion conflict more than doubled from 1965 to 1970. Moreover, such disputes showed a relatively steady rate of increase through the 1950s and 1960s.

The most serious effort in recent years to obviate conflict in the construction industry was carried out under the leadership of John Dunlop, both before and during his tenure as Secretary of Labor. A formal result was the establishment in 1971 of the Construction Industry Stabilization Committee (CISC) by Executive Order of the President. In the words of Daniel Quinn Mills, who served as secretary of CISC:

> The committee, provided by the President with legal authority to involve itself in negotiations in an orderly manner, held out the hope of moderating the rates of negotiated wage increases short of a wage freeze and formal controls. The long-term contribution of such a policy as that suggested by the establishment of the Stabilization Committee will depend on the

degree to which it can combine short-term actions with steps toward long-term reforms in the structure and operation of collective bargaining in the industry.[20]

Like other mechanisms in the past, the CISC has been beset by problems of implementation. The much-publicized veto by President Ford of the so-called common-situs picketing bill in 1975 undermined the progress made toward stability in the industry, the bill being at least part of the *quid pro quo* demanded by the unions for their collaboration in CISC.

Most industries that exceeded their twenty-five-year mean (mandays idle per 1000 workers, Table 9.2) in the 1968–1973 period did so because of a combination of noncontract-related strikes, discussed in the next section of this chapter, and large-scale contract-related strikes. In the combined transportation-communications-utilities category, two nationwide airline strikes in 1969, a national telephone strike in 1970, and two major interstate trucking strikes in 1970 added to the totals piled up in these sectors (and in the railroads) in connection with work-rule disputes. A nationwide strike, conducted jointly by all unions with company contracts, occurred at General Electric in 1969. And the 12.3 million man-days idle accumulated in the General Motors strike of 1970 added enough weight to the already large volume of strike activity from noncontract sources to increase the transportation equipment industry's strike index by almost one-third compared to the overall twenty-five-year mean.

STRIKES AND GRIEVANCES

Even though the focus of the previous section of this chapter was on the economic causes and organizational context of strikes, it should be clear that the resolution of conflicts, whatever the causes, depends on the maturity of the collective-bargaining process. The word "maturity" has a positive connotation in most industrial-relations circles. Conceptually, however, it may be viewed more neutrally as signifying the institutionalization of conflict.[21] Part of this process—and by far the most effective—is the growth and elaboration of grievance procedures.

By the mid-sixties, major collective-bargaining agreements reflected the almost universal adoption of grievance procedures and grievance arbitration, giving rise to the notion that strikes or lockouts during the term of agreement are universally outlawed.[22] On the contrary, in the absence of an absolute ban, work stoppages may occur during the term of an agreement for a number of reasons, including the breakdown of grievance machinery.[23]

Although the comparison has to be made with care because of the different number of agreements covered and certain other temporal differences, the Bureau of Labor Statistics reported that absolute-ban provisions occurred in 45 percent of all agreements in 1963, compared to 35 percent in 1973. Significantly, this decline covered a period when arbitration was rapidly extending its scope. Within each industry a majority of agreements have limited bans. In 1973 the exceptions were ordnance, paper, chemicals, stone/clay/glass, electrical equipment, instruments, communications, and utilities.[24] One would think that a preponderance of limited bans would be related to strike frequency during the term of the contract, but the two are not so closely related as this logic suggests. For example, all 45 agreements in textile and apparel have limited bans, while electrical equipment is split most evenly; yet the latter ranks fairly high in short strikes, while textile and apparel are low in any strike measure one chooses. In short, some contracts have provisions that are seldom invoked, while some unions conduct strikes in spite of absolute bans.

A somewhat different estimate emerges from a Bureau of National Affairs (BNA) sample of 400 contracts, representing a cross section of industries, unions, number of employees covered, and geographical areas. BNA reported that unconditional strike bans remained stable at 57 percent from 1970 to 1973, in contrast to a steady increase from the 48 percent reported in 1960. Conditional bans increased slightly, from 33 percent in 1970 to 35 percent in 1973. Conditional bans appear in 50 percent or more of contracts in apparel, petroleum refining, lumber, and construction. Forty-three percent of these conditional bans provide the right to strike when a grievance is processed through the final step of the procedure without resolution of a dispute. This particular provision is found in contracts in almost all industries, but mainly in lumber, primary metals, machinery, transportation equipment, and construction.[25] Again, there seems to be only partial correspondence between types of contract clauses and what actually happens in the industry.

Whether legal or illegal, strikes occurring during the term of a contract tend to be shorter than those resulting from contract negotiations. A link between grievances and such "short" strikes is suggested by James Kuhn's comparative study of collective bargaining in the United States and Australia.[26] He found a tendency for Australian workers to carry on short strikes over grievances that were handled by regular procedures in the United States. Conversely, long strikes at contract negotiation time, like those occurring in the United States, were obviated for the most part in Australia by a system of compulsory arbitration and by the preoccupation of Labor Party leaders with public opinion. While Kuhn's was a cross-national study, it suggests differences in context that deserve exploration on an interindustry basis in the United States.

In 1968 the BLS annual *Analysis of Work Stoppages* introduced a data series on strike activity by duration that made it possible to explore interindustry differences by length of strikes. The measures we calculated were mean man-days idle per thousand *union members* for the period 1968–1972. Since strikes are relatively infrequent phenomena compared with the scope of industrial activity, a single year's events may have an inordinate effect on the relative position of an industry in these calculations.[27] Furthermore, after a period of relative constancy, the events of a single year may upset the balance among industries. The first of these points will be amply illustrated below. As for the second, even though the number of strikes varied from 1968 through 1971, just about half in each year occurred at contract renegotiation time, an additional 13 percent in connection with negotiating a first agreement, and about one-third during the life of an existing contract. In 1972, however, largely because of numerous flare-ups in the coal industry, these proportions changed to 44, 13, and 40 percent, respectively.

We experimented with several operational definitions of "short." The two major ones, strikes of one day and strikes of six days or less, showed a general correspondence by industry for man-days idle per thousand union members. The disparities are probably due to the events of a single year. The food industry, for example, ranked fifth in one-day and fifteenth in six-or-less. While several events may have contributed to the difference, it can be largely explained by one: the Amalgamated Meatcutters and Butchers closed down the meat-packing industry for one day in 1971 in protest over the administration's decision to disallow the retroactive payment of wage increases during the ninety-day wage-price-rent freeze of that year.

The instruments industry, which is both very small and mostly unorganized, produced 4,500 man-days idle in 1968, compared to 100 or less in each of the succeeding four years, enough to place it third and seventh, respectively, in the one-and six-day rankings.

With due regard to such extreme cases, the rankings of the eight industries highest in short strike activity were as follows:

Industry	Rank, 1-day	Rank, 6-day
Mining	1	1
Transportation, Communications, Utilities	2	2
Instruments	3	7
Electrical Equipment	4	4
Food	5	15
Transportation Equipment	6	6
Machinery, exc. electric	7.5	3
Government	7.5	16
Tobacco	13	3

Using both measures, the major industries involved in short strikes during the five years in question were mining; transportation/communications/utilities; electrical equipment, and transportation equipment. Transportation, etc., aggregates several disparate three- and four-digit Standard Industrial Classification categories, including the railroads, shipping, airlines, stevedoring, telephones, and energy producers. Railroad and other transportation strikes are particularly sensitive to the injunction process, so that a one-day strike may be simply the first day of a long dispute over new contract provisions or a one-day protest over work rules.

To get the flavor of "noneconomic" disputes and thereby the character of worker dissatisfaction in this and other short-strike industries, we examined the detailed information produced by BLS for "major" strikes —those involving 10,000 workers or more occurring *during* a contract period for the years 1968–72: [28]

1. In four out of the five years, there were five railroad strikes on crew-size issues, involving firemen, trainmen, and switchmen.

2. The Communications Workers carried on three short major strike in 1970 alone, two over work-classification assignments and one over protection against crime in the areas of particular work assignments.

3. There were two longshoremen's strikes in New York–New Jersey, both over the issue of hiring new men.

All of these major strikes–in railroads, communications, and stevedoring–are aggregated in the data under "transportation, communication, and utilities."

4. Each year there were strikes in coal—over health and safety, payment of disability benefits, arrest of pickets, welfare-fund administration, the discharge of union officials, and intraunion matters connected with the criminal conduct of union officers.

5. There were four major strikes at one General Electric location in Louisville, Kentucky, alone—over a disciplinary action, over work assignments and back pay, and over the wage scale of sixteen floorsweepers. These four strikes lasted a total of twenty-five days (two less than six days and two more than six days).

6. In 1968, 1969, and 1972 there were major auto-industry strikes, all at General Motors, over job classification, production standards, and unresolved grievances. In 1968 there were two strikes in Flint over local unresolved issues. In 1969, over a period of eighty-seven days, there were stoppages staggered over various plants in six states "in protest of the merger of GM's Chevrolet and Fisher Body divisions . . . [which] created some different pay scales for similar jobs." And in 1972 there was a series of short stoppages (in the course of fifty-nine days), nationwide, concerning production standards, which came to an end when "grievances and other issues were settled according to conditions at the various plants."

7. In 1968 and 1969 there were five major one-day teachers' strikes directed toward influencing state legislatures. An additional long strike occurred in New York City in the showdown between the union and a decentralized school district over teacher dismissals.

These "major" strikes indicate in a general way that issues of job security—including work classifications—of production standards, and of the piling up of grievances of all kinds will, if left unresolved over a period of time, culminate in what might be characterized as the "showdown" of a strike or a series of stoppages. The most widely publicized examples in recent years were the 1972 events at the General Motors plants in Lordstown and Norwood, Ohio, imbedded in the strike statistics quoted above as "grievances concerning production standards."

While journalists and other publicists produced reams of prose about the alienation of workers in general and the disaffection of young workers in particular, these events had more specific causes—namely, the management tactics of the company's Assembly Division (GMAD), created in 1968 to combine the operations of the Chevrolet and Fisher Body divisions. Each takeover by GMAD involved the consolidation of union locals, layoffs, and new local plant contracts, and all but one were accompanied by strikes. The basic issue at Lordstown and Norwood, as at many other locations where both "quickie" and long-drawn-out strikes occurred, was the tightening of production standards in the name of "efficiency," which was viewed by the union as a breach of its original contract.

In fact, however, there are less-publicized walkouts over grievances, some too brief to enter the official strike statistics, which report only stoppages of at least one shift. With the growth of grievance machinery and arbitration these have diminished, but the flavor of an earlier style is still evident in the approach of a relatively small union in the electrical industry, the United Electrical Workers (UE). In the UE's national contracts with GE and Westinghouse, as well as in contracts with smaller firms, arbitration provisions are limited to discharge and discipline cases. If the Union requests arbitration on other issues, the company has to agree, but if issues are not resolved by the parties, the union, which is free to strike under the contract, does not hesitate to do so.

If, for example, a worker complains that he has been assigned to a job outside of his classification, and if the shop steward agrees with the worker, everyone in the affected department will simply walk out. The union's position is that grievances short of discipline and discharge are best settled on the spot, and that this approach has minimized both the delays and the costs associated with arbitration, as well as an otherwise inevitable tendency for grievances to pile up.[29]

In procedural terms, the trade-offs between grievance systems with and without arbitration can be illustrated by the history of another small independent union, the Allied Industrial Workers, which covers the western half of Michigan, including seventeen locals in Grand Haven, a small industrial town of 10,000, about which field data were collected for this volume. Historically, this union's birth was the by-product of an early split in the leadership of the United Auto Workers; a major tenet of its longtime president was strong objection to arbitration because of the delays, the costs, the necessity of compromise, and the avoidance of responsibility by both parties.

In the period after World War II, and through the middle sixties, few strikes over unresolved grievances actually occurred. Whereas companies had been in general agreement with the union in this relatively conservative town that the lack of arbitration reduced the number of grievances they had to deal with, their position began to change when the custom arose of banking grievances as union bargaining chips in contract negotiations.

What finally undermined the nonarbitration stand of the union, however, was the takeover by merger of many of the shops it had organized. The AIW is a union without a clearly defined jurisdiction. Where it had agreements with multiplant companies that normally bargain with other unions demanding arbitration clauses, the pressures for arbitration became irresistible.[30]

CONCLUSION

The materials we have presented on interindustry strike patterns, in respect of both long and short strikes, provide a sense of organized workers' concerns, whether or not one is prepared to treat collective bargaining and collective worker actions as legitimate forms of worker participation in their workaday worlds.

Our inclination is to regard the organized actions of organized workers as being vital in a democracy, whether they are undertaken directly, "on the floor," in Gary steel mills, in small job-shops in Grand Haven, Michigan, or indirectly, in joint labor-industry councils, in national contract negotiations, or in the corridors of Congress. We see very little in the efforts of intervention enthusiasts that addresses the issues joined in strikes in even a remote way. The hostility toward unions evidenced in large portions of the literature meanwhile is subversive of a vital structure of carefully conceived arrangements that, we believe, is more often strengthened than weakened by strikes.

In between, there are those who believe that unions do well in their place but that they cannot "do it all," or that the constraints upon their leaders require paraunion mechanisms—Quality of Working Life Committees, and the like—to do for workers and managers (especially the chores in connection with work redesign) what collective bargaining makes difficult. Actually, collective bargaining can make for difficulties for reasons that are arguably good and sufficient. There was not handed down on Mount Sinai, for example, a sacred commandment prohibiting job ladders or job jurisdictions or seniority "bumping" procedures that may simply disappear when skill hierarchies are leveled and job classifications are blurred by job redesign.

The discussion of the relationship between participation, collective bargaining, work dissatisfactions, and the prospects for intervention schema is best pursued after more detailed attention has been given to worker grievances and the issues joined in grievance and arbitration procedures, subjects to which we now turn.

10. Workers' Grievances and
Managers' Responses*

One of the quintessential differences between the efforts conducted by investigators in the two principal approaches to work inheres in their different conceptions of managers and workers.

In the mainstream and the tributaries that may be identified within the human-relations tradition, little attention has been given to managers' and workers' concerns with their rights as such. To the extent that conflicts over rights have been recognized, they have been perceived, rather condescendingly, as reflections of managers' psychological needs. From this perspective, many organizational problems stem from managers' preoccupation with authority, control, and power; they may be aided in mastering these "dysfunctional" preoccupations by professionals skilled in sensitizing executives and supervisors to the untoward effects on subordinates of the hierarchies, rules, and impatient commands induced by executives' own anxieties, conformity needs, and paranoid distrust of workers.

Investigators in the industrial-relations and human-resources fields have been far more inclined to view the conflicts in organizations as reflections of conflicts over distributive justice and legal rights than as displaced psychological urges. From this perspective, workers and managers are best helped by structural devices that enable them to engage in trades of quids and quos without psychologizing very much about deeper-going processes at play in the unconscious of individuals in the parties. Investigators in this tradition do not, of course, deny that workers and managers have personalities, but they emphasize that workers are free members of a democratic society as well as the contractual members of an organization owned by others, and that there

---

* The arbitration data discussed in this chapter were originally analyzed by Patricia
  Bonfield under my direction; our presentation of these materials borrows from a
  memorandum she prepared.   I.B.

are at least as many limits on the willingness of employees in America to check their rights, privileges, and immunities at the workplace door as on their willingness to repress their feelings.

In this chapter we elaborate upon this second, less psychological theme through an examination of one type of relevant data.

MANAGERS, INDUSTRIAL CITIZENS, AND CONFLICT RESOLUTIONS

Writing some forty years ago on what he termed "the tradition of inequality," R. H. Tawney observed that

> of course, the distinction between the majority who are mainly dependent on wages, and the minority, who are largely concerned with proprietary interests, is not the only significant line of division in the economic system. There is also the familiar division between the directed and the directors; between those who receive orders and those from whom orders proceed; between the privates and the noncommissioned officers of the industrial army and those who initiate its operations, determine its objectives and methods, and are responsible for the strategy and tactics on which the economic destiny of the mass of mankind depends.[1]

A quarter of a century later, Ralf Dahrendorf somewhat similarly observed,

> I would here merely assert this: in postcapitalist as in capitalist industrial enterprises there are some whose task it is to control the actions of others and issue commands, and others who have to allow themselves to be controlled and who have to obey.[2]

Later on he sharpens the point:

> The incumbents of certain positions are endowed with the right to make decisions as to who does what, when, and how; the incumbents of other positions have to submit to these decisions. . . . For the industrial worker, the labor contract implies acceptance of a role which is, *inter alia*, defined by the obligation to comply with the commands of given persons.[3]

Tawney and Dahrendorf are pointing to the relations of superordination and to a basic conflict of interest which, in their view, is endemic to twentieth-century enterprise. Dahrendorf, however, goes on perceptively to suggest that the conflict between capital and labor, both within and outside the workplace, has become organized, routinized, "institutionalized," or, in the newest idiom, "diffused." We may add that a good many potentially explosive conflicts have thereby been, in the same new idiom, de-fused, as well.

As Dahrendorf sketches it, the process of institutionalization began with the organization of interest groups both within industry and throughout the greater polity. While, in the stage of organization, "conflict [may have developed] a greater visible intensity, organization itself [had] at least two side effects which [operated] in the opposite direction." Organization at once presupposed "the legitimacy of conflict groups" and thereby removed "the permanent and incalculable threat of guerilla warfare." At the same time, it made "systematic regulation of conflict possible."

> Organization is institutionalization, and whereas its manifest function is usually an increasingly articulate and outspoken defense of interests, it invariably has the latent function . . . of inaugurating routines of conflict which contribute to reducing the violence of clashes of interest.[4]

Hence, Dahrendorf suggests, it is no surprise that in the industrial arena we have subsequently seen contending parties come to agree on certain rules of the game and on the need for the creation of institutions that provide "a framework for the routinization of the process of conflict"— such as collective-bargaining bodies and systems of conciliation, mediation, and arbitration.[5] Any observer of the recent industrial-relations scene in the United States would have to agree that such mechanisms as "the contract" (or, more typically, "the agreement"), "collective bargaining," and "conciliation, mediation, and arbitration" are more than a little functional in regulating conflict between "those who receive orders and those from whom orders proceed."

The use of arbitration has increased markedly in recent years. From 1960 to 1972, the number of requests for arbitration panels directed to the Federal Mediation and Conciliation Service (FMCS) almost quintupled (from 2,835 to 13,005).[6] Together, the two principal agencies supplying arbitration services at the national level—FMCS and the American Arbitration Association—correctly anticipated their combined requests for arbitration panels to exceed twenty thousand in 1972.[7] "Arbitration's growth," according to a National Representative of the FMCS, is indicated by [the fact that] more than 95 percent of major labor contracts now [provide] for arbitration."[8]

At the same time that arbitration is assuming an ever larger role in the resolution of management-labor disputes, arbitration decisions are becoming more visible elements in an emerging "common law of the shop."[9] As conflict becomes increasingly institutionalized, arbitrators are to a considerable extent assuming *de facto* roles as "interpreters" of reality and "enforcers" of industrial justice in the world of work.

In addition to providing "a framework for the routinization of the process of conflict" in the workplace, arbitration may have other latent functions. A survey of arbitration decisions accordingly provides us with another vantage point from which to survey dissatisfactions in the organized corner of the labor market.

In the preceding chapter we attempted to adduce clues to worker dissatisfaction from industry-specific strike data. An analysis of samples of formally filed workers' grievances and the dispositions made of them would unquestionably offer additional and probably better clues to the character of modern organized workers' experiences, their reactions to their circumstances, and managers' ways. Unfortunately, we have not been granted access to study grievances by means of systematic and intensive observational techniques.[10] The next best thing, to use materials on grievances in published arbitration cases (as we have done), is second best by an appreciable margin. Consider that relatively few formal grievances actually reach the arbitration stage; they are either resolved or withdrawn at earlier steps in the ingenious grievance and bargaining process.[11]

Even had we obtained extensive data on grievances, by number and type, from parties to labor-management agreements, the information would not have obvious meaning: while some grievances are meritorious, others are inventively concocted by the parties to serve their individual and mutual needs for exchangeable quids and quos in day-by-day bargaining. Still other grievances are juggled in connection with formal precontract negotiations.[12]

The fact that arbitration is expensive, time-consuming, and in some ways precedent setting militates against its being used, in the fashion of grievances, as part of regular bargaining. The cases that come before arbitrators are likely to be "real" ones, with merit and substantive significance to the parties.[13] The fact that only about 4 percent of all labor arbitration decisions are published [14] considerably limits what one may make of arbitration awards: the publication of awards is very much under the control of busy arbitrators and, in some instances, of their clients. But, since the cases are published largely for use as indicators of trends in important domains of industrial relations by unions, employers, and other arbitrators, they may be taken as the equivalent of physicians' vital signs, since they are carefully selected by informed editors who keep their expert fingers on the industrial pulse. The widespread use of published arbitration awards by the parties to labor-management agreements and by arbitrators themselves as important grist for their respective mills, if not exactly as binding precedents, suggests that these awards may be usefully examined by researchers who are mindful of their limitations as data.[15]

In accordance with this logic we have examined the contents of arbitration awards published by the Bureau of National Affairs in 1953–54, 1962–63, and 1971–72. The middle period, 1962–63, was chosen in order to examine developments prior to and after practical restrictions on arbitration were almost entirely removed by the Supreme Court in the Steelworker "Trilogy" cases.[16] Prior to these decisions, the issue of arbitrability under existing agreements, of whether a dispute over contract interpretation was arbitrable in the first place, was a matter for courts, not arbitrators, to decide. The effect of these cases was to resolve doubts about arbitrability in favor of arbitration and to leave to arbitrators, rather than to less technically competent and organizationally cognizant judges, the responsibility for determining the merits of grievances.[17] By selecting 1962–63 as the middle date in our two-decade time period, we built into our sample of cases the fullest "before and-after" effects of the landmark "Trilogy" decisions. Again, our essential purpose in this chapter is to consider the grievances that come to arbitrators as clues to workers' dissatisfaction and to make rough inferences about managers' performance from the description of events provided as part of arbitrators' awards.

THE NATURE OF GRIEVANCES

Table 10.1 suggests that during the years under review, grievances clustered within from three to six categories.[18] In 1953–54, slightly more than two-thirds were concerned with pay rates and other compensation; hours and overtime; employee benefits; job protection; and discharge, discipline, and plant rules. Another significant proportion was concerned with arbitration itself, an issue that virtually disappeared after the "Trilogy" cases.

In 1962–63 and 1971–72, the substance of grievances seems to have become increasingly concentrated. In the latter fiscal year, the three categories of "employee benefits," "job protection," and "discharge, discipline, and plant rules" alone accounted for almost two-thirds of all major issues.[19]

The data suggest that while the matters resulting in worker grievances changed markedly during this twenty-year time span, they seemed to become increasingly concentrated in two major categories of longstanding (and by no means irrelevantly) "instrumental" concern—namely, job protection and "discharge and discipline."[20]

We explored in some detail awards involving "discharge, discipline, and plant rules," the single largest among grievance categories, accounting for almost one-third of all reported cases in 1971–72. During each of the three time periods considered, 70 to 75 percent of reported cases involved discharge, with the remainder involving discipline.

The sample in the present section includes all cases coded in this category by the BNA for the time periods surveyed. The units of analysis

TABLE 10.1.   Grievances [a] Grouped by Major Issue—Percentage Distribution

Major Issue	Year 1953–54	1962–63	1971–72
Interunion Relationship; Jurisdictional Disputes	—	4.1%	7.4%
Union Security	2.0%	1.1	[b]
Collective Bargaining Contracts	3.4	1.1	1.8
Arbitration	13.7	17.4	3.2
Supervisors	1.0	[b]	[b]
Wages; Other Compensation	12.1	6.0	5.6
Hours, Overtime, Premium Pay	10.2	4.0	2.9
Employee Benefits	11.5	7.6	15.7
Job Protection: Layoffs, Work Assignments, etc.	18.3	22.9	17.2
Discharge, Discipline; Plant Rules	17.5	24.6	30.8
Promotion, Demotion	4.4	4.3	2.9
All Others	5.9	6.9	12.5
Total	100.0%	100.0%	100.0%
N =	(498)	(751)	(727)

[a] Except for arbitration, excludes grievances by companies (1953–54 N = 1; 1962–63 N = 5; 1971–72 N = 10).
[b] Less than 1 percent.

Source: Bureau of National Affairs, *Labor Arbitration Reports*, Vols. 11, 20, and 29.

are (a) the BNA decision abstract as it appears at the beginning of each relevant case, (b) BNA classification notations as they appear at the beginning of each relevant case, and (c) the "award" section as it appears at the conclusion of each relevant case.

On the basis of the content of these units, the following were coded:

1. Management actions (i.e., discharge, discipline, other).

2. Nature of awards (i.e., grievance sustained—with or without qualification; grievance denied; mixed award—namely an award concerning a number of workers and in which some workers' grievances were sustained, others' denied; and "other," which includes, for example, the interpretation of a contract clause).

3. Management's charge(s) against the worker, or workers.

4. Reason, or reasons, given by arbitrators for sustaining workers' grievances—when in fact grievances were sustained.

5. Whether or not plant rules were involved.

Coding includes multiple charges and reasons for sustaining grievances but does not include multiple mentions of the same charge or reasons for sustaining grievances within the same case.

In effect, then, this information is at least indicative of management actions against which workers grieve; of arbitrators' perceptions of the validity of workers' efforts to contest management actions; of managements' perceptions of workers' behavior; and of arbitrators' perceptions of management behavior.

In Table 10.2 management charges against workers involving "discharge, discipline, and plant rules" during the years under study are tabulated first by number of cases and second by number of charges. Charges themselves are indicative of what managers consider most bothersome or problematic about workers, of the manner in which managers tend to perceive workers, and of the conceptual framework within which managers view them.

Historically, the greatest percentage of charges have involved (a) insubordination (e.g., refusal to accept job assignments or job transfers; refusal to work overtime; refusal to obey, or disputing, management instructions; leaving one's post; insulting one's supervisor; usurping management's function); and (b) job- or workplace-related misconduct

TABLE 10.2. **Management Charges against Workers in Discharge and Discipline Cases—Percentage Distribution**

	Year		
Charge Against Worker	*1953–54*	*1962–63*	*1971–72*
Absenteeism/Tardiness/ Malingering	6.9%	11.1%	12.5%
Incompetence/Negligence/Low Production	17.6	11.1	10.9
Disability—Mental/ Physical/Other	5.9	4.3	4.7
Fighting/Troublemaking	7.8	9.6	9.3
Insubordination	22.5	27.4	23.0
Work Stoppage/Picketing/Union Activities and Related	12.7	9.1	4.7
Misconduct—Other— Job/Workplace Related	15.7	19.2	26.5
Misconduct—Other— Nonjob/Workplace Related	8.8	2.9	3.1
Miscellaneous Charges	1.0	1.4	—
Other	1.0	3.8	5.4
Total	99.9%	99.9%	100.1%
N =	(102)	(208)	(257)
Mean Charges Per Case	1.2	1.1	1.2

Percentages do not always sum to 100 percent because of rounding.

(e.g., misrepresentation on one's employment application; theft of company or co-worker property; gambling; failure to observe rules; disloyalty to the company; conflict of interest). Charges of insubordination have remained relatively constant; charges of job-related misconduct have increased noticeably. In 1971–72 the two categories together accounted for approximately one-half of all management charges against workers.

Other categories of charges are relatively unpopulated. However, within them we find overall increases in the percentage of charges of absenteeism/tardiness/malingering and fighting or troublemaking; and decreases in the percentage of charges of incompetence/negligence/low productivity; work stoppage/picketing/union activities; and nonjob- or workplace-related "misconduct."

The percentage distribution of cases (not reproduced here) in which various charges against workers have been made is generally parallel to the distribution of charges. Historically, insubordination and job- or workplace-related misconduct have been mentioned in the greatest number of cases. The percentage of cases in which charges of insubordination have been made has remained fairly constant, varying from slightly under to slightly over one-fourth of all cases; in contrast, the percentage of cases in which job- or workplace-related misconduct has been charged has consistently increased, from 17 percent in 1953–54, to 21 percent in 1962–63, to 30 percent in 1971–72.

Once again, other categories are relatively small. However, there have been increases in the percentage of cases charging absenteeism/tardiness/malingering; a decrease in the percentage of cases charging incompetence, negligence, low productivity, work stoppage/picketing/union activities and related, and nonjob- or workplace-related misconduct; and a fairly constant percentage of cases charging fighting and/or troublemaking.

MANAGERS' AND WORKERS' PERFORMANCE

In the previous section we tallied the grievances of workers in order to identify some of the dissatisfactions of organized workers; arbitrators, as we saw, sustained the workers' grievances in the all-important area of discharge, disciplines, and plant rules in roughly half of all the cases.

In Table 10.3 we have tabulated the main reasons arbitrators have given for sustaining workers in each of 259 cases won by workers under six categories. The workers have been sustained when managers use pretexts for charges against workers, lack evidence and act frivolously or inconsistently, fail to investigate "facts" in support of charges against a worker, overlook extenuating circumstances or employees' past records,

TABLE 10.3. Reasons Worker Grievance Sustained—Percentage of Cases [a]

Reason Grievance Sustained	Year		
	1953–54	1962–63	1971–72
Management Violation/Circumvention of Contract; Pretext	11.9%	11.1%	7.6%
Management Unreasonableness/Arbitrariness	54.8	51.5	49.2
Management Inconsistency	16.7	28.3	16.1
Management Incompetence/Dereliction	28.6	27.3	33.1
Positive Personal Qualities/Record of Employee	19.0	21.2	16.1
Other	33.3	13.1	19.5
N (Cases) =	(42)	(99)	(118)
Mean Number of Mentions per Case	2.0	1.6	1.5

[a] The base for these percentages is the number of cases for each time period. Percentages do not sum to 100 because of multiple reasons invoked by arbitrators.

themselves violate rules applied to employees, or otherwise act in bad faith.

Table 10.4 reports the results of a content analysis of all the reasons mentioned by arbitrators in their awards in these cases. It should be noted that the problems in sampling arbitration cases are less relevant here because we are considering the distributions of assessments by arbitrators within an identifiable universe of 259 cases.

It is clear that the bulk of cases won by workers reflected experiences with managers perceived by arbitrators to have been unreasonable or arbitrary in their exercise of authority or incompetent or derelict in the technical-legal sense. These arbitration cases will be further discussed in Chapter 12 in which our concern will be with the logics applied to the roles of managers and workers in American society. Our purpose here is simply to report on efforts to identify the complaints of organized members of the work force that are sufficiently important to the grievants to cause them to involve themselves and their unions with the expensive and time-consuming paraphernalia of arbitration.

It turns out that managers are and have been far more than just a little concerned with what are taken to be their rights—a crucial matter, yet one that is almost totally ignored by those who seek to humanize workplaces through the application of social-science technology and who

TABLE 10.4.   Reasons Mentioned by Arbitrators for Sustaining Worker Grievances—Percentage Distribution [a]

Reason Grievance Sustained	Year		
	1953–54	*1962–63*	*1971–72*
Management Violation/Circumvention of Contract; Pretext	8.5%	6.8%	5.0%
Management Unreasonableness/Arbitrariness	35.4	34.8	34.8
Management Inconsistency	9.8	18.6	11.0
Management Incompetence/Dereliction	17.1	18.0	24.3
Positive Personal Qualities/Record of Employee	12.2	13.7	11.6
Other	17.1	8.1	13.3
Total	100.1%	100.0%	100.0%
N (Mentions) =	(82)	(161)	(181)

[a] The base for these percentages is the number of mentions by arbitrators for each time period. Percentages do not sum to 100 because of rounding.

seek to go behind managerial claims to consider managerial motives in psychological perspective. The cases provide considerable evidence that managers are inclined to be quick on the draw or the trigger.[21] They also direct our attention to a concern on the part of the workers with the implications of their dependence, a matter which comes sharply into focus when their jobs may be held hostage by employers who are bent, reasonably or unreasonably, upon maintaining their authority, their rights to manage.[22]

CONCLUSION

It is rather too easy, in our judgment, to write off managers' actions in the cases we have discussed as rooted more in their psyches than in their problematical roles as responsible stewards of others' wealth as well as managers of men's and women's working lives. If it is indeed the case that the impetuousness and precipitousness of managers in our cases may be attributed to misguided, "nonlogical" sentiments much more than to role conflict in a society both democratic *and* industrial, then there is a need for far more sophisticated therapeutic interventions than have been suggested by the best known of work reformers.

An alternative view seems patently more practical: efforts are needed to improve the design of machinery now in place in many work settings and to upgrade the quality of the grease that reduces bureaucratic frictions so that workers are protected from the impulsiveness (perhaps more than the guile or the ineptness) of managers who have logical sentiments rooted in their legal roles, as well as nonlogical sentiments anchored in their psyches. But nonlogical sentiments, we recall, were imputed to workers by human relationists long before they were imputed to managers. There is evidence that we still view workers and managers quite differently along precisely these lines, that we lose track of other conflicts between managers and workers' interests while attending to the interesting psychological conflicts that may be observed between "individuals' and organizations' needs." In Part IV we consider the implications of this two-way view of managers and workers for work-reform prospects.

PART IV
ALTERNATIVE PERSPECTIVES ON MANAGERS AND WORKERS

In Parts II and III we attempted to differentiate among the sources
of workers' concerns and discontents over which managers have
relatively little, some, and considerable control. The evidence adduced
up to this point suggests that while overall worker dissatisfaction is
significantly related to concern about matters either beyond or only
marginally within the scope of managers' capacities, it is also influenced
by "local" work experiences. These sources, we have suggested, are
more amenable to well-advised interventions than are the dissatisfactions generated by larger socioeconomic trends. In between are
concerns about developments that once were under management control
(and may grow to be again in the future) but are now, like the average
educational achievements of their employees, only marginally
manipulable.

Among the currently manipulable items, we have argued, are
issues having to do with supervision and workplace resources. Others,
like those having to do with superordination and subordination
and those discernible in labor-management conflicts, are not so easily
factored into overall assessments of worker reactions because the
underlying issues suggested in such conflicts are not included among
those addressed in attitude surveys. And surveys, as we have seen,
lend themselves to statistical analyses of the linkages only between
the discrete dissatisfactions actually considered by investigators and
the sum of discontents to which the parts add up.

The fact that we cannot put all the demonstrable sources of
dissatisfaction into a single ranked list is unfortunate but not
necessarily fatal to our effort in this study, for many of these issues
can be inferred from studies of worker behavior. It is not stretching
credibility, after all, to suggest that workers' attitudes may be
inferred from their actions in the workplace as well as by their
responses to survey questions.

In this part of our study we turn to the responses of managers
to the opportunities for reform identified by the latter-day human
relationists and to some of the reasons why these responses are
unenthusiastic. We question the contention that managers are stupid,
inept, or both when they neglect to manage workers more effectively
and democratically or, even more surprisingly, when they neglect to
take the by no means radical advice of the current generation of
work reformers. Some of the data, especially those bearing on
grievances, may indeed seem to invite such a reaction, but we would
caution against it on the simple ground that it requires one to ignore
or deny a number of more evident reasons, described in the chapters
that follow.

We also question a wholly psychological explanation that conceives of managers as slaves of "nonlogical sentiments," analogous to the motives for so long attributed to workers. Evidence that managers have deep-seated unconscious needs to be tyrannical, for example, is at least as scarce as concrete and persuasive evidence that workers are emotional midgets or submissive seekers after benevolent corporate father-figures.

Without being able to assign it a weight, we consider the highly problematic quality of the relationships between worker satisfaction and productivity to be an important factor in accounting for managers' apparent disinterest in work reforms. To believe, as many managers do, that productivity is in fact related to satisfaction and to suspect that the "true" relationship is really there to be discovered in due course is not to affirm (1) that productivity is the only concern of managers, (2) that improved worker satisfaction is the main stepping stone to corporate productivity gains, or (3) that worker productivity rates are so low that they require the investments entailed by efforts to raise them by raising worker morale.

While these considerations hint at an explanation of managers' reactions, it is helpful to balance the promises of reformers against pictures of managers less simplified than the ones that occur in many reformers' works. To this end we look first, in Chapter 11, at the fate of several interventions. The results do not prove much—but they suggest persuasively (1) that much is at stake in organizations and that worker morale issues will regularly give way to other issues, and (2) that the most frequently proposed workplace reforms have prerequisites for their success that are virtually unattainable, even given good intentions on the part of interested parties.

Next, in Chapter 12, we return to data on grievances before arbitrators, to demonstrate that the logic by which would-be reformers (and many of the rest of us) view managers and workers is two-valued, obscuring a number of important issues that need to be joined before discussions of work, discontent, and reform can be coherent and productive. The results of our examination of this two-valued logic lead us to compare the differential judgments typically made of workers' and managers' behavior. In Chapter 13 we examine wherein both workers and managers are disposed to be rational and loyal in their respective roles.

In all, we seek in this part to understand the character of the diagnoses of reformers and the effects—and side effects—of the remedies they most typically prescribe.

11. Managers' Responses to Interventionist Opportunities

In Chapter 5 we explored issues that have to do essentially with income distribution, and we argued that managers, as such, have relatively little control over the forces shaping the gross patterns of income distribution in American society. An examination of workers' responses to questions involving working conditions over which employers *do* have considerable powers of initiative led us, in the immediately succeeding chapters, to be more pointedly concerned about the roles employers actually play in their organizations as suppliers of resources and as leaders, in short as managers.

Clues to workers' dissatisfactions adduced from strike and arbitration materials pointed thereafter to additional areas in which human-relations and other interventionist ideas might conceivably be relevant. As we have indicated, however, interventionists' schema rarely address the matters that emerge in strikes and in grievances, in large measure because these involve at least as many questions about such intractable issues as economic interests and rights (the rights of managers as well as workers) as about psychological and motivational issues in the usual sense of these terms.

In this chapter we return to the more proximal working conditions that occupied us in Part III, conditions at the level of the individual enterprise, which many reformers are wont to argue offer prospects for remediation. These are the conditions, we have emphasized, that have received most attention from managers who give any serious thought to the matter of worker discontent and from their social-science advisors and consultants since the earliest days of the human relations movement. These are also, and quite consistently, conditions addressed in the densely populated professional courses, generally called Human Behavior in Organizations, taught to aspiring business leaders and managers.[1]

Thus it has been a major theme in the literature, both technical and

157

popular, and in academic programs, conferences, and workshops since the early experiments at Western Electric's Hawthorne works that managers could do a great deal to increase the satisfactions of workers by granting workers "the authority they need to do their work"; by "defining workers' responsibilities clearly"; by more frequently assigning workers "to do the things they do best"; by increasing the "challenge" in workers' jobs; by helping workers to "develop their abilities"; by promoting conditions conducive to "friendly relationships among workers"; and by hiring workers only after being assured that job candidates have realistic conceptions of what their prospective jobs will entail.[2]

As we have seen in Part II, workers' expressions of satisfactions with their jobs vary quite consistently with their favorable judgments on just such matters. Reformers, meanwhile, have gone well beyond such findings to argue that interventions designed to improve working conditions not only would increase workers' satisfactions and their productivity but that their mental health would improve as well. Hardly a writer among them has failed to note the likely favorable effects on workers' psyches of reductions in general workplace stress, interpersonal conflict, boredom, and modifications in rules and supervisory arrangements that conflict with needs for "self-actualization." Indeed, scarcely a writer fails to quote liberally, if carelessly, from a major study of the psychologically unsettling consequences of life in auto plants by Arthur Kornhauser.

These results (Table 11.1) are essentially in line with, though they certainly do not prove, the optimistic assertions of work reformers and latter-day human relationists. Note, for example, the independent effects of educational achievements in a study of the effects of work.[3] But

TABLE 11.1.   Percentage of Educational Groups at Two Lowest Occupational Levels Who Have High Scores on Selected Mental-Health Components

Mental-Health Components	Young		Middle-Aged		
	Some high school or less	High-school graduates	8th grade or less	Some high school	High-school graduates
Life satisfaction	25	11	38	33	18
Self-esteem	18	11	22	14	12
Personal morale	25	21	19	32	59
Sociability	32	47	21	44	59
N =	(57)	(19)	(81)	(57)	(17)

Source: Arthur Kornhauser, *Mental Health of the Industrial Worker* (New York: Wiley, 1965), p. 137. Used by permission.

human-relations and organizational-development specialists have been incomprehensibly slow in providing us with data in support of their claims about work and mental health. They have, moreover, neglected those few rigorous investigations whose results do buttress their arguments. These studies strongly support premises regarding the likely outcome of reforms, if they do not confirm the validity of assumptions underlying the techniques they prefer. "Humane" concerns as well as concerns with efficiency could and probably do motivate some employers,[4] and intriguing if limited evidence suggests that managers could serve as well as be served by reforms targeted upon proximal issues.[5]

The underlying question of workers' psychological functioning and well-being off the job is by no means trivial. That proximal conditions *are* subustantially related to workers' psychological functioning, away from as well as at work, seems indeed to be the case.[6] Thus, Melvin Kohn and Carmi Schooler successfully "disentangled the intercorrelated dimensions of occupation by survey responses to a large [representative] sample of [3101 employed] men who work in many occupations," inventorying their job conditions, and statistically differentiating the psychological concomitants of each facet of occupation.[7]

In the execution of their study, these researchers focused on ten aspects of psychological functioning that "deal with subjective reactions to the job itself, valuation of self-direction or of conformity to external authority, orientation to self and to society and to intellectual functioning."[8] They examined a dozen occupational conditions and measured. the statistically independent effects of each of the conditions that were significantly related to more than one facet of psychological functioning, as follows:[9]

1. Ownership/nonownership
2. Bureaucratization (indexed by numbers of levels of supervision)
3. Position in the supervisory hierarchy
4. Closeness of supervision
5. Routinization of the work
6. Substantive complexity of the work
7. Frequency of time-pressure
8. Heaviness of work
9. Dirtiness of work
10. The likelihood of a sudden and dramatic change in a man's income, reputation, or position
11. The likelihood of being held responsible for things outside one's control
12. The risk of loss of one's job or business

These twelve occupational conditions define what the investigators suggestively refer to as "the structural *imperatives* of the job."[10]

After tests of alternative explanations for the pattern observed in their results, the investigators conclude that while all twelve job conditions have significant impact on psychological functioning, "substantive complexity of the job" (an index made up of seven ratings by respondents and investigators, listed above as the sixth of the twelve job conditions) is especially potent.[11] In support of their belief "that there is a continuing interplay between man affecting job and job affecting man," they have presented several strands of evidence, none of which, as they point out, is definitive, but all of which are consistent.

> In fact, for the one occupational condition about which we have sufficient historical data to make a precise assessment—the substantive complexity of work—we find that the job has a substantially greater impact on men's psychological functioning than the reverse. . . . Not only the conditions that determine occupational self-direction, but all structural imperatives of the job that elicit effort and flexibility, are conducive to favorable evaluations of self, an open and flexible orientation to others, and effective intellectual functioning. Men thrive in meeting occupational challenges.[12]

From a parallel study of work and "alienation,"[13] Kohn concludes that the variable, "control over work process"—encompassing the "closeness of supervision," the "routinization of work," and the "substantive complexity" of jobs—has an appreciable effect on the measures of each of three dimensions of alienation.[14]

The centrality of the job in determining other aspects of men's lives also emerges from this study:

> A man's job affects his perceptions, values, and thinking processes primarily because it confronts him with demands he must try to meet. These demands, in turn, are to a great extent determined by the job's location in the larger structures of the economy and the society. It is chiefly by shaping the everyday realities men must face that social structure exerts its psychological impact.[15]

While the items used by survey researchers to "capture" workers' attitudes toward proximal work conditions vary, there is little significant difference between the themes in Kohn's "self-direction" items and his "substantive complexity of the job" index as against the "challenge" items in the Working Conditions Survey. Kohn's work helps to underscore in dramatic ways the significance to workers, managers, and the nation of the so-called proximal work issues in the current study.

The evidence is strong then that proximal issues are important to the psychological functioning of workers. The results could easily be used by would-be reformers to make even more forceful arguments in defense of interventions in the work setting. One may accordingly ask whether, and with what consequences, the suggested interventions have been attempted. One may also ask what might account for observed failures of interventions when they have delivered less than promised. Finally, one may ask what might account for the general lack of attempts to intervene in manipulable work arrangements despite suggestive evidence that the interventions would be likely to have salutary consequences. We turn now to these related questions.

INTERVENTIONS AND THEIR CORRELATES

It needs to be reemphasized that one must be wary about interpreting the available evidence on interventions of the type endorsed by workplace reformers.

First, studies of interventions and their effects are almost always of a very low scientific order. In their survey for the National Science Foundation, Katzell and Yankelovich located "only nine intervention studies which satisfied [their] requirements" from an even nominally scientific point of view.[16] Fourteen others were less adequate, though better than nine additional "miscellaneous" ones.[17]

Second, even the interventionist-investigator [18] who is given a broad mandate for change rarely has control during the experiment over the variables that any sensible worker would identify as potent in determining the prospects for reforms favored by most "change agents."

Third, even the most persuasive reformers have no significant controls over managers and workers. This impotence is characteristic, not withstanding the agreements and "contracts" intervenors typically seek to elicit in advance from the two parties in work experiments.[19]

Fourth, it is evident that work reformers are not inclined (in Max Weber's marvelous characterization of biases) to trip over "inconvenient facts . . . and for every partisan opinion there are facts that are extremely inconvenient."

Overlooking flaws in the reports by interventionists, we would agree with Katzell and Yankelovich that "the overall message to be learned" from these studies is that:

> Efforts to redesign jobs have not produced results that are generally persuasive in validity or consistent in direction, although there are tantalizing bits of evidence, including the results of four prototype experiments, which suggest the potential value of the approach to both the quality of working life and economic performance. Those who wish to experiment should be prepared to make major job changes, for it is apparent that to do less is likely to be ineffectual. Moreover, evidence also suggests that such experiments are likely to succeed only if (a) workers are pscyhologically ready for it, which is more likely to be true of young, affluent, and better educated workers, and (b) the production technology lends itself to such change.[20]

Even if we leave aside the perversity of *some* workers and the misgivings of *some* unions [21] to which *some* of the failures may directly or indirectly be attributable, the review of the evidence by Katzell and Yankelovich points to the overridingly important role of managers in shaping the content and the results of interventions calculated to address proximal work issues. A report by Edward M. Glaser, Carrol E. Izard, and Mary Faeth Chenery, of the Human Interaction Research Institute, on their efforts to intervene in the "planning, staffing and organizing" of "Crown" Laboratories' new plant (1973) in "Centerton, U.S.A." makes the point very well. Glaser and Izard are behavioral scientists; Ms. Chenery is an authority on management.[22]

THE "CROWN" CASE

The "action researchers," as they call themselves, sought to shape developments in a new industrial plant in accordance with QWL [Quality of Working Life] principles.[23] These principles produce a schema that is almost indistinguishable from those endorsed by intervention enthusiasts. Thus, the scientists worked out careful agreements with "Crown's" top-level executives at their West Coast headquarters as well as arrangements with the local production and personnel managers in the Southeast to permit small teams of plant employees to help plan "the design, structure and organization" for a new production process. The intervenors helped to screen section and department manager candidates, acted as resource agents in solving organizational problems, contributed to conflict resolutions, and facilitated communications, "goal attainment," and overall development needs. They also observed and participated in problem identification, problem solving and feedback regarding the development of managerial styles and team functioning. Finally, they interpreted and documented intervention methods.[24]

Evaluation of the results of these preparatory efforts and the concrete arrangements that were actually installed were conducted in accordance with criteria developed and articulated by J. R. Hackman [25] and by Glaser himself.[26] The authors' own statement of "positive developments" deserves an almost extant presentation:

1. The initial production runs were successful, which is an unusual achievement. The plant was licensed in November 1974 by the Bureau of Biologics of the Food and Drug Administration to ship its first product, with three other product licenses granted by July of 1975.
2. The plant performance has exceeded company expectations for quantity of production and yield of finished product from the raw material. . . .
3. . . . there is evidence of broadly-felt ego-involvement among the total workforce with the company, the plant and its problems. Workers are

committed to the goal of high quality products. Personnel appreciate the unusual opportunity to have a "say" about their work. They feel that management usually is responsive to their ideas, and there is widespread concern about plant goals and problems. . . .

4. The plant has weathered great frustrations, pressures and irritations in the start-up and "debugging" phase from May 1974 to about May 1975. After that time, the Centerton organization began to settle down and mature in a generally healthy, productive way.

5. Some of the focal points of the QWL improvement effort, such as the development of a responsive managerial climate that would pay heed to needs, suggestions or criticisms from any member of the workforce, have been internalized as the general style of work at Centerton, even though no longer a QWL thrust *per se*.[27]

On another side, they report the following "dubious or negative" developments:

1. The early enthusiasm for creating an innovative QWL program has been blunted. While the management climate of the plant still is more responsive to employees' needs, suggestions and criticisms than in a traditionally managed manufacturing plant. . . . the many intervening factors and difficulties have led to a diminution of concern for QWL improvement considerations.

2. While some managers and supervisors have maintained a style that sincerely invites participation by the task teams in the design, structure and organization of their work, others have reverted to a more traditional authoritarian approach that is short on upward communication and defensive with regard to suggestion or criticism. The Centerton plant manager's initial support of participative management has shifted toward a philosophy of "manage in whatever way is comfortable for you so long as you get good results." Thus, those whose customary management style tends to be authoritarian are no longer unequivocally encouraged to learn new ways of stimulating ego-involvement on the part of the workforce by respectfully and appreciatively inviting their participation.[28]

It would be difficult, and perhaps unfair, for their readers simply to fault these social scientists, though their otherwise sympathetic critics, charged with evaluating the results of the experiment, are devastatingly critical in the draft report cited in note 23. The investigators, perhaps to their credit, do not agonize much over the failures of the company to meet fully the key conditions specified for the conduct of their interventions and the research based thereupon. The *real* blame for the negative effects quite apparently lies close to management's doorstep, if not actually in the executive suite. And the bill of particulars, in the authors' words, is instructive:

1. In February 1974 . . ., CMS was sold to a foreign multinational company. . . . In the Fall of 1974, the HIRI P-O learned that at least some

influential members of the local management at Centerton had inferred (correctly or incorrectly) that the new corporate top management did not regard the QWL effort with favor, and this perception understandably affected commitment to that effort at Centerton.

2. The new plant had only a few people who were experienced and technically competent in the plant's primary production functions (extraction and processing of biological products). Thus managers and supervisors were occupied with learning to perform the complex technical activities of their jobs and had little time to develop new management styles or commit themselves to the QWL program.

3. Because of severe financial problems at the time the new management took over the company, there was great pressure for cost cutting and for getting the plant into production as quickly as possible. Start-up was delayed for four months because of numerous problems. Frequent 12– to 16–hour workdays drained managers' and supervisors' energies.

4. The HIRI project was on a very tight budget, which sharply limited the amount of time the PD and PI could spend at the plant.

5. Prior to the beginning of the Centerton project the HIRI PI had accepted a scientific exchange fellowship in the U.S.S.R., scheduled to begin July 1, 1974. The date appeared compatible with the original plans for plant start-up in January 1974. . . . However, technical problems delayed start-up until June 1974, and it was not feasible to change the PI's fellowship arrangements. . . . Although the PD tried to substitute for him during this period, he had not had time to establish close relationships with Centerton staff, and the budget would not support frequent travel between the PD's Los Angeles office and the Centerton plant.[29]

The point in presenting the "Crown" experience is not to question the essentially attractive idea that increased worker participation, and at least some forms of work redesign,[30] will increase workers' satisfactions and perhaps even their productivity.[31] Rather, we wish to highlight the fact that managers themselves have misgivings about the usefulness of reforms, about the implications of reforms for their own status and careers, and about long-term commitments.

We wish, in the same vein, to highlight the fact that whatever the short-term gains, interventions focusing on worker participation and work redesign only rarely lead to sustained experimental efforts. It is interesting to note, in this specific connection, that virtually none of many celebrated and well-documented work redesign efforts since the 1950s has been revisited by the investigators who initially reported on their great benefits.[32] It is likely that a majority of even the most promising experiments died in their infancy, a conclusion that is suggested, perhaps unintentionally, in Richard Walton's description of the fate of eleven of the most celebrated of the recent workplace experiments.[33] Walton's review of special interest: he is director of research as well as a professor at the Harvard Business School, is a leading member of the international committee on work reforms mentioned in an earlier chapter, and, with Einar Thorsrud of Norway, Louis Davis of UCLA, and Albert Cherns of Great Britain, is a member of the inner circle of spokesmen for the interventions concerning us in this volume and for the perspectives from which workplace reforms are viewed.

His review of eleven work-redesign, work-enlargement, and worker-participation experiments shows quite clearly that the contents of QWL packages like that delivered to "Crown" Laboratories, with or without the promises of higher output, will be opened, tried, and discarded by managers in all but exceptional cases.[34]

Three of the intervention experiments, Walton reports, "have returned to conventional patterns. . . . Many others have regressed somewhat after a few years. . . . Several other innovative plants . . . are still successful and evolving in the direction that they were launched." [35] In the third category he includes a pet-food plant (Gainesburger) in Topeka, Kansas, about which a great deal has been written and said in TV documentaries, in scholarly books and periodicals, in business journals, and in the popular press. The Gainesburger case is, however, a rather special one in that the plant involved is for practical purposes a runaway shop (its product was previously manufactured in a unionized plant in Kankakee, Illinois) where nearly all of the strict prerequisites for success set down by interventionists were present.[36]

In addition to the seven restrictive prerequisites considered below, Walton identifies seven developments in the efforts that went amiss, unintentionally pointing to some serious contradictions between the humane objectives of reformers and the objectives of managers. We may summarize these as follows:

1. The lapses of managers who failed to follow through on efforts that had heightened the expectations of workers. These expectations, we may safely surmise, were born of dissatisfactions that led workers to be enthusiastic participants in experiments in the first place.

2. Managers who were simply unwilling to reduce supervision "and materially increase workers' influence in critical decisions," despite the reduced needs for preexperimental traditional controls.

3. Managers who failed to reduce turnover to a threshold level (10 percent) beyond which a requisite "bank of necessary skills" is too depleted for the redesigned and "enlarged" work to be effectively executed.

4. Managers who accepted new appointments, and thereby drained the pool of qualified, trained successors committed to work redesign.

5. Managers who lost their consultants to other clients.

6. Managers who could not "contend" with the expansion of work to be performed by the relevant work unit or by the larger plant.

7. Managers who could not maintain a "steady state" in the ex-

perimental operation when "pressures developed" for greater "predictability . . . and certainty" and for "less movement of personnel, more specialization among workers, and closer supervision." [37]

Walton's list of his research findings is a most revealing one. The success of some reforms is contingent upon conditions that the reforms themselves are intended to produce, suggesting that inventive changes may be enmeshed in what may perhaps be viewed as the dialectics of enterprise.

Other issues, like the one referred to last in Walton's list, are attributed to "technical problems." Such problems, in the testimony of one of Walton's informants, "induced a certain amount of unexpected stress in the social system." [38] The assertion is an intriguing one: the firm is not just an equilibrated microeconomic system, and managers are understandably concerned with stability and continuity even if, as with other concerns, the achievement of stability is purchased at a price. It is one of managers' important functions, as has been argued at Harvard since the time of Elton Mayo and Chester Barnard, that they manage social systems as well as economic systems. It is remarkable that the latter-day human relationists do not see the nearly contradictory quality of the logics underlying their views of managers as managers and managers as agents of change. They simplify greatly what they have long recognized as the need for executives to perform balancing acts: in the balance, stability will predictably be assigned very considerable weight over potentially beneficial reforms that are, almost by definition, disruptive and disequilibrating.

One inevitable conclusion, supported however unwittingly by Walton's assessment, is that reforms require a veritable revolution in managers' thinking. As is clear in Walton's list, the structure and the function of labor and other markets would have to be substantially altered in order for proposed interventions to take hold in most cases.

This impression is reinforced by a reading of Walton's conceptions of managers' roles. Consider this brief catalogue of what may too easily be deplored as wrong-headedness or as treatable elements of what some have called bureaupathology:

> Two of these companies came under new, severe, and long-term competitive pressures that resulted in new initiatives and influence patterns emanating from the top. Higher management began emphasizing cost reduction and near-term results, insisting upon discipline and compliance with their programs, and in general providing an inhospitable environment for the innovative work system.

> Authoritarian decisions and "do it" commands tended to erase the premise that a subordinate could freely challenge superiors in unguarded dialogue. Politically-based influence techniques undermined the premise that a person's influence would be a function of his expertise and information. And,

as cliques formed to exercise influence, interpersonal relationships were corrupted, trust was eroded, and the sense of "community" began to deteriorate.[39]

Walton and other latter-day human relationists are inclined to wring their hands over such "politically based" managerial styles. Such labeling, however, obscures more that it reveals: aspiring executives have much at stake in their careers, and a good many of the responses Walton implicitly abhors may be quite serviceable, at a particular juncture, to key organizational leaders. We may report, in this context, the experience of a UAW local union president with a succession of plant managers in one of the subsidiaries of a major chemical company. The first manager appealed to this sensible man that he collaborate in efforts to increase production, an appeal to which the union leader responded constructively if not with alacrity. Two years later a successor made a similar appeal that the local union get behind "a push to upgrade product quality," the new boss having a weather eye to opportunities to attract favorable headquarters attention. After two and a half years, the second manager, like the first, was promoted and replaced by a third who saw executive career benefits in increased output. When we interviewed the local union leader he was facing reelection and was much troubled by his opponent's urges that he be unseated for failing to represent rank-and-file impatience with confusions in work standards.

It is not necessarily so appalling that local agreements reached between the parties in one plant location, according to which union members' pay envelopes are fattened by their bargained share of the productivity gains generated by reforms, are coveted by leaders of locals in other plants. One does not need a research grant to learn that the demands for interlocal pay parity are often unaccompanied by equivalent productivity gains; differences in production processes in different plant locations, among other factors, may make for different productivity patterns.

Nor need one automatically complain, as Walton does, that the workers in a "reformed" plant will withdraw their psychological investments in innovative work designs upon discovering that fellow workers elsewhere gradually receive rewards accorded originally only to collaborative workers in the reformed setting, who, in Walton's words, have "allowed [management] the freedom necessary to conduct the experiment." While many Americans would like to see income distributed in the future strictly on the basis of productivity, others would prefer a reexamination of the logic supporting the present allocation of income shares before agreeing that future allocations should be linked exclusively to output. The issue is a bit more value-laden than Walton's formulation allows.

That there is some recognition, at least, of deeper-going issues than may be usefully joined in reformists' perspectives is in fact evident in Walton's own view about the interunion local question. He asks us to consider the implication of the foregoing statement about allowing managers the freedom to experiment:

> It suggests that the equity concept is so strong that even though employees may be intrinsically rewarded by taking on high responsibility and making high contributions, their extrinsic reward must also be in line with their relatively high work inputs. If this is not the case, their sense of injustice will cause them to scale down their level of involvement.[40]

Walton, however, stops short of indulging a worker's claim to the status of *homo economicus*, to minimize his costs and seek to realize a profit thereby. It is as if views about distributive justice are informed by peculiar ideas. "Equity" is a "concept," and injustice is something that workers may in some cases "sense." The *realities* of inequity and injustice are not absolutely denied in such a formulation; they are consigned to a surreal universe of discourse in which the concept or sense of a thing displaces the thing itself.

Work reformers' conditions meanwhile are difficult to meet, as we see from Walton's list:

1. Small towns. "They provide a community context and a work force that is more amenable to the innovation."
2. Small work force.
3. New plants. "It is easier to change employees' deeply ingrained expectations about work and management in a new plant culture."
4. Geographic separation of the experimental unit from other parts of the firm's facilities.
5. "The use of outside consultants as change agents provides objectivity and know-how."
6. A significant factor in several cases: long lead times, implicit in start-ups, allow large blocks of time for the "training and acculturation" of participants.
7. No unions, or where union-management relations are "positive."[41]

We may note here that the characteristics of settings in which experiments have purportedly been successful are not very much different from those identified in connection with the application of Scanlon Plans. These plans, deservedly named after their inventive author, provide for worker bonuses from worker-produced savings and are not tied to company profits. A consequence, as a leading labor expert points out, is that

> the employees cannot lose or gain bonuses by management decisions in other areas such as purchasing and inventory control, which affect the income statement. The workers' fortunes are related to problems they can do something about, and they need not worry about "accounting." [42]

The plan has been successfully operated in a few unionized firms, typically small ones.[43] Even in smaller plants, the plan has often gone awry, however, in the wake of mergers and management successions, and for other reasons advanced by Walton.

Just prior to his list of seven conditions favorable to experimentation and to the continued application of work reforms, Walton writes, "Where the external labor market is favorable, a firm can tailor the work force to the innovative system, in terms of both a capacity for development of multiple skills and a receptivity to cooperative social patterns." [44] This formulation evokes memories of Winston Churchill's response upon hearing that Hitler—referring to England—intended "to wring the chicken's neck": "Some neck! Some chicken!" The equivalent here would be: "Some tailor! Some development!"

The conditions Walton and many other interventionists commend are not only difficult to meet; some of them, like reduced turnover, may be as much a condition for success as a desired result. And, apropos the seventh item, Ted Mills, formerly of the National Commission on Productivity, reported (to participants in a 1974 Chicago conference on "The Changing Work Ethic") findings from a private corporation survey that 80 percent of 150 work experiments meeting minimal criteria for inclusion in the study were undertaken specifically to avoid unions.

CONCLUSIONS

The evidence, then, is that proximal issues *are* important to workers, as judged by an examination of their responses to the Working Conditions Survey. Furthermore, we have noted, both from our own analysis of the Working Conditions Survey and from Kohn's work, overall satisfaction with work is strongly influenced by proximal working conditions. We have also seen, in Kohn's reports, that there are impressively strong relationships between satisfaction with proximal working conditions and both workers' psychological functioning and the degree to which they are "alienated." These findings support the long-argued positions of the most reputable of dedicated reformers.

The results of interventions actually informed by these findings, however, could impress no one. Leaving aside flaws in research design and the potential role of self-serving manipulations of data by researcher-activists, this review and that by Katzell and Yankelovich support none of the optimistic urgings of the intervention fraternity.

The disjunctions between the apparent promises in these interventionist schemes and the outcomes discussed in this chapter, we contend, are largely attributable to factors best linked to American managers and the realities in terms of which *their* recognitions, priorities, concerns, and diagnoses were and are formed. Some of these measures of what is material to managers are hinted at in the recounting of the Crown Laboratories' story. More general indications of executives' basic concerns and enthusiasms are visible just below the surface of Walton's impatient discussion of "what might have been" in the cases he examined.

In the following chapter we pursue further the question of managerial misgivings about reforms in the workplace. The question is "Why don't managers *do* something about what are far more than just nominally relevant work-related issues?" And "Why, after so many years of pro-interventionist efforts, after so many surveys, and after so much concern has been expressed by managers, does almost nothing *happen* regarding those work issues about which managers do have fairly wide margins for initiatives?"

12. The Rights and Roles of Managers and Workers*

We have emphasized that the worker discontents most readily identified from behavioral and attitudinal data vary greatly in their vulnerability to intervention by managers. The evidence also indicates, however, that a number of conditions affecting overall worker satisfaction that are vulnerable to some managerial manipulations are not often the objects of systematic interventions or even of much active concern among those who mind the store.

A few of the reasons for managers' apparent indifference to opportunities to exercise their oft-asserted rights in their workers' and their own interests may be perceived in the work of Richard Walton and other friendly social-science consultants, as we saw in Chapter 11. We do not question the civilized intentions of these social scientists; our own sense of the serious difficulties facing interventionism do not stem from the mischievous motives of those hell-bent for humanization, self-actualization, and other transcendental ends. Nor do they stem from fears that Americans will be more than marginally manipulated by behaviorists.

Indeed, a neglected reason for the failure of a large number of socio-scientific intervention programs to survive inheres in the refusal of American workers to be "had" by would-be social science exorcists.[1] More problematic, as we see it, is a questionable tendency (among social scientists not much less than others) described by Eugene Linden in a trenchant and apposite article on the reasons we have neglected, for at least three-quarters of a century, to attempt to converse with chimpanzees:[2]

* The arbitration data discussed in the middle third of this chapter were originally analyzed by Patricia Bonfield under my direction; our discussion of those data borrows from a memorandum she prepared. I. B.

To start with, our perceptions of other species have been limited by a laboratory tunnel vision in science that has been part of . . . the cure orientation in science. Operating under Francis Bacon's thesis that nature best reveals her secrets when tormented, we have tended to dissect and study animals with the idea of seeing how they might solve our problems, medical or social, rather than attempting to understand them in their own right, in their own environment.

When we eventually got around to comparing human and animal behavior, we studied animals as if they had no reason or language, while we studied humans knowing we did. Thus the disparate investigations tended to perpetuate the assumptions on which they were based, and our approach to animal and human communication eventually resurfaced as the explanation for the differences between the two: Man is different because that is the way we look at him.[3]

The conceptual framework in which an issue is discussed bears heavily on both theoretical and empirical outcomes; as every researcher knows, the way in which a question is posed limits the possible answers. Paraphrasing Marx, Bertell Ollman put it this way:

our knowledge of the real world is mediated through the construction of concepts in which to think about it; our contact with reality, insofar as we become aware of it, is the contact with conceptualized reality.[4]

To take the terms in common use just as they are is to confine oneself within the boundaries describing the ideas expressed by those terms. The very "language of concepts" includes unexamined assumptions related to the ultimate question of *cui bono*.

The Italian Marxist Antonio Gramsci applied this notion to the problem of "false consciousness" among workers:

because of social and intellectual subordination, this [working] class *borrows* a world view of another class and asserts this borrowed world view in words although in action a contradictory world view is manifested.[5]

What he is suggesting here, and elsewhere in his writings, is that the terms of discourse invented by groups with power in a society come to dominate the way in which people think about the issues and problems in that society, no matter what their particular interests may be. Gramsci may extend the logic rather further than will suit the tastes of some, but the point will not be much blunted by the argument that the notion of false consciousness can too readily be pressed too far.

The fact is—as we suggested at the volume's outset—that the logics and categories we employ in discussions of workers and managers are fundamentally different, and they are different in ways that obscure some important dimensions of the very realities they are intended to characterize. Consider that the best-intentioned change agents are either implicitly or explicitly convinced that managers are ultimately both rational and humane or, rather, that they *could* be, with social-science help, more rational and, thereafter, more humane—which is to say more democratic and so on. By reducing social structural and related issues to questions of motive, they restrict the discussion of worker malaise almost entirely to educational or therapeutic solutions.

Gainsaid in this diagnosis, and limiting almost totally the utility of the resulting prescriptions, are the categorical differences in the roles of the two groups in the economic drama and in the conventional languages used to describe them. These roles are recognized at some level of consciousness by change agents, no less than the rest of us, as being "natural," beyond discussion or dispute. These distinguishable roles, moreover, are enshrined in the law both specifically and generically.[6]

In our own earlier work on labor-management and human-resources questions, we have been averse to two-valued logic; its boundaries are simply too constraining, too obscuring, and (to make our values explicit) grotesquely unfair to the great mass of citizen-workers. To pretend that millions of employees can ultimately be treated far better than they are while consigning them conceptually—i.e., by definition—to a different category from employers, by a taxonomy drawn from the laws of property and from Darwin, may be likened to the errors that would result in a laboratory if the magic of preliterate cultures were confused with Newtonian mechanics (a confusion that never, certainly, occurred to Claude Lévi-Strauss while writing a book which, its frightening title notwithstanding, is an admiring statement of the nature of the savage mind).[7]

GRIEVANCES REVISITED

Some readers will recall from Chapter 10 that there have already appeared in arbitration awards some signs of the gross differences between the ways we view employers and employees in America. Our own reading of these holdings led us to pursue the matter, the better to determine whether there are suggestions, at least, that the two-valued logic, employed in the present instance by arbitrators, has consequential implications for workplace reforms.

Our reasoning was as follows: work reforms are urged by enthusiasts who assume that the obstacles to change inhere in the motives of workers, workers' representatives, and managers, not in the webs or structures of the institutionalized roles in which they are incumbents. The parties to employment relationships, according to this logic, are far freer to act in novel ways than they do but for the encumbrances that therapeutic, cure-oriented programs are designed to dissipate; it is not *necessary* that those who play critical economic and workplace roles perform in only stereotyped ways.

If, as we believe, arbitrators have legally defined roles as institution builders, then we should be able to identify, through a careful reading of their awards and holdings, the structures of the institutions they help to build. Next, we should be able to infer the restrictions and the freedoms of workers that flow from the efforts of these legally licensed social architects. Finally, we should be able to compare these constraints and allowances with those that flow from the more social-psychological perspectives of interventionists. As it turns out, workers may be likened to Linden's animals; our "cure orientations" help in "perpetuating the assumption" that workers are "different," not so much in actual fact as "in the way we look at" them.

MANAGERS' AND WORKERS' ROLES

Arbitrators, we have implied, have an immanent public role as well as the narrower professional one inherent in their dealings with their contesting clients. The "Trilogy" decision mentioned in Chapter 10 said as much in elevating arbitration to a position of sociolegal significance. If there were any doubts on the matter, they were demolished by the later decision of the Court in the *Gateway Coal* case.[8] While Justice Douglas, the champion of arbitration in the earlier cases, dissented in *Gateway*, the Court held against workers' rights to strike and in favor of arbitration (and the Gateway Coal Company) over the alleged falsification of mine records dealing with the adequacy of air flow into a deep mine.

Critics of the decision, including Justice Douglas, have argued that arbitration in health and safety matters would impede the enforcement of relevant laws, "since an arbiter is not bound to apply the law but rather the collective bargaining agreement [and] an incorrect arbitration award [by a nonexpert] based on an erroneous interpretation of relevant statutes or the exclusive consideration of the contract may result in serious injury or loss of life."[9] Further, as Justice Douglas pointed out in his dissent, "An Arbiter seeks a compromise, an adjustment, an accommodation. There is no mandate in arbitration to apply a specific law."[10] Judge Hastie, in his majority opinion from the lower (Third Circuit) court, stated:

> Considerations of economic peace that favor arbitration of ordinary disputes have little weight here. Men are not wont to submit matters of life or death to arbitration and no enlightened society encourages, much less

requires, them to do so. If employees believe that correctible circumstances are unnecessarily adding to normal dangers of their hazardous employment, there is no sound reason for requiring them to subordinate their judgment to that of an arbitrator however impartial he may be. The arbitrator is not staking his life on his impartial decision. It should not be the policy of laws to stake theirs on his.[11]

Until the Congress speaks differently to the questions involved, Justice Powell's majority opinion in *Gateway* has promoted arbitrators to policy levels in America, a fact that makes their awards and accompanying observations more important than even the "Trilogy" decision would have suggested.

It is well to keep this public-interest role of arbitrators clearly in mind in examining the differences in the *assertions* by arbitrators about what managers "should" and "ought" to be and do and *descriptions* of what managers in fact have done, that have been coded from their awards and tabulated in the tables in this chapter.

Readers will recall the damaging logic by which arbitrators found managers culpable in those cases in which the award went to grieving workers. Some readers may indeed be tempted to make much of the ineptitude of managers noted by arbitrators in these cases. We wondered in fact whether arbitrators' holdings were informed by an increasingly generalized hostility toward them born of critical impatience with managerial codes, on one side, and by growing sympathies for "noble" workers, on the other. A close examination of the arbitration materials reveals that arbitrators' criticisms of managers notwithstanding, it is quite the other way around.

Thus we examined a stratified random sample of one-half of all BNA-reported "Discharge, Discipline and Plant Rules" cases that were denied and an equal number of cases in which workers were sustained, with or without qualification, for the years on which we reported in Chapter 10. The sample includes all usable cases under ground rules established to avoid bias: no presiding arbitrator should be duplicated within the same year; no company should be duplicated within the same award category (i.e., "denied," "sustained") within the same year; and the sample should consist of an equal number of cases denied and sustained in each year under study. The samples on which our analysis is based were accordingly distributed as follows: [12]

1953–54:	Denied:	cases = 21; arbitrators = 21
	Sustained:	cases = 21; arbitrators = 21
	Total:	cases = 42; arbitrators = 42
1962–63:	Denied:	cases = 49; arbitrators = 49
	Sustained:	cases = 49; arbitrators = 49
	Total:	cases = 98; arbitrators = 98

1971–72:   Denied: cases = 68; arbitrators = 68
             Sustained: cases = 68; arbitrators = 68
             Total: cases = 136; arbitrators = 136

The content analysis itself is based upon methods suggested by Ralph K. White.[18] Extrapolating from White's personal-value and propaganda definitions to the workplace, following his procedures, and using the "decisions"/"discussion" sections of arbitration awards as the units of analysis, the presence (yes/no) of the following were coded: (1) descriptive references to management and workers and their actions; (2) role-related references to management and workers (i.e., specific references to the effect that "management should . . ."/"workers should . . ."); and (3) general value references (i.e., values mentioned more or less gratuitously and without specific reference to management/worker action or roles).

Table 12.1 shows the consolidated results of coding all the positive and negative statements made by arbitrators about the specific actions of both workers and managers that were received and reported in the cases in our sample. The units in the table are cases sorted by year and subclassified according to whether the ultimate award in a given case went to labor or management. Once again, we have sampled cases from *within* the universe of BNA-reported cases.

Table 12.1 shows that in the three time periods sampled, the percentage of total awards containing positive references to management fluctuated between 74 and 84 percent; the percentage containing positive references to workers increased from 55 percent in the earliest year studied to 62 percent in the two later time periods. The percentage of awards containing negative references to management fluctuated between 60 and 66 percent while the percentage of negative references to workers fluctuated between 88 and 93 percent.

There is an interesting asymmetry in the data. When arbitrators are making judgment calls on managers they tend to be positive about them in cases awarded to them and negative about them in cases awarded to workers. This even-handedness, however, does not extend to their judgments about workers. No matter how cases were decided, negative references to workers always outweigh positive ones: in each of the three time periods, there are more positive references to workers in cases awarded to them than in cases awarded to management, but even here the percent of negative references is greater.

Overall, then, arbitrators evidence noticeably less positive perceptions of labor than of management, and this is so regardless of the merits of the cases upon which they have ultimately made their awards. More detailed analysis suggests that the generally positive and negative views of managers and workers are rooted, respectively, in two entirely

TABLE 12.1. **Positive and Negative References to Management and Worker Action, by Year and Award (Percent of Cases)**

	Year					
	1953–54		1962–63		1971–72	
	Award to:		Award to:		Award to:	
Reference to:	Mgt.	Labor	Mgt.	Labor	Mgt.	Labor
Management Action						
Positive	95.2%	52.4%	95.9%	71.4%	89.7%	66.2%
Negative	42.9	85.7	40.8	91.8	30.9	88.2
Worker Action						
Positive	47.6%	61.9%	53.1%	71.4%	51.5%	72.1%
Negative	90.5	85.7	93.9	91.8	97.1	80.9
N =	(21)	(21)	(49)	(49)	(68)	(68)

different sets of perspectives. Because these two sets are so closely parallel to the different views of workers and managers suggested in our opening chapters they bear closer scrutiny.

WORKERS AND MANAGERS: TWO PERSPECTIVES

According to Table 12.2, over the years arbitrators made the largest number of positive statements concerning management's "generosity," which, in the present context, refers largely to management's giving knowledge, instructions, and warning.

Second, awards have tended to refer to management's justness and fairness; since this reference is closely associated with awards in favor of management, it may be to a large extent an artifact of arbitrators' needs to identify a rationale for sustaining managers' positions. Third in order of frequency, arbitrators have referred positively to managers' decisiveness and firmness, and, fourth, to their carefulness and self-control. There were also a few favorable mentions of managers' trustworthiness and reliability; their attentiveness to and consistency in respect to the applicability of past practices, rules, the grievance procedure, the labor-management agreement, law, etc.; and their intelligence (e.g., evidences of logic and objectivity).

Compared with the base period, there appears to be a growing tendency on the part of arbitrators to refer positively to managers' giving knowledge, instructions, and warnings, and to their being decisive and firm. Not only have such positive references increased noticeably, but, whereas in the earliest period they were more likely to appear in awards in favor of management, these favorable qualities are increasingly likely to be imputed to managers in cases awarded to workers as well.

A similar shift in perceptions appears to have taken place in regard to managers' decisiveness and firmness; whereas, in the earliest time period, positive references to these traits were most likely to appear in awards in favor of management, they were quite likely later to appear in awards in favor of both management and labor; indeed they were more likely to appear in *both* types of cases in the latter than in the former periods.

On the negative side, arbitrators were likely to suggest, in awards to workers, that managers were *not* just or fair; that they did *not* give knowledge, instructions, warnings; that they were in general ungenerous, given to wavering and indecisiveness; that they were uncontrolled, careless, or inclined to violate established practices, rules, grievance prodcedures, the contract, the law, etc. Compared with the base period,

TABLE 12.2. Categories of Positive and Negative References to Management Action, by Year and Award (Percent of Cases)

	Year					
	1953–54		1962–63		1971–72	
	Award to:		Award to:		Award to:	
Reference	Mgt. (N = 21)	Labor (N = 21)	Mgt. (N = 49)	Labor (N = 49)	Mgt. (N = 68)	Labor (N = 68)
Positive						
Generous	42.9%	23.8%	73.5%	40.8%	66.2%	52.9%
Just, Fair	81.0	14.3	59.2	12.2	57.4	17.6
Decisive, Firm	23.8	4.8	32.7	22.4	19.1	22.1
Careful	38.1	4.8	22.4	4.1	25.0	8.8
Trustworthy	9.5	—	14.3	14.3	13.2	5.9
Obedient[a]	14.3	4.8	14.3	10.2	5.9	2.9
Intelligent	14.3	4.8	14.3	10.2	5.9	2.9
Total:						
Any Positive	95.2	52.4	95.9	71.4	89.7	66.2
Negative						
Not Generous	14.3%	23.8%	20.4%	28.6%	5.9%	27.9%
Not Just, Fair	19.0	66.7	4.1	67.3	5.9	61.8
Not Decisive, Firm	4.8	4.8	4.1	14.3	10.3	20.6
Not Careful	—	28.6	4.1	18.4	4.4	25.0
Not Trustworthy	4.8	19.0	—	4.1	—	10.3
Not Obedient	9.5	38.1	10.2	28.6	7.4	20.6
Not Intelligent	14.3	52.4	8.2	36.7	8.8	39.7
Total:						
Any Negative	42.9	85.7	40.8	91.8	30.9	88.2

[a] E.g., obedient to past practice, rules, law, etc.

an increasing percentage of arbitrators referred to managers' lack of decisiveness and firmness while a decreasing percentage referred to managers' injustice, unfairness, violations of past practice, rules, etc., and to their acting unintelligently.

Together, the substance of positive and negative references to management reveal heightened attention by arbitrators to such managerial functions as imparting information, instructions, and warnings, and to such managerial traits as decisiveness and firmness. There is some diminution, in arbitrators' perceptions at least, in justice, fairness, intelligence and attentiveness to procedural forms among managers.

The positive and negative references to workers are of a qualitatively different order (Table 12.3). On the positive side, workers historically have been referred to in terms of their being appropriately "at work," "working," "achievers," or "working well," traits to which approximately one-third of all arbitrators make references. Workers have also been referred to in more positive terms, though in a far smaller percentage of cases, as being trustworthy, reliable, truthful, or intelligent (e.g., evidencing logic or objectivity in their actions).

On the negative side, workers have been seen to be disobedient, a flaw to which references are made in from a third to nearly two-thirds of all cases. They are also characterized in terms of absenteeism; whether they are not working or not working well or competently; whether they are trustworthy, reliable, or truthful; whether they are careful or self-controlled; whether they are intolerant (e.g., harboring ill will or anger); and whether they are friendly and cooperative with management.

One may reasonably infer from all this that arbitrators' assumptions concerning American managers have to do primarily with their sense of justice and fairness; with whether they give instructions, information, and provide fair warnings; and whether they are decisive and firm. One may as well infer that our value expectations or background assumptions in America concerning workers, as reflected in these awards, have to do primarily with the realms of obedience, loyalty, work performance, and competence; trustworthiness and reliability, truthfulness, carefulness, and self-control; intelligence; and tolerance, or perhaps better, toleration. One may also infer that arbitrators tend increasingly to focus upon worker obedience.

The essential trend over the periods examined, then, clearly illustrates an increase in concerns about the maintenance of relationships of superordination and subordination between workers and managers in the most literal of the senses implied in the treatment of the subject by Max Weber. Where one of the authors, in company with Eli Ginzberg, could report evidence of "the reach of democracy" in a study of arbitration cases in the early 1960s, we here see evidence—to mix

TABLE 12.3. Categories of Positive and Negative References to Worker Action, by Year and Award (Percent of Cases)

	Year					
	1953–54		1962–63		1971–72	
	Award to:		Award to:		Award to:	
Reference	Mgt. (N = 21)	Labor (N = 21)	Mgt. (N = 49)	Labor (N = 49)	Mgt. (N = 68)	Labor (N = 68)
Positive						
Work/Work Well	19.0%	52.4%	32.7%	38.8%	23.5%	45.6%
Trustworthy	4.8	9.5	10.2	18.4	4.4	16.2
Achievers	14.3	9.5	18.4	4.1	8.8	13.2
Intelligent	—	14.3	16.3	16.3	8.8	7.4
Friendly/Cooperative with Management	4.8	4.8	10.2	10.2	5.9	7.4
Total: Any Positive	47.6	61.9	53.1	71.4	51.5	72.1
Negative						
Not Obedient	42.9%	28.6%	71.4%	53.1%	60.3%	47.1%
Don't Work	42.9	42.9	59.2	36.7	48.5	30.9
Not Trustworthy	42.9	9.5	26.5	12.2	45.6	19.1
Not Careful	28.6	19.0	24.5	30.6	20.6	26.5
Not Intelligent	28.6	14.3	36.7	12.2	32.4	10.3
Not Tolerant	14.3	14.3	12.2	30.6	10.3	10.3
Not Cooperative with Management	23.8	9.5	24.5	18.4	10.3	11.8
Not Mannerly	9.5	—	8.2	22.4	8.8	8.8
Physically Aggressive	4.8	9.5	4.1	16.3	2.9	8.8
Not in Good Health	9.5	19.0	10.2	14.3	8.8	10.3
Total: Any Negative	90.5	85.7	93.9	91.8	97.1	80.9

clichés—either that workers are hoist with their own petards or that their reach has exceeded their grasp. Such, at least, are the images conjured up by arbitrators' highly differentiated views of their worker and manager clients.

The point may be pursued considerably further. Consider the normative statements made by arbitrators about the parties. Where the data presented above refer to the reasons adduced by arbitrators for their awards and to their immediate, if differentiated, reactions to the deportment of the parties, it is possible by analyzing the *obiter dicta* to identify the roles attributed to the parties. One is tempted to call them *arbiter dicta*, in order to distinguish arbitrator cases from full-fledged law cases. The fact is, however, that the courts have invested heavily in arbitration.

Arbitrators are involved now in work that is strongly affected with a public interest; it is no longer far removed from the law. Like judges, they make no bones about how the roles of the antagonists should be characterized in more or less legal terms. The *obiter dicta* combined with the rationales of the awards themselves provide an indication of values regarding manager and worker behavior, as it is and as it ought to be, in the perspectives of arbitrators. These may be summarized as follows:

Management is commended by arbitrators for being and are encouraged further to be—

1. just and fair (overall decrease in "mentions" by arbitrators from the base period)

2. "generous" in giving knowledge, information, warnings, and other things (overall increase over the base period)

3. dominant (historically relatively high)

4. decisive and firm (overall increase over the base period)

5. intelligent (steady historical decline)

6. careful and self-controlled (historically relatively high)

7. obedient to rules, etc. (noticeable decrease from the first two time periods studied)

8. trustworthy, reliable, truthful (noticeable decrease from the first two time periods studied)

9. friendly and cooperative toward workers (noticeable decrease from the first two time periods studied)

Workers are commended by arbitrators for being and are encouraged further to be—

1. at work, working well (historically high)

2. obedient (noticeable overall increase over the base period)

3. trustworthy, reliable, truthful (historically relatively high, slight decrease from the base period)

4. careful and self-controlled (historically relatively high)

5. intelligent (historically relatively high)

6. friendly, cooperative with management (historically relatively high)

7. tolerant (overall increase over the base period)

CONCLUSIONS

The sum of the findings in this section, when juxtaposed with the awards themselves (see Chapter 10) and the views of arbitrators regarding the facts in the cases conceived to be dispositive, may be stated as follows: (1) managers are greatly concerned about the authority to manage the enterprise with a minimum of worker misbehavior, a judgment in which arbitrators join; (2) managers tend to be quick on the trigger in efforts to secure employee obedience; (3) neither managers nor arbitrators, so far as we can determine from extensive clinical evidence [14] are even slightly less concerned about worker responsiveness and obedience today than over the past twenty-year period; (4) managers, in their eagerness to secure themselves and their operations against what they regard as untoward worker conduct, rarely come before ideologically hostile third-party arbitrators; they tend to enjoy the benefits of arbitrators' logics regarding managers' and workers' roles and appear to lose the cases awarded to worker grievants only when they have been deplorably poor managers.

We see nothing in these arbitration materials suggesting that managers are contending with new and insoluble problems. We see even less that would suggest a promising role for interventions of the type commended by enthusiastic workplace reformers. Heavy-handed and occasionally stupid leadership is not likely to yield to the various therapies prescribed. More importantly, abiding concerns with management's rights, managerial authority, and the responsive subordination of democratic citizens are unlikely to be diluted in solutions generally labeled "worker participation" in the intervention literature. Like strike activity, grievances by workers are part and parcel of collective bargaining. And collective bargaining *is* an important form of "worker participation," however reluctant many work reformers are to concede the fact.

The argument, finally, that arbitration cases really involve supervisors at lower levels and not managers, and that when an employer loses arbitration cases it is because of the defects of underlings, will be attractive to few intelligent Americans and compelling to none. Obviously one may sympathize with adroit and sensible managers who must contend with ineffective help. Even champions of the working class among intellectuals have been heard to rant like angry lunatics over the performance of, for example, their clerical co-workers. But it would ill serve good, able, intelligent, technically competent managers who deserve a measure of worker loyalty to ignore their responsibilities in the "chains of their commands"; good managers, moreover, probably emphasize competent command, not the chains, in their use of the familiar expression.

In the next chapter we consider briefly the loyalty issue itself, an issue that is generally explored only in respect to employees. We will suggest that employers may, by objective standards, be disloyal to employees, even as workers absent themselves from and quit their jobs. The fact is that most of us in America see significant elements of worker disloyalty in the limited data available on absenteeism and turnover; our two-valued logic leads us, again, not only to condone somewhat comparable behavior by managers but, in many instances, to encourage what in their employees we deplore.

13. Exit, Voice, and Loyalty

The evidence adduced in Chapters 11 and 12 suggests that would-be work reformers have overlooked the two-valued character of their diagnostic model of workers and managers. Where in Part III the prescriptions of reformers could be challenged on theoretical and empirical grounds, in these chapters they were questioned on logical grounds.

First, the evidence does not suggest that the conflicts managers perceive to exist between their interests in the maintenance of their authority and their employees' interests in equity and due process may be usefully reduced, in logical terms, in accordance with a psychological calculus; the conflicts may not, that is, be reduced to questions of deep-seated motives.

Second, the evidence from follow-up studies of innovations indicates far less clearly than reformers would have us believe that corporate clients will act systematically on the opportunities to deal even with the workplace problems that most probably lie within their purview. Employers apparently do not agree that the gains from applications of reformers' plans and experiments compare favorably with those to be achieved by the very traditional management styles that are often scathingly criticized by workplace "humanizers." The fears of managers in unorganized firms that their workers will join unions adds a little to their interest in reforms, but the interest is rarely translated into efforts of the magnitude commended by reformers.

Third, the evidence strongly suggests that reformers confuse, in the fashion of what psychologists call the mote—beam mechanism, the specks in workers' eyes with the rather larger splinters in their own and managers' eyes.

In this chapter we pursue further the question of whether the differentiated views applied to workers and managers may not be pushed too far and, thereby, to the disadvantage of more sensible, practical and realistic views.

ABSENTEEISM AND VOLUNTARY QUITS

In 1970, Albert O. Hirschman pondered the uses of "voice" and "exit," respectively, as modes of handling sundry dissatisfactions in many types of marketplace. After developing a line of analysis stressing the virtues of "voice," Hirschman urges that economists in particular, and social scientists in general, attend to the benefits in facilitating more "voice" at the expense of "exit." [1] The thesis is that it is better to work within social systems for reform than to quit them.

Hirschman's ideas have particular applications to strike behavior and absenteeism (both forms of "voice") and to employee "quits" (a form of "exit"). While neither Hirschman nor others would treat all strikes, absences, and quits as the result of work dissatisfactions, it is clear that employers and others are concerned with the costs of both excessive absenteeism and "dysfunctional" turnover—i.e., employee turnover above and beyond the (highly variable) number that individual managers regard to be necessary for an enterprise's vitality.

Over the years, concern about turnover and quit rates has varied in intensity. In the 1950s the growth of pension and benefit plans gave rise to a fear in some quarters of a "new industrial feudalism" [2] that might be responsible for an observed decline in the quit rate. Optimum allocation of manpower, in conventional economic theory, requires voluntary mobility; a declining trend in the quit rate may therefore reflect "a growing sclerosis in labor market adjustments." [3]

Studies of this phenomenon have led researchers to a variety of conclusions in the search for potentially revealing correlates of quit-rate variations. Pencavel, for example, came to what he termed a "timid" conclusion:

> There does appear to be limited evidence supporting the thesis that growing wage supplements have contributed to the decline in the quit rate, but this is far from being a complete explanation, and changes in the industrial and demographic composition of the manufacturing work force are at least of equal importance. [4]

Pencavel used data for the decade 1953–1962; in 1965–66 the quit rate took an upward turn, but even before that some attention was being paid to worker dissatisfaction as a causal factor. [5] The typical study of quit rates (or other aspects of turnover) is based on monthly data for manufacturing industries published by the Bureau of Labor Statistics in *Employment and Earnings*. There is actually very little reason to believe that global measures of job satisfaction and industry quit rates, uncontrolled for occupation, would show much relationship. The crude

TABLE 13.1. Mining and Manufacturing Industries,[a] Ranked by Percent Very Satisfied with Job, 1969, with Quit Rates per 100 Workers, 1969.

Industry	Percent Very Satisfied	Quit Rate
Stone, Clay, Glass, Concrete	56%	2.2
Primary Metals	53	1.5
Printing and Publishing	50	1.9
Electrical Machinery	50	1.8
Fabricated Metal Products	48	2.3
Mining	46	2.5
Food and Kindred Products	46	3.2
Transportation Equipment	42	1.3
Miscellaneous	41	2.8
Chemicals	36	1.0
Furniture and Fixtures	36	3.4
Lumber Products except Furniture	33	3.1
Paper and Allied Products	33	2.0
Machinery, except Electrical	31	1.3
Apparel	25	2.5
Leather Products	23	3.2
Rubber and Plastics	20	2.7

[a] Instruments and Related Products, Tobacco, Textile Mill Products, and Petroleum are omitted; WCS sample size insufficient.

Source: Job satisfaction data from *Working Conditions Survey* (late 1969). Quit rates for November 1969 from *Employment and Earnings* 16 (February 1970), Table D-2, pp. 160–164.

exercise in juxtaposition in Table 13.1 suggests—ecological fallacies aside—that these measures seem to vary independently.

Under different economic conditions workers will be differentially inclined to leave the labor force, to accept another job, or to search for another job. The relative proportions of quits for these reasons may also be expected to vary according to interindustry differences in wages, demographic distributions, typical length of tenure, secular trends, and cyclical and seasonal variations in employment.[6]

It seems reasonable to believe that in good times quit rates will be higher as workers seek to maximize their advantages, and in fact the business cycle has a "ubiquitous effect." [7] But Flanagan, Strauss, and Ulman found that

when the influence of changes in relative hours, relative earnings rates, and the age, sex, and racial composition of the work force over the 1958–1972 period is controlled . . . we find that the quit rate *declines* at the rate of .01 per quarter (.04 per year), indicating that the positive trend in quits observed in the simple cyclical models . . . is an artifact of movement in the other variables.[8]

In an interindustry comparison, Flanagan *et al.* put particular stress on the demographic composition of the work force. It is and has long been a fact that young workers quit their jobs more frequently than older workers. For some observers this behavior, together with absenteeism, is a sign of youths' disloyalty toward duly constituted authority and their undisciplined contempt for and utopian dreams about "the system," as it is and as it could be, respectively.

Such an interpretation is hard to support, however, since young workers have always been more prone than their older co-workers to change jobs. Their so-called job-shopping tendencies are just that: they move about in search of the more stable types of employment typically allocated to mature white males. While a formal labor market in the European tradition does not exist in the United States, our young workers are clustered in temporary, low-paying, dead-end jobs; the only way they can improve their positions—an aim entirely in accord with widely held values incidentally—is to move on.

It is a tenable hypothesis that younger workers in America "remain young" longer nowadays. Such an inference may be readily drawn from data on rising average age at first marriage and the average age of parents of firstborn children; young people otherwise behave in the labor market now pretty much as they did in earlier times.[9] The labor-market option to change jobs that goes with freedom from family obligations may simply be the valued property of larger numbers of workers for longer periods in the life cycle, a possibility reflected in aggregated data on quits. Such workers can practice both "voice" and "exit" reactions without devastating effects on their families during periods in which labor markets are tight and with relatively fewer problematic consequences when markets are loose. Occupational maturity may be said to vary, sociologically speaking, with the business cycle. When times are good—and especially if the entering cohort is small—workers may become established in jobs at an earlier age than if, as in the 1970s, unemployment is high and the number of young workers is unusually large.

The labor-market behavior of women and minorities is not quite so readily or parsimoniously understood. The members of these groups have been disproportionately allocated—or relegated—to the least stable segments of the labor market and to jobs where turnover is the expected rather than the unusual event. In viewing the upward secular trend of the quit rate in the mid-1960s, perhaps the most important point is that these types of jobs increased at a faster rate than did jobs with better prospects for establishment.[10]

But whether one focuses on the supply side or on the demand side, industry data on quits and satisfaction do not yield much insight. On an individual-firm basis, however, when occupational structure and organizational features are controlled, the influence of micro working conditions on quit behavior may emerge. A Princeton study of the Trenton labor market found that small, well-managed firms were able to hold on to their workers in a period of great expansion during the early 1950s.[11] A questionnaire study of workers in ten shops in an aerospace plant was conducted in the 1960s,[12] presumably when the economic climate was favorable to those seeking "exit." The survey-type items were cast in equity terms; that is, they were explicitly comparative: "My supervisor expresses the same appreciation to me when I do a job as to others in the group who do the same work." There were significant differences between the low-turnover and high-turnover shops in responses to items on pay, supervision, security, advancement, working conditions, and both "intrinsic" and "social" aspects of the job.

> The findings suggest that when an employee perceives inequitable treatment, he will feel frustrated and he will not contribute his best efforts toward the management-perceived primary goals of the organization. If the inequity is excessive, he will actually separate himself from the organization.[13]

ABSENTEEISM

If quit behavior is not easily analyzed and conclusions about it must needs be fuzzy, the matter of absenteeism is downright obscure. Judging from the tone in which it is discussed in the popular press it is a matter of great concern to managers but is in general a poorly understood phenomenon. A meeting of "experts" called by the Organisation for Economic Cooperation and Development concluded that—apart from evidence that absenteeism was on the rise in European countries— there were no data worthy of serious consideration and very few attempts to come to terms with the problem.[14] Our own informal interviews uncovered a consensus that absenteeism was much higher in Western Europe than in the United States, a conclusion bolstered by the willingness (and in some cases eagerness) with which European managers have gone into business in the United States (see Chapter 14).

Recent surveys in the United States have shown no increase in absenteeism from 1972 to 1974. Unlike the quit rate, absenteeism data show no evidence of a cyclical relationship. It is noteworthy that workers under twenty-five have a rate of *full-week* absence about half that of workers over forty-five, but their *part-week* absence rate is higher.[15]

Hedges suggests that young workers are substituting part-week absence for the paid vacation time that their low seniority obviates.[16] She does not speculate about the older workers, but it seems clear that chronic illness may play a part in their greater tendency to full-week absence.

Flanagan *et al.* found that absence rates tend to be higher in industries in which the weekly hours of work, percent female, and percent nonwhite are relatively high. In their regression equation, the coefficient of the relative-hours variable implies that an industry with an hours-of-work schedule 9 percent higher than the average for manufacturing would have an absence rate one percentage point higher than the manufacturing average, all other things being equal. The coefficients also imply that a 1 percent increase in the proportion of the work force that is nonwhite will have twice the impact on the absence rate of the same increase in the proportion female. In either case, however, the impact is small: the proportion of nonwhite workers would have to increase by over 10 percent to raise the absence rate by 1 percentage point. Workers in high-wage industries appear to quit less frequently but are at least as prone as workers in lower-paying industries to be absent.[17]

We doubt that it is possible persuasively to differentiate the causes of absenteeism. The summary data embody different proportions of dissatisfaction, disability, and the increasingly complex demands of everyday life, but the precise weights may be impossible to calculate at present. Where the strain of the work activity is palpable, as in the much-maligned assembly-line case, it may well be that high absenteeism is, in the words of the OECD *rapporteur*, the "brake which intervenes before maladjustment and exhaustion." [18] Furthermore, there have certainly been changed definitions of sickness: "In the past, you were said to be sick when you couldn't stand up any longer." [19] Nowadays, if the employer provides only a few or no sick days, workers who do not feel well will stay home, even with a pay loss, and may indeed be well advised in the event.

One of the factors in absenteeism, however, is less seldom the subject of commentary. Thus, personal business in advanced industrial societies takes up a great deal of time—one must deal with institutions, arrange for repairs of durable goods, obtain health care, etc. Especially if all the adults in a household are working, someone has to be absent from work to attend to these chores. When the operation of the society requires more free time, usually spent in activities that are free only in the nominal sense, then people will take this time. And, although employers may fume about the fact, they schedule work and pass on the incidental costs in resigned acceptance to the way things are. It is perhaps not surprising that women have historically been more prone to absenteeism; their jobs are usually less well paid than the men to whom they are related, and, like good maximizers, they take the time off since the loss to family income is less.

MANAGERIAL EXITS

On management's side, there is evidence of exit behavior as well. This behavior is not generally considered in juxtaposition to that reflected in the quit rates of workers, although the effects of managers' exits on workers can be more appalling than the effects of workers' exits on managers.

Thus, Sidney Cobb and Lawrence Hinkle, physicians at the University of Michigan and at Cornell, respectively, have investigated the physical and emotional ills of victims of layoffs and plant shutdowns; Alfred Slote has documented, in case-study fashion, the detailed reactions and experiences of nearly thirty employees and their families who were among the more numerous victims of an auto–plant shutdown.[20] Slote tells of ex-employees' anxieties, illnesses, and psychological breakdowns. One contributing element is a consequence of the short notice that is often involved.

Consider Tables 13.2 and 13.3, from a 1964 survey of manufacturing

TABLE 13.2.   Notice Given When Employee is Discharged for Circumstances Beyond His Control

	Percent of Companies		
Notice Time Given	Blue-Collar Employees Only	White-Collar Employees Only	Both Blue- and White-Collar Employees
None	16%	6%	6%
1 day	9	a	1
2 days	8	–	2
3 days	18	–	2
5 days (1 week)	36	9	20
10 days (2 weeks)	9	59	21
15 days (3 weeks)	–	7	a
30 days (1 month)	a	15	3
Varies, no set practice	2	3	45
Total	100%	100%	100%
N =	(110)	(110)	(316)

a Less than 1 percent.

Source: *Personnel Practices in Factory and Office: Manufacturing*, Studies in Personnel Policies, no. 194 (New York: National Industrial Conference Board, 1964), p. 139.

TABLE 13.3.   Notice Given When Employee is Laid Off for Any Reason

Notice Time Given	Percent of Companies		
	Blue-Collar Employees Only	White-Collar Employees Only	Both Blue- and White-Collar Employees
None	13%	9%	12%
1 day	14	2	5
2 days	18	2	5
3 days	31	a	10
4 days	a	—	a
5 days (1 week)	18	32	31
10 days (2 weeks)	2	44	8
15 days (3 weeks)	—	5	2
30 days (1 month)	—	2	—
Varies; no set practice	3	5	27
Total	100%	100%	100%
N =	(131)	(131)	(295)

a Less than 1 percent.

Source: *Personnel Practices in Factory and Office: Manufacturing*, Studies in Personnel Policies, no. 194 (New York: National Industrial Conference Board, 1964), p. 139.

companies by the National Industrial Conference Board. Table 13.2 shows that blue-collar workers in 87 percent of 110 cases received five days' notice or less about discharge, and only three days' notice about layoff in 76 percent of 131 cases; these cases overlap substantially with those of 185 companies in which 72 percent of employers require five or more days' notice from workers who intend to resign from their jobs. Meanwhile 87 percent of 508 surveyed employers send flowers when a worker dies, but only 27 percent of 427 employers have severance-pay programs for both blue-collar and white-collar workers; 19 percent have such programs for white-collar workers only.

The managers in these instances are presumed to behave in accordance with sound economic principles, not whimsically, as are the managers whose bankruptcy cases "filed and pending" in the period 1905–1973 are reported in Table 13.4. Employees also suffer when managers walk or are pushed through the exit door, as were employees of the firms that failed in 1974 (Table 13.5). The objection that failure occurs for reasons unconnected with managerial acumen and that the exits of managers are not fairly juxtaposed with those of lazy or otherwise undependable employees gains little force from a listing of the causes of failure (Table 13.6).

TABLE 13.4. Bankruptcy Cases Filed and Pending: 1905 to 1973 (In thousands)

Year	Filed	Pending	Year	Filed	Pending
1905	17	28	1961	147	124
1910	18	25	1962	148	134
1915	28	44	1963	155	148
1920	14	30	1964	172	157
1925	46	60	1965	180	162
1930	63	61	1966	192	169
1935	69	65	1967	208	185
1940	52	55	1968	198	184
1945	13	21	1969	185	179
1950	33	38	1970	194	191
1955	59	56	1971	201	201
1960	110	95	1972	183	197
			1973	173	189

Source: U.S. Bureau of the Census, *Statistical Abstract of the United States, 1975* (Washington, D.C.: U.S. Government Printing Office, 1976), Table 815, p. 493.

TABLE 13.5. Commercial and Industrial Failures, with Estimated Associated Employment, 1974

Industry	Number	Liabilities (000)	Estimated Employment
Mining and Manufacturing			
Mining: Coal, Oil, Misc.	9	$ 10,102	3,375
Food and Kindred Products	100	65,429	15,000
Textile Mill Products and Apparel	301	230,823	45,150
Lumber and Lumber Products	202	113,510	15,150
Paper, Printing, and Publishing	195	63,998	29,250
Chemicals and Allied Products	39	8,720	14,625
Leather and Leather Products	34	11,554	12,750
Stone, Clay, and Glass Products	50	25,506	7,500
Metals, Primary and Fabricated	109	39,914	54,500
Machinery	228	141,870	114,000
Transportation Equipment	83	62,936	41,500
Miscellaneous	207	59,462	77,625
Total Mining and Manufacturing	1,557	833,824	430,425
Wholesale Trade	964	274,893	73,800
Retail Trade	4,234	1,069,656	156,393
Construction	1,840	526,598	64,400
Commercial Service	1,320	348,166	30,000
Total	9,915	$3,053,137	755,018

Source: Dun and Bradstreet, *The Failure Record, 1974.* Employment estimated from median establishment size, U.S. Bureau of the Census, *County Business Patterns, 1972* (Washington, D.C.: U.S. Government Printing Office, 1973), Table 1C, p. 29.

TABLE 13.6.   Causes of 9,915 Business Failures in 1974, Percentage Distribution by Industry

Underlying Causes	Manufacturers	Wholesalers	Retailers	Construction	Commercial Services	All
Neglect	2.3%	1.2%	1.6%	2.4%	1.7%	1.9%
Fraud	0.4	1.8	0.9	0.7	1.0	0.9
Lack of Experience in the Line	14.6	13.7	18.3	11.5	15.5	15.6
Lack of Management Experience	12.0	10.8	13.9	16.9	15.9	14.1
Unbalanced Experience	19.3	22.7	22.9	23.9	21.5	22.3
Incompetence	48.6	46.3	37.6	40.3	38.3	40.7
Disaster	1.1	0.8	1.1	0.5	0.6	0.9
Reason Unknown	1.7	2.7	3.7	3.8	5.5	3.6
Total	100.0%	100.0%	100.0%	100.0%	100.0%	100.0%
Number of Failures	1,557	964	4,234	1,840	1,320	9,915
Average Liabilities Per Failure	$835,532	$285,159	$252,635	$286,195	$263,762	$307,931

Source: Dun and Bradstreet, *The Business Failure Record, 1974*, pp. 12–13.

There are, in addition to failures, of course, the often disruptive and almost always disequilibrating effects on employees of mergers and acquisitions, after which whole new personnel and related systems are introduced into the lives of employees. While the dust may settle in due course, it was our experience in interviews with middle managers and employees at two "acquired" plants in Grand Haven, Michigan, that there are many more highly problematic than moderately happy outcomes for workers whose companies had been the objects or victims of takeover. Table 13.7 tells the story for 1972, a not terribly active merger year. The estimates of workers affected are conservative; insofar as acquisitions are more numerous among the *larger* firms, a midpoint esti-

TABLE 13.7. **Acquisitions and Mergers, 1972, with Estimate of Workers Affected**

Acquired Companies		Median Establishment Size		Estimate, Number of Workers Affected
Industry	Number		Midpoint	
Food and Kindred Products	67	100–249	175	11,725
Textile Mill Products	15	250–499	375	5,625
Apparel	32	100–249	175	5,600
Lumber Products except Furniture	21	50– 99	75	1,575
Furniture and Fixtures	23	100–249	175	4,025
Paper and Allied Products	17	100–249	175	2,975
Printing and Publishing	36	50– 99	75	2,700
Chemicals	46	250–499	375	17,250
Petroleum	5	250–499	375	1,875
Rubber and Plastics	31	250–499	375	11,625
Leather Products	12	100–249	175	2,100
Stone, Clay, Glass	20	100–249	175	3,500
Primary Metals	21	500+	1000	21,000
Fabricated Metal Products	60	100–250	175	10,500
Machinery, except Electrical	81	250–499	375	30,375
Electrical Machinery	77	500+	1000	77,000
Transportation Equipment	33	500+	1000	33,000
Instruments and Related Products	40	500+	1000	40,000
Miscellaneous	30	100–249	175	5,250
Mining	23	100–249	175	4,025
Trade (Wholesale and Retail)	290	20– 49	35	10,150
Services and Others	380	50– 99	75	28,500
Total	1,360			397,360

Source: U.S. Federal Trade Commission, *Statistical Report on Mergers and Acquisitions* (No. 6-15-16) (Washington, D.C.: U.S. Government Printing Office, 1973), Table 3, p. 2; and U.S. Bureau of the Census, *County Business Patterns, 1972*, U.S. Summary (Washington, D.C.: U.S. Government Printing Office, 1973), Table 1C, p. 29.

mate of 1,000 as the average number of employees for these firms may be too low.

The point is not that managers and their principals have no rights in these matters. The point is precisely the opposite. They *do* have rights, to act in accordance with their definitions of their situations, their assessments of their options, and their conceptions of the costs and benefits of the decisions they wish or feel compelled to reach. Our two-valued logic endorses these freedoms, and we, including employees, often applaud the resulting consummations when they work out well.[21]

When they do not work out well, as they often do not for workers, we neither implicitly nor explicitly castigate managers, nor do we pursue intervention programs by change agents calculated to improve managers' performance as rational economic agents. Our logic thus distinguishes quite fastidiously between managers and managed and draws us to cures for the pathologies in the latter group while we seek to draft ever more lenient bankruptcy regulations, to locate subsidies for marginal employers, to lighten the "bureaucratic" regulatory and tax burdens on merger-bound executives, to arrange emergency tariffs for distressed victims of foreign competition, and to pass "Buy American" acts, thereby sparing domestic producers. The number of jobs to be guaranteed by such interventions is never specified, it should be noted, though workers are generally implicated as major beneficiaries by intervention-seeking managers. Unions are not uncommonly directly engaged, or friendly parties to these attempts.

MANAGERS IN AND OUT OF TEXTBOOKS

One explanation for the popularity of this peculiarly two-valued logic derives from the widespread belief that managers are essentially rational economic agents who, with the help of social scientists, can deal with neurotic or misguided employees. A thoroughgoing confrontation of the first half of that thesis is well beyond the authors' ken, as it is well beyond the scope of this volume: this is, after all, not a book about economic theory. We may point out, however, that the evidence supporting the view of rational, efficient managers is at best ambiguous, especially in respect to employer exits and related types of decisions bearing in essential ways upon employees.

Thus Stanley E. Boyle and Philip W. Jaynes, in a staff report to the Federal Trade Commission on mergers, wrote that the results were

> largely of a neutral or negative nature. . . . There is no evidence, for example, that the conglomerates have made many improvements in the operations of acquired firms. . . . The alleged qualities of corporate syner-

gism, if they exist, are not detectable in our data. . . . Our sampled firms have not consistently or substantially expanded market positions. . . . [But] their effects are not entirely neutral. . . . Adverse consequences . . . can best be summarized as those associated with a loss [to owners and prospective owners] of information . . . [because] data relative to these corporations obscure many significant elements of the firms' activities . . . a loss that also obscures the performance of firms.[22]

One does not see much by way of social returns flowing from mergers, then, in exchange for the costs borne by the unsettled victims of take-overs.

It would be difficult indeed to demonstrate an alternative hypothesis, that managers really do care very much about the ways in which human-capital resources are exploited. It is equally difficult to demonstrate that employers act expertly to exploit these human resources effectively. It is in fact easier to be skeptical than to be assured that the view of managers as thoughtful marginal-cost and marginal-revenue calculators is an accurate one.

MANPOWER PLANNING AND UTILIZATION

Faith that managers behave over the long run in accordance with the logic attributed to them either in the conventional wisdom or in our economic models may, like most faiths, be difficult to refute; market forces will, indeed, lead some managers to observe closely the precise intersections of their marginal cost and marginal revenue curves. But, by and large, short-term behavior patterns in large corporations do not conform very closely to the script laid down for managers in textbooks.

Consider the results of three studies of the manpower perspectives of private-sector managers, studies that are critical, by the way, to an understanding of managers' willingness to be passive or negative toward the problem of work in America.

First, Diamond and Bedrosian examined data on ten entry level and "near-entry" level jobs in each of five white-collar and four blue-collar occupations, together with one service occupation, in the New York and St. Louis Standard Metropolitan Statistical Areas (SMSA). Their concern was with the role of employers' hiring standards in the development of labor-market imbalance. Though hiring requirements were quite specific, the authors report, they were unrelated—across the two cities, the fourteen industries, or the twenty companies—to employees' job performance. In only three of the twenty categories were there even slight differences in worker performance attributable to, for example, the educational achievements required by employers. Material differences between hiring standards and real job requirements were, however, as-

sociated with and "appeared to be an important cause of costly turnover in a major segment" of the firms "in virtually all of the twenty
groups." [23]

A second study, by Heneman and Seltzer, was designed to gain a
sense of the approaches to manpower planning and forecasting, and
the techniques applied, by the managers of sixty-nine Minnesota firms
employing 500 or more workers.[24] The results may be considered as
follows:

1. Forecasts of manpower requirements were not undertaken at all
in 50 percent of the firms. Among a fifth of the firms, forecasting efforts
were undertaken for the first time only one year before the study, and
only one third sought to forecast manpower supplies.

2. "Sales" was the only determining factor viewed by the managers of half the firms in which some forecasting was undertaken.

3. About 90 percent of the firms used forecasts for recruiting, but
only one-third related manpower forecasts to budget plans, training,
or transfer and promotion programs; only one-tenth of the firms used
the forecasts in plans for production, space, and facilities. The use of
such forecasts in plans for acquisition and expansion or in product
pricing was reported even less frequently.

4. Twenty percent of the firms were able to produce no employment
data breakdowns; 30 percent had none on separations and hires; 60
percent had none on the ages of their employees.

"In brief," report the investigators, "manpower seemed to be almost
completely isolated from other types of planning." [25]

A third study, targeted upon the deficiencies in national data on
absenteeism noted earlier in this chapter, uncovered substantially the
same shortcomings in the manpower analyses of managers. Thus, Hedges
reports that "fewer than two-fifths of all workers worked in firms
keeping records on absences." [26] This reflects the more remarkable fact
that managers of 60 percent of the 500 manufacturing firms did not
consider unscheduled absences among production workers a "very
serious" or even a "moderate" problem. Fewer than one-seventh of the
500 employers, furthermore, applied such worried expressions to unscheduled absences among their white-collar workers.

These investigations and one by Piore,[27] in which the haphazard
responses to labor-market developments by managers in eighteen manufacturing plants and eleven corporate headquarters are reported, suggest
that manpower issues stand far lower on the agenda of managerial concerns than work-reform enthusiasts would have us believe. The facts
in these studies, moreover, help to explain the developments lamented
by those in social-science ranks who have described the seemingly subversive or, in Walton's usage, regressive developments encountered
by change agents.

The need to take account of the human problems in organizations, urged by behavioral scientists for over forty years, has been well covered by others, especially by the "managerialists" and behaviorists with whom the "marginalists" did battle. It is sufficient here to state that those who aspired over the years to recast the orthodox economists' model of the firm focused on the prepotent roles of unemployment and market imperfections in their assessments of the forces contributing to management nonrationality.[28]

That market imperfections provide managers with very wide margins to make economically uninformed judgments, at least in the short run, is readily seen in data on subcontracting and on plant-location decisions, both of which have significant implications for workers and their families. Thus, Margaret Chandler and Leonard Sayles conducted an examination of decisions to farm out plant-maintenance and construction work and reported that

> complex cost calculations were not employed universally [in determining whether it is cheaper to contract-out or to do the work inside] but rather were limited to about three-fifths of the group. Of the remaining 40 percent, about 30 percent made rough computations, and slightly over 10 percent made absolutely no cost calculations. Surprisingly, the character of the computing system had no relationship to conclusions regarding relative cost. . . . Size of plant seemed to have some relationship to estimates of the relative cost of contracting-out versus in-plant operations. A significant majority of the larger plants considered contracting-out cheaper than inside work.[29]

The evidence suggests that the standards applied to location decisions are often particularly hazy and bear little relation to academic conceptions. Thus, the homes and hobbies of top executives are described by *Business Week* observers and by Leonard Yaseen, head of Fantus Company, a consulting firm specializing in corporate moves, as among the most critical location considerations: "There is very little that can be done," says *Business Week*, to curb the executive with his eye on a specific location. In Yaseen's words:

> The decision-making process is his, and when it comes to moving, his decision is sometimes a very personal thing. . . . Unfortunately, a good many executives react by moving the corporation to somewhere near their own residence or community. It's a very unsatisfactory way of solving their relocation problems.[30]

Business Week cites J. Roger O'Meara, a research specialist of the Conference Board, to the effect that more than half of thirteen major corporations that moved out of New York City from 1968 to 1972 were "influenced" by the chief executive officers' places of residence. He points out, meantime, that

We never have any trouble with choosing a location for a branch plant, because the chief executive isn't personally involved. He treats it very scientifically because he isn't going to have to move to that little town of 26,422 people.[31]

Russel Poylo, head of a relocation service called National Home Settlers, probably understates the consequences of decisions to get closer to top executives' ski lifts, hunting lodges, and trout streams: [32] "People are upset," he reported to *Business Week's* correspondent, "because they think the top six or seven higher-ups have made things a lot more convenient for themselves at the expense of the employees as a whole." [33]

Consider, finally, that the annual turnover rates among 135,000 "truly policy-level executives"—exclusive of retirement—"has risen from close to zero prewar to an estimated 20,000-plus today." This 15 percent figure may be compared with the upper limit of 10 percent placed on *labor* turnover as a prerequisite for successful workplace innovations by reputable work redesigners. "This penchant for job hopping among policy-level managers," according to an expert, "appears to be increasing at a rate of 20 percent annually. And demographic projections indicate such turnover among experienced executives will get worse before it gets better." [34]

CONCLUSION

It is not necessary to argue that managers are simply ignorant, totally self-serving or hopelessly cynical, as the foregoing discussion might mistakenly be taken to imply. Like union leaders who are skeptical of "quick solutions," there are many managers who recognize complexity for what it is and market imperfections for what they are, and who have their eyes open—as high-turnover young workers do—for better jobs and better circumstances otherwise. And as we have been at pains to stress, especially in our discussion of trade-offs, workers are themselves a heterogeneous lot; their interests in job facets form a complicated mosaic.

But the circumstances of employer exits of all kinds are unambiguously relevant to employees, including some managers-as-employees, whose lives are touched significantly if not totally disrupted by the exits of their employers. Our categorical schema, in America, make much of managers' rationality, their roles as superordinates, their rights as property owners' representatives, their needs for residential and other incentives, and so on. These schema clothe managers with a protective shield not unlike the shield some of them enjoy, certainly in the short run, from the pressures of the market, a shield made up of tariffs, subsidies, and the rest.

In the next chapter we compare the constraints upon union leaders with those on managers. There we will note that the logic we apply to union leaders' potential roles in respect to worker satisfactions is more akin to that applied to the men and women they represent than to that applied to those who manage, with equally problematical results. Again, the point is not that managers are wrong and that workers and their representatives are right. It is, rather, that we use different standards in discussing the parties, standards that lead us to absolve one and to attempt to criticize or apply treatments to the other for actions that have more in common than our two-valued logic leads us to recognize. To overlook this aspect of labor-management relations is to reduce one's capacities for comprehending the limits on the prospects for workplace reforms.

PART V

INDUSTRIAL RELATIONS
HERE AND THERE;
PRODUCTIVITY EVERYWHERE

While many questions bearing on the nature of worker dissatisfaction and the prospects for improving worker morale have been left unattended in our investigation, there are two that need to be addressed even in a restricted effort to move toward a "middle-range" coupling of the two main approaches to our subject.

On one side, we have made much out of both the explicit and the implicit misgivings of many human relationists (and many more work-reformers) toward unions, misgivings about which we, in turn, have doubts. Many of the ablest human-relations and interventionist spokesmen, on another side, have identified the resistant inclinations of unions as among the major causes of the failures of reforms. In Chapter 14, accordingly, we conduct a brief discussion of the interests of unions and their members. It is our view that the actions of unions are far too readily maligned and that the roles of unions in the workplace are generally and unhelpfully viewed in accordance with the same two-valued logic discussed in Part IV.

In Chapter 15 we consider a pair of propositions argued lately with considerable fervor, even though the evidence is unclear. The first proposition is that Europeans are well ahead of Americans in combating the social and private costs of workplace discontent; the second is that lessons learned from Western Europe (and Japan) could and should be applied with alacrity by efficiency-minded and humane leaders in American public and private life. A thoroughgoing consideration of the relevant evidence would require an extensive separate study of developments overseas. Still, it is possible to identify a few of the reasons for contesting the presumption that the transfer of foreign achievements, so viewed by their American admirers, would be easy for managers and workers of goodwill.

In Chapter 16, finally, we suggest that the productivity question itself is a far more complicated one than the formulations in work reformers' discussions about workers' performance make evident.

14. Unions and Worker Participation

The current discussion of worker discontent is not about blue-collar dissatisfaction alone. It is, indeed, a novel element in the discussion that considerable attention today is being paid to the so-called woes of white-collar workers, including those of managers.[1]

Still, concern about job-related discontents tends to focus on the blue-collar worker's world. While a few change agents address the strains in the occupational lives of America's officeworkers and middle managers, most attend to the organizational and psychological issues in settings populated by those who wear blue (or, in recent times, gray) collars. The published literature on which we drew in Parts II and III, for example, is largely about blue-collar workers. In this literature the unions to which blue-collar workers belong have been accorded different treatments depending upon the tradition to which investigators and commentators belong. In the industrial-relations and human-resources tradition they have tended to be viewed, as by the eclectics in between, in either neutral or positive terms. But the publications and discussions on "worker participation" point to the conclusion that collective bargaining is consigned to a *residual* and highly problematical category in the mainline, human-relations view of worker discontent.

Put differently, "worker participation," whatever it is meant to denote, is most decidedly *not* meant to refer to collective bargaining. The recognition that employers might well consult with union leaders and urge their collaboration in experimental efforts to redesign work in unionized shops does, of course, appear in a paper here and a book there. But the references to American unions are rare and either unenthusiastic or grudgingly reluctant.[2] In the main, unions are seen as unprogressive agencies led by unrepresentative and backward-looking leaders who are out of touch with the rank-and-file and bent upon preserving the *status quo* for workers and their own positions for themselves.

It is our purpose in this chapter to consider some of the facts relevant to a judgment of whether or not unions and their leaders are as negligent in their representational roles and as conservative and stubborn about work reform as their critics would have us believe.

PARTICIPATION AND WORK RULES

The generally low level of worker involvement in union meetings and union elections is typically taken as evidence that unions do not and cannot represent their members. Periodic investigations of corrupt labor-management practices in a few settings distract attention from the effective implementation of labor-management agreements. Most important, the differentiated interests in wages and fringe benefits, for example, of older and younger, male and female, and white and non-white workers are taken as further evidence of the difficulties facing union leaders, even when they are really interested in representing the rank-and-file.

It is hard to see why some employers and social scientists think that *they* can overcome these differences in interests. They seem to sense opportunities to deal with shared irritations over "meaningless" work, in the apparent hope that the remedies they prescribe will reduce the disparate claims and demands of workers with different attributes.

Union leaders and most workers simply do not view their worlds that way. The *packaged* nature of worker concerns does not emerge from survey questions on such global concepts as "hierarchies of need." What we observe, in the event, is a complex network of worker interests according to their age, sex, race, skill, and seniority, interests that are adjudicated in an unending pattern of trade-offs.

The delicate balance thus achieved is threatened by efforts to enlarge work. Take, for example, the attempt to level the skills among worker groups that is a critical part of many reform prescriptions. The world in which workers live is *stratified*, especially by skill, and the stratification *system* is valued, all other things considered, by those who regard themselves to be in the system's upper levels.[3]

Furthermore, skill differentiations are only a part of the law, customs, and workrules of the shop that workers respect. As James Kuhn, in company with one of the present authors, once wrote:

> . . . work rules are formal and informal arrangements in the shop, sanctioned by custom, tradition, and bargains. They are the oral and written regulations that govern work activities, crew sizes, and job assignments. Work rules set the amount, quality, and manner of work a man must do. They establish the standards by which one can tell how fast is fast, how fair is fair, and how reasonable is reasonable. Most are

mutually beneficial. They allow foremen and workers a necessary and useful degree of flexibility in meeting unforeseen, unpredictable daily work difficulties.

Since most work rules are established through give and take, they can be changed in the same way. Having bargained for work rules, and thus created an "investment" of rights and benefits, workers are but prudent managers of their capital. Work rules are the coin of the bargaining realm; a coin that both managers and workers try to use profitably.[4]

These rules and customs protect systems, systems that have integrity (and, correspondingly, a large measure of legitimacy) because they are the results of bargains to which workers, not just union "reps," are the active and interested parties.

It is one sign of the problems interventionists must face in their endeavors as change agents that these carefully negotiated arrangements are often ignored, deplored, or viewed with suspicion in favor of new arrangements whose potential utilities are unclear.[5] Outside the organized sectors of the economy, we suggest, committees to redesign work in "humanistic" ways *may* be able to do *some* creditable work. While contending with well-developed "interaction systems" [6] in such settings, change agents are not dealing with parties whose contracts with each other call for structural relationships, underwritten by state and federal laws, in which the public has an interest paralleling those of the signatories to labor agreements. As the Supreme Court has pointed out,[7] the public has well-developed interests in minimizing the disruptions caused by overt conflicts among the parties in organized settings when the bargaining machinery breaks down.

In organized shops, furthermore, workers are ever mindful that working conditions are of a piece: the evidence from work rules and other disputes suggests that workers do not separate out the sundry elements, or job facets, of their daily and weekly obligations except for the need to identify the *quids* and *quos* required to make bargains. The "whole" may be dismembered for exchange purposes; a piece here and there may be renegotiated or "sold," to be sure. But the integrity of the whole is rarely obscured in bargaining relationships.

One needs to grasp firmly, as the slogan's devotees only rarely grasp it, the principle that the "quality of working life" involves important questions of distributive justice. Noneconomic improvements in working conditions, of the type emphasized by reformers, are not free goods; rather, they are among the returns to productive efforts and must be netted out by the parties in an accounting scheme in which the costs and benefits of a large number of improvements must be assigned weights.

A union leader bent on work redesign, for example, knows full well that the net costs of any benefits to workers will be paid in the coin of the bargaining realm by hard-headed management negotiators who do not have unlimited funds. Intervention-minded observers typically regard the reluctance of unionists to follow the reformers' urging and break open the "package," the final, inclusive settlement, as only the result of indifference, corruption, stubbornness, short-sightedness, or of other egregiously negative qualities. The inescapable fact, however, is that work reforms with putatively humanitarian consequences will far more often than not simply unsettle a highly structured and carefully constructed, complex agreement in unionized organizations.

The agreement, meantime, is the object of great concern among both workers and managers. Observers are inclined to subsume these agreements under the malignant rubric "status quo." Observers rarely see the status quo—let's call it the social contract—for what it really is: a system of arrangements, procedures, methods and work rules that have been hammered out over time between unions and managers (and, in other sectors, sometimes without unions) involving long lists of bargains and adjustments. These accommodations lead to job classifications and other elements of social and organizational predictability and stability in which both workers and managers have considerable investments, including some that may be vaguely and intractably psychological but which, like other investments, may also be fundamentally and concretely economic in nature.

Among the other virtues these accommodations possess is their utility as grease in the bureaucratic machine, as was noted earlier on, reducing the friction among the moving parts of an organizational apparatus. These accommodations may not be written off by well-intentioned third parties as simply "politics" or the result of "Luddite" attitudes. Not, that is, if one wishes to understand the phenomena one seeks to modify.

It may be added that efficiency and productivity gains are among the ends of managers; they are not the only ends. Nor need efficiency and profitability always stand to each other in a relation of identity. Stability, predictability, and collaboration also rank high among organizational consummations devoutly to be wished.[8] The ways to profit, meanwhile, almost like the peace of God, surpasseth all conventional understanding, a point to which we will return in our concluding chapter.

VALUES AND TECHNIQUES

Beyond emphasizing the psychological or nonlogical resistance of workers, myopic observers misread the realities of work and mislabel their observations. Consider that workers themselves have engaged, individually and in concert, in the "enrichment," "enlargement," and "restructuring" of their work for a very long time. As Mathewson pointed out in 1930, his respondents—managers and workers—spoke "generously" and "unreservedly" about their "restrictive" work practices.[9] Like many modern-day work reformers, Mathewson had great interest in nonunion workers. But he had no difficulty in recognizing work practices as the results of agreements and processes that made their work far more acceptable to employees.

If the practices were restrictive, they were no more restrictive than those of managers who cap oil wells, limit production, or tie up markets. Unlike the moderns, Mathewson made his observations while working as a bench assembler, laborer, machine operator, conveyor assembler, and unskilled mechanic on different shifts in forty-seven different localities and while living with working people in their homes; the objectivity Mathewson possessed does not come as easily to "activist researchers" with personal, short-term economic and professional stakes in the outcomes of their involvement as change agents.

The two-valued nature of the logic underlying the prescriptions of reform enthusiasts is thus discernible in the attribution of positive qualities to the techniques they use and to the work redesigns their techniques suggest. When a consultant reforms work, the results are "humanizing" in their consequences; they may, it is hinted, even lead to productivity increases. When workers and, most typically, their first-line supervisors negotiate to change work practices, however, the results are either overlooked entirely or deplored as resulting in wasteful featherbedding.

Thoughtful study of a great many work rules, however, supports the view that the more spontaneous arrangements are at least as likely as those wrought with the help of work humanizers to facilitate stable production. They may even contribute to productivity increases. Even such notorious cases as those involving the "unnecessary resetting of advertising copy"—the so-called bogus-type rule in the printing trades —and the presence on diesel locomotives of "firemen who tend no fires" have their origins in rational exchanges between workers and managers concerned with job performance and the job benefits that bring them together in the first place, exchanges the terms of which may be renegotiated when they no longer are valued by the parties.[10]

Work reformers are not only inclined to overlook the little adjustments in work tasks, manning arrangements, and work procedures; they also overlook some of the larger efforts along these lines. As James Kuhn recently reminded two work-reform enthusiasts, "It would be a surprise to Thomas Gleason and Anthony Scotto of the east coast Longshoremen or to Harry Bridges and his dockworkers" and to "the trainmen, firemen and engineers who have struggled with massive technological and work changes on the railroads" to learn that unions, as reformers strongly imply, are rarely involved in work restructuring.[11]

The reader may gain a sense of the efforts of some managers and union leaders to reform American workplaces from a review by James Healey and his colleagues of collective-bargaining efforts under problematic, modern conditions in the auto, electrical appliance, airlines, textile, farm equipment, steel, meat-packing, longshoring, and glass container industries.[12] The review supports the view that newspaper headlines about strikes, about corruption in some unions, and about absenteeism in Michigan auto plants are obscuring a much more promising set of developments involving millions of workers and their employers.

Bargaining, to be sure, is often difficult: one or another party to labor agreements can be balky over interests deeply felt; and equity, justice, efficiency, and productivity are simultaneously served only with imagination and patience when they are among exchangeable values.

However, there is not a shred of evidence to support the condescending view that American workers and managers are hopelessly incompetent in defining and pursuing their preferences in the workplace, as the currently popular thinking suggests.[13] Nor is it the least bit clear that the more frankly antiunion sentiments among many reformers are sensibly informed.

It is a reasonable estimate that reformers' misgivings about work-rules bargaining reflect concerns with management prerogatives, prerogatives that are felt by many to be of the order of divine rights, higher up in organizations and perhaps unwittingly among social-science work reformers. The fact is, however, that the rights of managers to manage people rather than property derives from a voluntary contract the terms of which are reached by parties who keep a weather eye on the prospects, so to speak, for a favorable balance of trade. Laws, meanwhile, have come to sanction collectively bargained exchanges among those in the marketplace who find such exchanges to be in their mutual interest.

THE RESPONSIVENESS OF UNIONS

The objection that collective bargaining is subversive of efficiency and even of workers' interests is typically coupled with charges that collective-bargaining results are costly and that workers themselves are dissatisfied with their unions.

The first charge must confront the fact that neither the social nor the organizational costs of work-redesign efforts by visiting consultants are low, as the reluctance of managers to reorganize production processes (and to wait patiently for reform-born economies) may be taken to demonstrate.[14]

The second charge is not easily supported either. Peter Henle mobilized the evidence on labor-management contract rejections handled by the Federal Mediation and Conciliation Service to show that "in 1967 contract rejections reached a total of 14 percent of all cases recorded as going to the 'joint meeting' stage. . . . This percentage gradually declined until it reached 10 percent in 1971 and 1972." [15]

Beyond rejecting the contracts submitted to them by their leaders, union members may petition the National Labor Relations Board to decertify their unions. A board-conducted election on continued representation is held if the petition meets the board's formal requirements. Although such cases increased during the 1960s, Henle estimated that "in 1972 only 10,000 workers terminated their union representation through the National Labor Relations Board, a small proportion of the 19 million union members in the United States." [16] And Henle concludes that the magnitude of neither contract rejections nor of decertifications indicates increased disaffection with the present structure of labor-management relations.

It should be added that there is some evidence that organized workers expressed more dissatisfaction with their unions in 1973 than in 1969. Quinn *et al.* reported that the percentage of union members reporting a problem with either union democracy or union management increased by nine points to 35 percent in 1973—that is to say, from the Working Conditions Survey to the Quality of Employment Survey.[17] In a search for clues to this increase, we controlled these responses for several items in the two surveys, with two suggestive results. First, whereas there was no significant difference in the incidence of union "problems" in 1969 by the respondent's view of his or her family income, in 1973 those who felt their family income to be inadequate were significantly more likely to mention problems with their unions.

Second, in both years the feeling that the worker was "exposed to danger" on the job was significantly related to the incidence of union problems. These findings are grounds at least for speculation that the impact of inflation on real earnings and heightened consciousness about industrial health and safety were implicated in Quinn's findings. Workers, by this logic, may have the realistic expectation that unions are obliged to respond by elevating safety issues, for example, to a higher place on the agenda of priorities for bargaining.

Work reformers, meanwhile, do not attend very energetically to opportunities for reform, either about safety or in other areas. There are, after all, a number of workplace problems where only public regulation affords unorganized workers protection. Table 14.1 provides an example, in this case of the underpayments revealed by the Bureau of

TABLE 14.1. Enforcement Statistics, Fiscal Years 1974 and 1975, Bureau of Employment Standards, Department of Labor

	Fiscal 1975		Fiscal 1974	
Violation	Underpayments	Workers Owed	Underpayments	Workers Owed
Minimum wage	$ 29,879,810	228,210	$22,486,666	138,370
Overtime pay	45,873,683	254,968	47,116,528	214,412
Equal pay	26,484,860	31,843	20,623,830	32,792
Age Discrimination	6,574,409	2,350	6,315,484	1,648
Wage garnishment	44,043	107	27,675	91
Total	$108,856,805	472,404	$96,570,183	357,278

Source: News release citing Bernard E. DeLury, Assistant Secretary of Labor for Employment Standards, U.S. Department of Labor, Office of Information, July 23, 1975, p. 2.

Employment Standards' enforcement procedures. While some employers caught in these tabulations have simply made mistakes, there is considerable room for old-fashioned equity in American workplaces, with or without complicated experiments in work design. Employers have unused opportunities to "humanize" the workplace by simply paying workers their due and by attending to such growing problems as job-related illness and injury.[18]

This is not to impute only evil motives to employers. Some actions or inactions are the result of honest errors; the mergers we referred to in Chapter 13 were legally undertaken; and safety standards can sometimes be improved only by making investments in equipment that marginal employers simply cannot afford.

The point is that at both micro and macro levels, managers have other imperatives than those perceived by dedicated interventionists. For personal, careerist, organizational, financial, business-cyclic, and other reasons, managers clearly place human relations fairly well down on the list of their concerns. Workers, too, we may assume, have differentiated objectives and, like employers, adapt their concerns and loyalties to wider-going conditions and their demands to realistic prospects.

As Richard Walton has written:

> The lesson we must learn in the area of work reform is similar to one we have learned in another area of national concern—the social services. It is now recognized that a health program, a welfare program, a housing program, or an employment program alone is unable to make a lasting impact on the urban-poor syndrome. Poor health, unemployment, and other interdependent aspects of poverty must be attacked in a coordinated or systematic way.

So it is with meaningful reform of the workplace: we must think "systematically" when approaching the problem.[19]

What Walton and other reform enthusiasts see less fully, however, is the extent to which organized workers, as our experiences suggest, know this lesson—as indeed do their representatives. In organized industries especially, workers are well aware that they and managers have agendas of concerns from which both parties make choices about priorities. The agenda items clearly reveal the parties' recognition of the firm as a system—economic, technical, legal, and political—in which trade-offs must be made.

Henle, dealing with the same subject matter, came to a more fundamental conclusion:

> Up to now, there is only limited evidence that dissaffection with work has interfered with the performance of the national economy. This may be in the process of changing as the bond that ties individuals to their work tends to loosen in a world of higher incomes, greater leisure, and more competitors for an individual's time. In such a world, if work is to retain its traditional attraction, management and labor may have to change some attitudes and techniques, perhaps even their basic approach to the work environment. However, the demonstrated adaptability of the nation's labor relations institutions provides some confidence that any such changes can be successfully adopted.[20]

UNION LEADERS AND UNION MEMBERS

None of this is to argue that unionists and union leaders always bargain with an eye to the multiple interests others have in their actions or that union leaders are free of the careerist impulses of the succession of executives discussed in an earlier chapter, who change signals in the workplace in pursuit of ends that become their personal means.

Not to put too fine a point on it, union leaders are not infrequently guilty of inventive or even deplorably self-serving strategies and tactics. Even the democratic votes of unionists may understandably offend voter groups; and not every case of union democracy is "the nice kind" that offends only displaced union leaders who have been voted out of their elected offices.[21]

The fact is, of course, that the edges of our own irritations with two-valued logic must cut both ways: we do not subscribe to the view that unionists are the sole and innocent victims of managers and of public ill will. "If it was so," said Tweedledee, "it might be; and if it were so, it would be; but as it isn't, it ain't." But fair play does not require one to overlook the structural limits on union leaders any more than we would wish to overlook the constraints, like the significant ones on managers, discussed in Chapters 4, 5, and 6. Once again, the point is that we in America tend to deplore the aspirations of union-office candidates in a democratic election, aspirations that compel them to honor the systematic perspectives of members. We tend *not*, however, to deplore the ambitions of those in oligarchic business structures who seek to prove their worthiness by managerial derring-do.

Let us consider these concerns of many union leaders:[22]

1. Worker expectations will be elevated by work redesigners "when there are few answers on the horizon."

2. "While workers have a stake in productivity, it is not always identical to that of management."

3. While both parties have interests in *productivity*, they do not necessarily define *efficiency* in the same way—a proposition that professorial readers who are pushed by deans and provosts to teach more and larger classes will quickly find congenial. Indeed, most of us could make the claim that we cannot overlook all of the issues having to do with quality in our concern with productivity.

4. While novel and specialized worker committees to improve the quality of working life may be forced to deal with *some* working conditions, they are not infrequently used by dissident or aggrieved workers as alternatives to the grievance process in respect to *other* conditions. These efforts are often attempts either to muddle matters or to speed them up, as the case may be. How, by the way, should new work modes be regarded if they were agreed to in the shop against union leaders' advice (and thereby become para-contractual arrangements) only to be the subject of grievances of the same workers later? Union leaders do not earn the respect (or the votes) of workers by reminding them, "We told you so!"

5. For a very long time noneconomic benefits have been traded off against economic benefits, a fact that ties union leaders to past agreements not to "mess around" with work procedures, at least in the eyes of management negotiators. And a union leader's negotiating role is not aided by a reputation for switching signals: in return for an acceptable agreement, leaders are supposed to keep the contract's beneficiaries "in line." Pressures in the economy, such as high unemployment or inflation, may force a reversal in these trade-offs as "the ability to trade off . . . with a good economic package has . . . become more limited," [23] but it does not usually help astute negotiators to "rush the cadence," as the Marines have it, to act out of phase with economic conditions.

6. Workers are not, as we have emphasized, a homogeneous group in most settings; they have *different* and *shifting* interests, a problem managers are generally pleased to let their unions address.[24] The problem can be tricky. "Constructive seniority," for example, is the phrase

used to describe an advantage for individuals who have suffered discrimination in the past: in effect, they may claim to be treated like workers with longer tenure in cases involving layoff. Nevertheless, the League of Union Women in Michigan filed *amicus curiae* briefs that supported a very limited scope for the play of "constructive seniority" in the UAW. Elsewhere, women and blacks in the same union have pushed for a *total* subordination of clauses protecting contractually senior co-workers during layoffs.

7. There are cases in which unions will help deal with troublesome worker behavior by bending even the most sacred and hard-won contract provisions.[25] Thus, according to a provision that was understandably never given any publicity in the 1970 UAW-Chrysler settlement, managers were permitted to pay new workers *under*-scale wages during the first year of employment, when absenteeism is highest, and to pay those who had near-perfect attendance records a bonus (equal to the withheld wages) at the end of twelve months. As UAW leaders confided, "This was a risky business—and it was done without the help of any professors." The latter was a reaction to the blistering the UAW and its leader, Leonard Woodcock received from all sides when Woodcock expressed impatience with well-intentioned but, in his judgment at the time, misguided academics who criticized the UAW's slow response to work-redesign efforts.

One could go on in this vein, but our purpose here is only to suggest that the union issue is not a simple one; unions have been obliged, as Salpukas points out, to limit their concerns with the proximal work issues that preoccupied us in Chapters 4 and 8, and over which managers may well have options: "Recurring major and minor recessions in the economy have not enabled unions to get too far away from bread and butter issues." [26]

Salpukas also reminds us that a union is limited by laws protecting contracts between workers and managers. While "there are no areas that are taboo in collective bargaining," there are practical limits to what can be pursued by way of working conditions after agreements are reached. Unions may be slow to get on the bandwagon in support of work reform, for less respectable reasons than those we have adumbrated. "Yet," writes Salpukas,

> given the thrust of management, which is still toward greater work fragmentation and adaptation of the worker to the plant, one must ask how seriously *management* will pursue the solutions without prodding from the labor movement. Also, the long-range answers to increased job satisfaction may mean no improvement or even a decline in productivity. Clearly those solutions will only be applied if union leaders begin to think that the overall satisfaction of their members is as worthwhile as enriching the paycheck.[27]

UNION DEMOCRACY AND "WORKER PARTICIPATION"

Irritated work reformers will be tempted to point to the constant affirmation in their writings that they favor "worker participation" and to charge that we are unfair in making so much of their low-level, if clearly stated, reservations, as well as their implicit misgivings about unions. Unions, one work reformer impatiently said to us, "are not, after all, the only form of worker participation, and unions, happily or unhappily, adequately or inadequately, represent the direct interests of only 22 percent of all employed workers."

We are not much impressed by such a formulation. Thus, borrowing his phrase, we may "pinpoint the ambiguities" in the view a representative reformer takes on the matter. Figure 14.1 is accompanied by the following formulation:

The curves portraying the direct effects of "constitutionalism" on productivity and on the quality of work life probably have a relatively small region of coincidence between them. . . . It can be hypothesized that situations characterized by only minimum rights would depress productivity as well as quality of working life because of the consequences of insecurity,

Figure 14.1: Effect of Constitutionalism in the Workplace on the Quality of Work Experience and on Productivity

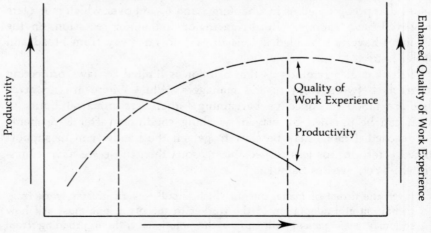

Source: Richard E. Walton, "Criteria for Quality of Working Life," in *The Quality of Working Life: Volume 1, Problems, Prospects, and the State of Art*, edited by Louis E. Davis and Albert Cherns (New York: Free Press, 1975), p. 100.

anxiety, and employee resentment on performance. Beyond some point, however, additional forms and degrees of constitutionalism will continue to improve quality, but at a price to productivity. At a still higher level of constitutionalism, the marginal effect on quality is zero or negligible.[28]

Readers can make up their own minds about the best balance to be struck between them, if indeed it is useful to apply traditional marginalist economic analysis to productivity and "constitutionalism." Readers can also decide whether there are identifiable limiting points— productivity apart—to the contribution of constitutionalism to the quality of work life, as Walton and others insist.

The view is not novel, of course. We tend to start these discussions with the premise that the present pattern of income distribution is a kind of footnote to the Ten Commandments. Thus, Walton writes elsewhere that productivity bargaining, a program urged by some reformers, is one of a package of reforms that would bring about new and desirable organizational equilibria:

> Productivity bargaining would revise work rules and increase management's flexibility, with a *quid pro quo* whereby the union ensures that workers share in the fruits of the resulting productivity increases.[29]

An alternative view would hold that workers may simply not wish to accept increases only in their absolute shares but might wish, in some sectors of the economy, to increase their relative shares and to reduce "management flexibility," especially if the exercises of such flexibility offends workers' collective sensibilities about their investments and their equity in the status quo. That, after all, is what many strikes, grievances, arbitration cases, and contract negotiations are all about, as we have already seen.

We might add that tough-minded managers may also feel that their companies' relative shares of productivity are too small and use their collective-bargaining skills to undo the allocations of productivity made between workers and managers in other days. Thus, workers in the "work-rule-ridden" organized building trades in New York City in 1976 yielded on *all* "restrictive practices," in order that the contractors who hire them may compete more effectively with unorganized contractors. These workers, interestingly, are *not* asking for a lump-sum payment in return for the considerable help they have given contractors in quest of building-code requirements that serve contractors' desires to add to their charges. This help was often made available as "payment" for restrictive practices.

About all such considerations, however, the champions of worker participation clearly have grave doubts. The acceptable difference between a few rights and maximum rights, we may presume, is management flexibility, a by now notoriously problematical difference defended by a few of King George's advisers in the late 1770s, before it was defended by Harvard Business School teachers, but deplored at the time by some of Harvard's most historically distinguished graduates.

Among the many questions that must be addressed in comparisons of collective bargaining arrangements with more ambiguous arrangements comprehended by the term "worker participation" is the question of whether local unions are really effective, whether industrial jurisprudence really obtains. Obviously much industrial jurisprudence *must* work well, in shop-level collective bargaining arrangements, if grievances are ever to come to arbitration.

Unfortunately, there are very few data available on the character of daily bargaining, on the degree to which pre–arbitration industrial relations are vital and viable, although the existence of work rules in most unorganized plants is *prima facie* evidence in the matter.

A few available classic studies, however, do point to great vitality in the local bargaining realm, much of it called implicit bargaining; but they do not bring us beyond "for instances": Gouldner's study of a gypsum mine,[30] Strauss and Sayle's study of a local mine,[31] Kuhn's study of rubber workers,[32] Sayle's study of auto workers,[33] Lipset, Coleman, and Trow's study of the International Typographers Union,[34] and, most recently, Gersuny's study of an "outlying facility" of the Ford Motor Company [35] come most readily to mind.

The author of the last of these studies compares the performance of two successive slates of union leaders in the management of grievances against punishments inflicted on workers by Ford managers. He concludes that the second slate was far more effective in getting penalties modified and, especially, in getting the penalties levied against black workers modified.

The results of Gersuny's research point to the relative efficiency of local unions in redressing punishments as a critical factor in the local's success in its representational role, a finding that suggests the need for members to be attentive to their interests in union elections. The findings do not point abstractly to deficiencies in the machinery but point to deficiencies in the intentions and capacities of people who work its levers and among those who elect them. Once again, the issues to be joined have to do with the vitality of a democratic people; and this vitality may be more or less admired depending upon the depth of one's commitment to democracy itself and to collective bargaining. The reader may accordingly draw conclusions, without further editorial comment, about the following observation by Peter Henle:

> Any widespread disaffection with union representation or with the labor relations system in general would be more evident in contests for local union offices. Unfortunately, very few studies have been undertaken to

measure this turnover, and none is available which provides comparable data over an extended period of time. One such study covering a specific locality indicated relatively high turnover; during 1963–66, more than half the local unions in the Milwaukee area changed presidents and 17 percent had two or more changes.[36]

CONCLUSION

The foregoing remarks on unions' roles in America, on the kinds of bargaining efforts in which they are engaged, on some of the complementarities in the roles of managers and union leaders and on union governance have been offered only to point up the fact that a great deal is lost in discussions of worker participation in which the roles of unions are slighted, ignored, or implicitly maligned.

New schemes, involving "quality of working life" committees, will conceivably serve workers and managers who seek new modes of communication in unorganized settings. And they may even offer some of the additional services provided to union members in other settings. There is, however, little reassuring evidence on the latter point: the essential hostility of many managers who pursue novel schemes toward unions should detract significantly from our confidence that "worker participation," even allowing for the ambiguities about its meaning among its protagonists, is an improved version of the rule of law organic to most collective-bargaining relationships.

In the case of unionized organizations, worker-participation schemes may augment, but are more likely to compete with, those structural arrangements that are organic to collective-bargaining arrangements. Where they do not compete disadvantageously with collective bargaining (and the grievance machinery that generally accompanies bargaining), these schemes will soon be merged with those standing arrangements that have long aided managers and workers to reconcile their interests satisfactorily.

A random sampling of contract agreements and of the work rules in accordance with which workers and managers live in most industries will show that work enlargement, work enrichment, and work restructuring take place in the ordinary, daily bargaining process and on a regular basis without the help of interventionist-consultants. We see no evidence that the work rules generated in collective bargaining procedures, explicit or implicit, are less to be admired than those instigated by third-party change agents.

A review of the machinery by which unions are governed suggests that there is room for some improvements on this score. But it is clear that neither managers nor enthusiastic work reformers would view more democracy in unions with equanimity. A little democracy, like a little constitutionalism, apparently goes rather a long way, as far as many Americans are concerned.

The discussion in this chapter, meanwhile, has brought us full circle to our concern in the initial chapter with two-valued logic, with the depth of managers' concerns about human-resource problems, and with the dim prospects for the best-laid plans of would-be workplace humanizers. We pass next to a consideration of the highly touted developments overseas and to an assessment of their relevance to the American case.

15. Work Reforms and Industrial Relations in Comparative Perspective

That the subject matter of this book has a comparative dimension is well known to Americans who attend to the daily news. Indeed some of our ablest journalists have made frequent and favorable references over the past decade to experiments and reforms overseas targeted upon worker morale and productivity problems reputedly parallel to those in the United States. These studies and reports imply that we have much to learn from European efforts to reduce labor-management conflicts, to improve working conditions, and to increase worker output.

Our own estimate is that American admirers of these efforts have overlooked a number of difficulties and misconstrued a number of relevant facts about Western European developments. A brief review of these difficulties and misconstructions suggests that one might best be careful in the use of Western Europe as a template for American reforms. A review suggests furthermore that U.S. workers and managers are ahead of Europeans in their application of a number of practices and techniques that apparently are relevant beyond particular national boundaries.

GENERAL OBSERVATIONS

Consider, first of all, that it is most difficult to order the work-reform, industrial-relations, and manpower-policy efforts of unions, workers, managers, employer associations, and political parties overseas into a revealing or suggestive scheme, for these interests are by no means all of a piece. Nor are the arrangements identical in all sectors of a given economy. And it is the case, as well, that the best-known Western European workplace experiments are parts of developments that cut straight across social systems: these developments do not involve only managers and workers in West European countries, and they are not readily extricated from their historical contexts in each country.

Second, it is hard to obtain data on the outcomes of the separate efforts of interested parties, even within a single company, to deal with problems (a) of collective bargaining, (b) of productivity, and (c) of work satisfaction. More clearly evident is the fact that one cannot look at work-reform experiments in isolation from the particular but wider-going industrial-relations *systems* into which they must be integrated.[1] Efforts to deal with the three problems in Western Europe are not usually coordinated by single, relevant, and interested record-keeping agencies in any one nation. Most of them are too new, furthermore, to have led to identifiable results. And the efforts themselves vary from country to country in their essential character, all the way from national programatic plans—involving parties, party platforms, and political leadership—to shopwide, plantwide, or companywide adjustments and experiments. The reform efforts can thus involve small work groups, local unions, national unions, industry associations, and national employer leagues.

Third, developments—especially the macro, programatic ones—are not constructively separable from cyclical economic trends in the social and economic life of each nation. A great many "reforms" are rooted in responses to business cycles, labor-market shifts, ways of allocating "social products" among interest groups, and plain, old-fashioned political realities.[2]

Fourth, it is clear that a great many of the reforms reflect changes in the fundamentals of union-management collective-bargaining relationships, a trend in the direction of the "implicit bargaining" and work-rules negotiations that have long characterized the American scene. It is precisely these developments in collective bargaining, outlined in the previous chapter, that are most readily overlooked or deplored by our domestic reform enthusiasts when they report on deficiencies in American work settings. They would also have us believe that European innovations are either independent of collective-bargaining arrangements or, at most, grafted on to them.

To conduct comparative analyses, one must accordingly confront the fact that a selection of the bases for comparisons involves controversy over the terms of such comparisons. Our position in such a controversy is anchored in the misgivings we have already expressed about two-valued logic which need no reaffirmation. It is sufficient simply to state that the West European cases hardly represent trailblazing reforms when compared with long-familiar American developments.

Fortunately, there is a burgeoning literature on work developments in Europe, Japan, and Australia, so that detailed review is unnecessary here. Four volumes in particular, together with their references and bibliographies, may be highly commended to interested readers.[3] In this chapter we have drawn on these works, on our own limited first-hand observations, and on those of a colleague on "The Humanizing of Europe's Assembly Line." [4] Our aim is to highlight a few considerations that lead us to the impressions reported in the concluding section of the chapter.

COLLECTIVE BARGAINING AND WORK REFORM

Changes in labor-management relations in the European Economic Community (EEC) countries have effectively moved the parties immediately concerned with work and its reform much closer to the system of bargaining in which the unionized 22 percent of American workers are involved than work reformers in the United States have recognized or allowed. Thus, it is clear from an Organisation for Economic Cooperation and Development study [5] that, with the exception of Belgium, the locus of collective bargaining has generally moved downward from national and industry-level bargaining toward bargaining at the level of the individual business enterprise. The logical consequence of a continuation of this trend would leave collective bargaining looking a good deal more like bargaining modes in the United States than those obtaining in most Western European countries prior to 1950.

It is also clear that while much is said in journals, newspapers, and TV documentaries about the reform of working conditions, the lion's share of bargaining efforts in EEC countries is over wages and wage-related questions, *not* over work procedures.[6] Indeed, though the drift to decentralized bargaining is clear—partly under the impact of American–based multinational corporations who bring the familiar U.S. system of industrial relations with them overseas,[7] and partly as a response to workers' demands for a larger role in bargaining efforts—it is even clearer that there is still a good deal less bargaining overseas than in the United States over proximal working conditions other than pay. Innovations in the area of workers' concerns, as we have noted earlier, may be far more readily credited to American workers and first-line supervisors who have imaginatively bargained over work rules than to forward-looking foreigners who speak of new human-relations discoveries.

It is also a fact, as Ginzberg points out, that what little real, experimental innovation does take place in Europe, along the lines endorsed by current work-reform enthusiasts, is essentially new neither overseas nor in the United States.[8] Popular endorsements of novel work-redesign, work-enlargement, or work-restructuring experiments at Volvo, Saab, Norsk Hydro, and Phillips tend to overlook the fact that these ventures are rooted in American and, later, English human-relations work (at the Tavistock Institute) in the period prior to 1950. And, to the extent that local bargaining is now involved in EEC countries, it is a manifestation less of newer than of older forces that were identified as early as 1904 by John R. Commons and other industrial-relations students in American shops.

Next, the scope of issues considered appropriate in collective-bargaining negotiations overseas has widened somewhat. A few work-redesign experiments aside, however, the expansions are into areas long since included in conventional U.S. collective bargaining. Thus, more attention has been turned in Western Europe to nonwork and nonwage issues: pensions, education, longer-term contracts, deferred compensation, wage adjustments, technological change, and subcontracting.⁹ And even expansions in the scope of bargainable issues to those that are relatively novel are enmeshed in regular, not new, collective-bargaining arrangements.

Consider, next, the arrangements in which more efficient working methods, "usually involving the removal of union restrictive practices," ¹⁰ are traded off for pay increases. These are usually called productivity agreements, and the process from which they result is called productivity bargaining. The term has taken on a voguish value in the United States among many who choose to ignore or who simply have not looked closely at the trade-offs that take place every day, week, and month in most unionized (and, to some degree, in nonunionized) United States settings. Generally, both parties in the United States gain in these bargains, as we saw in the previous chapter, but the public hears very little about them. Pressure from managers for productivity gains without the provision of reciprocal or near-reciprocal gains for workers is well known in union circles as a "speed-up" or "stretch-out". In a few celebrated cases, like the Lordstown strike, we may even come to hear about the matter outside the firm's walls when quieter, national exchange of quids for quos have not been concluded.¹¹

Productivity bargaining gained its current vogue in the United States from an agreement reached in 1960 among the British Transport and General Workers' Union, a number of engineering unions, and the managers of a subsidiary of the Standard Oil Company of New Jersey.¹² The parent company had encountered more seriously restrictive practices in their U.K. than in their U.S. operation and moved to reduce their uneconomic effects. By 1969, 4.5 million workers in the United Kingdom were covered by 1500 such agreements.

According to Dufty, the United Kingdom's National Board on Prices and Incomes reported that "lower costs" did result from such agreements in three-quarters of the cases,¹³ but that there has been a marked decline in the amount of productivity bargaining in recent years.

Dufty instructively offers four possible explanations. First, he writes, many of the agreements were in fact

> spurious in the sense that they achieved little or nothing in the way of higher productivity or that wage increases granted were much higher than the increased productivity. . . . Such agreements were devices to circumvent the government's prices and incomes policy. When the official incomes policy collapsed in 1969 the need for subterfuges of this sort disappeared.[14]

Next, he suggests, the usefulness of these agreements diminishes with their success to the degree to which the bargains merely "buy out" restrictive practices. This view he regards as being "perhaps an unduly restricted and cynical view of productivity bargaining."

As students of the American scene, we do not view such a development cynically. As we have pointed out, we find it most difficult to locate "restrictive" work rules in the United States that did not begin with an exchange of real values; many of the resulting rules could be bought back by managers who, in the event, had to find a price deemed equivalent under new circumstances to the "goods" that were originally sold in exchange for the rule. That American workers have discovered such selective uses for the marketplace should not surprise a detached observer. American managers, after all, have been excellent instructors in the selective uses of markets.

Dufty also points out that Western European unions become less interested in agreements that are inherently labor displacing when unemployment rates creep upward,[15] and that the "left-wing notion that productivity bargaining is a capitalist plot to persuade the workers to discard their armor of restrictive practices"[16] has some credibility. Thus, these agreements have in some cases limited the "mobility and moral powers of shop stewards."[17]

British workers are like the rest of us, we may suppose, in their unwillingness to depend on the economy's well-being as the guarantor of the equities they seek to protect; these equities and the other social and economic circumstances favored by workers are not, as we argued in Part II, solely in the hands of even the best-intentioned of managers. Today's agreements to increase productivity in exchange for wage benefits cannot be protected from the business cycle tomorrow by work reformers or by managers. Nor can work reformers who endorse productivity bargaining designed to eliminate work rules[18] expect the plaudits of employees when their companies are later merged with other companies whose managers are less solicitous, or when managers fail because they could not manage a firm's other interests, or when the "good" managers with whom they engage in productivity bargaining transfer to other companies, leaving workers without their "armor."

Beyond productivity agreements, there are a host of other arrangements that are innovative as compared with the arrangements they displace in Western Europe; they are not, however, innovative by American standards. It is something of an irony that favorable publicity has attended European reforms that shift bargaining activities nearer to the actual workplace. Americans have been known to mutter, after all, over the failures of local union members to ratify hard-won agreements between their unions' national leaders and corporation executives in the electrical appliance, rubber, glass, auto, steel, and transportation industries.

There is also a certain irony in the fact that though changes are occurring in collective-bargaining arrangements overseas, these are not the changes that have most fascinated American observers. Indeed, the changes in industrial-relations practices, so "American" in their character from many points of view, are neither so admirable in the eyes of work reformers nor so newsworthy as changes in the role of workers in the management of enterprises and experimental changes in the design of work processes.

WORKERS IN (OR NEAR) MANAGEMENT

It is impossible to review fully in this volume all the European attempts to increase workers' involvements in decision making. These plans vary in the numbers and powers of workers who sit on councils and committees concerned with an enterprise's comings, goings, and doings. They are sufficiently new in their environments, meanwhile, to make summary statements vulnerable to oversimplification. A few strands among the numerous developments are beginning to become clear, however.

In almost no European country are these councils and committees officially linked to unions, and they tend to be more useful to management and labor in nations, industries, and firms in which collective bargaining about issues directly of concern to workers where they work is weak or nonexistent.[19]

Dufty, after his review of OECD member countries, notes that "there seems to be a fairly close relationship between the strength of the trade union movement and the process and significance of works councils" despite the lack generally of official linkages.[20] "The more formal work counsels of continental Europe," he writes, "are tending to accrue more powers of co-determination to a greater or lesser degree in all cases except Italy, where they have been submerged by the recently developed enterprise level collective bargaining structure."[21]

Though it is most clearly the case in Germany, as the powers of worker-councils under codetermination plans increase, the councils' activities more nearly approximate collective bargaining.[22] While one must hedge any bets on the subject, the most defensible conclusion is that worker representation/participation of the newer Western European types will both influence and be limited by collective-bargaining practices in each nation. Any synthesis of the new with the old will resemble the bargaining and representational arrangements in the U.S. steel, rubber, and auto industries more than those of Western Europe circa 1950. This is by no means to suggest that international differences will disappear. The central tendencies of nations also count for a great deal, as studies of the convergences and divergences among industrialized nations make clear.[23]

Dufty's summary, though brief, is a compendium on the subject and it serves to highlight the distinguishable roles of nations' social and economic organizations in shaping worker-participation pattern among OECD countries. It deserves extensive citation:

> The concept of worker directors has made little progress where there is a strong private enterprise philosophy, as in Japan and the English-speaking countries. At the other end of the political spectrum it has not flourished where there are strong Marxist or radical socialist trade union federations, in Belgium, France and Italy for example, because the idea of worker directors is incompatible with the outright rejection of capitalism which is favoured by these federations. The existence of powerful social or Christian democratic parties seems to be a necessary condition for legislation requiring worker representation on boards of directors. Worker directors have been firmly established in Germany for many years and recent pressures have been in the direction of increasing the proportion from a third to a half to bring all industry in line with the coal and steel sector. Recent legislation has introduced worker directors into Norway and Sweden and movements in the same direction have occurred in the Netherlands. In all cases the political motivation has been strong and action has been influenced by the articulation between the unions and the political parties with which they are associated. Although no action has been taken in the UK, due to the predominant private enterprise philosophy mentioned above, the entry of that country into the EEC and the prospect of European company legislation have aroused considerable discussion. The trade unions have come out in favour of worker directors on supervisory boards in equal numbers to those nominated by the shareholders but with the unions having direct control over them. Official employer opinion remains opposed to both supervisory boards and special interest group representation of any kind.[24]

It is important to note in all this, not that all industrial systems or industrial-relations systems converge on a point, but rather that they diverge around central tendencies. Also, as Dufty's assessment suggests, outside the United States the nexus of councils, unions, and parties is highly developed, a point that is simply ignored in popularly expressed admirations of worker-participation patterns overseas.

In Western Europe the impact of the wider-going social, economic, political, and cultural environments is perhaps more conspicuous than in the United States; partisan political struggles, after all, are not generally as subtle as collective bargaining negotiations. Industrial class conflicts are not left to the parties to collective-bargaining agreements to deal with by themselves in countries in which national labor parties seek to win elections. In the United States there are some equivalent environmental pressures on managers and workers, but their adjudication tends to be in the local, fragmented style characteristic of other conflicts in a pluralistic system.

As for the degree of worker participation, the difference between the United States and Western European countries is not so great when one considers the subjects that are bargainable in accordance with decisions of the National Labor Relations Board and the courts. As we noted previously, the scope of arbitration has been greatly expanded. Even legislation designed to be regulatory—like the Fair Labor Standards Act, the Equal Employment Opportunity Act, and the Occupational Safety and Health Act—have broadened the opportunity for unions to bargain in areas formerly reserved to managers unilaterally. As one expert puts it, these developments have brought participation in America to the point where "the importation of a European or Scandinavian model would almost be carrying coals to Newcastle"; the mutual accommodations that result, however, occur "without the increasing bureaucracy emanating from co-determination, worker participation, and worker control systems abroad." [25]

The "American way" in this context is, of course, rather more litigious than is the European political route to conflict resolution. This difference goes well beyond variations between the industrial-relations systems in the United States and Western Europe; it is rooted in the different historical roles of class conflict in the Old and New Worlds. Even so, the net differences among the present-day industrial-relations systems are not nearly as great as the admiring references to Western Europe would have us believe.

One may doubt, finally, whether many work reformers would hold any serious brief for the highly politicized aspects of industrial-relations systems in Western Europe or that they could sell many American workers, managers, or union leaders on the virtues of the class conflicts that underlie them.[26]

WORK-REDESIGN EXPERIMENTS

The first conspicuous fact about joint efforts of Western European unions and managers to redesign work—for purposes of either enriching or enlarging it to the end that work becomes less boring—is that they are few and far between. Indeed, while book-length case studies are available, a decently comprehensive overview of experiments in all the EEC countries is presented by Dufty in six pages of his book [27] and by Ginzberg in eight.[28]

The second conspicuous fact about these experiments is that they have developed in response to forces and circumstances rather different from those in which American workers and managers have recently found themselves. As conditions in a given Western European nation come increasingly to approximate those that prevailed in the United States in the early 1960s and again since 1970, however, it is reasonable to expect that work-experimentation efforts will decline. As—and if— employment levels go down, so will experiments lose their appeal.

Consider that Western European work experiments are reflections of Europe's tight labor-market conditions; as in the United States, interest in worker morale quickens appreciably when employers are vulnerable to the more genuinely autonomous actions of workers. Workers can absent themselves, quit their jobs, or strike consistently for improved working conditions when the demand for their labor services is at a peak. The pace of economic development in Western Europe from 1950 to 1970 so far exceeded their manpower capacities that most fully developed European economies were even obliged to import "guest workers." In the United States meanwhile we have had a succession of boom-and-bust periods.

Not until recently have most industrialized European nations had to endure the threats to their workers' well-being that have become predictable, cyclical aspects of the working conditions of millions of Americans since World War II. Older, not less than younger, better-educated workers have accordingly been able until very recently to act upon their irritations, a fact that has forced some European managers, especially those in larger enterprises, to focus on worker morale. A tight labor market is as close, realistically speaking, as disaffected workers can come to economic paradise.

The fact that labor (and Communist) parties play leading parts in these nations' politics has served to quicken managerial concerns: discontented workers in Western Europe can vote with their ballots as well as with their feet. Radicals have not objected to work-reform experiments, though their essential commitments are ostensibly more revolutionary than reformist. Thus, we asked three high-ranking staff personnel at the headquarters of the Confédération Générale du Travail, the French Communist–led trade union, why their organization appeared to be supportive of work redesign efforts and the intervention movement generally. One of them said:

American radicals, whose commentaries we read in various journals, are really very silly to take these management efforts in Europe, *or* in America, as seriously as they do. We feel that most work is unpleasant and could be made a little less so by various experiments. Our members are too well informed and disciplined to take managers' efforts to subvert workers' membership in our party ranks seriously, however. So, we accept all the "job redesign" we can get while we keep our eyes on membership discipline and the more important underlying issues in a capitalist economy. Work redesign has no bearing upon workers' appraisals of their circumstances as workers, increases in the particular satisfactions that may come of experiments notwithstanding.[29]

French businessmen also talked freely to us of the need to reduce worker alienation—10,000 French white-collar workers, led by a youthful woman, were on strike over working conditions in French banks as we spoke—as did Italian and Norwegian businessmen.

In May and August 1974, the Western European states were still enjoying economic boom; employment levels were very high, and the left, with its "mixture of undisciplined socialists and disciplined communists,"[30] was a significant threat in the eyes of all. "Work experiments [were] essential"; they were calculated, as a French Harvard Business School graduate in an international consulting firm put it, "to cool out the Marxists."

A deeply felt hope in all this in 1974 was that the Communist Party's disciplined Marxists, at least in France, were the best *organized* hope for dampening the strike fever then visible all over Western Europe, and that work redesign might help assure individuals that less tedious work is one of the best possible nonpecuniary by-products of sustained economic growth.[31]

In Norway, where Einar Thorsrud, one of the world's leading work reformers, has sought to facilitate collaborative union-management experiments, there were widespread fears in the late 1960s and beyond, in upper-middle-class circles, of increased Labor Party demands for worker membership on corporate boards.

> We know of Einar Thorsrud's work and his enthusiasms about workplace reforms [one of the top leaders of Norway's Employer Association (Norsk Arbeidgiversforening) told us] and so we encouraged him with "support" to do what you Americans call "his thing." It was our essential purpose, in doing this, to attempt to stop or, more likely, to delay legislative efforts in the Storting [Parliament] to have employees represented on corporate boards of directors! I did not personally think it would work, but I thought it not very costly to try to avoid "the worst." As you well know, it did not work. A third of the members of our boards of directors are now elected by employees.[32]

Einar Thorsrud is one of many Western European intervention enthusiasts, an admired spokesman for employed men and women whose working conditions he feels could be far more rewarding, and a member of the international group of change agents described in Chapter 2. We do not know how aware he is of the uses to which persons of somewhat devious intentions have put, or tried to put, his work, but it may be doubted that he would care very much one way or the other, for his teachings have had wide influence among managers and labor leaders in Norway. This may be taken to reflect the realistic concerns of managers about worker morale in an economy with the world's tightest labor market, one of the world's highest living standards, and proven oil reserves in the North Sea so large that they give great economic support to long-standing and well-organized social-democratic demands, in and out of the Labor Party, for a higher "quality of life." The situation in Sweden is only a little less favorable to work reformers whose programmatic efforts are also substantially integrated into a larger industrial democratic program.[33]

Since the political and economic facts in Western Europe seem so supportive of reformist experimentation, one may wonder not that work-redesign experiments have been conducted at all but that there have been so few of them, an issue to which we turn next.

LIMITS ON OVERSEAS REFORMS

We are in a position to offer only a few impressions about why the work-reform movement in Western Europe has had such a modest reach. First, given the tendency for collective bargaining to become somewhat more decentralized, European managers and union leaders find it difficult to integrate what amounts to two systems, conceived and operated separately.

Second, we note that Western European managers have sought to head off more profound political changes, like those requiring worker representation at top levels of an enterprise. Insofar as they have failed to do so, their enthusiasm for workplace reform, except in Scandinavia, has predictably been dampened.

Third, the evidence that work-reform experiments have "worked" economically, that they have yielded greater worker productivity as a function of improved worker morale, is unimpressive.[34] This fact has not been lost on European managers, who, even before the advent of Europeanized human-relations efforts, were well aware of the costs of faulty manpower planning—in the form, for example, of severance payments and of relatively low output even among the least militant of employees. Where employers have developed concerns about such issues as absenteeism, as in Germany, their solution is simply to hire enough workers to keep production moving rather than become involved in attempts to treat worker morale.[35]

European managers will confide privately that they are inclined to dismiss worker productivity as a "big issue in profits." As one German manager put it to us in an interview,

> Profits are determined by such things as exchange rates, the profitability of particular industries, and what their competition is. . . . As far as cooperation is concerned, it is long-term stability and growth that insures it and not the other way around.

According to another German business leader, productivity is not an appropriate measure in the international market:

> For an individual plant, you need competition, which involves cost-consciousness, internal competition between units, and investments in labor-saving equipment. However, capital intensity has a limit.

His own company is now going in what he called "the Swiss direction" —that is, to specialized products of superb quality—which hardly puts him in a position to mechanize his operations further. This is a problem, he told us, because

> the volume of a market is a key to productivity. In any case I am concerned not with the productivity of workers, but with productivity of management. Management decisions are important because one reaps the adverse effects of mistakes for a long time.

He was personally restive about the time it takes to effect change in German industry, given present management structures.

Another German manager complained to us not about workers but about "the mentality of German purchasers [that] requires highly finished goods of much better quality than in other countries." Furthermore, he complained, "German managers are less flexible; there is a time lag in their adjustments."

CONCLUSIONS

Many American admirers of European work-reform efforts have been unaware of the slippage in these efforts and of the movement in the direction of U.S. collective-bargaining patterns. One reason is that they have often seen themselves, correctly, to be helping European managers (as they have sought to help American managers) to *avoid* collective-bargaining arrangements. When they have recognized the union implications, they have also recognized that work reforms may embarrass European union leaders who have been too preoccupied with party politics to attend adequately to workers' company or shop-level needs.

That private-sector managers have abiding reservations about a world in which the quality of working life is a principal agenda item may be seen in the fact that many Europeans (and others) are currently showing increased interest in managing American workers under the very American conditions that offend reformers. We will comment further on this apparent paradox in our concluding chapter.

Before we pass, in the next chapter, to a brief review of the heightened interest of foreign investors in their American undertakings, we cite the following statement by way of summarizing the discussion in this section. The statement's authors are among the leaders of the "quality of working life" movement:

> Managements, then, have often approached unions to share in experiments aimed at enhancing quality of working life. Outside Scandinavia, unions have tended at best to maintain a neutral posture. Strongly ideological unions have opposed such measures. Even where they are not ideologically opposed, unions face special problems in cooperating in this field. Where there is no tradition of workplace bargaining, issues of work allocation and organization have remained outside the unions' purview; they have neither the knowledge nor the machinery to engage in it. And, even where workplace bargaining is common, the union is not set up to deal with matters which fall outside its normal range. The union can demand safeguards such as a guarantee against redundancies or can, as in the case of the Italian unions, demand that jobs be upgraded while leaving management to work out how.
>
> Clearly, unions are likely to be in a far stronger position if they choose to demand enhanced quality of working life for their members and persuade managements to comply. But if this is in the context of bargaining, this would allow management to obtain a *quid pro quo*. Not surprisingly, unions prefer to be in a position to exact their own quid.[36]

There is, we emphasize, a certain irony in the facts to which Davis and Cherns allude and in the related facts to which we have been attending in the foregoing pages.

Thus, a great many work humanizers and not a few managers see work reforms as aids in warding off collective bargaining; they hold up European experiments as examples. The facts, however, support the judgments, first, that there are relatively few efforts to reform work along the lines in question; second, that the more substantial (and, to some, perhaps praiseworthy) developments overseas have more to do with expansion in the traditional scope of bargaining issues than with end runs around unions; and third, that America-bound foreign managers-investors have a better-developed interest in the well-established ways of American workers, managers, and union leaders than in the ways of the modern heirs of the Harvard Business School's human relations tradition.

16. Productivity, Efficiency, and Stability

In this chapter we discuss two topics that will serve to round out our overall analysis. The essential facts about recent foreign investments in the United States suggest that a number of foreign observers are a good deal less myopic about American workers and their ways— especially their unions—than are American work-reform enthusiasts. The facts also suggest that reform enthusiasts themselves have been selective in their assessments of developments overseas. We may pursue both of these themes by picking up in this chapter approximately where we left off in the discussions of developments overseas (Chapter 15) and of American collective bargaining (Chapter 14).

As we noted in Chapters 2 and 3, reformers have not been at all averse to linking their programmatic ideas to workers' productivity, either by implication or by explication. It is therefore useful to discuss some of the complexities in the vexed matter of productivity in order to view the putative linkages between worker satisfaction and worker productivity in the "macro-micro" perspective as well as in the narrower version of the human-relations perspective. The comments on productivity *per se* in this chapter thus carry us well beyond the discussion of Chapter 3 of the relationships among worker productivity, attitudes toward work, and morale.

THE RELEVANCE OF FOREIGN DEVELOPMENTS

We pointed out in the preceding chapter that discussions of changes in Western European manpower management tell only a part of the story. Specifically, we read regularly of work-enlargement, work-enrichment, and autonomous work-group experiments, but these marginal developments are rarely considered in the larger context of the evolution of industrial-relations systems in Western Europe in the direction of collective-bargaining arrangements in the United States. The limited vision of work reformers, however, reflects their generally unfavorable attitudes (and those of their corporate clients) toward collective bargaining, toward the union leaders who represent American union members, or toward both the principles and the practices involved.

In contrast, foreign investors see great advantages in the American labor market and in American-style industrial relations. These circumstances are encouraging to those who seek to humanize the workplace. The facts of the matter support the inference that the *lack* of worker-oriented reform at all levels, from workplace to marketplace, help to make the United States attractive to foreign investors.

Consider, first, the implicit dissatisfactions with their domestic conditions that have led foreign managers to make investments in the United States whose book value by mid-1974 reached $22 billion.[1]

Among the motives underlying these investments are the desire to get closer to American markets, to bypass tariff barriers, and otherwise to simplify a number of essentially nonlabor problems.[2] There is also the fact that "depressed" stock prices and the dollar's depreciation make U.S. corporations attractive buys. There are, however, other reasons more relevant to our interests in this volume, and some of them should unsettle many work-reform enhusiasts, especially the minority who seek work reforms as important first steps down the road to major social reforms.

Business Week collects these reasons under the heading "Disenchantment at Home." As the magazine's foreign-department editor puts it, foreigners are experiencing "uneasiness about the future of private enterprise in their own nations because of government regulations, labor's growing role in corporate management, and, in the case of Italy and France, leftist political trends." Foreign managers are concerned over what they regard as "constraints" on their growth at home.[3] Neither the threats to private enterprise nor the constraints on corporate growth are seen, apparently, to be nearly so troublesome in the United States as in Canada, Japan, Britain, Switzerland, Italy—or Scandinavia.

"More important" are the facts that the "costs of labor, energy and materials are going up faster in most other industrial countries than in the U.S." Furthermore, European managers perceive American workers to be more productive:

> In Italy, says Aldo Cardarelli, head of European operations for General Telephone & Electronics Corp., "Labor costs at our plant outside Milan are pretty much the same as at our Huntsville or Albuquerque plants, yet their output in the U.S. is more competitive. . . . The answer has to be in the productivity of the workers."[4]

A British company, ICI, is delighted to note that the "freedom to hire, fire, and move workers from job to job makes for higher productivity in the U.S. than in Britain," and is consequently putting $70 million into an herbicides plant near Houston.[5]

Fortune's Sanford Rose points out, in a discussion of the advantages of foreign investments in the United States, that our labor is cheaper, more "tractable,"and more readily "available."[6] American unions are content to represent their members in bargaining and grievances rather than try to help run the economy through labor parties or through worker representatives on boards of directors. Large numbers of low-seniority, low-wage young workers are available in the United States. And finally, according to Rose, a good deal is made of America's more qualified managers.

Consider that while many work reformers are bent upon heading off unions in American plants, American collective-bargaining agreements do not seem to faze foreign investors. It is not lost upon Western European and Japanese executives that while many firms have been organized by unions, American executives have avoided implicating themselves in long-term worker-management arrangements from which they cannot extricate themselves when economic conditions are favorable to hardnosed management bargaining postures. We do not in the United States have Japan's "career employment" system, for example, a system from which many Japanese employers have long sought relief by such strategems as subcontracting.[7] The reader will recall that the new German employers had no difficulty ridding themselves of unwanted reforms at the formerly American-owned plant in "Centerton" (Chapter 11).

The inclination to compare a small number of contemporary Western European experiments directed toward the "humanization" of work with those in the United States ought to be resisted. The divergent political, social, and economic histories of the United States and the Western European nations have produced gross differences in the respective roles of unions, in the rights of managers, and in the more profound philosophical premises that inform "industrial democracy" as a working concept in the Old and New Worlds.

The strategic political significance of trade unions in England, Germany, Norway, Sweden, and, in large measure, in France has led to extraordinary elaborations on Bismarckian reforms, thus nationalizing many issues still bargained over in the United States by separate unions and companies; has made faulty manpower decisions very costly to Western European employers who, for example, pay high severance and other costs of human-resources misallocation; and has led in several nations to requirements that corporations bank part of their retained earnings in state depositories, with highly political unions having considerable influence over the disposition of the funds.

In passing, one may note that hardly any of Western Europe's advanced industrial economies have reached even their twenty-fifth birthday. As some critics from the left might see it, there is a sense in which we in the United States are prisoners of an industrial-relations system evolved by a slower process, which has not forced and crystallized questions addressed by a handful of widely celebrated work innovations in Western Europe's social democracies. Many Western European nations have been aided (or harmed, depending upon one's viewpoint regarding managements' rights and of the reason for inflation) until very recently by high levels of employment, a circumstance that facilitated (perhaps even necessitated) all types of reforms in the workplace.[8]

The problems are similar in all industrial countries. In the USSR, for example, there are very serious problems like those we have treated under our "underutilization" rubric. Soviet social scientists, in fact, commend work redesign as an important way of enlarging and enriching jobs for the legions of youths whose educational achievements exceed job requirements by allegedly wide margins.[9] Soviet managers are not, however, encumbered by most of the constraints affecting their American and Western European peers.

All in all, we are not so taken with experiments overseas as are those who make guided tours through the showpiece settings. Our investigation, limited as it is, leads us to argue that the business cycle, more than any other single factor, has pushed Western Europeans to deal with worker malaise, and that the dealings look far more like collective bargaining and wage negotiations than like work enlargement and work enrichment.

It is a fair bet that the story would be very different if economic circumstances changed in ways that went beyond the visible impact of unemployment on imported workers in the major European economies. These imported workers function as a shock-absorber for the European left in each country as well as for Europe's managers: imported workers get the most "alienating" jobs in peak economic periods and the bulk of the unemployment during troughs; native workers get the best of their labor parties' policies and the best jobs (and a few massages, at the margins, by work reformers and intervention agents) when economic conditions are booming. These booms "sustain" managers' concerns with workers' well-being in order in the short run to avert work stoppages and in the long run to slow down radical macroscopic social and economic reforms.

MANAGERS, WORKERS, AND PRODUCTIVITY

There is no hard evidence that foreign managers in general or foreign investors in particular know something about productivity, management, and workers that we don't know in the United States.

One may wonder, though, whether they and the American managers who have essentially ignored the work of behavioral scientists for so long are better informed about the complexities involved in productivity than the rest of us, would-be reformers in particular.

That one could be readily confused is quite understandable; it is sometimes as difficult to know what we are talking about on the subject of productivity as it is to speak sensibly. Indeed, if doublespeak afflicts our discourse about managers and workers, then the only word for discourse about productivity would have to be "multispeak." In Humpty Dumpty's semantic calculus we would be obliged to pay "triple-time" rates each time we use the word.[10] A brief discussion of the productivity matter will help the reader to understand our misgivings about the emphases work reformer assign to *workers'* productivity.

In economics, productivity is a ratio of input to output for a given industry or sector in the economy. The most common measure is output per man-hour.[11] While economists have attempted to account for changes in this ratio over a period of time by introducing ever more sophisticated measurements of critical variables, "no credible econometric model has yet been constructed," as one economist puts it, because "the productivity variable is so complex."[12]

Even without a model, Kendrick puts capital investment and research and development activity high on his priority list of factors underlying both GNP and productivity growth. Renshaw, while pointing to the positive association between changes in productivity and changes in total output, is far less certain of how these phenomena are related:

> Our knowledge with regard to how to promote improvements in productivity is rather meager and, in terms of certainty, about on a par with our knowledge of how to control inflation.[13]

One depressant of productivity is clearly underutilization of capacity. In short-run terms, Solow called the cyclical relationship between output and productivity a "puzzle":

> When output stagnates or falls away from a peak, productivity (output per man-hour) tends to fall, or to rise slower than trend; when output revives, productivity rises faster than trend.[14]

One solves the puzzle by discarding the assumption of full utilization of capital stock. Some employment, meanwhile, is overhead, which is much slower to decline. Solow suggests that a reduction of 6 percent in capital utilization is associated with a 1 percent reduction in employment, but that allowing for the overhead factor, the true elasticity is closer to one-quarter:

The strong impression remains that labor is more nearly the fixed factor in the short run, and variations in output are reflected substantially in the changing intensity of use of existing plant and equipment.[15]

The use of changes in output per man-hour as a measure of the economy's health has an interesting relationship to what we have elsewhere called the "confidence game." In this game the management players make decisions favoring economic expansion only when they feel confident; investments (and jobs) are held hostage to the public policies business leaders regard as confidence-building. In the case at hand, unused plant capacity and underutilized workers cause the output per man-hour to decline. After a period of layoffs, even if capacity utilization fails to rise, the man-hours figure comes into alignment with the capacity being used; productivity, accordingly, then "increases."

It was this phenomenon that accounted in part for the ebullience of the stock market in early 1976. Slow economic growth had helped to bring interest rates down and was correctly seen by most to act as a restraint on wage settlements. The slowness of the recovery signaled that employers were not rehiring workers at a rapid rate and that productivity, therefore, promised to show faster-than-usual growth. This, as one alert observer recently noted, is the kind of thinking that generates confidence:

> Some prognosticators believe the climb in output per man-hour this year could be as much as 5 percent. If average wage increases—for the larger nonunion sector as well as organized labor—come in at only 7 percent, the rise in unit labor costs this year will be only 2 percent.[16]

Apart from the fact that unit labor costs are low in manufacturing, once one leaves manufacturing and the primary sector (agriculture, mining, and construction) the measurement problems become acute. Since measures of output in physical units are not available in such industries as health or education, the usual solution is to use dollar values for output and man-hours for input. The results are self-evidently tautological.

The whole question of productivity differentials between goods and services, one that has encouraged some work reformers to urge action in the service sector, is contaminated by the concept of technology and technological change (of which more later). Baumol, for example, describes the "cost disease" created by the expansion of the service sector in a fashion he regards as being productive of "unbalanced growth," with illustrations (given his well-known interest in the economics of the arts) like the impossibility of improving the productivity of string quartets.[17]

The whole position, however, is based on an essential but problematic assumption—that economic activities can be grouped, with only a slightly nominalist bias, into two types: technologically progressive activities in which innovations, capital accumulation, and economies of scale make for a cumulative rise of output per man-hour, and all other activities. The assumption of this dichotomy obscures both facts and trends.

First, there are the contributions of the service sector to the productivity of the goods sector, through such activities as improving the health (or education) of workers.[18] On the other side of the balance sheet are the social costs that have not been attributed to production. The magnitude of these costs is becoming evident in the complaints of industry that the cost of pollution control is diminishing their profits and therefore their incentives.

If we take such costs into account, leaving aside the pollution-control device makers, losses in productivity in the goods sector would be greater. In fact, simple maintenance, let alone environmental improvement, counts *against* productivity. On the nation's railroads, for example, output per man-hour has been spuriously high as a result of too little maintenance.[19] The cumulative effects appear in the form of breakdowns and derailments, which are charged, in effect, to other accounts.

Generalizing from such phenomena, Renshaw points out that "large reductions in one input can sometimes mean only a modest increase in total welfare if the reductions are in large measure offset by increases in other inputs." [20] This caution is particularly timely when we recall that the technological advances largely responsible for the quantum leaps in productivity in the past were rendered feasible by cheap and abundant energy. The constraints in energy supply (and the general rise in the cost of materials) put some cost limits on the substitution of machines for workers. Furthermore, there has been a slowing of the pace of innovation. In Renshaw's view, one implication of the decline in the growth rate of GNP from 1965 to 1973 is that

> persons engaged in research and development are now finding it more difficult to discover and invent new products and productive processes that are unambiguously superior to older commodities and ways of producing goods and services.[21]

While this slowdown may be viewed by some as inevitable, other students of the field are searching for ways to counteract "underspending" on research and development. They assume a continuing connection between innovation and productivity with such desirable outcomes as a more competitive trade position and faster economic growth.[22]

From this point of view, private investment in research and development has been too small. Government has focused on defense and space technology, which absorbed over 55 percent of its R & D expenditures during the early 1960s. This percentage decreased, but even in 1970 the figure was about 43 percent. Whatever the spillover effect, the contribution to economic growth is considerably less than the contribution of a dollar of civilian R & D.[23]

Meanwhile, the indicators used to measure general scientific advance have declined. According to a report by the National Science Foundation, "The number of patentable ideas of international merit has been growing at a greater rate in other countries than in the United States." [24] It is important, furthermore, that private-industry R & D is concentrated largely on products, not processes; on development ($21 billion in 1976), not on research ($5.5 billion in 1976). And much of the expenditure on research is aimed at fairly modest advances in the state of a particular art. Industries seem to be loath to make heavy investments for uncertain returns, and their desire to minimize risk contributes some of the impetus to the search for appropriate points of governmental intervention.

One public-policy response to the potentially productive role of technological advance is to afford employers the benefits of subsidy-like tax expenditures such as the investment tax credit. Workers whose jobs are to be enlarged in the interest of satisfaction and productivity might be understandably skeptical of some employers' real concern in the matter, however, since corporate tax benefits tend to have a bigger effect on the bottom line than on the production line. Thus, the *Wall Street Journal* noted on August 11, 1976, that the

. . . profits of Aluminum Company of America dropped 62 percent last year but the bottom line would have been much worse if the investment tax credit hadn't made it possible for the large aluminum maker to avoid paying all U.S. taxes for 1975. Still, recession-weakened demand forced the company to cut its 1976 capital spending budget 29 percent from last year to $382 million.[25]

Other aids to both productivity and profit innovation through the application of technology are often viewed with similarly stout entrepreneurial reservations; as the *Wall Street Journal* suggests, there are easier ways to make money. Those who drum away at the theme that American workers are apostates from the Protestant ethic might, for example, look at the backsliders among the putatively faithful employers in America's economy.

The search for enhanced productivity and economic growth through investment and innovation runs into other barriers. On a comparative basis, as Renshaw points out, there is a peaking effect. The United States remains the country with the highest absolute level of output per worker. Faster rates of growth in productivity experienced by other industrialized countries are due, in effect, to the low levels from which they started. The United States could not hope to reap the same advantages by similar increases in investment.[26]

New industries, new plants, and new equipment are of course more productive than old industries, plants, and equipment. But new industries also tend to have higher ratios of nonproduction to production workers (N/P ratios). This is another ambiguity in this most ambiguous of subjects: those "newer" industries whose "production functions" have been most radically transformed by technology seem to require a greater proportion of professionals, managers, and technicians and an enlarged clerical staff to support them! George Delehanty concludes that rising N/P ratios have been associated with increased productivity, although he allows that "there is room within the unexplained variance in N/P for . . . bureaucratic expansion," with the attendant possibility that increases in overhead costs may be simply wasteful and inefficient.[27]

As soon as the notion of a "nonproduction" worker is introduced we find ourselves in the same dilemma as in assessing the contribution of the service industries. One thing we do know is that one manager's efficiency is another manager's waste. Most discussions of productivity simply assume that tasks are rationally defined and managed in profit-making enterprises, overlooking the decision about what is being produced. A typist's efficiency in producing letters may be improved, but as Leon Greenberg has reminded us, "It might be even more productive . . . to evaluate and reduce the need for letter writing and multiple copies." [28]

To summarize, productivity can be imagined in the center of a ring of connotations. Insofar as it is related to profit, the concept involves labor costs, capacity utilization, and the effectiveness/efficiency with which capacity and resources are used.

Next, a few items are related to both productivity and profit: innovation, technological change, and the efficiencies that come of better-managed employees, whether human-relations logics or others are among those applied by managers.

Finally, there are a number of institutional arrangements that aid profit-seekers in the short run but that can and sometimes do subvert productivity. Tariffs can have such restrictive effects even though imposed to help producers through difficult times in competitive international markets. "Captured" regulatory agencies can help protect the arbitrarily noneconomic ways of producers through the congenial rates they schedule and the nominal character of their enforcement activities.

The behavior of oligopolists, meanwhile, points to the conclusion that managers can act on the urges to go beyond the limits prescribed in "profit-maximizing" roles.[29] Walter Adams points out, after consulting relevant studies, that there is a difference between the advantages accruing to large-scale integrated production—in steel making, for example—and the administrative leviathans that result from combining functionally separate plant units. As he puts it:

> To the extent that profit figures are valid as measures of comparative efficiency, it seems that, in a number of cases, medium-sized and small firms outperform their giant rivals. Moreover, a breaking down of huge firms does not necessarily have fatal effects on efficiency *or* profitability.[30]

Adams quotes Joe Bain on the subject as follows:

> In estimating multiplant economies, Bain concluded that in 6 out of 20 industries, the cost advantages of multiplant firms were "either negligible or totally absent"; in another 6 industries the advantages were "perceptible" but "fairly small"; and in the remaining 8 industries, no estimates could be obtained. (*Barriers to New Competition*, Cambridge, Mass.: Harvard University Press, 1956, pp. 73, 85–88ff.) These findings hardly support the contention that existing concentration in American industry can be explained in terms of technological imperatives.[31]

The fact that not all managers elect to follow the route to profitability mapped out in textbooks which applaud the working out of market forces is not news. Our own interest in the matter derives from our concern with the two-valued logic used to judge the behavior of workers and managers. Thus, it is fair to recognize workers' interests in stability as well as productivity and to argue that managers who stoutly avoid opportunities to be more productive are also protecting a status quo in which they have considerable investments. It is simply unfair to castigate unproductive workers alone as transgressors against the imperative of the Protestant ethic.

Nor need the backsliders in management be drummed out of the faith straightaway for their differentiated view of the believers' creed. The Protestant ethic, after all, can make room for the principle that there are as many mansions in Adam Smith's house as in God's.

Consider that as one moves from smaller to larger corporate units there are relevant qualitative changes. For a small unit, stability is important in the larger environment, but as one goes up the size hierarchy it becomes less exogenous: major problems of stability occur inside the larger organizations because of the nature of processes of production. One simply does not increase productivity in one segment of an organization alone, and the problems inherent in raising productivity overall are complicated indeed.

Consider, further, while momentarily conceding a high positive correlation between satisfaction and productivity, that the most logical source of productivity increases often inheres in work-force *reductions*. But job security is among the job facets noted as "most important" by respondents to the *Working Conditions Survey*.

It is also frequently argued, as we have stressed, that work rules are to blame for productivity losses. Many of these rules protect workers' equity, however, and the provision of equity to workers is itself a kind of efficiency. As the conventional logic in the allocation of stock options to managers goes, people with more equity have greater incentives. The denial of the application of that logic to the equities that concern workers is, of course, simply another case of doublethink. Work rules facilitate organizational stability, a fact that even the most orthodox of believers affirm, even as they deny the sound economic instincts of workers with investments in stability.

CONCLUSION

In all, it would be something of an embarrassment for managers to be obliged to live by the simpleminded conceptions of efficiency and productivity that have suffused recent discussions of the economic benefits imputed to work reforms. Thus, "satisfaction" requires job security in exchange for productivity, skill, and loyalty. But managers' loyalty as well as their skill and productivity is just as important as workers'. Loyalty especially cuts two ways; and it strikes us that the last of management's aims is to be loyal to its work force. Ultimately, that would be a kind of capitalism that no one could understand, least of all its most articulate proponents.

Many orthodox social scientists overlook all this, as do some Marxists who share a view of managers as an undifferentiated crowd of rational, production-minded decision makers. The rationality of American managers is, by and large, not of the type represented by the engineers who Veblen thought should run the American economy. Nor is it well represented by Max Weber's conception of legal-rational bureaucrats. The closest most American managers come to Weber's version of rationality is in accounting offices. If Weber were alive, as Sam Goldwyn might say, he would probably turn in his grave at the way in which accountants, the most important of the capitalist technical experts in his related theories of the Protestant Ethic and bureaucracy, have been driven from their temples and into desperate quests in legislative corridors, Bahamian banks, and courtrooms for tax havens, tax dodges, tax deductions, and taxonomic exercises in artful avoidance—even evasion—of liabilities.

Otherwise, what we have in abundant numbers are not Veblen's engineers and Weber's legal-rational bureaucrats but Veblen's "financiers," Sloan's marketers,[32] confidence-game players, wheelers, dealers, stealers, as well as a very large number of able leaders who seek to balance the possibilities of productivity gains against the disruptive effects on their firms of new technology, new risk-taking ventures, and new unknowns. The textbookish management skills that Americans conspicuously admire most and that business schools are pleased to impart are not necessarily the critical ones in making corporate winners.

These realities are of course recognized by most leading business-men. Perhaps equally aware are the social-science consultants who are able to sell their human-relations nostrums to clients who can effectively exploit scientific findings for public-relations purposes, in support of a far more simplified view of productivity (and of workers' exaggerated roles in productivity) than either the behavioral-science data or a tech-nically competent assessment of the productivity matter will sustain.

17. A Concluding Overview

Few thoughtful Americans would seriously maintain that the work ethic is dying. The outraged and frustrated cries of the unemployed are familiar to every politician, and the evidence from recent studies of welfare recipients demonstrates that the able-bodied minority among them exhaust all other avenues of support before they subject themselves to the humiliations that accompany public assistance. Employable welfare recipients, furthermore, hopefully attend any and all programs designed to improve their employment prospects.[1] And it is a mockery of the agonized competition for jobs between those protected by equal rights regulations and those protected by union seniority clauses to hold that people are less "work-oriented" now than in other days.

But the demonstrated eagerness of Americans to work should probably not be exploited by a civilized people. Even a little job dissatisfaction, though only vaguely linked to productivity, deserves the attention of a thoughtful and humane citizenry. The recent promotion of work-related discontents to the level of a cause in many American quarters ought accordingly to be endorsed and even praised.

Most good causes, however, enlist some allies whose conceptions of the problems are oversimplified, whose collection of relevant information is incomplete, whose reading even of relevant information is too narrow and too selective, and whose reform proposals are consequently vulnerable to skepticism. While such allies often come by their views and recommendations honestly, they can mislead others who are even less informed but who are equally dedicated to the cause. Good causes are especially vulnerable when the popular media seize upon and generalize freely from the work of less scrupulous experts and commence to raise hopes to unrealistic heights. The work-reform movement is among the causes in America that have suffered along just these lines.

While many experts have sought to fathom employee reactions to work, the relation of these reactions to performance, and the usefulness of a variety of tactics for improving morale, only one segment of this body of investigators and theoreticians has gained much popular attention. It is also the case, perhaps understandably, that the work of the most zealous but least radically threatening representatives of this contingent of experts has gained the lion's share of attention. It is unfortunately also the case that a number of the experts to whom attention is most readily paid have been inclined to market their expertise without guarding against compromising their scientific obligations to be cautious. Finally, it is the case that the movement to reform work includes among its more articulate spokesmen a number of persons whose aims are less to serve discontented workers as such than to design arrangements that may suffice to dampen workers' interests in alternative arrangements.

Thus, the work reform movement's leaders in the academy and in the media have been very much taken with a modern version of the human-relations approach founded at the Harvard Business School in the 1930s, according to which much worker discontent is attributable to immediately proximal working conditions, which are within the scope of management to change. Workers, it is argued, are more satisfied, less prone to unionize, and probably more productive—all other things being equal—if they are supervised in democratic rather than autocratic ways; if they work at jobs that are more challenging by virtue of their being enriched and enlarged; and if they play somewhat more participative roles in decisions affecting their tasks, obligations, and rewards. Managers, it is argued further, can combine a sense of *noblesse oblige*[2] with trained social-scientific sensibilities, the better to design organizations with social relationships that are gratifying both to workers and to managers' rational economic ends.

According to what may be construed as a competing industrial relations view, the problem of worker discontent is a far more complex matter. The prospects for harmonious labor-management relations are evaluated more skeptically (if not misanthropically) in this view, and the rights and interests of workers and managers are regarded as being in material, rather than psychological, conflict. In this view there is a need for more legalistic machinery than is provided in the "solidarities" astute managers can engineer on behalf of anomic workers, and a need as well for more hard-headed economic bargains than are conceived to be required in the social-psychological views of human relationists.

It is also an essential element in the competing perspective that workers' attitudes are influenced by macroscopic social and economic developments to a far greater degree than is made clear by modern human relationists. Finally, worker attitudes and actions are viewed by industrial-relations and human-resources students as being directly affected by the forces that distribute the population among occupations and among income groups and by changing economic conditions, especially business cycles, that affect the fortunes of employees in labor markets.

The two views do not lend themselves readily to a synthesis in the classical, theoretical sense of the word. It has been our position, however, that more data relevant to crude tests of validity could be juxtaposed than are considered by the promoters of either view. Such tests have been conducted in this volume; they approximate "critical experiments" whose results complement and supplement those of others who work at different levels of analysis.

In the remainder of this chapter we review the questions pursued in each of the five parts of our investigation and the tentative conclusions supported by assessments of the data. The review is presented in essay form, without references to the chapters, tables, percentages, or statistical correlations included in the preceding chapters.

SATISFACTION AS ATTITUDE

Work satisfactions, we have noted, are most often the subject of attitude surveys. The bulk of the data regularly mobilized in support of conclusions about the state of morale among research populations is thus confined to issues that have attracted the attention of social scientists as researchers, consultants, and interested parties.

The results from a pair of recent national probability surveys by University of Michigan investigators highlight the difficulties facing a would-be theorist. In a series of interview questions these investigators elicited sentiments about matters that have essentially been ignored for many decades. Specifically, the questions cast light upon the effectiveness of respondents' managers as resource-users and resource-suppliers. The replies to these questions are consistent with the hypothesis that worker satisfactions vary directly with managerial competence, though by themselves they cannot confirm it. Managers who are "legitimate," along the lines conceived by Max Weber, are more likely to be managing contented workers than those who are not. Even the ablest, most legitimate managers, however, cannot be assured of their work force's happiness in a society in which workers' feelings about their jobs are influenced by many more factors than individual employers can control.

Next—questions about managers' legitimacy and other generally unexplored issues quite aside—it is possible to measure worker attitudes only in relative terms. The fact is that there are different thresholds of satisfaction and dissatisfaction among workers depending upon the specific content and wording of survey items. It is also clear that worker satisfactions and dissatisfactions as expressed in surveys may be ordered and explained to only a modest degree and can be linked to worker performance only in accordance with a speculative model that requires the interpolated roles of a number of contingencies; the relationships are anything but direct.

Finally, it is not clear that the most frequently mentioned organizational causes of dissatisfaction—causes anchored in size and technology, for example—are as relevant to dissatisfaction as many commentators believe, even if it is supposed that managers could and would manipulate them. There is, admittedly, some intriguing evidence that their memberships in different units of work flow have bearings upon workers' attitudes and behavior. This evidence suggests, furthermore, that these flows, influenced as they are by the way specific production methods are employed, could be designed by managers in ways that would have positive effects on workers' dispositions to grieve and on their attitudes toward work, toward their colleagues, and toward their supervisors. This evidence is suggestive but scanty, just as evidence is scanty that managers would tinker much with work flows if a really strong case could be made for adjustments.

One may conclude that managers could expect to reap *some* increases in worker satisfaction by making adjustments in what have been demonstrably offensive arrangements and by facing and managing more rationally the issues that are sifted in survey researchers' nets. It is quite clear, though, that a good deal of unexplained variance remains in the data.

INTRA- AND EXTRAORGANIZATIONAL SOURCES OF DISCONTENT

The observation that a number of extraorganizational as well as intraorganizational forces are relevant to worker sensibilities suggests that a preliminary paradigm can be constructed for the understanding of managerial options vis-à-vis worker discontents.

The model, whose essential elements are derived from a reading of the best-demonstrated conclusions of investigations from the human relations and industrial relations traditions, is readily applicable to survey data; it requires that one look at the forces impinging on the macroscopic, mezzoscopic, and microscopic levels of workers' circumstances. The linkages that cut across the three analytical levels are workers' skills and their occupations. The skills possessed by workers are significant in shaping their reactions and are differentially touched by the forces operating at each of the analytical levels.

An application of the model to survey data reveals that workers are predictably discontented with the unfavorable experiences rooted in developments at each level. While interventions of the type commended by human-relationist reformers might well increase overall job satisfactions, they can by no means be expected to yield a wholesale discount in discontent. Untouched by the workplace changes favored by work reformers are the mezzoscopic and macroscopic forces that collectively appear to account for more of workers' overall discontents than do those in the workplace itself.

Thus, managers no longer have the controls over the educational achievements of their work forces that they had in the 1950s. They can try to undo the demoralizing effects of underutilized formal education only by paying higher wages to some underutilized workers. Other underutilized workers, who do not enjoy even the advantages of relatively higher-skilled jobs in a skill-conscious society and who consequently enjoy fewer dollar gains to offset their "objective" underutilization, are and will remain unhappy.

Next, a part of overall job satisfaction and dissatisfaction stems from survey respondents' comparisons of their lot with that of people in other occupations, transcending the differences attached to specific jobs. But it is only over the jobs in their enterprises that employers typically have manageable controls. They do not control the terms of socially defined coercive or invidious comparisons, though they may indirectly influence these terms in the aggregate by their advertising and other expressions bearing upon cultural norms and values.

Finally, managers could perform more effectively than they do, or so it would appear from survey responses. The facts suggest that workers are often supervised by managers whose leadership and related capacities are limited. They are also dissatisfied about work scheduling and about the equipment and information provided them by managers. The facts also suggest that jobs are satisfying to the degree to which they are challenging. The challenge of the job, in turn, is related to the skill level of the job and to the worker's formal educational achievement.

SATISFACTION AND BEHAVIOR

Data on workers' and managers' behavior can be additionally revealing of the interests of the parties and the effectiveness of the devices used in labor-management relations for their reconciliation.

It is clear from a study of arbitration cases, for example, that managers are as concerned with enforcing discipline as ever they were in putatively rougher days. Indeed, their zealous defense of their "rights to manage" can lead to excesses in their behavior, excesses that give precious little assurance that most managers' "orientations" are vulnerable to the gentle therapeutic directions and ministrations stressed by work reformers.

The fact of the matter is that work reformers are inclined, in their emphasis on managers' and workers' psychologies, to gainsay the material conflict between managers' rights to manage and workers' rights to due process and need for protection against the unilateral and arbitrary exercise of power over their occupational and personal lives. While work reformers insist that novel "quality of working life" committees are both good and useful things, data on strikes and grievances in a sample of arbitration cases suggest that workers derive important protections from their participation in old-fashioned grievance processes against managers who (apparently not uncommonly) are unreasonable, arbitrary, or derelict in their roles.

Findings like those about managers and proximal working conditions and about conflicts over the exercise of managers' authority lead one to wonder about the extent of managers' real interest in human-resource problems in general and in work reforms in particular. To put this in another way, it is clear that, while managers cannot manipulate all the levers that regulate the flow of worker discontent, they can influence a number of the intraorganizational arrangements that affect workers for better or worse. They can even do so without concern for problems of invidious comparison. Highly skilled workers do not suffer marginal losses in their exalted positions, after all, when lesser-skilled co-workers are supervised equitably, are provided with adequate tools, are given sufficient information to perform their chores, or are treated with civility and fairness by managers concerned with the maintenance of law and order in their shops and offices. The implicit question remains: Why *don't* managers avail themselves more frequently of opportunities to manage workers more effectively? The question is not so easily answered, but some facets of the general problem can be examined.

THE LOGICS OF MANAGERS AND WORKERS

Consider the evidence that work-reform experiments, targeted upon issues that managers *can* join, tend not to "take." Evidence collected by leaders of the reform movement itself suggests that managers' commitment to work reform is not very great even in cases in which workers have expressed interest in the reform program and in which productivity gains may realistically be anticipated. The evidence supports considerable skepticism about the degree to which managers wish to manage at all in ways designed to utilize people effectively; they rarely engage in manpower planning and are clearly reluctant to construct even the least compromising of the conditions requisite to the success of work-reform experiments.

Further examination of managers' performance, as discernible in arbitration cases, confirms these suspicions. Indeed, a review of the holdings of arbitrators reveals that these agents of the public interest in peaceful labor-management relations have helped to sanctify a view of workers and managers in America according to which different standards are applied to the two groups. This two-valued view favors managers even when arbitrators sustain workers' grievances. Thus managers may be exonerated and even praised for actions that are deplored when they occur among workers. When workers quit their jobs in boom periods, adding to "turnover rates," we wring our hands over their lack of loyalty. When a manager leaves one company for a better position in another company, we see the effective operations of the market for valued skills and rationally self-interested behavior in pursuit of the American dream of mobility.

Overall, we do not find much evidence that either managers or workers fit the perspectives of those who urge work reform. Managers are concerned as often about their authority as about their opportunities on the human-resources front; they are apparently mindful of the costs of reform and of the modesty of the rewards reform would bring their firms. They are also apparently unconcerned either with workers' discontents or with the marginal implication of these discontents for the well-being of their enterprises.

In these circumstances, when their discontents are highly developed and when business and other conditions afford them the opportunity, workers will grieve, will strike, will quit their jobs, and sometimes will absent themselves from work. We find little evidence that their actions are less rational than those of managers who sometimes do not manage people very well and only infrequently give thought to improvements in working conditions beyond those forced upon them by labor-market conditions or regulatory legislation.

In unionized work-settings, workers are protected against a number of untoward actions by managers that are simply not included in most studies of worker discontent. Indeed, many studies of discontent are conducted by social-science investigators who view unions as obstacles to the implementation of inventive and progressive work reforms. This view we find to be informed more by prejudice than by detailed investigative control of data on collective bargaining and on the well-developed capacities of many managers, workers, and union leaders to enlarge, enrich, and restructure work quite without the help of change agent-consultants. Once again, a two-valued logic can get in the way of a sensitive, empirically rigorous, and ideologically neutral appraisal.

In the meantime, there is no compelling evidence that unions do *not* serve to protect workers' rights and interests. On one side, complaints by managers about restrictive work practices have increased over the years. Workers, it thus appears, are enlarging work in their own way. They have negotiated millions of work rules; they have grieved against the unilateral violation of these rules by managers; and hundreds of thousands have joined strike actions, as in the great steel strike of 1959, to protect the bilateral character of work-rule agreements.

On another side, the law requires that unions be more democratic than corporations, and the evidence suggests that the law is largely satisfied on the point. There is the "practical difficulty," as some see it, that democrats in unions may, like other democratic citizens, act upon their political freedoms in ways not especially admired either by work reformers or by citizens generally. The times are—in these as in many other respects—out of joint.

Consider, in this connection, that the use of arbitration in the steel industry in place of strikes at contract-expiration dates ran afoul of partisan politics in the United Steelworkers Union. Thus the union's elected leaders were accused, in the union's 1977 election campaign, of collaborating rather too much in the adjudications of rights, privileges, and immunities of workers about which opposition candidates promise a tougher bargaining line. As it turned out, a majority of bona fide steel-worker critics lost their bid to redirect bargaining relationships with steelmakers as established union leaders secured the electoral endorsements of USW members outside the nation's steel mills, including mushroom pickers in North Carolina caves who never before the USW came along "have had it so good."

CODA

It was one of our purposes to explore an alternative to a prevailing view of work that states that managers, in seeking to maximize (or at least to optimize) efficiency and productivity, must overcome (or yield to) forces that limit the commitments of workers to work industriously. Our long associations with managers, aspiring executives, and the world in which they operate had left us skeptical of this perspective. Our skepticism has been reinforced by the experiences in our investigation. Our doubts about what is so often made of human relations findings, by themselves, are immeasurably larger than when we embarked upon our research. When these findings are combined with findings emanating from an industrial relations–human resources perspective, however, the results are a good deal more instructive.

We have been struck, for example, by the power of *occupational* attributes in predicting workers' attitudes and by the fact that these attributes receive almost no systematic attention as variables in studies of workers as *job* incumbents. We have also been struck by the impact of managers' capacities *as managers* in contributing to worker disaffection.

A second major aim of this study was to examine work and workers as though they were at the center of a whirlpool, the rings of which represent distinctive sets of forces: those stemming from organizational and from technological characteristics and imperatives; those stemming from the means, methods, and modes of managers; and those stemming from the reach of democracy and from growing concerns over equity in America. Such an approach inevitably leaves one vulnerable to charges commonly leveled at eclectics. We have accordingly tried to be sensitive to the risks of oversimplification.

Thus, we have sought to be mindful of the possibility that when one elects to study simultaneously the effects and the correlates of forces and factors that operate along what is customarily regarded as a macroscopic-microscopic continuum, one is likely to do injustice to in-depth research focused on one point along this continuum or, in our metaphor, in one of the rings of the whirlpool to which we likened the forces impacting on workers. These risks, we believed, were worth taking; the results were, as we have noted, far more complementary and supplementary to those who work at different levels of analysis than they were subversive of others' results.

A third aim of this study was a negative one: we aspired to show what we believed to be some gross oversimplifications in the most popular approaches to work in the twentieth century. Thus, we were disturbed by the regular reappearance of the view that behavioral-science findings based on studies at the organizational level can be assembled into a package of prescriptions and proscriptions for managers which, if attended to, would reduce worker dissatisfaction and the putatively offensive worker behavior it engenders and thereby increase worker productivity.

These remedies, we have argued, are for the most part unacceptable to managers for one set of reasons and, when applied without a weather eye to a number of neglected issues, are intrinsically and inherently deficient for another set of reasons. An examination of the apparent effects of major extraorganizational forces and their correlates revealed many of these reasons and helps, we suggest, to provide a more realistic conception of policies for intervention in the workaday world.

Our thesis has been that little is likely to come of the renewed urgings by many social scientists that our policymakers, managers, and, in lesser degree, union leaders get on with the most conventionally proferred reforms to improve the quality of working life. Our reasoning may be outlined here.

First, the relations among worker attitudes toward working conditions, worker behavior patterns, and working conditions themselves are far from being of the order that would persuade employers, cost-conscious or otherwise, to engage in experimentation or reform. The evidence from programmatic interventions is similarly not reassuring. In some instances the experiments are flawed. More often they are discontinued in the short run, even when they are apparently productive of desired changes in workers' attitudes, behavior, or both, for lack of employer interest, sympathy, good sense, or need.

Second, and among the principal reasons for the failure of innumerable experimental efforts to affect either worker performance or attitudes in enduring ways, are the trade-offs between productivity on the one side and workplace stability and other employer objectives on the other. Efficiency for managers (no less than for workers who seek to protect allegedly inefficient work rules, for example, in the interest of their *own* definitions of efficiency and equity) is a multidimensional consummation. It comes in many guises, involves a variety of stakes, and often competes unsuccessfully with employers' needs for stability and predictability.

Next, it is not altogether clear that many employers take very seriously the inefficiencies social scientists attribute to work malaise or that they confound productivity with profitability; imperfect markets and alternative routes to efficiency and profit are among the factors apparently taken into the short-run account managers make of their circumstances.

Important but neglected evidence of what is downright indifference among managers may be read in the pitiful quality of data on worker behavior in American firms, in the cyclical quality of managers' interests in reform, and in the regular association between managers' interests in reform and their apprehensions about collective bargaining.

On another side, it may be noted, are the sources of some worker discontent that are common to members of an age group, a sex cohort, a racial group, a skill classification, or an occupation. These are *differentiated* discontents born of conditions that are largely beyond employers' control. While a manager here and an employer there has been an active party to some of the more vicious aspects of the development of America's much-admired pluralistic social system, most could argue with other innocents that they were just doing their job in a world rife with conflicting and sometimes equally valid claims on their imaginations and resources. To the extent that dissatisfactions among workers reflect the differential vulnerability of members of different races, sexes, age groups, and occupations, they are not *directly* amenable to the control of individual employers on a firm-by-firm basis.

Employers play important parts, to be sure, in the unfolding American drama. But they did not, as employers, unilaterally write seniority clauses into union contracts that offend those first fired during layoffs; they did not single-handedly invent housing segregation or suburbanization and the disastrous effects of these social developments on the reading, writing, and ultimately the critically important occupational skills and opportunities of inner-city blacks; and they did not, by themselves, determine that the sanguinary trades practiced by skilled crotch sawyers in a slaughterhouse and hospital surgeons who perform sex transformations would be so very differently rewarded.

Put another way, the logic by which distributions of advantages, opportunities, job security, prestige, and, finally, income are determined is not the exclusive domain of employers. But the resulting inequalities and inequities are reflected in both the behavioral and the attitudinal responses of employed Americans. It should not be surprising that reforms focused only on the most proximal causes of worker discontent have only trivial consequences.

Indeed, we submit that to improve some of the worst working conditions on behalf of those most damaged by them would substantially unsettle a balance of rewards and deprivations in which currently favored races and sexes—as well as skill, age, and occupational groups—have more than marginal interests. We have accordingly been surprised by the tendency among reformers bent upon work redesign to overlook the probable effects on *satisfied* workers of arrangements calculated to reduce the dissatisfactions of others in a labor force whose members are demonstrably given to coercive and invidious comparisons. While one may applaud whatever marginally egalitarian impulses are at play among aspiring reformers, it is hardly practical to expect openhanded generosity among "haves" toward "have-nots."

Paralleling almost precisely our reason for misgivings about the prospects for reform in the quality of working life is what we call sectorialization of the economic and social system. Where once there were a few organized competing and conflicting interests, there are now many. The strains among the sectors quite obviously are greater when the economic pie grows only slowly, as events since 1973 in respect to equal employment opportunity have made vividly clear.

Whether one sees this inadequately conceptualized development as the flawed work of self-made men, themselves the products of unskilled labor, or as the predictable heritage of a "people of paradox" [3] may be debated, along with other possible explanations. The facts are, however, that workers in America do not see themselves as a homogeneous whole with respect to many issues that are joined even across similar work-settings. Witness the increased solidarity of particular groups of workers and managers, of which joint, long-time lobbying efforts in the steel industry offer cases in point. Even more to the point, consider the "well-advanced" program of former Labor Secretary John Dunlop by which it was sought

> to enlist the aid of unions and management in specific areas of industrial relations [embracing] the whole spectrum of basic political policy. Its goal was to provide a vehicle through which the dominant influence groups in the economy could harmonize their differences and arrive at a common position that would then serve as a guide to Government in running the country. . . . The principal instrument of collaboration was the President's Labor Management Committee, a summit organization, in which George Meany and seven other ranking unionists sit alongside the heads of General Motors, General Electric, United States Steel, Alcoa, Mobil Oil, The First National City Bank, The Bechtel Group and Sears Roebuck.[4]

The effort foundered over the ill-fated situs-picketing bill in the construction industry and Dunlop's ensuing resignation. As A. H. Raskin suggests, it might have "atrophied" anyway,

> but the frequency with which corporate magnates and union chiefs make common cause in Congress these days on import curbs and on stretch-outs of environmental time limits indicates that the idea of a shadow economic cabinet is not dead. . . . [One of the] most interesting heritages of the committee [is the] vastly improved climate for top-level communication it engendered between labor and industry. The union dissatisfaction is with the Ford Administration, not with the good faith of the executives representing the giant multinationals which the unions condemn so regularly in their pronouncements.[5]

The ultimate effects on other Americans of comfortable relations between some labor-management groups may be saluted or deplored, depending upon one's view of the public interest. The issues are not new ones and in any event need not be explored fully here. The essential point of such a collaboration of worker representatives and managers will not be much blunted by those who see top-priority and readily remediable workplace problems behind exotic dog-food blenders and glass-fabricating devices, behind complicated pulp grinders and glucose-bottle fillers, or plain old ordinary buffers, mops, and brooms.[6] Workers are at the same time a heterogeneous lot and members of large groups with patterned and rather well-perceived interests.

If they are too unconscious of their status as commodities to act upon their interests as a class in Marxian or neo-Marxian terms, they are highly conscious of the effects of foreign-product "dumping," of the benefits of protective tariffs secured by their employers' lobbyists, of the advantages of job-creating building codes, defense contracts won by managerial bid-writers, interstate highway construction appropriations, and court decisions overturning the impulse of Equal Employment Opportunity commissioners to unsettle hard-won seniority rights. Shared irritations over such aggravating work conditions as those associated with amateurish supervision, for example, simply do not support a larger view that reforms will even marginally touch the core of worker insecurity, anxiety, and distemper. Neither can packages of reforms be constructed that fit the multiple conditions of citizens of so highly sectorialized an economy.

Finally, we doubt whether managers can undo, by most proposed interventions, the results of their errors or of earlier, sound business logics that were pushed too far. It was in this connection that we examined the relevant correlates of the underutilization of workers in jobs for which only the educational requirements have been upgraded. A significant degree of underutilization is undoubtedly inevitable in a society in which the occupational structure has stabilized while educational achievements have bounded upward; neither the occupational structure's shape nor the educational achievements of the work force are realistically amenable, at this late date, to much amelioration by the nation's business leaders. The problems inherent in *significantly* "enlarging" jobs in order to make them more challenging for those millions of underutilized workers are mind-boggling.

The errors of managers—and occasional questions about their ethics—do little, of course, to enhance the confidence of their employees, though the usual view taken of "confidence" in our economy is, as we have suggested, generally of another sort. Thus, it has been almost an obsession with many that we must all bend our will to assure that businessmen are confident. The most adroit of the players in that game have effectively—indeed, in almost extortionate ways—used problematic business confidence to political advantage by holding hostage the fortunes needed for investment and growth pending favorable government actions—depreciation allowances, tax credits, and the rest [7]—to obtain all manner and means of leverage. Recent data suggest that the familiar one is no longer the only confidence game in town, however, and that workers' unhappiness with the quality of working life is in no small measure a function of managers' increasingly questionable legitimacy. As Max Weber emphasized, the bigger part of legitimacy is rooted in technical competence and bureaucratic virtuosity; Americans see some room for doubt about their employers on both counts. Some wise observers of the business scene, happily, are not unmindful of the problem.[8]

QUO VADIS?

It may be America's curse or its genius that we wish to reform as many things as possible while changing things as little as possible. Thus, the widespread interest in worker discontent, like the concern with poverty and government corruption, is admirable, but like our efforts to deal with social and political disorders, our efforts in the workplace tend to focus on the symptoms rather than on the first causes of pathology.

Our reluctance to change things in substantive and substantial ways cannot be simply ascribed either to the shortsightedness of businessmen or to "capitalistic" greed, although there is clearly no shortage in America of either commodity. Consider, for example, that we would probably reduce the dissatisfaction of those whose education has been significantly underutilized if our occupational structure changed over the next ten years as radically as it did in the 1960s (a matter discussed in Chapter 6), and if unemployment levels were sufficiently low to encourage risk-taking job-hoppers at the lower economic reaches to follow the example of the nation's top corporate decision makers (Chapter 13). But the desire of some Americans for low unemployment levels runs directly counter to the yearnings of others for appreciably lower inflation rates. Economists recognize that the order of magnitude among the complex trade-offs involved here may be only crudely gauged, but no responsible scientist denies that labor costs are of a piece with other strands in the economic web. The point is that well-intentioned rationalists—socialists no less than "establishment" economists—can disagree about the weights that should be assigned to the costs and the benefits of specific social and economic undertakings.

Beyond the reasoned disagreements among reasonable souls, there are of course the other problems to which we have referred earlier. Those workers whose satisfactions are predictable from their skills, for example, will not generously suffer rapid and subversive shifts in the structures that protect their invidious claims and the benefits attaching to their positions; and managers, for another example, will always listen to social scientists in whose tables and graphs they may find the trappings of scientific expertise, the better to dress their rights—never mind their power—in the legal-rational raiment of authoritative leadership. Business leaders, no less than emperors in the cliché, we may suppose, are anxious to be enrobed.

There are thus essentially two related reasons why we continually seek to study worker dissatisfactions while doing little to make changes that would affect a number of the critical conditions in which these dissatisfactions are rooted. On one side, we in America have reservations about essential, which is to say "fundamental," changes; on the other, however, we feel an obligation to cluck our tongues, to express our concern, to take dim views, and to view with alarm when we see troubles and symptoms of troubles. We are, after all, a reasonably compassionate people.

One is reminded of Paul Samuelson's invitation to readers of his text to ponder the arrangements that assure higher incomes to plastic surgeons than to cardiac surgeons. Some will suggest that Samuelson's conundrum is a kind of metaphor, that Americans have a well-developed instinct for the capillary rather than the jugular, for cosmetic reform over radical revision—in short, for the social equivalent of "nose jobs." The difficulties on the road to critics' preferred major, substantive changes in workaday life, in short, are very numerous indeed. A nation whose war against poverty turned, early on, into skirmishes against the poor, will certainly not do more for relatively better-situated employed Americans whose jobs afford few pleasures than for those whose circumstances are so often linked to *un*employment.

It is not our disposition to be quite so angrily accusative of Americans' motives, to be so totally despairing of their willingness or ability to share more of the social product and loosen up their bureaucracies. We take a little heart, for example, from the fact that an integrated jury, made up essentially of workers, acquitted James Johnson, a black worker, of murdering his white foreman. Johnson was suspended from his job at Chrysler's Eldon plant for refusing to participate in a speed-up. Nat Hentoff summarizes the case, in a review of the book in which the full story is told, as follows:

> The jury, which—at the insistence of Cockrel [Johnson's lawyer]—had been taken to see the conditions under which Johnson worked, found James Johnson not responsible for his acts. The next year—and who could have predicted this?—Johnson "was awarded workman's compensation for the injuries done to him by Chrysler." [9]

Hentoff notes with understated sadness that Johnson "collects the money at Ionia State Hospital." We thus emphasize that we take a *little* heart in the prospects for better work-days ahead. One of our hopes focuses on the Occupational Health and Safety Act, legislation targeted upon problems that need not be interpreted in complex psychological terms and that are very much more often directly amenable, if work satisfaction is not, to expeditious intervention schemes.

The facts of the matter are good ones on which to end our report; we would urge that work in America can be made considerably less hazardous to health. We urge further that efforts to improve menacingly dangerous working conditions be regarded as the best *starting* point for improving other working conditions. Because sorely needed reforms—like those focused on pollution in our environment—require an effective partnership of managers, workers, citizens, and public officials, successful participation in efforts to complete these reforms could conceivably be a paradigm for reform writ larger.

Consider that since 1972, when the first annual data on work-related injuries and illnesses were gathered, one out of every ten private sector employees has suffered a nonfatal injury or illness or was actually killed because of hazards in the work environment. This means that in 1974, 5,900 workers were killed on the job and over 2 million were sufficiently affected to lose time from work.[10]

A small sample study conducted at the University of Washington, however, showed that diseases suffered by *three* of every ten factory and farm workers appeared to have been caused by working conditions and that 90 percent of these work-related health conditions had not been reported in official government records.[11] The passage of the Occupational Health and Safety Act in 1972 coincided with the beginning of serious public interest in the question, but the incidence of work-related illness, in contrast to the incidence of accidents, is still vastly underreported.[12] Silicosis and black-lung disease among miners have taken their toll over the years, but the long-term effects of many toxic substances are just now emerging as health hazards.

In each of recent years, moreover, we have had a new health hazard revelation—1973 was the year of asbestos, when cases of cancer were discovered not only among long-time asbestos-plant workers but among their households' members as well; 1974 produced the first news of death from a rare liver cancer unquestionably linked to vinyl chloride, a chemical used in manufacturing for twenty-five years; in 1975, we had kepone, a pesticide linked to neurological disorders, sterility, and liver cancer. In 1977, it was benzene, believed to cause leukemia. Altogether, about 153,000 workers were said to be exposed to benzene in 1,200 workplaces.[13] In this instance, the Department of Labor issued an emergency standard to cut down exposure. Typically, some large benzene producers said that "the link between benzene and leukemia hasn't been established sufficiently to justify the massive cash outlays necessary to meet the new standards." [14] They said the same sorts of things in 1974, the year of vinyl chloride, but six months after tough new rules took effect, the industry, far from an immediate close-down, "surprised itself" by managing to meet the rules with no closings, four new plant openings, and lower prices than the previous year.[15]

Therein lie some clues that deserve attention; we might then return, later, to worker morale problems with the lessons that may be learned from following these suggestive clues.

Notes

NOTES FROM PREFACE/ACKNOWLEDGMENTS

1. May 8, 1977.
2. *American Scientist*, May–June, 1976, p. 254.

NOTES FROM CHAPTER 1

1. Reinhard Bendix, *Work and Authority in Industry: Ideologies of Management in the Course of Industrialization* (Berkeley, Calif.: University of California Press, 1974). See especially Chapter 5.
2. *Work in America*. Report of a Special Task Force to the Secretary of Health, Education and Welfare (Cambridge, Mass.: MIT Press, 1973).
3. See "Hearings on Worker Alienation" before the Subcommittee on Employment, Manpower and Poverty of the Senate Committee on Labor and Public Welfare, 92d Congress, 2d Session (1972).
4. This council was formed at Columbia University's Arden House in 1972. Its members are leading social-science consultants on workplace reforms. Its American leader is Louis Davis of the school of management at UCLA.
5. Richard Walton, "How to Counter Alienation in the Plant," *Harvard Business Review* 50 (June 1972), pp. 70–81.
6. The word normally used in connection with such managers is "democratic." A decent respect for the word has led us, in later chapters, to distinguish between the forms of employee participation endorsed by work reformers, on one side, and the types of institutional reforms urged by social reformers, on the other.
7. Only 32 percent of the top 161 personnel and industrial-relations executives from a panel of companies surveyed by the Bureau of National Affairs in 1966 conducted training programs of any type for their first-line supervisors more than once per month. Twenty-seven percent did nothing at all in this allegedly critical area. Bureau of National Affairs, *Personnel Policies Forum*, Survey No. 78 (February 1966), p. 8. The matter itself is rarely pursued by the Bureau or by others who influence management thinking.

In a later study, by the National Industrial Conference Board, spokesmen for only 53 of 302 surveyed companies reported "great interest" in relevant behavioral science findings generally. About half reported "moderate interest" while 30 percent reported "little" or "no interest." Harold M. F. Rush, *Behavorial Science: Concepts and Management Application*, Personnel Study No. 216 (New York: The National Industrial Conference Board, 1969), p. 60.

8. For a brief discussion of differences in these approaches, especially between social scientists with reservations about the adequacy of marginal economic analysis and neo-orthodox economists in the study of managers and workers, see Fritz Machlup's Presidential Address at the 1966 meetings of the American Economics Association: "Theories of the Firm: Marginalist, Behavioral, Managerial," *American Economic Review* 57 (March 1967), pp. 1–33.

9. See, as Adam Smith's twentieth-century editor, Edwin Cannan, suggests, E. Chambers, Encyclopedie, vol. ii, 2nd ed. (1738), and 4th ed. (1741). Dr. Cannan's annotation appears on p. 5 of *The Wealth of Nations* (Modern Library, 1936). For Adam Smith's version of the intellectually numbing effect of factory-type labor, see *ibid.*, pp. 734–735.

10. William Felkin, *A History of the Machine-Wrought Hosiery and Lace Manufacturers* (London: Longmans, Green, 1867), p. xiii and Chapter XVI. For more recent discussions, see F. O. Darvall, *Popular Disturbances and Public Order in Regency England* (London: Routledge & Kegan Paul, 1934); and Malcolm I. Thomis, *The Luddites: Machine-Breaking in Regency England* (New York: Schocken Books, 1972).

11. See James Kuhn and Ivar Berg, "*Bargaining and Work-Rule Disputes*" *Social Research* 31 (Winter 1964) pp. 466–481, and, by the same authors, "The Assumptions of Featherbedding," *Labor Law Journal* 13 (April 1962), pp. 277–283.

12. For inventive efforts toward such syntheses, see Bendix, *Work and Authority*, and Clark Kerr et al., *Industrialism and Industrial Man Reconsidered: Some Perspectives on a Study over Two Decades of the Problems of Labor and Management in Economic Growth* (Princeton, N.J.: The Inter-University Study of Human Resources in National Development, 1975). An early intellectually compelling effort, by Karl Marx, focused on the problems of alienation attributable to the estrangement of workers from their work and therefore from themselves, under conditions that reduced labor to a commodity. The perspective Marx developed still informs a great deal of the research on work. Finally, for a recent social-psychological study of the effects of factory and other experiences incidental to the industrialization process, see Alex Inkeles and David H. Smith, *Becoming Modern: Individual Change in Six Developing Countries* (Cambridge, Mass.: Harvard University Press, 1974).

13. It is interesting to note in passing that the view of managers as rational economic agents is widely shared. Thus, in a review of a most interesting and provocative book, written in a Marxist, not a human relations, vein, a sympathetic critic chides the author, Harry Braverman, for failing to see

managers' uses of "human relations" as part of an overall rationalistic utilitarian strategy in the service of "the highest practicable profits for the corporation." We have some doubts about the strategy, detailed in later chapters, but we doubt more fundamentally that managers are seriously concerned with either human-resource strategies or human-relations tactics. See Maarten deKatt, in a review of Harry Braverman, *Labor and Monopoly Capital: The Degradation of Work in the Twentieth Century* (New York: Monthly Review Press, 1974), *Review of Radical Political Economics 7* (Spring 1975), pp. 84–90. For an earlier, more favorable view, from the Right, of the same applications of behavioral science, see the classic discussion by Chester Barnard in *The Functions of The Executive* (Cambridge, Mass.: Harvard University Press, 1938), *passim.* DeKatt's view differs from those of one of America's principal managerialists only in the judgments he makes about the *legitimacy* of management; management's *role* is the same in the two views. The Barnard work is among those discussed in the assessment by Bendix, *Work and Authority,* Chapter 5.

14. John Dunlop brought a similar perspective to bear in his seminal work, *Industrial Relations Systems* (New York: Henry Holt and Co., 1958). For a theoretical statement of work relationships among essentially rational managers and workers, see Neil Chamberlain, *A General Theory of Economic Process* (New York: Harper, 1955). For some specifications of Chamberlain's view of economic relationships as bargaining relationships, see his book, *The Firm: Micro-economic Planning and Action* (New York: McGraw-Hill, 1962), especially Chapters 11, 17 and 18. We owe intellectual debts to Thorstein Veblen, as well; few scholars have written more trenchantly about the functions of the executive.

15. William M. Leiserson, "The Economics of Restriction of Output," in Stanley B. Mathewson, *Restriction of Output Among Unorganized Workers* (Carbondale, Ill.: Southern Illinois University Press, 1969), p. 166. The first edition was published by Viking Press in 1931. The 1969 edition, cited here, includes a pertinent introduction by Donald F. Roy, whose work on quota restrictions, worker incentives, and worker strategies and tactics constitutes several critically important chapters in the literature on work. Roy's materials will be cited later.

16. A whirlpool has been described as a "revolving current in an ocean, river, or lake. It may be caused by the configuration of the shore, irregularities in the bottom of the body of water, the meeting of opposing currents or tides or the action of the wind upon the water." William Bridgwater and Seymour Kurtz (eds.), *The Columbia Encyclopedia* (New York: Columbia University Press, 1956 ed.), pp. 2317–2318. This description, if all of the causes outlined in it were acting more or less simultaneously, would apply, in metaphorical terms, to the many factors operating on workers and jobs.

17. See Thomas Fuller, *The Profane State: The Rigid Donatists* (London, 1642), book 5, ch. 11: "That faith is easily wrought which teacheth men to believe well of themselves."

18. We will note in Chapter 11, however, that when a work reform program

appears to collapse, as at a pharmaceutical plant in North Carolina, the
change agents are roundly criticized while the underlying model's validity
stands totally unchallenged by "outside" evaluators.

NOTES FROM CHAPTER 2

1. For more fully developed efforts see, for example, Reinhard Bendix, *Work
   and Authority in Industry: Ideologies of Management in the Course of
   Industrialization* (Berkeley, Calif.: University of California Press, 1974)
   and Charles Perrow, *Complex Organizations: A Critical Essay* (Glenview,
   Ill.: Scott Foresman, 1972), pp. 61–204.

2. For one meticulous discussion of the labor theory of value, both Marxian
   and pre-Marxian, and of the Marxian notion of exploitation, complete with
   tables, graphs, symbolic notations, and even the slain deer and beavers
   who figure prominently in economic theory, see Paul A. Samuelson, "Understanding the Marxian Notion of Exploitation: A Summary of the So-
   Called Transformation Problem between Marxian Values and Competitive
   Prices," *Journal of Economic Literature* 9 (June 1971), pp. 399–431. For a
   Marxist review see Maurice Dobb, *On Economic Theory and Socialism*
   (London: Routledge & Kegan Paul, 1955), pp. 273–81.

3. The debate over the meanings of terms like alienation and estrangement,
   in and out of the Marxist tradition, involves a considerable and fascinating
   literature. For a most helpful and accessible discussion see Richard
   Schacht, *Alienation* (Garden City, N.Y.: Doubleday, 1970), for which the
   distinguished philosopher Walter Kaufman has written a valuable introduction. For a discussion that takes account of detailed social-science
   findings, see Melvin Seeman, "Alienation Studies," in Alex Inkeles (ed.),
   Annual Review of Sociology 1 (1975), pp. 91–123.

4. For a fine, brief discussion of the last of these functions, see Kenneth
   Boulding, "Man as a Commodity," in Ivar Berg (ed.), *Human Resources
   and Economic Welfare: Essays Presented to Eli Ginzberg* (New York:
   Columbia University Press, 1974), pp. 35–49.

5. A. G. Zdravomyslov, V. P. Rozin and V. A. Iadov, eds., *Man and His
   Work: A Sociological Study* (White Plains, N.Y.: International Arts and
   Sciences Press, 1970) (originally published in Moscow in 1967). The Eng-
   lish text has been translated and edited by Stephen P. Dunn.

6. We leave aside here the complicated views regarding unorganized workers
   among proponents (and practitioners, especially in the labor movement)
   of this second "macro" or institutional version.

7. We will consider this issue later. For a well-executed example of this line
   of analysis, see Robert J. Flanagan, George Strauss, and Lloyd Ulman,
   "Worker Discontent and Work Place Behavior," *Industrial Relations* 13
   (May 1974), pp. 101–123.

8. These efforts will receive specific attention in Chapter 5. For a brief and
   lucid discussion of their place in economic theory, see Michael Piore, "The

Importance of Human Capital Theory to Labor Economics: A Dissenting View" in Gerald Somers (ed.), *Proceedings of the Twenty-Sixth Annual Winter Meeting of the Industrial Relations Research Association*, 1973, pp. 251–258. For a sensible statement of the aspirations of and difficulties in the human-capital approach, see T. W. Schultz, "Human Capital: Policy Issues and Research Opportunities" in *Human Resources: Colloquium 6, Economic Research, Retrospect, and Prospect* (New York: National Bureau of Economic Research and Columbia University Press, 1972), pp. 1–97.

9. See Bendix, *Work and Authority*, pp. 254–340. For a recent effort to make "Taylorism" less distasteful, and to give Taylor a bit more intellectual credit than has been accorded him by critics, see Peter F. Drucker, "The Coming Rediscovery of Scientific Management," *Conference Board Record* 13 (June 1976), pp. 23–27.

10. For a recent and relevant example, see "The Anachronism of Taylorism," in *Work in America*, Report of a Special Task Force to the Secretary of Health, Education, and Welfare (Cambridge, Mass.: MIT Press, 1973), pp. 17–20.

11. Among this group, it was Henderson who explicated the relevance of the Newtonian physical-science notion of "system" for social science. His approach, in the tradition of Pareto and Marshall, was related to their development of "equilibrium" theories of society and economy—theories that led a generation of social scientists to view conflict as an unnatural disturbance of what would otherwise be harmonious, integrated social systems. Exit Marx, unions, and criticisms of management, among other elements of the radical critique. See Ralf Dahrendorf, *Class and Class Conflict in Industrial Society* (Stanford, Calif.: Stanford University Press, 1959).

12. Thus, the playful taps that workers gave each other at the Hawthorne works, called "binging," were seen as sanctions calculated to bring a "rate-buster" back in line, to preserve group integrity and the production quotas that served the workers' social system. The quotas, meantime, were interpreted as the outcome of workers' distrust of management, distrust born of "nonrational," that is, unconscious, "confusions" about those in authority.

13. This idea, or an earlier version by Frederick W. Taylor, had once been challenged by American businessmen who felt that any such heresy should be resisted on the grounds that *ownership*, not *technical competence*, was the source of managerial legitimacy. Taylor was hauled before a congressional committee when his heretical notions received some currency.

14. Chester Barnard, *The Functions of the Executive* (Cambridge, Mass.: Harvard University Press, 1938).

15. The operative term here is "more"; Barnard's democracy considerably revises the doctrine of "consent of the governed."

16. These experiments have recently been reviewed by H. M. Parsons, who reports, after reassessment of both reported and previously unreported data, that the behavior of the Hawthorne workers could more easily be interpreted by reference to earnings than to the sociopsychological factors

adduced by the investigators. His reanalysis appears to demolish the asserted potency of the "Hawthorne Effect" at Hawthorne. See "What Happened at Hawthorne?" *Science* 183 (March 8, 1974), pp. 922–932. See also Alex Carey, "The Hawthorne Studies: A Radical Criticism," *American Sociological Review* 32 (June 1967), pp. 403–416.

17. For a discussion of the apologetics, see the provocative article by Edward S. Mason, "The Apologetics of 'Managerialism'," *Journal of Business* 31 (January 1958), pp. 1–11.

18. See Elton Mayo, *The Human Problems of an Industrial Civilization* (Boston: Harvard University, Graduate School of Business Administration, 1946); and *The Social Problems of an Industrial Civilization* (Cambridge, Mass.: Harvard University Press, 1945). Also, T. N. Whitehead, *Leadership in a Free Society* (Cambridge, Mass.: Harvard University Press, 1936). The underlying assumption in all of this, that worker satisfactions are related to worker productivity, will concern us in the next chapter.

19. Elton Mayo and George F. Lombard, "Teamwork and Labor Turnover in the Aircraft Industry of Southern California," *Business Research Studies*, No. 32 (Boston: Harvard Business School, 1944).

20. Clinton S. Golden and Harold J. Ruttenberg, *The Dynamics of Industrial Democracy* (New York: Harper, 1942), p. 58. *E.g.*, "Management, as a general principle, gets the kind of union leadership it deserves. A tough management begets tough union leaders, while a patient, friendly, cooperative management begets a like type of union leadership."

21. A notable exception was the systematic study of authoritarianism by psychologists and social-psychologists. See T. W. Adorno *et al.*, *The Authoritarian Personality* (New York: Harper & Row, 1950), an effort that has inspired much research.

22. For a sensible discussion, see Edgar H. Schein, *Organizational Psychology* (Englewood Cliffs, N.J.: Prentice-Hall, 1965).

23. Hoke Simpson, in conversation with one of the authors, 1975.

24. See, for example, Clark Kerr and Lloyd H. Fisher, "Plant Sociology: The Elite and the Aborigines," in Mirra Komarovsky (ed.), *Common Frontiers of the Social Sciences* (New York: Free Press, 1957), pp. 281–309. While Kerr and Fisher are skeptical of the humaneness of market processes, they make more room for industrial workers' interests and less for the utility of the corporatist, medieval-like social system of workers and managers commended in the early human-relations literature.

25. See Schein, *Organizational Psychology*, and Chris Argyris, *Personality and Organization* (New York: Harper & Row, 1957).

26. See, for example, John R. Maher (ed.), *New Perspectives in Job Enrichment* (New York: Van Nostrand, 1971). Maher is a Columbia University-trained social psychologist employed by the IBM World Trade Corporation.

27. Interested readers may consult the advanced mimeographed assignments given to participants at a conference held at Columbia University's Arden House campus in the fall of 1972 on work and the roles of consultant-investigators concerned with work, available from Louis Davis, Chairman, Center for Quality of Working Life, University of California, Los Angeles.

The result of these discussions was the formation of the International Council for Quality of Working Life.

28. These are topics discussed, for example, at conferences on "The Changing Work Ethic" in Chicago and New York in December 1972 and April 1973, respectively, sponsored by The Urban Research Corporation of Chicago.

29. Ironically, federal and state affirmative-action requirements have elevated the personnel function, since it is the personnel office that must perform "utilization analyses" of "protected" and unprotected groups, an analysis requisite to equal-opportunity goal-setting for employee promotions and new hiring. The irony resides in the fact that such rational procedures were *not* compelled by the marketplace's pressures, a fact of relevance in assessing managers' interest in intervention programs generally.

30. The classic Marxist critique gainsays a great deal of what is discussed in this volume on the grounds that the materials we assay are not targeted upon the role of private property, in what should be viewed in a totally political-economic perspective. A number of the issues that Marxists would insist be considered, meantime, are joined in later "institutional" sections of the present volume.

31. See Robert Blauner, *Alienation and Freedom: The Factory Worker and His Industry* (Chicago: University of Chicago Press, 1964), and Chapter 3, below.

32. Argyris, *Personality and Organization.*

33. Leonard Sayles, *Behavior of Industrial Work Groups: Prediction and Control* (New York: Wiley, 1958); and James W. Kuhn, *Bargaining in the Grievance Process* (New York: Columbia University Press, 1961).

34. Kuhn, *Bargaining in the Grievance Process.*

35. Abraham Zaleznik, *Worker Satisfaction and Development* (Boston: Harvard University, Graduate School of Business Administration, 1956).

36. Other frequently cited conclusions regarding work and workers' discontents are available in competent summaries. For the most recent, see Lyman Porter, Edward E. Lawler III, and J. Richard Hackman, *Behavior in Organizations* (New York: McGraw-Hill, 1975). For a fine summary of one of the important perspectives, see George Strauss et al., *Organizational Behavior: Research and Issues* (Madison, Wisc.: Industrial Relations Research Association, 1974). For examples of two overviews of the industrial-relations perspective, see the articles by Harold Wilensky and Reinhard Bendix in Conrad Arensberg et al. (eds.), *Research in Industrial Human Relations: A Critical Appraisal* (New York: Harper, 1957); and Sherman Krupp, *Patterns in Organizational Analysis: A Critical Examination* (New York: Holt, Rinehart, 1961), respectively.

NOTES FROM CHAPTER 3

1. George Strauss et al., *Organizational Behavior: Research and Issues* (Madison, Wisc.: Industrial Relations Research Association, 1974). See,

especially, Chapter 1, pp. 1–18, and Chapter 8, pp. 193–220. For a parallel, somewhat more didactic discussion of issues related to satisfaction studies, see Robert P. Quinn, Stanley E. Seashore, *et al.*, "The Personal, Corporate, and Societal Implications of Employment: Some Issues of Strategy, Theory and Methods" (Ann Arbor, Mich.: Survey Research Center, 1971), mimeo. This paper also explicitly addresses the place of outcomes of research in public policy and in private policy.

2. For a book-length review of research and a bibliography, see Lyman Porter, Edward E. Lawler III, and J. Richard Hackman, *Behavior in Organizations* (New York: McGraw-Hill, 1975), especially Part 3, pp. 221–310.

3. Quinn, Seashore, *et al.*, *Implications of Employment*, p. 23.

4. *Ibid.*, p. 24. Emphasis in the original. The discussion by Quinn and his associates is of special interest because it reflects not only wide experience with other studies but, as we shall see, their own meticulous exploitation of two sets of data on the satisfactions and dissatisfactions of national probability samples of employed Americans in 1969 and 1973. For another helpful discussion of the policy implications of productivity-performance-attitude materials, see Robert P. Quinn, Graham L. Staines, and Margaret R. McCullough, *Job Satisfaction: Is There a Trend?*, Manpower Research Monograph, No. 30 (Washington, D.C.: U.S. Government Printing Office, 1974).

5 Quinn, Seashore, *et al.*, *Implications of Employment*, p. 24.

6. Cited from Vroom, *Work and Motivation* (New York: Wiley, 1964), pp. 183, 186 in Quinn, Seashore, *et al.*, *Implications of Employment*, pp. 29–30.

7. Frederick Herzberg *et al.*, *Job Attitudes: Review of Research and Opinion* (Pittsburgh: Psychological Service of Pittsburgh, 1957), p. 99.

8. *Ibid.*

9. Cited in Quinn, Seashore, *et al.*, *Implications of Employment*, pp. 30–31. We may note, from a 1972 Gallop Poll, that 57 percent of the "total public" allowed as how "they could produce more each day if they tried"; the figure for professional people and businessmen was 70 percent. See Ivar Berg, " 'They Won't Work': The End of the Protestant Ethic and All That," *Columbia University Forum* 5 (Winter 1973), p. 19.

10. Raymond A. Katzell, Daniel Yankelovich, *et al.*, *Work, Productivity, and Job Satisfaction: An Evaluation of Policy-Related Research* (New York: The Psychological Corporation, 1975), pp. 151–153. Emphasis added.

11. Quinn, Staines, and McCullough, p. 51.

12. Quinn, Seashore, *et al.*, *Implications of Employment*, pp. 31–32. Porter and Lawler have developed a promising conception along the "third factor" line. They suggest that a key variable in a "feedback" process involves the effect workers' efforts have on the values of the rewards received and the perceptions the recipients of these rewards have of their equity. The model is constructed from data on a sample of managers. See Lyman W. Porter and Edward E. Lawler III, *Managerial Attitudes and Performance* (Homewood, Ill.: Irwin-Dorsey, 1968). For our own view of equity as a factor, see Part II.

13. A number of colleagues have urged us to be more skeptical of the utility of worker-satisfaction surveys, a matter to which we will address ourselves later. We may say that while many workers undoubtedly hesitate to be critical of circumstances that reflect in some measure on themselves, they apparently "hesitate" to do so in different proportions. While measurements of satisfactions in an absolute sense are clearly problematical, as noted by Quinn, Staines, and McCullough, and Quinn and Seashore, measures of worker satisfactions *are* suggestive of *relative* differences among different worker-respondents.

14. Quinn, Staines, and McCullough, *Job Satisfaction*, pp. 1–2.

15. *Ibid.*, p. 27.

16. For an overview, see Chris Argyris, *Personality and Organization* (New York: Harper & Row, 1957). The "general principles" here allow, of course, for variations. Thus, there are, in the vast literature on work, cases of workers who favor opportunities for daydreaming over not inconsiderable challenges in their work, who are ruggedly individualistic and therefore offended by the pressures of co-workers' norms; of workers, like bridge-building Mohawk Indians, who enjoy coping with occupational hazards; and of workers who thrive upon, and self-servingly exploit, ambiguities in organizational demands. See, for example, the following studies whose very titles will suggest the variations around the mean: Melville Dalton, *Men Who Manage* (New York: Wiley, 1959); Donald Roy, "Quota Restriction and Goldbricking in a Machine Shop," *American Journal of Sociology* 57 (March 1952), pp. 427–442; "Work Satisfaction and Social Reward in Quota Achievement: An Analysis of Piecework Incentive," *American Sociological Review* 18 (October 1953), pp. 507–514; "Efficiency and 'the Fix': Informal Intergroup Relations in a Piecework Shop," *American Journal of Sociology* 60 (November 1954), pp. 255–266. See also Melville Dalton, "The Industrial Rate-buster: A Characterization," *Applied Anthropology* 7 (1948), pp. 5–18. Finally, see Leonard Sayles and George Strauss, *The Local Union* (New York: Harcourt, Brace and World, 1967); James W. Kuhn, *Bargaining in the Grievance Process* (New York: Columbia University Press, 1961); and Ivar Berg and James Kuhn, "The Assumptions of Featherbedding," *Labor Law Journal* 13 (April 1962), pp. 277–283.

17. "Enough facts have accumulated," they write, "to indicate that conditions which improve job satisfaction are *likely* to reduce avoidance behavior such as turnover and absenteeism [attributable to dissatisfiers]." Katzell, Yankelovich, *et al.*, *Work, Productivity*, p. 152. Emphasis added.

18. Porter *et al.*, *Behavior in Organizations*, pp. 43–44. Emphasis in the original. These authors' references to relevant empirical studies have been omitted from the citation.

19. J. Thad Barnowe, Thomas W. Mangione, and Robert P. Quinn, "The Relative Importance of Job Facets as Indicated by an Empirically Derived Model of Job Satisfaction," *The 1969–1970 Survey of Working Conditions: Chronicles of an Unfinished Enterprise* (Ann Arbor, Mich.: Survey Research Center, University of Michigan, 1973), pp. 263–320. Our own

efforts to exploit portions of the same data lead us to the same conclusions. See Chapter 4.

20. For a useful discussion of motives involved in "mid-career" changes, see Dale L. Hiestand, *Changing Careers after 35* (New York: Columbia University Press, 1971). We return to this issue in Chapter 4.

21. For one relevant critical treatment, in theoretical terms, of the "organization man" thesis, see Mayer N. Zald, *Occupations and Organizations in American Society* (Chicago: Markham, 1971), especially pp. 81–82. For a useful discussion of bureaucracy and the view of social scientists toward bureaucracy, including those of the human-relations school, see Charles Perrow, *Complex Organizations: A Critical Essay* (Glenview, Ill.: Scott, Foresman, 1972). For a provocative presentation of social-science reservations about bureaucracy, see Alvin W. Gouldner, "Metaphysical Pathos and the Theory of Bureaucracy," in Amitai Etzioni (ed.), *Complex Organizations* (New York: Holt, Rinehart, 1962), pp. 71–82.

22. The idea has received its fullest popular expression in the work of Eric Trist, Albert Cherns, and others from the Tavistock Institute, a human relations organization in the U.K. For examples of the detailed positions of these latter-day intellectual descendants of the approach founded at the Harvard Business School in the 1930s, see Louis E. Davis and Albert B. Cherns, eds., *The Quality of Working Life*, 2 vols. (New York: Free Press, 1975), Chapters 1–4, pp. 4–104; Chapter 15, pp. 220–241.

23. Sherrill Cleland, *The Influence of Plant Size on Industrial Relations* (Princeton: Industrial Relations Section, Department of Economics and Sociology, Princeton University, 1955), pp. 61–63. A "small" plant in this study employed fewer than 500 workers. The study covered the period 1951–1953.

24. Porter *et al.*, *Behavior in Organizations*.

25. Geoffrey K. Ingham, *Size of Industrial Organization and Worker Behavior* (Cambridge, Eng.: Cambridge University Press, 1970), p. 143. Emphasis in the original.

26. Many small-business types are not exactly outside large organizations, as the outraged expressions of franchised automobile dealers and service-station operators, over the years, make clear. While many of these persons are legally defined as independent businessmen, their "renegotiably" renewable franchise contracts leave them quite vulnerable to the initiatives of large supplier corporations. For example, readers may compare Harvard human-relations professor Theodore Levitt's paean to the managers who developed the McDonald's fast-food franchise system, "Management and the 'Post-Industrial' Society," *The Public Interest* 44 (Summer 1976), pp. 69–103, with the report by Clark Bell of the Chicago News Service of the desperate efforts of McDonald's franchisees to protect themselves from the fearful tactics used against them by the very managers Professor Levitt extols. *Detroit Free Press*, August 29, 1976, pp. 1B and 6B.

27. From the author's preface to the first edition, Karl Marx, *Capital*, Vol. 1 (New York: Modern Library Edition).

28. Robert Blauner, *Alienation and Freedom: The Factory Worker and His Industry* (Chicago: University of Chicago Press, 1964). The book has appeared in both hard and soft covers. The sixth impression appeared in 1973. A list of important books and monographs significantly influenced by this study would be very long, indeed. For one prototypic and itself influential example, see Richard H. Hall, *Occupations and the Social Structure*, 2nd ed. (Englewood Cliffs, N.J.: Prentice-Hall, 1975), pp. 54–60, 191–192, 215, 217–218. It is our sense that the substitution of "control" enables investigators to eat their cake and have it as well, to offer an apparently radical critique while commending work reforms. The reader, in such instances, is left to choose (or wonder about) a role for capitalism in the play of affairs.

29. Blauner, *Alienation and Freedom,* p. 5.

30. *Ibid.,* p. 6. While we reexamined these data, reported first in *Fortune* in May 1947, pp. 5–6, 10, 12, and in June 1947, pp. 5–6, 10, we became fascinated with the prospects for refinements in sociological and economic theories in which the "separation of ownership from control," in the modern corporation's management, is treated as though it is entirely distinguishable from the "separation of the worker from the means of production" in the workplace. We would suggest that the two social-structural developments are special cases of a general process of structural differentiation.

31. Dorothy Wedderburn and Rosemary Crompton, *Workers' Attitudes and Technology* (Cambridge, Eng.: Cambridge University Press, 1972). In this study of 400 textile workers, the findings on one subset whose job tasks parallel the chemical industry workers' in the Roper survey are, however, consistent with Blauner's findings.

    From a 1967 survey study of a cross section of the U.S. labor force targeted on discovering the impacts of technological *change,* the investigators report first that "technological advance changed relatively few jobs to a significant degree—about 2 to 3 percent a year;" and, second, that the overriding majority of workers view machine and machine-related changes in their jobs with great equanimity or satisfaction. See Eva Mueller *et al., Technological Advance in An Expanding Economy: Its Impact on a Cross-Section of the Labor Force* (Ann Arbor, Mich.: Institute for Social Research, 1969), p. 10 and *passim.*

32. Leonard R. Sayles, *Behavior in Industrial Work Groups: Prediction and Control* (New York: Wiley, 1958), and Kuhn, *Bargaining in the Grievance Process.*

33. William H. Form, *Blue-Collar Stratification: Autoworkers in Four Countries* (Princeton, N.J.: Princeton University Press, 1976).

34. See E. C. Wegner and Leonard R. Sayles, *Cases in Organizational and Administrative Behavior* (Englewood Cliffs, N.J.: Prentice-Hall, 1972); and George Strauss and Leonard Sayles, *Personnel: The Human Problems of Management,* 3d ed. (Englewood Cliffs, N.J.: Prentice-Hall, 1972), pp. 313–322.

NOTE FROM INTRODUCTION TO PART II

1. See Lester C. Thurow, *Generating Inequality: Mechanisms of Distribution in the U.S. Economy* (New York: Basic Books, 1975), pp. 75–128.

NOTES FROM CHAPTER 4

1. Robert J. Flanagan, George Strauss, and Lloyd Ulman, "Worker Discontent and Work Place Behavior," *Industrial Relations* 13 (May 1974), pp. 101–123.
2. Among the key structural factors affecting workers' experiences are those embodied in labor markets, factors that shape the demand for workers of different attributes and thus the opportunities for different workers to obtain and hold jobs of diverse character.
3. Jerome M. Rosow (ed.), *The Worker and the Job: Coping with Change* (Englewood Cliffs, N.J.: Prentice-Hall, 1974), p. 3. It is indeed the case that fundamental predispositions, or response sets, can have a marked effect on the ways in which survey questions are answered. For an interesting discussion of methods for handling this problem, see Walter R. Gove *et al.*, "Response Bias in Community Surveys of Mental Health: Systematic Bias or Random Noise?" *Social Science and Medicine* 9/10 (September–October 1976), pp. 497–502.
4. See especially John H. Goldthorpe *et al.*, *The Affluent Worker: Industrial Attitudes and Behavior* (Cambridge, Eng.: Cambridge University Press, 1968).
5. George Strauss, "Workers: Attitudes and Adjustments," in Rosow, ed., *Worker and Job*, pp. 73–98, especially pp. 82–92.
6. Thus the underlying sources of job satisfaction may not have changed, but the measurements of the relative statistical effects of explanatory factors depend on the variances of these factors in the sample being analyzed, and these variances may change with changing times. See Arne L. Kalleberg, "Work Values and Job Rewards: A Theory of Job Satisfaction," *American Sociological Review* 42 (February 1977), p. 136. This article contains several ingenious suggestions for identifying and establishing further some of the links our ideal model would include.
7. Thus, for example, the kinds of jobs in which women are concentrated lead to a seemingly better fit between their educational achievements and their job requirements, in part because discriminatory practices simply exclude them from a number of jobs in which mismatchings occur more regularly. A hasty look at relevant data could lead the observer *simply* to see more economic rationality in the uses made of women's than of men's educational achievements. See Chapter 6.
8. For a formal statement, complete with indifference curves describing the penchants of the id, ego and superego, see Harvey Leibenstein, *Beyond*

Economic Man: A New Foundation for Microeconomics (Cambridge, Mass.: Harvard University Press, 1976).

9. Daniel Yankelovich, *The New Morality: A Profile of American Youth in the 70's* (New York: McGraw-Hill, 1974), p. 105.

10. It is not obvious, for example, how best to interpret the data just cited. The numbers who actually *would* trade a fifth of their incomes for training opportunities might be considerably fewer than the numbers replying to a question about trade-offs. Moreover, in Bacon's words, "As it asketh some knowledge to demand a question not impertinent, so it requireth some sense to make a wish not absurd."

11. It has been demonstrated that these economists' and sociologists' views are coterminous, not contradictory, in a presentation in which the author aspires to show that occupational differences in the processes governing wage attainment "can be predicted from and explained in terms of forces which lead to occupational segmentation of labor markets." Ross M. Stolzenberg, "Occupations, Labor Markets and the Process of Wage Attainment," *American Sociological Review* 40 (October 1975), pp. 645—665. A parallel effort has been conducted by one of the authors. See Marcia Freedman, *Labor Markets: Segments and Shelters* (Montclair, N.J.: Allanheld, Osmun, 1976). For an early review of the literature on the subject, see Bruce McKinlay, *A Functional Classification of Occupations* (Eugene, Ore.: University of Oregon Press, 1971).

12. See Flanagan *et al.*, "Worker Discontent." See also Malcolm Getz and Yuh-ching Huang, "Consumer-Revealed Preference for City Size" (Nashville, Tenn.: Vanderbilt University, Department of Economics, 1975), mimeo; and the references in Chapter 6 to the human-capital literature and the underutilization of manpower.

13. For a discussion of the often implicit differences in the meaning of "development" and "growth," see Peter L. Berger, *Pyramids of Sacrifice: Political Ethics and Social Change* (New York: Basic Books, 1974), pp. 9–65.

14. For a current review of the major classification schemes, see Bruce McKinlay, "Review of Literature and Research on Characteristics of Jobs that are Considered Common: Review of the Literature and Research" (Columbus, Ohio: The Center for Vocational Education, Ohio State University, 1977), mimeo.

15. Ivar Berg, *Education and Jobs: The Great Training Robbery* (New York: Praeger, 1970); Marcia K. Freedman, *The Process of Work Establishment* (New York: Columbia University Press, 1969). For an example of the use of skill level as a critical independent variable in an analysis of worker responses to their occupational experiences see the study, cited in a similar context in the preceding chapter, by William H. Form, *Blue-Collar Stratification: Autoworkers in Four Countries* (Princeton, N.J.: Princeton University Press, 1976).

16. For details of these scales, see addendum to Chapter 6.

17. Berg, *Education and Jobs*, Chapters 2–4.

18. With these data we cannot, of course, "time-order" these attitudes or experimentally observe a change for any individual in one attitude when another is varied. We consider that, for example, being very satisfied with the job (for *whatever* reason) may cast a glow of satisfaction on the respondent's sense of the challenge it provides. Our analysis of these possibilities, which always exist in such correlational studies led us to the conclusion that the relations persist mainly in the direction argued in the text. In addition, Quinn and his associates have already thoroughly explored the entire terrain afforded by the Working Conditions Survey. See the results mentioned in Chapter 3.

19. Mayer N. Zald, *Occupations and Organizations in American Society* (Chicago: Markham, 1971).

20. As we shall see in Chapter 6, one of the most useful critiques by an economist of the work of colleagues who study the "private" rates of returns to educational investments is that most research in this lively area fails to examine the full-time, part-time and full-year, part-year earnings patterns in different occupations. See Richard S. Eckaus, *Estimating the Returns to Education: A Disaggregated Approach* (Berkeley, Calif.: Carnegie Commission on Higher Education, 1973).

21. Arne Kalleberg, "On the Relationship Between Occupations and Job Satisfaction," revised version of a paper presented to the Southern Sociological Association, Miami, April 1976 (Bloomington, Ind., mimeographed, 1976). Relevant aspects of Kohn and Schooler's work will be discussed in Chapter 11. Kalleberg defines occupations in terms of job complexity, income, and the security and stability of tenure where we use skill.

NOTES FROM CHAPTER 5

1. The sample had a small number of responses that may be regarded as "errors": among the 353 workers who perceived family income to be inadequate, seventeen workers nevertheless reported it to be "comfortable."

2. Daniel Yankelovich, "The Meaning of Work," in Jerome M. Rosow (ed.), *The Worker and the Job* (Englewood Cliffs, N.J.: Prentice-Hall, 1974), pp. 44–45.

3. *Ibid.,* p. 44.

4. Angus Campbell, Philip E. Converse, and Willard L. Rogers, *The Quality of American Life: Perceptions, Evaluations, and Satisfactions* (New York: Russell Sage Foundation, 1976) pp. 431–432. See also Yankelovich, "Meaning of Work," p. 44.

5. We recognize that people construe the adequacy of their incomes by the relative standards of their neighbors, friends, and social groups. The logic and methods by which they come to select one reference group rather than another involves questions well beyond the scope of this study.

6. The literature on wage determination is as voluminous as the subject is

complicated. For a lucid discussion of the economic and related roles of unions, for example, in determining incomes, see Derek C. Bok and John T. Dunlop, *Labor and the American Community* (New York: Simon & Schuster, 1970).

7. This is the thrust of the recent assessment in William Serrin, *The Company and the Union* (New York: Knopf, 1973), in which the UAW is portrayed as a union that has grown out of touch with its rank-and-file members. It should be noted that the dollars loaned by GM to the UAW are actually in payment of health-benefit obligations on which striking workers would have been obliged to default. Readers will have to make up their own minds about GM's logic in doing this. Serrin's judgment, noted above, may seem a bit harsh in the event.

8. For a discussion see Bok and Dunlop, *Labor and the American Community*. The Kefauver Committee in the early sixties found that the objective of General Motors in setting its prices was to fix them at a level that guaranteed a 20-percent return after taxes on net worth if its plants operated for 180 days or thirty-six weeks in the year: GM's break-even point was so low that it could make profits even while operating at 40 to 45 percent of capacity. These calculations are made by General Motors for five-year periods. Cited in Daniel Bell's review of *Sloan: My Years at General Motors* in *New York Review of Books* 2 (March 1964).

9. A detailed, lucid application of this basic sociological paradigm by an economist to income differences may be found in a masterful treatment of the difficulties that inhere in so-called marginalist theories of income distribution: Lester C. Thurow, *Generating Inequality: Mechanisms of Distribution in the U.S. Economy* (New York: Basic Books, 1975), pp. 20–128.

10. The Center for Political Studies, *1972 American National Election Survey*, Inter-University Consortium for Political Research, Ann Arbor, Michigan.

11. Burkhard Strumpel, "Inflation, Discontent and Distributive Justice," *Economic Outlook USA* 1 (Summer 1974).

12. Lester Thurow, "Toward a Definition of Economic Justice," *Public Interest* 31 (Spring 1973), p. 69.

13. *Ibid.*, p. 67.

14. See Richard A. Easterlin, "Does Money Buy Happiness?" *Public Interest* 30 (Winter 1973), pp. 3–10, who compared thirty surveys from nineteen countries and concluded that although more money for an individual typically means more happiness, raising the incomes of all does not increase the happiness of all; there is, in fact, a "hedonic treadmill."

15. Patricia C. Smith, "Strategy for the Development of a General Theory of Job Satisfaction," Cornell University, 1963, mimeographed. Cited in Donald P. Schwab and Larry L. Cummings, "Theories of Performance and Satisfaction: A Review," *Industrial Relations* 9 (October 1970), pp. 408–430.

16. William A. Rushing, *Class, Culture, and Alienation: A Study of Farmers and Farm Workers* (Lexington, Mass.: Lexington Books, 1972).

NOTES FROM CHAPTER 6

1. See Richard B. Freeman, *The Overeducated American* (New York: Academic Press, 1976). Freeman's 1976 assertions about "overeducation" may be compared with his own earlier report on the responsiveness of students to the realities of the marketplace and their willingness to alter plans in the face of these realities. See Richard B. Freeman, *The Market for College-Trained Manpower: A Study of the Economics of Career Choice* (Cambridge, Mass.: Harvard University Press, 1971), pp. xix–xxvi and *passim*.

2. Ivar Berg, *Education and Jobs: The Great Training Robbery* (New York: Praeger, 1970).

3. Theodore W. Schultz, *The Economic Value of Education* (New York: Columbia University Press, 1963).

4. Edward F. Denison, *The Sources of Economic Growth in the United States and the Alternatives before Us* (New York: Committee on Economic Development, 1962).

5. Gary S. Becker, *Human Capital* (New York: National Bureau of Economic Research, 1964).

6. The major theoretical and empirical literature that has grown out of these initial efforts is treated in Mary Jean Bowman, "The Human Investment Revolution in Economic Thought," *Sociology of Education* 39 (Spring 1966), pp. 111–137; W. L. Hansen, ed., *Education, Income and Human Capital* (New York: National Bureau of Economic Research, 1970); Theodore W. Schultz, "Human Capital: Policy Issues and Research Opportunities," *Human Resources*, Fiftieth Anniversary Colloquium Series (New York: National Bureau of Economic Research, 1972); and Andre Daniere, "The Economics of Higher Education," *Annals of the American Academy of Political and Social Science* 404 (November 1972), pp. 58–70. The latter is a commendably cogent and readable overview of many of the issues in "human capital" discussions. Constructive criticisms of the prevailing approach in this literature may be found in R. S. Eckaus, *Estimating the Returns to Education: A Disaggregated Approach* (Berkeley, Calif.: Carnegie Commission on Higher Education, 1973); and Michael J. Piore, "The Importance of Human Capital Theory to Labor Economics: A Dissenting View," *Proceedings*, 26th Annual Winter Meeting, Industrial Relations Research Association (New York, 1973), pp. 251–258. For a helpful recent review, see Mark Blaug, "The Empirical Status of Human Capital Theory: A Slightly Jaundiced Survey," *Journal of Economic Literature* 14 (September 1976), pp. 827–855.

7. Orion White, Jr., and Gideon Sjoberg, "The Emerging 'New Politics' in America," in M. Donald Hancock and Gideon Sjoberg (eds.), *Politics in the Post-Welfare State* (New York: Columbia University Press, 1972), p. 15.

8. Burton A. Weisbrod, "External Benefits of Public Education: An Economic Analysis," Industrial Relations Section, Dept. of Economics, Princeton University, 1964, pp. 24–26. Among other possible socioeconomic benefits

we ignore in this chapter are the production skills added to less-educated fellow workers by their collaboration with better-educated peers, and the dissemination of new information into economic activities by better-educated workers as ex-learners and as readers. These aspects of the utilization of workers await further research.

9. For a discussion, see Berg, *Education and Jobs*, Chapters 2 and 3. We will here simply agree that education makes important noneconomic contributions to society, indeed, but that we are concerned with its economic role.

10. Communication from our colleague, Rendig Fels, upon reading an earlier draft of this chapter.

11. Berg, *Education and Jobs*. Some economists had difficulty understanding that the effort was a sympathetic one, designed to help clarify marginalist assumptions about the relationship between earnings, performance and education. Thus, though we were examining the hypotheses of other economists, not our own, we were informed by one noted economist that we had not proven *our* thesis! Another economist described *our* crude test of *his* favored marginalist position as a "much read diatribe," though he was unable to gainsay the doubts in the matter that our assessments supported. See Jack Embling, *A Fresh Look at Higher Education: European Implications of the Carnegie Commission Reports* (New York: American Elsevier, 1974), p. 207.

12. Paul Taubman and Terence Wales, *Mental Ability and Higher Educational Attainment in the Twentieth Century*, National Bureau of Economic Research Occasional Paper 118 (Berkeley, Calif.: Carnegie Commission on Higher Education, 1972).

13. In a careful analysis of difficulties, Eckaus observes: "The rate of return estimates are not robust and, on close and intensive examination, are shown to be quite sensitive to the assumptions made in the calculations, the level of occupational aggregation and the type of comparisons made. While calculated rates reveal something about [the relationship between education and] the distribution of income, their full import still remains so obscure that they cannot be used to form policy for the allocation of resources to education." Eckaus, *Estimating the Returns to Education*, p. 76.

14. The distinction is drawn by an economist. See Carnegie Commission on Higher Education, *College Graduates and Jobs* (New York: McGraw-Hill, 1973); and Margaret S. Gordon (ed.), *Higher Education and the Labor Market* (New York: McGraw-Hill, 1974).

15. See R. S. Eckaus, "Economic Criteria for Education and Training," *Review of Economics and Statistics* 46 (May 1964), pp. 181–190; J. K. Folger and C. B. Nam, *Education of the American Population*, 1960 Census Monograph (Washington, D.C.: U.S. Government Printing Office, 1967); James G. Scoville, *The Job Content of the U.S. Economy, 1940–1970* (New York: McGraw-Hill, 1969); V. Lane Rawlins and Lloyd Ulman, "The Utilization of College-Trained Manpower in the U.S.," in Gordon (ed.), *Higher Education and the Labor Market*, pp. 195–235; and Carnegie Commission, *College Graduates and Jobs*, p. 3.

16. Methodological definitions, assumptions, and detailed data are presented in an addendum to the present chapter. It is sufficient to state here that GED is a 6-point scale, theoretically distinct from years of schooling and applicable to job requirements. In some of the tables that follow, GED 5 has been divided into two categories to facilitate the matching process. The methods and rationales for our specific procedures also appear in the addendum.

17. We do not suggest that the standard has virtues, as such. We simply wish to avoid a lengthy discussion of the pros and cons of "radical" versus "conservative" measures. The median standard *does* offer the advantage of identifying what is likely to be a reference-group standard for employed Americans, a probability borne out in some degree by our examination of survey data in Chapters 4, 7, and 8.

18. Since our meanings have now been made clear we will discontinue the use of quotation marks about the terms underutilization, match, and mismatch in our exposition.

19. See especially Freeman, *The Overeducated American*. We suggest that there are no "overeducated" Americans. The larger question of the use of Americans' education requires adequate discussion of education's *non*economic roles. We prefer to think of Americans, in the work conditions we and Freeman are concerned about, as being underutilized rather than overeducated.

20. J. K. Folger, H. S. Astin, and A. E. Bayer, *Human Resources and Higher Education: Staff Report of the Commission on Human Resources and Advanced Education*, (New York: Russell Sage Foundations, 1970), p. 39.

21. Michael F. Crowley, "Professional Manpower: The Job Market Turnaround," *Monthly Labor Review* 95 (October 1972), pp. 9–15.

— 22. Carnegie Commission, *College Graduates and Jobs*, pp. 3–4.

23. J. Folger, "The Job Market for College Graduates," *Journal of Higher Education* 43 (March 1972), p. 215.

24. Neal H. Rosenthal, "Projected Changes in Occupations," *The U.S. Economy in 1985: A Summary of BLS Projections*. BLS Bulletin 1809 (Washington: Government Printing Office, 1974), Chapter II, pp. 18–26.

25. Joseph Froomkin, *Supply and Demand for Persons with Postsecondary Education* (Washington: Joseph Froomkin, Inc., 1976), p. 21.

26. Survey Research Center, University of Michigan, *Survey of Working Conditions* (Washington, D.C.: U.S. Government Printing Office, 1971), p. 406.

27. Anne M. Young, "Employment of Recent College Graduates October 1972," *Special Labor Force Report 169* (Washington, D.C.: U.S. Government Printing Office, 1974). This survey was not repeated in subsequent years. In October 1975, however, 107,000 college graduates aged 16–24 were unemployed. "Students, Graduates and Dropouts in the Labor Market, October 1975," *Monthly Labor Review* 99 (June 1976), Table 1, p. 38.

28. A. J. Jaffe and Joseph Froomkin, *Technology and Jobs* (New York: Praeger, 1968); and Stephen P. Dresch, "Demography, Technology and

Higher Education: Toward a Formal Model of Educational Adaptation," *Journal of Political Economy* 83 (June 1975), pp. 535–569.

29. Rawlins and Ulman, "Utilization of College-Trained Manpower."

30. Richard B. Freeman, "Overinvestment in College Training?" *Journal of Human Resources* 10 (Summer 1975), p. 309.

31. Dresch, "Demography, Technology and Higher Education," pp. 537–539.

32. Stephen P. Dresch, "Ability, Fertility and Educational Adaptation," in Julian L. Simon (ed.), *Research in Population Economics*, Vol. 1 (Greenwich, Conn.: JAI Press, 1977).

33. Stephen P. Dresch, "Human Capital and Economic Growth: Retrospect and Prospect," paper prepared for the U.S. Congress, Joint Economic Committee, October 15, 1976, p. 21.

34. For a discussion, see Lester C. Thurow, *Generating Inequality: Mechanisms of Distribution in the U.S. Economy* (New York: Basic Books, 1975), Chapters 4 and 5.

35. Denis F. Johnston, "The Aging of the Baby Boom Cohorts," *Statistical Reporter*, Number 76–79 (March 1976), pp. 161–165.

36. Howard N. Fullerton, Jr., and Paul O. Flaim, "New Labor Force Projections to 1990," *Monthly Labor Review* 99 (December 1976), Table 3, p. 7.

37. Johnston, "The Aging of the Baby Boom Cohorts," p. 162.

38. Dresch, "Human Capital and Economic Growth," p. 40.

39. Berg, *Education and Jobs*, Chapter 3.

40. *Ibid.*

41. Ann Miller, *Occupations of the Labor Force According to the Dictionary of Occupational Titles*, Statistical Evaluation Report No. 9 (Washington, D.C.: Office of Management and Budget, February 1971), p. 34.

42. U.S. Department of Labor, *Selected Characteristics of Occupations Supplement to the Dictionary of Occupational Titles*, 3rd ed. (Washington, D.C.: U.S. Government Printing Office, 1966), p. A-5.

NOTES FROM CHAPTER 7

1. Robert P. Quinn and Martha S. Baldi de Mandilovitch, *Education and Job Satisfaction: A Questionable Payoff* (Ann Arbor:, Mich.: Survey Research Center, University of Michigan, 1975).

2. For details on GED, once again see addendum to the preceding chapter. For a caution against this type of "translation," see Sidney A. Fine, "The Use of the Dictionary of Occupational Titles as a Source of Estimates of Educational and Training Requirements," *Journal of Human Resources* 3 (Summer 1968), pp. 363–375.

3. Quinn and Mandilovitch, *Education and Job Satisfaction*, p. 26.

4. *Ibid.*, pp. 39–40.

5. Charles B. Knapp and W. Lee Hansen, "Earnings and Individual Variations in Postschool Human Investment," *Journal of Political Economy* 84 (April 1976), pp. 351–358. It is a reasonable guess that a number of Knapp's and Hansen's respondents made job-related investments in schooling even as they acquired experience and seniority.

6. For a thoughtful discussion of the question, based on similar types of data, see Angus Campbell, Philip E. Converse, and Willard Rogers, *The Quality of American Life: Perceptions, Evaluations and Satisfactions* (New York: Russell Sage Foundation, 1976), Chapter 5.

7. Ivar Berg, *Education and Jobs: The Great Training Robbery* (New York: Praeger, 1970), Chapter 7. These are the same data upon which Robert Blauner drew in a study discussed in Chapter 3 in the present volume.

8. For definition of SVP, see addendum to Chapter 6.

9. Herbert H. Hyman, Charles R. Wright, and John Shelton Reed, *The Enduring Effects of Education* (Chicago: University of Chicago Press, 1975).

10. *Ibid.*, p. 74. Emphasis added. The "advantaged" and "less advantaged" respondents to which references are made are "the highly educated in lowly circumstances," and "the uneducated who have arrived at a high station in life," respectively. The former, consequently, are those living under "stringent conditions."

11. The following observations are taken from a longer assessment in Frederick Mosteller *et al.*; Ivar Berg, "Knowledge Beyond Achievement: A Seventies Perspective on School Effects—A Review Symposium on *The Enduring Effects of Education*, by Herbert Hyman, Charles Wright, and John Reed," *University of Chicago School Review* 84 (February 1976), pp. 283–289.

12. See Richard B. Freeman, "Overinvestment in College Training?" *Journal of Human Resources* 10 (Summer 1975), pp. 287–311, and *The Overeducated American* (New York: Academic Press, 1975).

13. See Samuel S. Peng and George H. Dunteman, "Equal Opportunity in Postsecondary Education: An Appraisal of Recent Evidence," Center for Educational Research and Evaluation, Research Triangle Institute, Raleigh, N.C., December 1975.

14. For recent discussions see Melvin Reder, "Human Capital and Economic Discrimination," in Ivar Berg (ed.), *Human Resources and Economic Welfare: Essays in Honor of Eli Ginzberg* (New York: Columbia University Press, 1972), pp. 71–86, and Lester C. Thurow, *Generating Inequality: Mechanisms of Distribution in the U.S. Economy* (New York: Basic Books, 1975), pp. 170–176.

15. The study by Hyman *et al.*, *The Enduring Effects of Education*, gives no credibility to the argument that our schools no longer "make them like they used to." Studies by the Educational Testing Service suggest secular declines in college board scores; it is not clear that these declines in scores are attributable to schools' declining capacities to educate youths, nor is it clear that the trend has continued into 1977.

16. Berg, *Education and Jobs*.

NOTES FROM INTRODUCTION TO PART III

1. For disturbing analyses, however, of the consequences for liberal values and for government by law of all these things, see Henry Kariel, *The Decline of American Pluralism* (Stanford, Calif.: Stanford University Press, 1961), and Theodore J. Lowi, *The End of Liberalism* (New York: Norton, 1969). In the second of these works, Lowi elaborates on Americans' fascination with administration and what he sees to be the false promises it has regularly held for them.
2. Louis Harris, *The Anguish of Change* (New York: Norton, 1973).
3. *Ibid.*, p. 162.

NOTES FROM CHAPTER 8

1. This is not to say that managers are *totally* straitjacketed. See Michael Piore, "The Impact of the Labor Market Upon the Design and Selection of Productive Techniques within the Manufacturing Plant," *Quarterly Journal of Economics* 82 (November 1968), pp. 602–620. Avoiding problems in the use of aggregated data on employers' uses of skill offerings in labor markets, this revealing study of one hundred and fifty managers in eighteen manufacturing plants and in eleven corporate headquarters observed their search for operating innovations in their production methods that "appear to be largely independent of labor market forces" (p. 606). The almost whimsical procedures followed by managers "appeared, nonetheless, to be consistent with the assumption of cost minimization" (p. 619).
2. Robert P. Quinn and Thomas W. Mangione (eds.), *The 1969–1970 Survey of Working Conditions: Chronicles of an Unfinished Enterprise* (The University of Michigan, 1973), p. 211.
3. All-purpose depreciation allowances, available to the competent as well as incompetent, do not help to reward those who make the most astute investments in work-related equipment, or, for that matter, in astute investments generally. The use of depreciation allowances as augmentations of "cash flow," in the meantime, contributes a little, at least, to those worker inefficiencies that may be linked to faulty tools and equipment.
4. Victor H. Vroom, *Work and Motivation* (New York: Wiley, 1964), p. 106.
5. For a thoroughgoing review, see Robert Dubin *et al.*, *Leadership and Productivity: Some Facts of Industrial Life* (San Francisco: Chandler, 1965).
6. See Robert Dubin, "Supervision and Productivity: Empirical Findings and Theoretical Considerations," and George C. Homans, "Effort, Supervision, and Productivity," in Dubin *et al.*, *Leadership and Productivity*, pp. 1–50 and 51–67 respectively; George Strauss and Leonard R. Sayles, *Personnel: The Human Problems of Management*, 3rd ed., (Englewood Cliffs, N.J.: Prentice-Hall, 1972), pp. 311–327; and James W. Kuhn, *Bargaining in the Grievance Process* (New York: Columbia University Press, 1961).

7. We have respected the wishes of our informants that the corporation's name not be mentioned. Data and quotations are from internal company reports the company generously shared with us. The data-analytic technique used in the study was Automatic Interaction Detector (AID). See J. A. Sonquist, E. L. Baker, and J. N. Morgan, *Searching for Structure* (Ann Arbor, Mich.: University of Michigan Survey Research Center, 1973).

8. Cited from an internal corporate report on the study described here. Emphasis added.

9. Once again, we are obliged not to reveal the name of the company.

10. The proportion of dissatisfied managers was only slightly smaller on most items than the proportion of dissatisfied workers in the WCS national probability sample of all workers on many parallel questions.

NOTES FROM CHAPTER 9

1. Robert Blauner, *Alienation and Freedom: The Factory Worker and His Industry* (Chicago: University of Chicago Press, 1964). We may remind our readers that we reviewed Blauner's treatment of the attitudes of workers in different industries in Chapter 3.

2. Clark Kerr and Abraham Siegel, "The Interindustry Propensity to Strike: An International Comparison," in Arthur Kornhauser, Robert Dubin, and Arthur M. Ross (eds.), *Industrial Conflict* (New York: McGraw-Hill, 1954); and James W. Kuhn, "Grievance Machinery and Strikes in Australia," *Industrial and Labor Relations Review* 8 (January 1955), pp. 169–176.

3. Angus Campbell, Philip E. Converse, and Willard L. Rogers, *The Quality of American Life: Perceptions, Evaluations and Satisfactions* (New York: Russell Sage Foundation, 1976), p. 297 ff.

4. The year 1946 was an exception: the figure was 1.04. U.S. Bureau of Labor Statistics, *Analysis of Work Stoppages, 1973*, Bulletin 1877 (Washington, D.C.: U.S. Government Printing Office, 1975), Table A–1, p. 4.

5. David Snyder, "Institutional Setting and Industrial Conflict: Comparative Analyses of France, Italy and the United States," *American Sociological Review* 40 (June 1975), pp. 259–278.

6. Arthur M. Ross, "The Prospects for Industrial Conflict," *Industrial Relations* 1 (October 1961), pp. 57–74.

7. Myron Roomkin, "Union Structure, Internal Control, and Strike Activity," *Industrial and Labor Relations Review* 29 (January 1976), pp. 198–217. Roomkin defined strike-proneness in terms of formal bargaining opportunities, omitting from his analysis all strikes conducted during the life of a contract.

8. Robert P. Quinn, Graham L. Staines, and Margaret R. McCullough, *Job Satisfaction: Is There a Trend?* Manpower Research Monograph No. 30 (Washington, D.C.: U.S. Government Printing Office, 1974).

9. Orley Ashenfelter and George E. Johnson, "Bargaining Theory, Trade

Unions, and Industrial Strike Activity," *American Economic Review* 59 (March 1969), pp. 35–49.

10. Robert N. Stern, "Intermetropolitan Patterns of Strike Frequency," *Industrial and Labor Relations Review* 29 (January 1976), pp. 218–235.

11. Snyder, "Institutional Setting and Industrial Conflict."

12. The relationships between strike activity and economic conditions are still not terribly clear, despite research stretching back to 1921 by Hansen, then by Rees, Levitt, Goldner, and Blitz in the fifties; and, more recently, by Weintraub; Ashenfelter and Johnson; Britt and Galle; Stern; and Flanagan, Strauss, and Ulman, as follows: Alvin Hansen, "Cycles of Strikes," *American Economic Review* 11 (December 1921), pp. 616–621; Albert Rees, "Industrial Conflict and Business Fluctuations," *Journal of Political Economy* 60 (October 1952), pp. 371–382; Theodore Levitt, "Prosperity versus Strikes," *Industrial and Labor Relations Review* 6 (January 1953), pp. 220–226; William Goldner, "Strikes and Prosperity," *Industrial and Labor Relations Review* 6 (July 1953), pp. 579–581; Rudolf C. Blitz, "Prosperity versus Strikes Reconsidered," *Industrial and Labor Relations Review* 7 (April 1954), pp. 449–456; Ashenfelter and Johnson, "Bargaining Theory" *(op cit.)*; David Britt and Omer R. Galle, "Industrial Conflict and Unionization," *American Sociological Review* 37 (1972), pp. 46–57; Stern, Intermetropolitan Patterns" *(op cit.)*; and Robert J. Flanagan, George Strauss, and Lloyd Ulman, "Worker Discontent and Work Place Behavior," *Industrial Relations* 13 (May 1974), pp. 101–123.

13. Our and others' recent interests in interindustry strikes were anticipated by Robert Hoxie in the twenties. See *Trade Unionism in the United States*, 2nd ed. (New York: D. Appleton, 1923), in which it is argued that bargaining patterns will vary by industry as a function of differences, for example, in industry structures.

14. Snyder, "Institutional Setting and Industrial Conflict," p. 270.

15. Kerr and Siegel, "The Interindustry Propensity to Strike." The industrial-environment variables in their original discussion remained to be tested in later works like those we have already cited.

16. Edgar Weinberg, "Labor-Management Cooperation: A Report on Recent Initiatives," *Monthly Labor Review* 99 (April 1976), p. 17. The realities of foreign competition are explored in A. F. Shorrocks, "Measuring the Imaginary: The Employment Effect of Imported Steel," *Industrial and Labor Relations Review* 24 (January 1971), pp. 203–215.

17. Shorrocks, "Measuring the Imaginary," p. 204. See the discussion of some of the implications of these developments in our introductory chapter.

18. The material here is adapted from U.S. Bureau of Labor Statistics, *Work Stoppages in Contract Construction, 1962–1973*, Bulletin 1847 (Washington, D.C.: U.S. Government Printing Office, 1975).

19. The electrical industry has a plan that has worked well since 1921: a Council on Industrial Relations renders private judicial determinations on a variety of dispute matters and has never had a decision violated. "Its success, however, is the product of many years of experience and may not

be readily duplicated in other branches of the industry." U.S. Bureau of Labor Statistics, *Work Stoppages* (Bulletin 1847), p. 15.

20. Daniel Quinn Mills, *Industrial Relations and Manpower in Construction* (Cambridge, Mass.: MIT Press, 1972), p. 271, fn. 3. For a discussion of the objectives of public policy and the problems of implementation, see Mills, Chapter 10. We may mention, in passing, that one of the by-products of New York City's tangled economic problems has been a willingness of the building trades unions there to yield, completely, on the enforcement of hundreds of working rules. Unionists, in the event, have concluded that they must compete more effectively with the labor market offerings of unorganized tradesmen for their own and the City's economic welfare.

21. See the discussion in Chapter 8. "Maturity" can, of course, have negative connotations to union leaders and members distrustful of demands for productivity, as well as to managers determined to maintain their traditional "rights."

22. Roomkin, in "Union Structure," as pointed out earlier, seems to be making this assumption in limiting his data-set to strikes occurring in connection with contract negotiations.

23. U.S. Bureau of Labor Statistics, "Grievance Procedures," *Major Collective Bargaining Agreements*, Bulletin 1425–1 (Washington, D.C.: U.S. Government Printing Office, 1964), p. 56. Courts, meanwhile, in a number of jurisdictions in 1977, have held that union *leaders* may be sued by employers when rank and filers participate in strikes barred by the labor agreement.

24. U.S. Bureau of Labor Statistics, *Characteristics of Agreements Covering 1,000 Workers or More, July 1, 1973*, Bulletin 1822 (Washington, D.C.: U.S. Government Printing Office, 1974), Table 72, p. 65.

25. Bureau of National Affairs, *Basic Patterns in Union Contracts* (Washington, D.C.: U.S. Bureau of National Affairs, 1975), pp. 90–95.

26. Kuhn, "Grievance Machinery and Strikes in Australia."

27. Several recent studies, including Stern, "Intermetropolitan Patterns," and Britt and Galle, "Industrial Conflict and Unionization," used two- or three-year means in which a single year may have an even greater effect than that described here.

28. U.S. Bureau of Labor Statistics, *Analysis of Work Stoppages*, Bulletins 1646, 1687, 1727, 1777, and 1877. (Washington, D.C.: U.S. Government Printing Office, 1970–1975). The most recent estimates by the Bureau, based on preliminary data covering the first three months of 1977 indicate that strikes were shorter than first-quarter disputes over the past decade though the average number of workers per strike (501) was larger. The average duration, 7.8 days per worker was in fact the shortest since 1966; not since 1952 have strikes "averaged more than 500 workers and lasted less than 10 days." U.S. Department of Labor, Office of Information, News Release, Wash., D.C.: April 29, 1977.

29. Personal communication from Robert Z. Lewis, general counsel, United

Electrical Workers. There is at least some indication that other unions want to move in this direction. See *Business Week*, March 22, 1976, p. 41, which reported that the Breweries & Soft Drinks Conference of the Teamsters Union broke off contract talks with Anheuser-Busch "when the company rejected a demand for the right to strike over unresolved grievances."

30. For a study of AIW in the early years, see Bob Repas, "Grievance Procedures Without Arbitration," *Industrial and Labor Relations Review* 20 (April 1967), pp. 381–387.

NOTES FROM CHAPTER 10

1. R. H. Tawney, *Equality* (New York: Barnes & Noble, 1965), pp. 69–70.

2. Ralf Dahrendorf, *Class and Class Conflict in Industrial Society* (Stanford, Calif.: Stanford University Press, 1959), p. 71.

3. *Ibid.*, p. 249.

4. *Ibid.*, pp. 65–66.

5. *Ibid.* In many respects, Dahrendorf's comments on the functions of the organization and the routinization of conflict are related to those of Georg Simmel, *Conflict and the Web of Group Affiliations* (New York: Free Press, 1955); and later, to Lewis Coser, *The Functions of Social Conflict* and *Continuities in the Study of Social Conflict* (New York: Free Press, 1956 and 1967, respectively). See also John Dunlop, *Industrial Relations Systems* (New York: Henry Holt, 1958); and Clark Kerr *et al.*, *Industrialism and Industrial Man* (New York: Oxford University Press, 1964).

6. James C. Power, "Improving Arbitration: Roles of Parties and Agencies," *Monthly Labor Review* 95 (November 1972), p. 16, Table 1.

7. *Ibid.*, p. 22, fn. 1.

8. *Ibid.*

9. Cf. *ibid.*, pp. 21–22; Ben Fischer, "Arbitration: The Steel Industry Experiment," *Monthly Labor Review* 95 (November 1972), p. 8 ff. Also, cf. citation of previous arbitration decisions in cases reported in the Bureau of National Affairs' continuing series, *Labor Arbitration Reports*—although it might be objected that previous awards may serve as much as "legitimations" as "common law." We will return to the issues in this paragraph in Chapter 12.

10. Such research has, in fact, been performed with suggestive results by William F. Whyte, Melville Dalton, Leonard Sayles, George Strauss, and James Kuhn. Readers will already have recognized the intellectual debts we owe these representatives of what we term the eclectic industrial-relations approach. See W. F. Whyte, *Money and Motivation: An Analysis of Incentives in Industry* (New York: Harper & Row, 1955), for an example. The others' relevant works have been cited elsewhere in this volume.

11. Some grievances, of course, are neither withdrawn nor resolved, as such, as the discussion in Chapter 7 made clear.

12. James W. Kuhn, *Bargaining in the Grievance Process* (New York: Columbia University Press, 1961); and Leonard Sayles, *Behavior in Industrial Work Groups: Prediction and Control* (New York: Wiley, 1958). A seasoned arbitrator has recently argued that many nondisciplinary grievances are "without merit." See Edward Lev, "Transcripts as Chastening Rods in Labor Arbitration," *Monthly Labor Review* 97 (October 1974), p. 55. Our concern, however, is essentially with disciplinary grievances.

13. Arthur M. Ross, "Distressed Grievance Procedures and Their Rehabilitation," *Labor Arbitration and Industrial Change* (Washington, D.C.: Bureau of National Affairs Books, 1963), pp. 104–132.

14. James A. Gross, "Value Judgments in the Decisions of Labor Arbitrators," *Industrial and Labor Relations Review* 21 (October 1967), p. 58.

15. Among the publishers are the Commerce Clearing House and the Bureau of National Affairs (BNA). The cases we have considered are from the latter's *Labor Arbitration Reports* (Washington, D.C.). For further discussions and illustrations of the use that may be made of arbitration cases as social-science data, see Eli Ginzberg and Ivar Berg, *Democratic Values and the Rights of Management* (New York: Columbia University Press, 1963), and Gross, "Value Judgments." In the first of these, the authors undertook to gain insights into the world of work and into the postures and positions of workers, worker representatives, and managers. For a similar approach, undertaken about the same time, see Philip A. Selznick, *Law, Society, and Industrial Justice* (New York: Russell Sage Foundation, 1969), which has had considerable influence on our thinking in the present investigation.

16. *United Steelworkers of America* v. *American Manufacturing Co.*, 363 U.S. 564 (1960); *United Steelworkers of America* v. *Warrior and Gulf Navigation Co.*, 363 U.S. 574 (1960); and *United Steelworkers of America* v. *Enterprise Wheel and Car Corp.*, 363 U.S. 593 (1960).

17. For highly influential arguments in favor of such an expanded role of arbitrators and for statements about the differentiated "common law of the shop" that the court holds arbitrators should apply, see Archibald Cox, "Reflections Upon Labor Arbitration," *Harvard Law Review* 72 (1959), p. 1482, and Charles Summers, "Reason, Contract and Law in Labor Relations," *Harvard Law Review* 68 (1955), p. 999. We will return to this issue in Chapter 12.

18. For present purposes, each grievance is classified only once, corresponding to what was judged to be its precipitating cause.

19. A survey of the last category indicated that grievances involving plant rules accounted for a relatively minor percentage of cases—an average of approximately 10 percent for the several years studied—and suggests that for the sake of simplicity the category may be subsumed under the larger "discharge and discipline" rubric.

20. It is our sense, from a lengthy discussion with the editor of *Labor Arbitration Reports*, Howard Anderson, that these are real increases and not the result of topical interests among the Bureau of National Affairs' staff.

21. The use of these metaphors is deliberate: the use of the term "economic capital punishment" to characterize discharge is part of the *lingua franca* of arbitration.

22. For an earlier discussion of the conflict between management interests and the extended reach of democracy, see Ginzberg and Berg, "Democratic Values," and Selznick, "Law, Society and Industrial Justice."

NOTE FROM INTRODUCTION TO PART IV

1. For a discussion of workers' interests in these measurements in disputes about working rules, see James Kuhn and Ivar Berg, "Bargaining and Work-Rule Disputes," *Social Research* 31 (Winter 1964), pp. 466–481.

NOTES FROM CHAPTER 11

1. While many business programs had hundreds of thousands of post–high school students registered for such courses in earlier times, the numbers of courses with titles and contents like the one alluded to in the text grew exponentially after the appearance of two independently sponsored foundation surveys of business education in which such "behavior science" materials were commended by the authors and their advisory panels in 1959. These courses, with few exceptions, borrow heavily from the logics and themes discussed in the section "Human Relations and Beyond" in our second chapter.

2. Quotations are used here because these specific and illustrative formulations of the general questions about proximal working conditions of forty years' standing are taken from items in the Working Conditions Survey.

3. Our selection of the particular table we have cited from Kornhauser's study is quite deliberate. Thus, most references to Kornhauser's study are to his own assertions about the singular effects of *work* on the mental health of his respondents. We may note, however, that Kornhauser's table shows significantly deleterious mental-health consequences attaching to workers' *educations* being, in our usage, underutilized. See our discussions in Chapters 6, 7, and 8.

4. That a majority of employers may have such highly laudable perspectives is suggested in the results of a poll of employers and union leaders by Raymond A. Katzell, Daniel Yankelovich, *et al.*, *Work, Productivity, and Job Satisfaction: An Evaluation of Policy-Related Research* (New York: Psychological Corp., 1975), Chapter 3.

5. We remind the reader that we have already indicated that the precise margins for such managerial reform are constrained by their influence over the skill hierarchies in their shops, mills, and offices, the character of which impact upon workers' perceptions of the challenge in their jobs.

6. It may well be that many workers survive psychologically as well as they do because they are matched with their jobs. Thus many, including employers, assume that "all correspondence between men's occupations and personalities results from processes of selective recruitment and modification of the job to meet incumbents' needs and values. This view seems to underlie, for example, the logic of personnel testing, where the object is to select job applicants whose personalities match those of successful job incumbents. This perspective may also underlie the greater attention sociologists have given to occupational choice than to occupational effects." Melvin L. Kohn and Carmi Schooler, "Occupational Experience and Psychological Functioning: An Assessment of Reciprocal Effects," *American Sociological Review* 38 (February 1973), pp. 97–118.

   It should be noted that the logic of personnel testing is made vulnerable to legal as well as scientific examination by the landmark case of *Griggs* v. *Duke Power*, in which it was held by the Supreme Court that educational and testing results must be validated against job performance if their use is to survive a list of their discriminatory employment consequences.

7. Kohn and Schooler, *Occupational Experience*, p. 97.

8. *Ibid.*, p. 99.

9. *Ibid.*, pp. 102–105.

10. *Ibid.*, p. 102. Emphasis in the original.

11. *Ibid.*, Figure 1, p. 112.

12. *Ibid.*, p. 116.

13. Melvin L. Kohn, "Occupational Structure and Alienation," mimeographed, (Washington, D.C.: National Institute of Mental Health, 1976). This study is based on the same data as the study of psychological functioning just cited.

14. See Melvin Seeman, "Alienation Studies," in Alex Inkeles (ed.), *Annual Review of Sociology* 1 (Palo Alto, Calif.: Annual Review, 1975), pp. 91–123.

15. Kohn and Schooler, "Occupational Experience," p. 117.

16. Katzell, Yankelovich, *et al.*, *Work, Productivity*, pp. 5–6.

17. *Ibid.*, "Job Design," pp. 134–197.

18. These roles often overlap.

19. In one case, involving investigators from the Academy for Contemporary Problems in Columbus, Ohio, a carefully negotiated agreement among the interventionists, a company, a union, and workers (whose condition were to be the subject of collaborative experiments) suddenly became a union election issue: an aspiring local union presidential candidate saw "Quality of Working Life Committees" to be thinly veiled substitutes for regular collective-bargaining machinery. Personal communication from one of the principal investigators, Columbus, Ohio, August 1975.

20. Katzell, Yankelovich, *et al.*, *Work, Productivity*, p. 184.

21. The worker/union questions will be addressed in a later chapter.

22. Edward M. Glaser, Carroll E. Izard, and Mary Faeth Chenery, *Improve-*

ment in the Quality of Worklife and Productivity: A Joint Venture Between Management and Employees. Final Report (Los Angeles: Human Interaction Research Institute, 1976). The amenities of research require that the company and location be disguised. The firm, a well-known producer of plasma fractions, was acquired by a large German chemical company.

23. *Ibid.,* Introduction. An evaluation of this effort was to have been undertaken by University of Michigan researchers at the Institute for Survey Research. At the time of this writing only a mimeographed draft report, by Veronica F. Nieva, Dennis N. T. Perkins, and Edward E. Lawler III, has been prepared. We thus depend, in our discussion, on the intervention agents' own report. The ISR draft report is *highly* critical of the interventionists for failing, essentially, to do right by the intervention model; its authors see *no* intrinsic difficulties whatever with the model itself when it is rightly understood and correctly applied.

24. Glaser *et al., Improvement in the Quality of Worklife,* pp. 2–8. These efforts were informed, in the technical sense of the word, by the authors-investigators' readings of studies and discussions, most of which were discussed in Chapter 3.

25. Cited in *ibid.,* pp. 76–77, from J. Richard Hackman, "Is Job Enrichment Just a Fad?" in *Harvard Business Review* 53 (September–October 1975), pp. 129–138.

26. Glaser *et al., Improvement in the Quality of Worklife,* pp. 93–110.

27. *Ibid.,* pp. 3–4. QWL stands for Quality of Work Life; DOL for U.S. Department of Labor; ISR for Institute for Survey Research; and HIRI for Human Interaction Research Institute.

28. *Ibid.,* pp. 4–5.

29. *Ibid.,* pp. 5–6.

30. The forms of work redesign about which we have the least confidence, in the American case, are those leading to significant orders of leveling in skill hierarchies, for reasons suggested in Chapters 4 and 5.

31. On the last point we have stressed *not* that there is *no* relationship between productivity and satisfaction, but that available evidence points to highly complicated relationships among different measures of productivity and satisfaction, and to a number of distal or macroscopic forces that influence satisfactions overall and over which managers have either no or very little control.

32. For a balanced review of the initial reports on innumerable American interventions and of the social-science literature on relevant laboratory experiments as well, see Paul Blumberg, *Industrial Democracy: The Sociology of Participation* (New York: Schocken, 1969), pp. 70–138.

33. Walton is a latter-day descendant, at the Harvard Business School, of the founders there of the human-relations movement. The discussion of a paper by Walton is adapted from Ivar Berg, "Working Conditions and Managements' Interests," in B. J. Widick (ed.), *Auto Work and Its Discontents* (Baltimore: John Hopkins University Press, 1976), pp. 96–108.

34. Walton's report, "Innovative Restructuring of Work," was presented at a meeting of the American Assembly at Columbia University's Arden House Campus; it was subsequently published in Jerome M. Rosow (ed.), *The Worker and the Job: Coping with Change* (Englewood Cliffs, N.J.: Prentice-Hall, 1974), pp. 145–176.

35. *Ibid.,* p. 165.

36. Walton indicates that, while he cannot vouch for the details he reports on other experiments, he can assure us about the validity of claims about Gainesburger because he was "closely involved as a consultant." *Ibid.,* p. 162. Walton's assurances in 1974 about the successful efforts at Gainesburger may be compared with a description of developments there by *Business Week* reporters on March 28, 1977, (pp. 78–82). According to *Business Week,* managers at Topeka have soured on Walton's experiments, are "stonewalling plant democracy" and have effectively torpedoed the innovations for the reasons discussed, in connection with other experiments, later in this chapter. Similar, and equally celebrated reforms in Sweden's Volvo plants, meanwhile, have contributed significantly to a 40 percent increase in labor costs! See *Time,* February 21, 1977, pp. 67–68.

37. *Ibid.,* pp. 167–168. Most of these managerial reactions are reported to have occurred at Walton's own Gainesburger site, though apparently in the period just after Walton's presentation at Arden House. See *Business Week,* March 28, 1977, pp. 78–82.

38. Walton reports that in one experiment turnover exceeded 10 percent because, according to an informant, "of the existence of unusual opportunities for overseas assignments." Ironically, such experiments are in part undertaken to *reduce* turnover, a fact that raises the question of whether working conditions must not be viewed in the context of competent labor market analysis. Work reforms that take no account of the firm's own internal labor market's functioning are simply naive. Equally naive are reforms introduced at one point in a firm's competitive history that take no account of the firm's changing experiences in product markets.

39. *Ibid.,* p. 168.

40. *Ibid.,* p. 169.

41. *Ibid.,* p. 161. Evaluators from the Institute for Survey Research who structured the Crown case are not so sure that new plants, third in Walton's list, are to be preferred for quality of work life experiments. Nor is it clear that expert innovators will use long lead times (number 6 in the list), very effectively.

42. James J. Healy (ed.), *Creative Collective Bargaining: Meeting Today's Challenges to Labor-Management Relations* (Englewood Cliffs, N.J.: Prentice-Hall, 1965), p. 50.

43. As Healy and his colleagues remind us, a protest that the Scanlon Plan is applicable only to small business may well be made, but that observers would recognize (in 1965) that "certain of [the Plan's] major principles [were] adopted almost intact in the Kaiser Steel Corp.–United Steelworkers Plan." Healy does not, however, take much exception to the protest. For

a parallel discussion of the Scanlon Plan, see Katzell, Yankelovich, *et al.*, *Work, Productivity*, pp. 355–368.

44. Walton, "Innovative Structuring of Work," p. 158. That managers are inclined to do just that, and to avoid labor market consideration, is the conclusion of Piore in a study cited in Part III. We will return to this issue in the next chapter.

NOTES FROM CHAPTER 12

1. For a now classic critique of efforts to liberate workers from "Ixion's wheel," see Daniel Bell, "Work and Its Discontents," in *The End of Ideology* (New York: Free Press, 1960).

2. Chimpanzees have recently been trained to use, with astoundingly high orders of subtlety and syntactic capability, a number of words in meslan, the American sign language for the deaf.

3. Eugene Linden, "Man Talks So Oddly!" *New York Times*, April 20, 1976, "Op Ed" page.

4. Bertell Ollman, *Alienation: Marx's Conception of Man in Capitalist Society* (Cambridge, Eng.: Cambridge University Press, 1971), p. 12.

5. Antonio Gramsci, *The Open Marxism of Antonio Gramsci*, ed. and trans. Carl Marzani (New York: Cameron Associates, 1957), p. 21.

6. Consider, for example, that corporations were invested with many of the legal rights of persons in the United States decades before chattel slaves were endowed with *any* such rights. For an early treatment, see Thurman Arnold, *The Folklore of Capitalism* (New Haven: Yale University Press, 1937).

7. Claude Lévi-Strauss, *The Savage Mind* (Chicago: University of Chicago Press, 1966); originally published in French in 1962. Irving Bluestone of the United Auto Workers sensibly objects to the term "humanized work." Workers, he points out, *are* human beings. He thus highlights what may be a slip in the minds of work reformers in the implicit reduction of workers to subhuman species in a linguistic shorthand according to which *work* is or is not human.

8. *Gateway Coal Co.* v. *United Mine Workers*, 94 S. Ct. 629.

9. Kenneth Kirschner, "Gateway to Problems: Arbitration of Strikes Due to Safety Disputes," *Industrial and Labor Relations Forum* 11 (Spring 1975), p. 111.

10. Cited in *ibid.*, p. 112.

11. Cited in *ibid.*

12. In cases in which there was a single arbitrator, arbitrator listed was used in analysis. In cases in which there were several arbitrators but in which one was designated as chairman, chairman was considered as spokesman and chairman was used in analysis. In the single case under study in which there were three arbitrators and none was designated as chairman (1953–54), the first arbitrator listed was used in analysis.

13. Ralph K. White, *Value Analysis: The Nature and Use of the Method* (New York: Society for the Psychological Study of Social Issues, 1951). In this monograph White established a fifty-personal-value code; provided operational definitions—and illustrations—for each of these values; provided adapted operational definitions—and illustrations—of the twenty-seven values found most useful in the analysis of propaganda and public-opinion materials; and provided procedural instructions.

14. This evidence was gathered in interviews with about three hundred and fifty managers and thirty-five local union leaders, mainly in off-the-record conversations in Grand Haven, Michigan, during March 1974; at the UAW's Walter and May Reuther Camp, Black Lake, Michigan, in July 1973; and at six of Columbia University's Arden House Executive Programs in the summers of 1972, 1973, and 1974.

NOTES FROM CHAPTER 13

1. Albert O. Hirschman, *Exit, Voice and Loyalty: Responses to Decline in Firms, Organizations and States* (Cambridge, Mass.: Harvard University Press, 1970). For an elaboration of Hirschman's applications of his ideas and an effort to address himself to the possibilities that exit and voice could be manipulated as "management tools," see his article, " 'Exit, Voice and Loyalty': Further Reflections and a Survey of Recent Contributions," *Social Science Information* 13 (February 1974), pp. 7–26.

2. Arthur M. Ross, "Do We Have a New Industrial Feudalism?" *American Economic Review* 48 (December 1958), pp. 903–920. Ross rejected the notion that benefits had unduly interfered with appropriate labor market operation.

3. John H. Pencavel, *An Analysis of the Quit Rate in American Manufacturing Industry*, Research Report Series No. 114 (Princeton, N.J.: Industrial Relations Section, Princeton University, 1970), p. 9.

4. *Ibid.*, p. 50.

5. See Lloyd Ulman, "Labor Mobility and the Industrial Wage Structure in the Postwar United States, " *Quarterly Journal of Economics* 79 (February 1965), pp. 73–97.

6. Llad Phillips, "An Analysis of the Dynamics of Labor Turnover in United States Industry" (Ph.D. dissertation, Harvard University, 1969), p. 339. For other studies showing the overall direct relationships between employment rates and quit rates see B. W. Anderson, "Empirical Generalizations on Labor Turnover," in Richard Pegnetter (ed.), *Labor and Manpower* (Iowa City: Center for Labor and Management, College of Business Administration, University of Iowa, 1974); and Fred L. Fry, "A Behavioral Analysis of Economic Variables Affecting Turnover," *Journal of Behavioral Economics* 2 (1973), pp. 247–295.

7. Robert J. Flanagan, George Strauss, and Lloyd Ulman, "Worker Discontent and Work Place Behavior," *Industrial Relations* 13 (May 1974), p. 113.

8. *Ibid.*, pp. 115–116. Emphasis in the original.

9. See Lloyd G. Reynolds, *The Structure of Labor Markets* (New York: Harper, 1951). Almost all the growth in the work force between 1975 and 1976 was made up of unmarried workers. Where 26.9 percent of all workers in 1970 were single or separated, the figures climbed to 31.2 in 1975 and to 32.4 in 1976.

10. Marcia Freedman, *Labor Markets: Segments and Shelters* (Montclair, N.J.: Allanheld Osmun, 1976).

11. Sherrill Cleland, *The Influence of Plant Size on Industrial Relations*, Research Report Series No. 89 (Princeton, N.J.: Industrial Relations Section, Princeton University, 1955).

12. Charles S. Telly, Wendell L. French, and William G. Scott, "The Relationship of Inequity to Turnover among Hourly Workers," *Administrative Science Quarterly* 16 (June 1971), pp. 164–172.

13. *Ibid.*, p. 171. The question of whether employees "correctly" perceive inequities in the treatment accorded them goes to the heart of the matter of workers' rationality in their behavior, a point we noted in the preceding chapter.

14. Organisation for Economic Cooperation and Development, "Absenteeism and Staff Turnover" (Report of Experts Meeting, Paris, October 17–19, 1973). We may note, in passing that work reforms at Volvo's experimental plant in Kalman, Sweden, have apparently helped cut absenteeism there to 15 percent—high by any standard, as *Time* notes, outside Sweden. The figure at "Volvo's Torslanda assembly plant just outside the Gothenburg headquarters runs to 20 percent daily." *Time*, February 21, 1977.

15. Janice Neipert Hedges, "Unscheduled Absence from Work: An Update," *Monthly Labor Review* 98 (August 1975), pp. 36–39.

16. Janice Neipert Hedges, "Absence from Work: A Look at Some National Data," *Monthly Labor Review* 96 (July 1973), pp. 24–30.

17. Flanagan *et al.*, *Worker Discontent*, pp. 120–121.

18. OECD, "Absenteeism," p. 11.

19. *Ibid.*, p. 15.

20. Sidney Cobb, Foreword, in Alfred Slote, *Termination: The Closing at Baker Plant* (Indianapolis, Ind.: Bobbs-Merrill, 1969), pp. xv–xx.

21. Thus we are acquainted with an executive who transferred his Grand Rapids, Michigan, position to a newly acquired plant in Grand Haven, Michigan, forty-five miles away, where he displaced a widely respected and admired family friend. He was himself squeezed out three years later by the parent company. He reported to us while unemployed that he "was glad that management still had the right to manage in America, and to make dispositions of people in accordance with its managerial principles."

22. Stanley E. Boyle and Philip W. Jaynes, *Conglomerate Merger Performance: An Empirical Analysis of Nine Corporations* (Washington, D.C.: U.S. Government Printing Office, November 1972). For a detailed discussion of the extraordinary difficulties in identifying the effects of merger, and therefore

of the difficulties in framing public policies towards mergers, see Peter O. Steiner, *Mergers: Motives, Effects, Policies* (Ann Arbor, Michigan: University of Michigan, 1975).

23. Daniel E. Diamond and Hrach Bedrosian, *Hiring Standards and Job Performance*, Manpower Research Monograph no. 18 (Washington, D.C.: U.S. Government Printing Office, 1970). These estimates are entirely in line with those by one of the authors. See Ivar Berg, *Education and Jobs* (New York: Praeger, 1970), Chapters 4–7 and 9.

24. H. G. Heneman, Jr., and George Seltzer, *Employer Manpower Planning and Forecasting*, Manpower Research Monograph no. 19 (Washington, D.C.: U.S. Government Printing Office, 1970).

25. By 1974 all but small firms had to "track" such information in order to comply with equal opportunity requirements. It is of immediate interest that government regulations, not the need to respond "rationally" to market forces, will induce businessmen to act somewhat more in accordance with their textbook images.

26. Hedges 1973, "Absence from Work," pp. 24–25.

27. Comments were made on the study by Piore in an earlier chapter.

28. Fritz Machlup, "Theories of the Firm: Marginalist, Behavioral, Managerial," *American Economic Review* 57 (March 1967), pp. 1–33.

29. Margaret Chandler and Leonard Sayles, *Contracting-Out: A Study of Management Decision Making* (New York: Columbia University Graduate School of Business, 1959), p. 36.

30. "When business moves where the boss lives," *Business Week*, September 30, 1972, p. 69.

31. *Ibid.*

32. Not all executives see fit to move their headquarters to suit their recreational needs. Some accept the costs of alternative arrangements. Thus, a former head of an American airline told the former chairman of a large manufacturing company that the latter's weekend trips to Norway (for salmon fishing) sounded like good fun, but added: "We bought a river in Colorado, my wife and I, for our fishing."

33. *Business Week*, September 30, 1972. William H. Whyte reports that of 38 moves by major corporations, in a small study he conducted, "31 moved to a place close to the top man's home. Average distance: about eight miles by road." As a check against the possibility that the observed results were by chance, moreover, Whyte "plotted the homes of the top executives of 95 corporations which have not moved from New York. The executives were distributed widely over the metropolitan area with roughly a quarter in New York City itself." *New York Magazine*, September 20, 1976, pp. 90–91.

34. The figures and quoted passages on executive turnover are from Arch Patton, "Ideas and Trends: The boom in executive self-interest," *Business Week*, May 24, 1976, p. 16. The title of Mr. Patton's article fits our use of his data well. In fairness to him, however, he does characterize these devel-

opments, the byproduct of the 1950s and 1960s boom, as "a devastating decline in the loyalty of the executive to his company."

NOTES FROM CHAPTER 14

1. Our own sense about the question of the pervasiveness of employee discontent is reflected, first, in the fact that blue-collar workers were not singled out for separate attention until we discussed the materials from arbitration cases; second, it is reflected in the fact that we have considered a few data on a large sample of white-collar managers, and, finally, in the fact that we have drawn some comparisons between the perspectives of blue- and white-collar workers (Chapter 7).

2. In one collaborative overview of job experiments and their logic, a very brief positive reference to unions is made by only one of the contributors. See John R. Maher (ed.), *New Perspectives in Job Enrichment* (New York: Van Nostrand Reinhold 1971), pp. 198–199.

3. We may add, not at all gratuitously, that one cannot logically speaking, eat one's cake and have one's cake; one cannot applaud mobility aspirations and the ambitions that inspire them while deploring the existence of the hierarchies through which admired "mobiles" move! It was clearly one of the problems, meanwhile, at "Crown" Laboratories, in the case described in Chapter 11, that the intervention scheme leveled the skill hierarchy in such a way that problems incident to shortages of needed skills were deceivingly attributed to technically incompetent personnel.

4. James Kuhn and Ivar Berg, "The Trouble with Labor Is . . . Featherbedding," *Columbia University Forum* 3 (Spring 1960), p. 23.

5. Sabbatical leaves are usually granted, upon application, as a privilege in most reputable universities in which they are granted at all. Most professors regard them as rights, however, quite in contravention of university statutes. Deans typically and simply do not manage in the matter. The "rights" thus claimed are won as *work rules*, protected by established practice and sanctified by a common-law-like principle. Professors ought not, in the event, look ungenerously on others' work rules.

6. See Elliot D. Chapple and Leonard R. Sayles, *The Measure of Management* (New York: Macmillan, 1961).

7. See Chapters 10 and 12.

8. For a classic study of "constructive compromises" over means and ends among managers in four firms, and for the implications for their employees, see Melville Dalton, *Men Who Manage* (New York: Wiley, 1959).

9. Stanley B. Mathewson, *Restriction of Output Among Unorganized Workers* (Carbondale, Ill.: Southern Illinois University Press, 1969), pp. 3–11.

10. A discussion of the "bogus-type rule" may be found in George E. Barnett, *American Economic Quarterly,* 3rd series, Vol. 10 (1909), Chapter 12. For a more general discussion of work rules and featherbedding, see S. Slichter, J. J. Healy, and E. R. Livernash, *The Impact of Collective Bargaining on Management* (Washington, D.C.: Brookings, 1960), pp. 320–

349; and Ivar Berg and James W. Kuhn "The Assumptions of Feather-bedding, *Labor Law Journal* 13 (April 1962), pp. 277–283.

11. "Industrial Conflict Resolution: A Comment" (Presented to a session of the meetings of the Industrial Relations Research Association, Atlantic City, N.J., September 1976, in which Richard Walton and Leonard Schlesinger presented a paper on "Quality of Work Life: Opportunity for a New Approach to Conflict Resolution").

12. James J. Healey (ed.), *Creative Collective Bargaining: Meeting Today's Challenges to Labor-Management Relations* (Englewood Cliffs, N.J.: Prentice-Hall, 1965).

13. We are perfectly willing to regard these preferences, on both sides, in economic terms and to impute economically rational motives to the parties in the workplace. Our objection would be to the two-valued logic by which workers' wants are seen to be nonrational when they appear to be subversive of earnings and that managers are rational when they wish, for example, simply and unilaterally to dispose of "obsolete" work rules.

14. See Chapter 11 in which managerial reactions to work-reform experiments are discussed.

15. Peter Henle, "Economic Effects: Reviewing the Evidence," in Jerome M. Rosow (ed.), *The Worker and the Job: Coping with Change* (Englewood, Cliffs, N.J.: Prentice-Hall, 1974), p. 137.

16. *Ibid.*, p. 139.

17. Robert P. Quinn, Thomas W. Mangione, and Martha S. Baldi de Mandilovitch, "Evaluating Working Conditions in America," *Monthly Labor Review* 96 (November 1973), p. 37.

18. These increased from 5.6 million to 5.9 million in the single fiscal year 1972–73. *Industry Week*, January 13, 1975, p. 55. Alleged violations of the National Labor Relations Act by employers in 1975 amounted to 20,311 cases, a 13 percent increase from 1974. Charges against unions went up 12 percent in the same period to 10,822. These figures are from an N.L.R.B. news release, Washington, D.C., Dec. 9, 1975.

19. Walton, "Innovative Restructuring of Work" in Rosow, *The Worker and the Job*, p. 149.

20. Henle, "Economic Effects," p. 144.

21. For a skeptical review, see Ivar Berg, "The Nice Kind of Union Democracy," *Columbia University Forum* 5 (Spring 1962), pp. 18–23.

22. Most of these are most conveniently discussed in Agis Salpukas, "Unions: A New Role?" in Rosow, *The Worker and the Job*, pp. 99–117.

23. *Ibid.*, p. 111.

24. Most managers in organized firms need only one drink to dissolve some of their hostilities to unions. The fact that union leaders have to deal with a heterogeneous worker group usually helps managers to see the advantages of a buffer group.

25. See Chapter 12.

26. Salpukas, "Unions: A New Role?" p. 110.

27. *Ibid.*, p. 117. Emphasis added.

28. Richard E. Walton, "Criteria for Quality of Working Life," in Louis E. Davis and Albert Cherns (eds.), *The Quality of Working Life, Vol. 1, Problems, Prospects and the State of the Art* (New York: Free Press, 1975), p. 100. Elsewhere, Rensis Linkert has written:

    It is essential that the group method of decision making and supervision not be confused with committees which never reach decisions or with *"wishy-washy," common-denominator sorts of committees* about which the supervisor can say, "Well, the group made this decision and I couldn't do a thing about it." Quite the contrary . . . *The supervisor is accountable for all decisions, for their execution, and for the results.*

    Rensis Likert, *The Human Organization* (New York: McGraw-Hill, 1967), p. 51. Emphasis added.

29. Walton, "Innovative Restructuring of Work," in Rosow, *The Worker and the Job*, pp. 148–149. We will return to "productivity bargaining" in the next chapter.

30. Alvin Gouldner, *Patterns of Industrial Bureaucracy* (New York: Free Press, 1954), and *Wildcat Strike* (Yellow Springs, Ohio: Antioch College Press, 1954).

31. Leonard Sayles and George Strauss, *The Local Union* (New York: Harcourt Brace, 1967).

32. James W. Kuhn, *Bargaining in the Grievance Process* (New York: Columbia University Press, 1961).

33. Leonard R. Sayles, *Behavior of Industrial Work Groups: Prediction and Control* (New York: Wiley, 1958).

34. Seymour M. Lipset *et al.*, *Union Democracy* (New York: Free Press, 1956).

35. Carl Gersuny, *Punishment and Redress in a Modern Factory* (Lexington, Mass.: Heath, 1973). For a discussion endorsing Gersuny's study but taking a more skeptical view of the adequacies of local bargaining, see Stanley L. Weir's review in *Contemporary Sociology: A Journal of Reviews*, 5:5 (September 1976), pp. 631–633. For an intriguing study of worker participation as conceived by workers in the U.S., Austria, Italy, Israel (in Kibbutzim) and Yugoslavia, see Arnold S. Tannenbaum *et al.*, *Hierarchy in Organizations* (San Francisco: Jossey-Bass, 1974). Tannenbaum and his colleagues make the important points that participation patterns valued by workers can be informal in character (p. 125) but that though they may value participatory arrangements, workers by no means ignore the fact that fellow workers can be as much instruments of control as can managers (p. 60). Worker participation, they also note, is *not* associated with lower levels of "alienation" (p. 162), of ulcer symptoms (p. 198) or with higher levels of "adjustment" (p. 157).

36. Henle, "Economic Effects," p. 139.

NOTES FROM CHAPTER 15

1. For two closely related treatments of industrial relations systems as systems, see John T. Dunlop, *Industrial Relations Systems* (New York: Holt,

1958), and Clark Kerr *et al.*, *Industrialism and Industrial Man* (New York: Oxford, 1964), pp. 192–239. For a brief discussion of the need to take institutional contexts into account, see Bogdan Denitch, "Notes on the Relevance of Yugoslav Self-Management" in Marie R. Haug and Jacques Dofny (eds.), *Work and Technology* (Beverly Hills, Calif.: Sage, 1977), pp. 141–160.

2. Thus the senior author learned in April, 1974, from M. David Dautresme of the Credit Lyonnais, of the need for work reforms in France, needs that were made "more recognizable" by a protracted strike of white collar bank employees that spring. The concern, widespread in France, at the time, was over the growing pressures from French socialists as France headed for its national elections in May 1974. By May 21, 1977 France was heading for a new election and M. Dautresme, Baron Guy de Rothschild (of Imetal), Max Mazerand (of Revillon Frères), in company with others were in New York "sounding out the possibility of new U.S. investments." Fears of a Communist election victory, according to the *Wall Street Journal*, prompted the visit by these top leaders who "would like to get more of their francs into U.S.-based assets before their country's general election next March [1978]." (May 21, 1977, p. 1.) There is now little discussion of work reforms even as palliatives in France.

3. Ronald Dore, *British Factory—Japanese Factory: The Origins of National Diversity in Industrial Relations* (Berkeley, Calif.: University of California Press, 1973); Norman F. Dufty, *Changes in Labour-Management Relations in the Enterprise* (Paris: Organisation for Economic Cooperation and Development, 1975); Solomon Barkin (ed.), *Worker Militancy and its Consequences 1965–75: New Directions in Western Industrial Relations* (New York: Praeger, 1975); and J. David Edelstein and Malcolm Warner, *Comparative Union Democracy: Organization and Opposition in British and American Unions* (New York: Wiley, 1976).

4. Eli Ginzberg, *The Manpower Connection* (Cambridge, Mass.: Harvard University Press, 1975), pp. 96–105. See also "Work Restructuring and Manpower Realities," pp. 88–94.

5. Dufty, *Changes.* The study's emphasis is on unionized industries and firms.

6. We should note at the same time that American unions are obliged to bargain over health and other issues that are elsewhere the subjects of national public policies.

7. For a comparison of the successes of U.S. and non-U.S. executives in non-American work settings, see Max Stever and Jack Gerrard, "Industrial Relations, Labor Disputes and Labor Utilization in the U.K." in John H. Dunning (ed.), *The Multinational Enterprise* (New York: Praeger, 1972), pp. 89–146. Among the significant consequences of the rise of multinationals are likely to be some additional convergence in the industrial-relations systems of different nations. For an assessment of the complexities, see Robert J. Flanagan and Arnold R. Weber (eds.), *Bargaining without Boundaries: The Multinational Corporation and International Labor Relations* (Chicago: University of Chicago Press, 1974).

8. Ginzberg, *The Manpower Connection,* pp. 95–96. See Chapter 2 in the

present volume for a discussion of the relationship of current work-reform proposals to the logics and propositions emanating from the early human-relations movement in the United States.

9. See Dufty, *Changes*, pp. 22–23.

10. *Ibid.*, p. 25.

11. When leading university professors moved to teach from three to two courses per term in the 1960s it was not called a slowdown. A reintroduction of the three-course load in times of economic straits would naturally be a speed-up, however.

12. For a report, see Alvin Flanders, *The Fawley Productivity Agreements* (London: Faber & Faber, 1964).

13. There is no certain way to deal with the productivity matter from secondary research sources, just as it is difficult to determine the contribution of labor to productivity gains in a randomly selected basic industry in the United States. The usual measure can mislead one because output per manhour goes up precipitously in periods of economic recovery as plant, equipment, and labor are employed more "intensively" and "extensively" than in periods of recession.

14. Dufty, *Changes*, p. 26.

15. *Ibid.*, p. 27.

16. *Ibid.*

17. *Ibid.*

18. We distinguish ongoing bargaining over work rules (typically the case in the United States) from formal contract negotiations that put an end to "restrictive practices" in wholesale fashion.

19. Dufty, *Changes*, p. 71.

20. *Ibid.*

21. *Ibid.*

22. *Ibid.*

23. See Dore, *British Factory*. See also a summary of the work of 25 years by the Inter-University Study of Labor Problems in Economic Development: John T. Dunlop *et al.*, *Industrialism and Industrial Man Reconsidered: Some Perspectives on a Study over Two Decades of the Problems of Labor and Management in Economic Growth* (Princeton, N.J.: Inter-University Study of Human Resources in National Development, 1975); and Wilbert E. Moore, *The Impact of Industry* (Englewood Cliffs, N.J.: Prentice-Hall, 1965), pp. 9–21. For a fine discussion of the impact of historical and institutional realities on modern German "efforts at industrial democracy" and co–determination, so-called, see Alfred Diamant's paper before the 1976 Annual Meeting of the American Political Association, "Democratizing the Work Place: The Myth and Reality of *Mittbestimmung* in the Federal Republic of Germany." (Bloomington, Ind.: Indiana University, 1976).

24. Dufty, *Changes*, pp. 71–72.

25. Douglas H. Soutar, "Co-Determination, Industrial Democracy and the Role of Management" (Presidential Address to the Industrial Relations Re-

search Association) in Gerald G. Somers (ed.), *Proceedings of the Twenty-Sixth Annual Winter Meeting,* December 28–29, 1973), p. 4.

26. It is equally unlikely that Americans would be enthusiastic about corporate board memberships. The idea was briefly mentioned in preliminary negotiations between the UAW and Chrysler in August 1976; it was reported only once, in the back pages of the *Detroit Free Press*; it was not, so far as we can judge, a real issue in the 1976 auto negotiations.

27. Dufty, *Changes,* pp. 57–63.

28. Ginzberg, *The Manpower Connection,* pp. 96–104.

29. From an interview, May 2, 1974.

30. From an interview, April 30, 1974.

31. By 1977 there is much less confidence, in and out of French business leadership circles that Marxists, in or out of the CGT or of the French Communist Party, will be cooled out in the largest sense. See note 2, above.

32. Interviews with an officer of Norway's national association of employers. His observations were repeated almost verbatim by top-level Norwegian managers in an insurance company, a manufacturing company, a ship-owner's trade association, and a chemical company.

33. For a description of the integration of work reform, collective bargaining, and social reform generally, see Diamant, "Democratizing the Workplace."

34. See Dufty, *Changes,* pp. 118–119.

35. The celebrated Volvo experiments, as we noted in Chapter 13, have contributed to a reduction in absenteeism at the Torslanda works, outside Gothenburg, to 20 percent daily. Still, that means "that Volvo in effect has to pay five employees to do the work of four. Some workers are absent an average of 65 days a year each." *Time,* February 21, 1976, p. 67.

36. Louis E. Davis and Albert Cherns (eds.), *The Quality of Working Life,* Vol. 1, *Problems, Projects and the State of the Art* (New York: Free Press, 1975), p. 391. Useful discussions of union interests in and reactions to work reform programs in Western Europe and elsewhere may be found in pp. 393–442. We would add that we are no more surprised by managers who mind their quos than by unionists who exact their quids in collective bargaining. The reification of unions in the Davis-Cherns passage serves to distract from an otherwise level-headed statement and brings us back to the two-valued logic delineated in earlier chapters.

NOTES FROM CHAPTER 16

1. *Business Week* estimates that by 1975 the figure was $25 billion; the figure for 1965 was $8 billion. "Preliminary" results of a "benchmark" study by the Commerce Department "indicate that foreign direct investment in the U.S. may actually be one-third higher" or about $32 billion. "Why Foreign Companies are Betting on the U.S." *Business Week,* April 12, 1976, p. 50.

2. *Ibid.* See also Sanford Rose, "The Misguided Furor about Investments from Abroad," *Fortune*, May 1975, pp. 170 ff. In the preceding chapter we noted that a team of French business leaders, concerned about the Leftist threat to the political status quo at home, and the prospects in the 1978 elections, has joined visiting teams from other countries in the spring of 1977 who seek to safeguard assets through American investments.

3. *Business week*, April 12, 1976, p. 50.

4. *Ibid.*

5. *Ibid.*

6. Rose, "Misguided Furor," p. 170 ff.

7. It is a good deal easier to subcontract work in the United States even when unions resist. In Japan, nearly half of the work force work under "career" arrangements. See Margaret K. Chandler, "Management Rights: Made in Japan," *Columbia Journal of World Business* 1 (Winter 1966), pp. 131–140. European managers, meanwhile, feel themselves plagued by national manpower policy provisions that require "discouragingly" high severance payments to workers whose jobs are terminated.

8. On one side Western European employers are faced, as we have noted, with threats from the political left. On the other, they have large numbers of "expendable" imported workers. Where one side pressures for reforms, the other constitutes a manipulatable management resource. For a fuller discussion, see Eli Ginzberg, *The Human Economy* (New York: McGraw-Hill, 1976), pp. 143–160.

9. A. G. Zdravomyslov, V. P. Rozin, and V. A. Iadov (eds.), *Man and His Work: A Sociological Study* (White Plains, N.Y.: International Arts and Sciences Press, 1970), pp. 263–283. Trans. and ed. Stephen P. Dunn (originally published in Moscow in 1967). The tables presented in these pages look in every respect like those we presented on underutilization in Part Two.

10. Humpty Dumpty used words to mean what he wanted them to mean, "neither more nor less." But, he added, "When I make a word do a lot of work like that, I always pay it extra."

11. There has also been some interest in a more inclusive measure called "total factor productivity." The term is something of a misnomer, since it includes capital and labor but not materials or energy.

12. John W. Kendrick, "Productivity Trends and Prospects." in *U.S. Economic Growth from 1976 to 1986: Prospects, Problems, and Patterns*, Vol. 1, *Productivity*, U.S. Congress, Joint Economic Committee (Washington, D.C.: U.S. Government Printing Office, 1976), p. 12.

13. Edward F. Renshaw, "Productivity," in *U.S. Economic Growth from 1976 to 1986*, p. 22.

14. Robert M. Solow, "Some Evidence on the Short-Run Productivity Puzzle," in J. Bhagwati and R. S. Eckaus (eds.), *Development and Planning: Essays in Honor of Paul Rosenstein-Rodan* (Cambridge, Mass.: MIT Press, 1973), p. 316.

15. *Ibid.*

16. Leonard Silk, "Virtues of Slower Growth," *New York Times*, February 4, 1976.

17. W. J. Baumol and W. E. Oates, "The Cost Disease of the Personal Services and the Quality of Life," *Scandinavska Enskilda Banken Quarterly Review* 2 (1972), pp. 44–50.

18. We will unoptimistically leave it to students of human capital (Chapter 6) to help resolve the contradiction inherent in this omission.

19. Renshaw, "Productivity," p. 23.

20. *Ibid.*

21. *Ibid.*, p. 33.

22. John Walsh, "R & D and Economic Growth: Renewed Interest in Federal Role," *Science* 193 (September 17, 1976), pp. 1101–1103.

23. Edwin Mansfield, "The Contribution of Research and Development to Economic Growth in the United States," *A Review of the Relationship between Research and Development and Economic Growth/Productivity* (Washington, D.C.: National Science Foundation, February 1971). On the spillover question, Mansfield says, "An enormous amount of verbiage and papers of dubious distinction have been produced on this topic. But so far as I know, the amount of penetrating, quantitative objective analysis has been surprisingly limited" (p. 40).

24. Philip M. Boffey "Science Indicators: New Report by U.S. Finds Performance Weakening," *Science* 191 (March 12, 1976), p. 1032. For the detailed statistics on R & D see *National Patterns of R & D Resources: Funds and Manpower in the United States, 1953–1976* (Washington, D.C.: National Science Foundation, 1976).

25. For a devastating argument against business tax breaks see Lester C. Thurow, "Business Doesn't Need a Tax Break" *Wall Street Journal*, April 29, 1977. The share of GNP going to corporate income tax has already been cut 35 percent while the share of other taxes has risen 46 percent. Depressed corporate spending on plant and equipment, Thurow notes, can hardly therefore be traced to corporate capital's falling share of GNP.

26. Renshaw, "Productivity," p. 42.

27. George Delehanty, *Nonproduction Workers in U.S. Manufacturing* (Amsterdam: North Holland Publishing Co., 1968), pp. 171, 217.

28. Leon Greenberg, "Definitions and Concepts," *Collective Bargaining and Productivity* (Madison, Wisc.: Industrial Relations Research Association, 1975), p. 3.

29. William J. Baumol, *Business Behavior, Value and Growth*, rev. ed. (New York: Harcourt, Brace, 1967). See also, J. Child, *The Business Enterprise in Modern Industrial Society* (New York: Macmillan, 1970), Chapter 5, "Conflicting Criteria of Business Performance," pp. 84–103.

30. Walter Adams (ed.), *The Structure of American Industry*, 4th ed. (New York: Macmillan, 1971), p. 487.

31. *Ibid.*, p. 486.

32. See Alfred P. Sloan, *My Years with General Motors* (Garden City, N.Y.: Doubleday, 1964).

NOTES FROM CHAPTER 17

1. See Leonard Goodwin, *Do the Poor Want to Work? A Social-Psychological Study of Work Orientations* (Washington, D.C.: Brookings, 1972). This may be a small apostasy from the most orthodox reading of the Protestant Ethic's imperative; as we noted in an earlier chapter, most Americans report that they could work a good deal harder than they do.

2. In the current argot, "social responsibility" and "corporate conscience" are used in place of more heraldic terms. Adolf Berle, for example, called it the "transcendental margin" in *The American Economic Republic* (New York: Harcourt Brace Jovanovich, 1963).

3. Michael Kammen, *People of Paradox: An Inquiry Concerning the Origins of American Civilization* (New York: Vintage Books, 1973).

4. A. H. Raskin, "After Dunlop," *New York Times*, January 3, 1976, p. 31.

5. *Ibid.*

6. These are among some of the tools used in jobs that have recently been the subject of reforms.

7. For a chilling version, see Arthur F. Burns, *The Management of Prosperity: The 1965 Fairless Lectures* (New York: Columbia University and Carnegie Presses, 1966). For a discussion, see Ivar Berg, "The Impact of Business on America" and "Business and American Ideology" in Ivar Berg (ed.), *The Business of America* (New York: Harcourt, Brace, 1968), pp. 3–33 and 146–162.

8. See, for example, *Business Week's* editorial, "Misplaced Loyalities," February 2, 1976.

9. Nat Hentoff, "Where Have All the Organizers Gone?" A review of Dan Georgakas and Marvin Surkin, *Detroit: I Do Mind Dying; A Study in Urban Revolution* (New York: St. Martin's Press, 1975) in *Social Policy* 6 (January/February 1976), pp. 56–57.

10. U.S. Bureau of Labor Statistics, *Occupational Injuries and Illnesses in the United States, by Industry, 1974*, Bulletin 1932 (Washington, D.C.: U.S. Government Printing Office, 1976), pp. 1, 5.

11. David Burnham, "Ills Linked to Job in Workers Study," *The New York Times*, May 12, 1975, p. 2.

12. U.S. Office of Management and Budget, *Statistical Reporter*, Number 77–7 (Washington, D.C.: U.S. Government Printing Office, April 1977), p. 253.

13. "Emergency Benzene Curb Is Set to Protect Workers till Permanent Rule Is Adopted," *The Wall Street Journal*, May 2, 1977, p. 16.

14. *Ibid.*

15. "Labor Letter," *The Wall Street Journal*, July 22, 1975, p. 1.

INDEX

Index